MORE LOST BOOKS OF THE BIBLE:

THE SECRETS OF ENOCH
&
THE APOCALYPSE OF BARUCH

the apocryphile press
BERKELEY, CA
www.apocryphile.org

apocryphile press
BERKELEY, CA

Apocryphile Press
1700 Shattuck Ave #81
Berkeley, CA 94709
www.apocryphile.org

The Book of the Secrets of Enoch first published in 1830 by the
Clarendon Press. *The Apocalypse of Baruch* first published in
1896 by Adam and Charles Black. Apocryphile Press
Edition, 2006.

Printed in the United States of America
ISBN 1-933993-19-7

THE SECRETS
OF ENOCH

*Translated from the Slavonic
by W.R. Morfill, M.A.*

*Edited by
R.H. Charles, M.A.*

PREFACE

THE Book of the Secrets of Enoch cannot fail to be of interest to students of Apocalyptic literature and of the origins of Christianity. It is with a view to help such that this the first edition of the book has been undertaken. In certain respects it will appeal also to specialists in Assyriology. So far indeed as it does so, I have been able to do little more than refer to the leading scholars in this department, as my knowledge of such subjects is very slight, and all secondhand.

This book has had a peculiar history. For more than 1200 years it has been unknown save in Russia, where acquaintance with it goes several centuries back. Further, by its present name it was never known in any literature save the Slavonic. Even in Slavonic the name was not quite constant, if we may trust one of the MSS. (B); for there it appears as 'The Secret Books of God which were shown to Enoch.' And yet the book was much read in many circles in the first three centuries of the Church, and has left more traces of its influence than many a well-known book of the same literature (see § 5), and it is undoubtedly of much greater importance in respect of exegesis. In its Greek form it passed current probably under the general designation of Enoch. Occasionally we find that it was not distinguished by those who used it from the older book which has come down to us through the Ethiopic. We have, in fact, in this book another fragmentary survival of the literature that once circulated under the name of Enoch.

That such a book had ever existed was not known in Western Europe till 1892, when a writer in a German review stated that there was a Slavonic version of the Ethiopic Book of Enoch. By Mr. Morfill's help it soon became clear that there was no foundation whatever for such a statement, and subsequent study showed that we had recovered therein an old and valuable pseudepigraph. The next step was naturally to secure its publication, and this was soon made possible through the kindness of the Delegates of the Press.

It will be generally understood that great difficulties beset such an undertaking, and particularly in the case of a book of whose existence there had never been even a surmise in the world of scholarship, and to which there was not a single unmistakable allusion in all ancient literature. The editor in such a case has to pursue untravelled ways, and if, in his efforts to discover the literary environment, the religious views, the date, and language of his author, he has fallen once and again into errors of perception or judgement, he can therein but throw himself on the indulgence of his critics.

The first edition of such a work must have many shortcomings. The editor will be grateful for corrections and further elucidations of the text.

In order to appreciate the value of this book in elucidating contemporary and subsequent religious thought, the reader should consult pp. xxix–xlvii of the Introduction.

In conclusion, I must express my gratitude to Mr. Morfill for his great kindness in undertaking the translation of the Slavonic texts, and for his unfailing courtesy and unwearying energy in the prosecution of the task. It is to him that I am indebted for the account of the Slavonic MSS. in § 2.

R. H. C.

CONTENTS

———◆———

INTRODUCTION

§ 1. SHORT ACCOUNT OF THE BOOK.

THE Book of the Secrets of Enoch has, so far as is yet known, been preserved only in Slavonic. It will suit our convenience to take advantage of this fact, and call it shortly 'the Slavonic Enoch,' in contradistinction to the older book of Enoch. As the latter has come down to us in its entirety through the Ethiopic alone, it will be no less convenient to designate it as 'the Ethiopic Enoch.'

This new fragment of the Enochic literature has only recently come to light through certain MSS. which were found in Russia and Servia. My attention was first drawn to this fact when editing the Ethiopic Enoch by an article by Kozak on Russian Pseudepigraphic Literature in the *Jahrb. f. Prot. Theol.* pp. 127–158 (1892). As it was stated in this article that there was a Slavonic Version of the Book of Enoch hitherto known through the Ethiopic Version, I at once applied to Mr. Morfill for help, and in the course of a few weeks we had before us printed copies of two of the MSS. in question. It did not take much study to discover that Kozak's statement was absolutely devoid of foundation. The Book of the Secrets of Enoch was, as it soon transpired, a new pseudepigraph, and not in any sense a version of the older and well-known Book of Enoch. In many respects it is of no less value, as we shall see in the sequel.

The Slavonic Enoch in its present form was written some-where about the beginning of the Christian era. Its author or final editor was an Hellenistic Jew, and the place of its composition was Egypt.

Written at such a date, and in Egypt, it was not to be expected that it exercised a direct influence on the writers of the New Testament. On the other hand, it occasionally exhibits striking parallelisms in diction and thought, and some of the dark passages of the latter are all but inexplicable without its aid.

Although the very knowledge that such a book ever existed was lost for probably twelve hundred years, it nevertheless was much used both by Christian and heretic in the early centuries. Thus citations appear from it, though without acknowledgement, in the Book of Adam and Eve, the Apoca-lypses of Moses and Paul (400–500 A. D.), the Sibylline Oracles, the Ascension of Isaiah and the Epistle of Barnabas (70–90 A. D.). It is quoted by name in the Apocalyptic portions of the Testaments of Levi, Daniel, and Naphtali (circ. 1 A. D.) [1]. It was referred to by Origen and probably by Clement of Alexandria, and used by Irenaeus, and a few phrases in the New Testament may be derived from it.

§ 2. THE SLAVONIC MANUSCRIPTS.

The Slavonic redaction of the text of the Book of Enoch, which is now for the first time translated into English, has come down to us mainly in two versions. It will be clear from the evidence in § 4 that they are translations from a lost Greek original. The manuscripts may be thus classified. I. First those in which we find the complete text, and of these two have been preserved; (*a*) a MS. in the possession

[1] The grounds for this date of the Testaments cannot be stated here, nor yet for the assumption some pages later that they sprang from a Hebrew original. These I hope to give at length in an edition of these Testa-ments.

of Mr. A. Khludov; this is a South Russian recension. The
MS. belongs to the second half of the seventeenth century,
and is found in a *Sbornik* or volume of miscellanies containing
also lives of the Saints and other religious treatises. This
text was published by Mr. A. Popov in the *Transactions of
the Historical and Archaeological Society of the University of
Moscow*, vol. iii. (Moscow 1880). It is unfortunately in
many places very corrupt. It forms the basis of the present
text, but where it is corrupt attempts have been made to
supply a sounder text from other MSS. It is marked by the
letter A in the critical notes to the present translation.
(*b*) A MS. discovered by Prof. Sokolov of Moscow in the
Public Library of Belgrade in the year 1886. This is a
Bulgarian recension, and the orthography belongs to the
middle Bulgarian period. This MS. is probably of the sixteenth century. It contains the account of the priesthood
of Methuselah and Nir, the birth of Melchizedek and the
Deluge. Though this legend does not belong to this Book
of Enoch, it is added as an Appendix. II. There is also
a shortened and incomplete redaction of the text of which three
MSS. are known; (*a*) that preserved in the Public Library of
Belgrade; a Serbian redaction, which was printed by Nova-
ković in the sixteenth volume of the literary magazine *Starine*
(Agram, 1884). Many of the readings of this MS. are
very interesting. It is of the sixteenth century, and is
cited as B. (*b*) That in the Vienna Public Library, which
is almost identical with the preceding; (*c*) a MS. of the
seventeenth century in the possession of Mr. E. Barsov of
Moscow.

Of the above MSS. I have direct acquaintance only with
A and B: of the other MSS. I have only an indirect knowledge through the text prepared by Prof. Sokolov, which is
based on all the above MSS. Unfortunately, however, this
text has not fully discriminated these sources. Accordingly,
to avoid misconceptions, this text which is designated as *Sok*,

is to be understood as representing all authorities other than
A and B.

Other fragments of the Book of Enoch are to be found in
Tikhonravov's Memorials of Russian Apocryphal Literature
(Памятники отреченной русской литературы), and Pypin's Memorials of Old Russian Literature (Памятники старинной русской
литературы). By allusions and citations in early Slavonic literature, we can see that these late manuscripts are only copies
of much earlier ones, which have perished. Thus Tikhonravov
cites from a fourteenth century MS.

The duty of the translator has been a comparatively simple
one—to present a text which would be of service to the
Western students of apocryphal literature. To this end all
philological questions have been subordinated, and therefore
my Slavonic friends must not blame me for not going more
into linguistic matters. These would be out of place on the
present occasion ; certainly the time for such a work has not
yet come in England. My translation will have served its
purpose by enabling my friend, the Rev. R. H. Charles, to
treat the subject as fully and learnedly as he has done from
the standpoint of Biblical apocryphal literature. In conclusion,
I must say that I am glad in however small a way to be able
to contribute to such studies through the agency of Mr.
Charles. I wish also to express my thanks to Professors Sokolov
and Pavlov of the University of Moscow ; to the former for
allowing me the use of his emendated text and furnishing me
with valuable notes on some obscure passages ; and to the
latter for the kind interest which he has taken in the book.

W. R. M.

§ 3. The Text followed in the Translation.

The formation of the text has been a matter of great
difficulty. As I have no knowledge of Slavonic, Mr. Morfill
has been so good as to furnish me with literal translations of
A, B and of Prof. Sokolov's text. The number of variations

which was unduly great at the outset has to some extent
been diminished by Mr. Morfill's critical acumen. This
careful scholar, however, I should remark, has conscien-
tiously refrained from all but obvious corrections of the text.
Starting then from his translations of the Slavonic MSS.
and of Sokolov's text, I resolved after due examination to
follow A in the main. B of course is followed when it
preserves the obviously better reading, and that it does
frequently. When both A and B are corrupt, I have fallen
back on the text of Sokolov. Occasionally I have been
obliged to follow one reading to the rejection of the others,
in cases where all the readings were equally probable or
improbable. In only two or three passages have I emended
the text, and that in the case of numbers, which are frequently corrupted in tradition through MSS. In all cases
the rejected variants are given in the critical notes below,
so that, in the event of the discovery of fresh critical
materials, the reader can revise the text for himself, and
in the process will reverse, no doubt, many of the editor's
judgements.

As regards the relative merits of A and B, though the
former is very corrupt, it is nevertheless a truer representative
of the original than B. B is really a short *résumé* of the
work—being about half the length of A. In the process of
abbreviation its editor or scribe rejected in some instances
and in others recast entire sections with capricious rearrangements of the text. For an example of the method pursued
occasionally in B the reader can consult the critical notes
on xl.

In A we find many interpolations. Thus in xx. 3 there is
a mention of the tenth heaven, and in xxi–xxii. 3 a description of the eighth, ninth and tenth heavens, though the rest
of the work directly speaks of and indirectly implies only
seven heavens. B omits all reference to this addition in A.
The reader will find many other like additions which have as

a rule been relegated to the critical notes or given in the text in square brackets.

The titles at the head of the chapters are given by A. I have enclosed them in square brackets, as they have no claim to antiquity. They are not given in Sokolov's text, nor are they found in B. A few titles do appear in B, but with one exception these consist merely of *Entry of Enoch into the first heaven, Entry of Enoch into the second heaven,* &c., &c., *Entry of Enoch into the seventh heaven.*

§ 4. THE LANGUAGE AND PLACE OF WRITING.

1. The main part of this book was written for the first time in Greek. This is shown by such statements, (1) as xxx. 13, 'And I gave him a name (i. e. Adam) from the four substances: the East, the West, the North, and the South.' Adam's name is here derived from the initial letters of the Greek names of the four quarters, i. e. ἀνατολή, δύσις, ἄρκτος, μεσημβρία. This fancy was first elaborated in Greek, as this derivation is impossible in Semitic languages. (2) Again, the writer follows the chronology of the LXX. Enoch is 165 years old when he begat Methuselah. According to the Hebrew and Samaritan chronologies he was 65. Josephus also (*Ant.* i. 3. 3), it is true, adopts the LXX chronology. (3) In l. 4 the writer reproduces the LXX text of Deut. xxxii. 35 against the Hebrew. (4) The writer frequently uses Ecclesiasticus, and often reproduces it almost word for word: cf. xliii. 2, 3—Ecclus. xxiii. 7 ; x. 20, 22, 24 : also xlvii. 5— Ecclus. i. 2 : also li. 1, 3—Ecclus. vii. 32 ; ii. 4 : also lxi. 2— Ecclus. xxxix. 25 : also lxv. 2—Ecclus. xvii. 3, 5. (5) lxv. 4 seems to be derived from the Book of Wisdom vii. 17, 18. So far as we can judge, it was the Greek Versions of Ecclesiasticus and Wisdom that our author used.

Some sections of this book were written originally in Hebrew. (See p. xxiv.)

2. This book was written in Egypt, and probably in Alexandria. This is deducible from the following facts. (1) From the variety of speculations which it holds in common with Philo and writings which were Hellenistic in character or circulated largely in Egypt. Thus the existent was created from the non-existent, xxiv. 2 ; xxv. 1 : cf. Philo, *de Justit.* 7 ; souls were created before the foundation of the world, xxiii. 5: cf. Philo, *de Somno,* i. 22 ; *de Gigantibus* 3; Wisdom viii. 19, 20. Again, man had seven natures or powers, xxx. 9: cf. Philo, *de Mundi Op.* 40. Man could originally see the angels in heaven, xxxi. 2: cf. Philo, *Quaest. in Gen.* xxxii. There is no resurrection of the body, l. 2; lxv. 6: so the Book of Wisdom and Philo taught. Finally swearing is reprobated by both, xlix. 1, 2: cf. Philo, *de Spec. Leg.* ii. 1. (2) The whole Messianic teaching of the Old Testament does not find a single echo in the work of this Hellenized Israelite of Egypt, although he shows familiarity with almost every book of the Old Testament. (3) The Phoenixes and Chalkydries, xii—monstrous serpents with the heads of *crocodiles*—are natural products of the Egyptian imagination. (4) The syncretistic character of the account of the creation, xxv–xxvi, which undoubtedly betrays Egyptian elements.

We should observe further that the arguments that make for a Greek original tend to support the view that the book was written in Egypt, especially when we take them in conjunction with the date of its composition.

§ 5. Relation of the Book to Jewish and Christian Literature.

The discoveries regarding the planets, &c., which Joel (circ. 1200 A.D.) in his Chronography assigns to Seth are, as we have shown on p. 37, most probably derived ultimately from this Book of Enoch. In like manner the statements regarding the sabbath and the duration of the world, which according to Cedrenus (circ. 1050 A.D.) were drawn from Josephus and the Book of Jubilees are likewise to be assigned to this book; for nothing of this nature appears either in Josephus or the Book of Jubilees. Cedrenus, we should remember, is largely dependent on Syncellus, and Syncellus is very often wrong in his references in the case of Apocalyptic literature (see xxxiii. 1, 2 notes). It is natural that these late writers should err regarding all facts derived from this book, inasmuch as it was already lost to all knowledge many centuries before their day. Let us now pass over these intervening centuries to a time when this book was still in some measure known. Now in the *Book of Adam and Eve* of the fifth century we find two passages drawn from our book which are quotations in sense more than in words. Thus in I. vi we read: 'But the wicked Satan ... set me at naught, and sought the Godhead, so that I hurled him down from heaven.' This is drawn from xxix. 4, 5: 'One of these in the ranks of the Archangels (i.e. Satan, cf. xxxi. 4) ... entertained an impossible idea that he should make his throne higher than the clouds over the earth, and should be equal in rank to My power. And I hurled him from the heights.' Again in the *Book of Adam and Eve*, I. viii: 'When we dwelt in the garden ... we saw his angels that sang praises in heaven.' This comes from xxxi. 2: 'I made for him the heavens open that he should perceive the angels singing the song of triumph.' See notes on xxxi. 2 for similar view in Philo and St. Ephrem. Again in I. xiv of the former book the words: 'The garden, into the abode of light thou longest for, wherein is no darkness,' and I. xi: 'That garden in which was no darkness,' are probably derived from Slav. En. xxxi. 2: 'And there was light without any darkness continually in Paradise.'

Next in the Apocalypse of Moses (ed. Tischend. 1866), p. 19, we have a further development of a statement that appears in our text regarding the sun: see xiv. 2–4 (notes).

In the anonymous writing *De montibus Sina et Sion* 4, we have most probably another trace of the influence of our text in this century. In this treatise the derivation of Adam's name from the initials of the four quarters of the earth is given at length. This derivation appears probably for the first time in literature in xxx. 13 (see note).

In the fourth century there are undoubted indications of its use in the Apocalypse of Paul (ed. Tischend. 1866). Thus the statement, p. 64, οὗτός ἐστιν ὁ παράδεισος, ἔνθα . . . δένδρον παμμεγέθη (sic) ὡραῖον, ἐν ᾧ ἐπανεπαύετο τὸ πνεῦμα τὸ ἅγιον is beyond the possibility of question a Christian adaptation of the Slavonic Enoch viii. 3: 'And in the midst (of Paradise is) the tree of life, in that place, on which God rests, when He comes into Paradise.' Again the words, p. 64, ἐκ τῆς ῥίζης αὐτοῦ ἐξήρχετο . . . ὕδωρ, μεριζόμενον εἰς τέσσαρα ὀρύγματα, and p. 52, ποταμοὶ τέσσαρες . . . ῥέοντες μέλι καὶ γάλα καὶ ἔλαιον καὶ οἶνον, are almost verbal reproductions of our text, viii. 5: 'From its root in the garden there go forth four streams which pour honey and milk, oil and wine, and are separated in four directions.' With two characteristic features of hell in this Apocalypse, i.e. οὐκ ἦν ἐκεῖ φῶς and ὁ πυρινὸς ποταμός (pp. 57, 58), we may compare x. 1 of our text: 'And there was no light there . . . and a fiery river goes forth.'

The peculiar speculation of St. Augustine in the *De Civ.* xxii. 30. 5 seems to be derived ultimately from xxxiii. 2 (see notes). Compare with xxxiii. 2 especially the words: 'Haec tamen septima erit sabbatum nostrum cuius finis non erit vespera, sed dominicus dies velut *octavus aeternus.*'

In the early part of the third and in the second century there is the following evidence of the existence of our text. Thus in the Sibylline Oracles, ii. 75 ὀρφανικοῖς χήραις τ᾽ ἐπιδευομένοις τε παράσχου, and 88 σὴν χεῖρα πενητεύουσιν ὄρεξον are too closely parallel to l. 5—li. 1, 'Stretch out your hands to the orphan, the widow [and the stranger, B om.]. Stretch out your hands to the poor,' to be accidental.

In Irenaeus *contra Haer.* v. 28. 3 we have the Jewish speculation in our text, xxxiii. 1, 2, reproduced to the effect that as the work of creation lasted six days so the world would last 6,000 years, and that there would be 1,000 years of rest corresponding to the first sabbath after creation. See text, xxxiii. 1, 2 (notes).

In Origen (according to Methodius; see Lommatzsch edition, xxi. p. 59) we find a reference to this speculation: χιλίων γὰρ ἐτῶν περιοριζομένων εἰς μίαν ἡμέραν ἐν ὀφθαλμοῖς θεοῦ, ἀπὸ τῆς τοῦ κόσμου γενέσεως μέχρι καταπαύσεως μέχρις ἡμῶν, ὡς οἱ περὶ τὴν ἀριθμητικὴν φάσκουσι δεινοί, ἐξ ἡμέραι συμπεραιοῦνται. Ἑξακισχιλιοστὸν ἄρα ἔτος φασὶν ἀπὸ Ἀδὰμ εἰς δεῦρο συντείνειν· τῇ γὰρ ἑβδομάδι τῷ ἑπτακισχιλιοστῷ ἔτει κρίσιν ἀφίξεσθαί φασιν. Whether this passage argues a direct knowledge of the Slavonic Enoch is doubtful. There can be no doubt, however, with regard to the direct reference in the *de Princip.* i. 3. 2 'Nam et in eo libello ... quem Hermas conscripsit, ita refertur: Primo omnium crede, quia unus est Deus, qui omnia creavit atque composuit: qui cum nihil esset prius, esse fecit omnia. ... Sed et in Enoch libro his similia describuntur.' Now since there is no account of the creation in the Ethiopic Enoch, Origen is here referring to the Slav. Enoch xxiv–xxx; xlvii. 3, 4.

The fragment of the Apocalypse of Zephaniah preserved in Clement, *Strom.* v. 11. 77, is likewise to be traced to our text: cf. xviii. (notes).

During the years 50–100 A.D. our text seems not to be without witness in the literature of that period. Thus in the Ascension of Isaiah, viii. 16, we read with regard to the angels of the sixth heaven: 'Omnium una species et gloria aequalis,' whereas the difference between the angelic orders in the lower heavens is repeatedly pointed out. Now in our text, xix. 1, it is said of the seven bands of angels present in the sixth heaven that 'there is no difference in their countenances, or their manner, or the style of their clothing.'

In 4 Ezra [vi. 71] the words 'ut facies eorum luceant sicut sol' are found in i. 5 'Their faces shone like the sun.'

With the Apocalypse of Baruch, iv. 3 'Ostendi eam (i.e. Paradisum) Adamo priusquam peccaret,' compare xxxi. 2.

In the Epistle of Barnabas xv. 4 τί λέγει τό· " συνετέλεσεν ἐν ἐξ ἡμέραις." τοῦτο λέγει ὅτι ἐν ἑξακισχιλίοις ἔτεσιν συντελέσει Κύριος τὰ σύνπαντα. ἡ γὰρ ἡμέρα παρ' αὐτῷ σημαίνει χίλια ἔτη, we have an exposition of the rather confused words in our text, xxxii. 2—xxxiii. In xv. 5-7, however, the writer of this Epistle does not develop logically the thought with regard to the seventh day; for the seventh day on which God rested from His works should in accordance with the same principle of interpretation as in xv. 4 have been taken as a symbol of a thousand years of rest, i.e. the millennium. In xv. 8, however, this writer shows his return to our text by his use of the peculiar phrase 'the eighth day': οὐ τὰ νῦν σάββατα [ἐμοὶ] δεκτά, ἀλλὰ ὃ πεποίηκα, ἐν ᾧ καταπαύσας τὰ πάντα ἀρχὴν ἡμέρας ὀγδόης ποιήσω, ὅ ἐστιν ἄλλου κόσμου ἀρχή. It may not be amiss here to point out that in the next chapter, in verse 5, the Ethiopic Enoch (lxxxix. 56, 66) is quoted as Scripture. The fact, therefore, that Barnabas does not quote our text as Scripture may point to his discrimination between the two books of Enoch to the detriment of the latter. Again in this Epistle, xviii. 1, the words ὁδοὶ δύο εἰσὶν ... ἥ τε τοῦ φωτὸς καὶ ἡ τοῦ σκότους are derived from our text, xxx. 15, 'I showed him the two ways, the light and the darkness.' Though the Two Ways are often described in early literature (see note on xxx. 15), only in Barnabas are they described in the same terms as in our text.

In the New Testament the similarity of thought and diction is sufficiently large to establish a close connexion, if not a literary dependence. With St. Matt. v. 9, 'Blessed are the peacemakers,' compare lii. 11, 'Blessed is he who establishes peace.' With St. Matt. v. 34, 35, 37, 'Swear not at all: neither by the heaven . . . nor by the earth . . . nor by

Jerusalem, . . . but let your speech be, Yea, yea : Nay, nay,'
compare xlix. 1, 'I will not swear by a single oath, neither
by heaven, nor by earth, nor by any other creature which
God made. . . . If there is no truth in men, let them swear
by a word, yea, yea, or nay, nay.' (See notes.)

With St. Matt. vii. 20, 'By their fruits ye shall know them,'
compare xlii. 14, 'By their works those who have wrought
them are known.' The words 'Be of good cheer, be not afraid,'
St. Matt. xiv. 27, are of frequent occurrence in our text, i. 8 ;
xx. 2 ; xxi. 3, &c. With St. Matt. xxv. 34, 'Inherit the
kingdom prepared for you from the foundation of the world,'
compare ix. 1, 'This place (i. e. Paradise) O Enoch, is prepared for the righteous . . . as an eternal inheritance.' Next
with St. Luke vi. 35 μηδὲν ἀπελπίζοντες, compare xlii. 7, 'Expecting nothing in return' Next with John xiv. 2, 'In my
Father's house are many mansions,' compare lxi. 2, 'For in
the world to come . . . there are many mansions prepared for
men, good for the good, evil for the evil.' With Acts xiv. 15,
'Ye should turn from these vain things unto the living God,
who made the heaven and the earth,' compare ii. 2, 'Do not
worship vain gods who did not make heaven and earth.' In
the Pauline Epistles there are several parallels in thought
and diction. With Col. i. 16, 'Dominions or principalities
or powers,' compare xx. 1, 'Lordships and principalities and
powers': with Eph. iv. 25, 'Speak ye truth each one with
his neighbour,' compare xlii. 12, 'Blessed is he in whom
is the truth that he may speak the truth to his neighbour.'
For other Pauline parallels with our text see pp. xxxix–xli.
With Heb. xi. 3, 'The worlds have been framed by the word
of God, so that what is seen hath not been made out of things
which do appear,' compare xxv. 1, 'I commanded . . . that
visible things should come out of invisible,' and xxiv. 2, 'I
will tell thee . . . what things I created from the non-existent,
and what visible things from the invisible.' For two other
parallels of Hebrews with our text see p. xli. With Rev.

i. 16, 'His countenance was as the sun shineth,' compare i. 5,
'Their faces shone like the sun': with ix. 1, 'There was
given to him the key of the pit of the abyss,' compare xlii. 1,
'Those who keep the keys and are the guardians of the gates
of hell.' With Rev. iv. 6, 'A glassy sea,' compare iii. 3, 'A
great sea greater than the earthy sea.' This sea in the first
heaven, however, may be merely 'the waters which were
above the firmament' (Gen. i. 7). With Rev. x. 5, 6, 'And
the angel . . . sware . . . that there shall be time no longer,'
compare lxv. 7, 'Then the times shall perish, and there shall
be no year,' &c.: xxxiii. 2, 'Let there be . . . a time when there
is no computation and no end; neither years, nor months,' &c.

Finally, in the Apocalyptic portions of the Testaments of the
XII Patriarchs, which were written probably about the beginning of the Christian era we find our text quoted directly or
implied in several instances. In Levi 3 we have an account of
the Angels imprisoned in the second heaven: ἐν αὐτῷ εἰσὶ πάντα
τὰ πνεύματα τῶν ἐπαγωγῶν εἰς ἐκδίκησιν τῶν ἀνόμων. This
must be rendered 'In it are all the spirits of the lawless ones
who are kept bound unto (the day of) vengeance.' With this
statement compare our text vii. 1, where the fallen angels in
the second heaven are described as 'the prisoners suspended,
reserved for (and) awaiting the eternal judgement.' Again, in
the same chapter of Levi, there are said to be armies in the
third heaven, οἱ ταχθέντες εἰς ἡμέραν κρίσεως, ποιῆσαι ἐκδίκησιν
ἐν τοῖς πνεύμασι τῆς πλάνης. With these compare the angels
of punishment in the third heaven in x. 3. The statement
from Enoch in Test. Dan. 5 τῶν πνευμάτων τῆς πλάνης. Ἀνέγνων γὰρ ἐν βίβλῳ Ἐνὼχ τοῦ δικαίου, ὅτι ὁ ἄρχων ὑμῶν ἐστὶν ὁ
Σατανᾶς is drawn from xviii. 3, 'These are the Grigori (i.e.
Ἐγρήγοροί) who with their prince Satanail rejected the holy
Lord.' In the Test. Napth. 4 the authority of Enoch is
claimed by the writer as follows: Ἀνέγνων ἐν γραφῇ ἁγίᾳ
Ἐνώχ, ὅτι καί γε καὶ ὑμεῖς ἀποστήσεσθε ἀπὸ κυρίου, πορευόμενοι
κατὰ πᾶσαν πονηρίαν ἐθνῶν, καὶ ποιήσετε κατὰ πᾶσαν ἀνομίαν

Σοδόμων. καὶ ἐπάξει ὑμῖν κύριος αἰχμαλωσίαν ... ἕως ἂν ἀναλώσῃ κύριος πάντας ὑμᾶς. This is a loose adaptation to later times of xxxiv. 2, 3, ' And they will fill all the world with wickedness and iniquity and foul impurities with one another, sodomy. . . . And on this account I will bring a deluge upon the earth, and I will destroy all.' The quotation in Test. Sim. 5 is probably derived from the same source, and that in Test. Benj. 9 ὑπονοῶ δὲ καὶ πράξεις ἐν ὑμῖν οὐ καλὰς ἔσεσθαι, ἀπὸ λόγων 'Ενὼχ τοῦ δικαίου· πορνεύσετε γὰρ πορνείαν Σοδόμων, καὶ ἀπώλησθε ἕως βραχύ, may confidently be traced to it. The words in Test. Juda 18 ἀνέγνων ἐν βίβλοις 'Ενὼχ τοῦ δικαίου, ὅσα κακὰ ποιήσετε ἐπ' ἐσχάταις ἡμέραις. φυλάξασθε οὖν, τέκνα μου, ἀπὸ τῆς πορνείας may likewise be founded upon it. The loose and inaccurate character of the quotations may in part be accounted for as follows.

Although it is a matter of demonstration that the main part of the book was written originally in Greek, it seems no less sure that certain portions of it were founded on Hebrew originals. Such an hypothesis is necessary owing to the above Enochic quotations which appear in the Testaments of the XII Patriarchs. For the fact that the latter work was written in Hebrew obliges us to conclude that its author or authors drew upon Hebrew originals in the quotations from Enoch. I have not attempted in the present work to discriminate the portions derived from Hebrew originals. For such a task we have not sufficient materials, and what we have, moreover, have not been preserved with sufficient accuracy.

§ 6. Integrity and Critical Condition of the Book.

In its present form this book appears to be derived from one author. We have in the notes called attention from time to time to certain inconsistencies, but these may in part be due to inaccurate tradition; for the book in this respect has suffered deplorably. There are of course occasional interpo-

lations— of these some are Jewish, and one or two are
Christian: xxxvii seems foreign to the entire text.

The text, further, has suffered from disarrangement. Thus
xxviii. 5 should be read after xxix, and, together with that
chapter, should be restored before xxviii.

§ 7. DATE AND AUTHORSHIP.

The question of the date has to a large extent been determined already. The portions which have a Hebrew background are at latest pre-Christian. This follows from the
fact of their quotation in the Testaments of the XII Patriarchs.
As I have remarked above (p. xxiv) it is impossible to
define the exact extent of such sections.

Turning, therefore, to the date of the rest of the book, we
can with tolerable certainty discover the probable limits of its
composition. The earlier limit is determined by the already
existing books from which our author has borrowed. Thus
Ecclesiasticus is frequently drawn upon : see xliii. 2, 3 (notes) ;
xlvii. 5 (note) ; lii. 8 (note) ; lxi. 2, 4 (notes), &c. The Book of
Wisdom also seems to have been laid under contribution : see
lxv. 4 (note). With this book our author shares certain closely
related Hellenistic views. Again, as regards the Ethiopic
Enoch, our author at times reproduces the phraseology and
conceptions of that book : see vii. 4, 5 (notes) ; xxxiii. 4
(note), 9, 10 (notes) ; xxxv. 2 (note), &c. ; at others he gives
the views of the former in a developed form : see viii. 1, 5, 6
(notes) ; xl. 13 (note) ; lxiv. 5 ; at others he enunciates views
which are absolutely divergent from the former : see xvi. 7
(note) ; xviii. 4 (note). It is noteworthy also that our author
claims to have explained certain natural phenomena, but the
explanations in question are not to be found in his writings
but in the Ethiopic Enoch : see xl. 5, 6, 8, 9 (notes). Finally
we observe the same advanced view on Demonology appearing
in the Slavonic Enoch and in the latest interpolation in the
Ethiopic Enoch ; see xviii. 3 (note).

Ecclesiasticus, the Book of Wisdom (?), and the Ethiopic Enoch (in its latest and present form) were thus at our author's service. The earlier limit of composition, accordingly, lies probably between 30 B.C. and the Christian era.

We have now to determine the later limit. This must be set down as earlier than 70 A.D. For, (1) the temple is still standing; see lix. 2 (notes). (2) Our text was probably known to some of the writers of the New Testament (see pp. xxi–xxiii; xxxix–xliii). (3) It was known and used by the writers of the Epistle of Barnabas and of the latter half of the Ascension of Isaiah.

We may, therefore, with reasonable certainty assign the composition of our text to the period 1–50 A.D. The date of the Hebrew original underlying certain sections of our text is as we have already seen pre-Christian.

The author was a Jew who lived in Egypt, probably in Alexandria. He belonged to the orthodox Hellenistic Judaism of his day. Thus he believed in the value of sacrifices, xlii. 6; lix. 1, 2; lxvi. 2; but he is careful to enforce enlightened views regarding them, xlv. 3, 4; lxi. 4, 5; in the law, lii. 8, 9; and likewise in a blessed immortality, l. 2; lxv. 6, 8–10; in which the righteous shall wear 'the raiment of God's glory,' xxii. 8. In questions affecting the origin of the earth, sin, death, &c., he allows himself the most unrestricted freedom and borrows freely from every quarter. Thus, Platonic (xxx. 16, note), Egyptian (xxv. 2, note), and Zend (lviii. 4–6 notes) elements are adopted into his system. The result is naturally syncretistic.

The date (1–50 A.D.) thus determined above makes our author a contemporary of Philo. We have shown above (p. xvii) that they share many speculations in common, but in some they are opposed. Thus our author protests against the Jewish belief in the value of the intercession of departed saints for the living; see liii. 1 (note). Philo undoubtedly taught this, *De Exsecrat.* 9.

§ 8. SOME OF THE AUTHOR'S VIEWS ON CREATION, ANTHROPOLOGY, AND ETHICS.

God in the beginning created the world out of nothing, xxiv. 2 [1]. (For a detailed account of each day's creations see xxv–xxx.) In this creation He made seven heavens, xxx. 2, 3 [2], and all the angelic hosts—the latter were created on the first day—and all animal and plant life, and finally man on the sixth day. After His work on the six days God rested on the seventh. These six days of work followed by a seventh of rest are at once a history of the past and a forecasting of the future. As the world was made in six days, so its history would be accomplished in 6,000 years, and as the six days of creation were followed by one of rest, so the 6,000 years of the world's history would be followed by a rest of 1,000 years, i. e. the millennium [3]. On its close would begin the eighth eternal day of blessedness when time should be no more, xxxii. 2—xxxiii. 2.

As regards man, all the souls of men were created before the foundation of the world, xxiii. 5, and also a future place of abode in heaven or hell for every individual soul, xlix. 2; lviii. 5; lxi. 2. The world was made for man's sake, lxv. 3. When Wisdom made man of seven substances, xxx. 8, at God's command, God gave him the name Adam from the four quarters of the earth—ἀνατολή, δύσις, ἄρκτος, μεσημβρία —xxx. 13. Man's soul was created originally good, while in the garden he could see the angels in heaven, xxxi. 2. Free-will was bestowed upon him, and the knowledge of good and evil. He was likewise instructed in the Two Ways of light and darkness, and then left to mould his own destiny, xxx. 15.

---

[1] Or else formed it out of pre-existing elements, xxv. 1, where we have an adaptation of the egg theory of the universe.

[2] Hell was in the north of the third heaven. It is possible, how-ever, that there were also seven hells; see xl. 12 (note).

[3] This millennium seems to be identical with a Messianic age, xxxv. 3 (note).

But the incorporation of the soul in the body with its necessary limitations biassed its preferences in the direction of evil, and death came in as the fruit of sin, xxx. 16. Men and angels will be judged and punished for every form of sin [1], xl. 12, 13; xlvi. 3; lxv. 6; but the righteous will escape the last judgement, lxv. 8; lxvi. 7; and will be gathered in eternal life, lxv. 8, and will be seven times brighter than the sun, lxvi. 7, and they will have no labour, nor sickness, nor sorrow, nor anxiety, nor need, and an incorruptible paradise shall be their protection and their eternal habitation, lxv. 9, 10. As for sinners there is no place of repentance after death, xlii. 2, but hell is prepared for them as an eternal inheritance, x. 4, 6. And there is no intercession of departed saints for the living, liii. 1.

In an ethical regard there are many noble sentiments to be found in our author, but generally in a very unliterary form. The Slavonic Version is, no doubt, partially to be blamed here. I will append here an outline of a man's ethical duties with sundry beatitudes according to our author. Every man should work; for blessed is he who looks to raise his own hand for labour, but cursed is he who looks to make use of another man's labour, lii. 7, 8. And men, likewise, should be unselfishly just; for blessed is he who executes a just judgement, not for the sake of recompense, but for the sake of righteousness, expecting nothing in return, xlii. 7. And men should also practice charity and beneficence. They should not hide their silver in the earth, but assist the honest man in his affliction, li. 2, and stretch out their hands to the orphan, the widow and the stranger, l. 5, and give bread to the hungry, and clothe the naked, and raise the fallen, and walk without blame before the face of the Lord, ix. Furthermore, men should not swear either by heaven or earth or by any other creature which God made, but by a word, yea, yea, or nay, nay,

---

[1] Observe that men will be specially punished for ill-treatment of animals, lviii. 4-6.

xlix. 1 ; neither should they avenge themselves, l. 4, nor abuse and calumniate their neighbour, lii. 2 ; but endure every affliction and every evil word and attack for the sake of the Lord, l. 3 ; li. 3. Moreover, they should shun pride : for God hates the proud, lxiii. 4; and walk in long-suffering, in humility, in faith and truth, in sickness, in abuse, in temptation, in nakedness, in deprivation, loving one another till they depart from this world of sickness, lxvi. 6. Finally, whereas one man is more honourable than another, either on the ground of cunning or of strength, of purity or wisdom, of comeliness or understanding, let it be heard everywhere that none is greater than he who fears God, xliii. 2, 3.

§ 9. The Value of this Book in elucidating contemporary and subsequent Religious Thought.

On the value of this book in elucidating contemporary and subsequent religious thought I shall be brief, save in the case of the doctrine of the seven heavens. This doctrine is set forth by our author with a fullness and clearness not found elsewhere in literature. Thus many gaps in our knowledge of this doctrine have been filled up. It will not be surprising, therefore, if we are thus enabled to explain certain mysterious allusions bearing on this conception in the Bible and elsewhere, which have hitherto been doubtful or inexplicable.

Some of the beliefs which appear in our text, and which in some instances are either partially or wholly elucidated, are as follows :

1. *Death was caused by Sin.* This was a comparatively late view : see notes on pp. 43, 44.

2. *The millennium.* This Jewish conception is first found in this book, xxxii. 2—xxxiii. 2, and the rationale of its origin is clear from this passage when taken together with statements on the same subject in later writers (see notes *in loc.*, and p. xxvii). Its origin was as follows. The account in Genesis of the first week of creation came in pre-Christian times to be regarded

not only as a history of the past, but as a forecast of the future history of the world so created. Thus as the world was created in six days, so its history was to be accomplished in 6,000 years ; for 1,000 years are with God as one day (cf. Ps. xc. 4 ; Jub. iv. 30 ; 2 Pet. iii. 8 ; Barnabas, *Ep.* xiv. 4 ; Iren. *contra Haer.* v. 28. 2 ; Justin M., *Dial. c. Tryph.* 80), and as God rested on the seventh day, so at the close of the 6,000 years there would be a rest of 1,000 years, i. e. the millennium.

3. *On the creation of man with freewill and the knowledge of good and evil*, see xxx. 15 (notes).

4. *The Seraphim.* In the Chalkidri [1], xii. 1, we have in all probability the serpents who are mentioned in the Ethiopic Enoch xx. 7 along with the Cherubim. They are a class of heavenly creatures, and like the Cherubim are formed by a combination of the members of different animals. The serpent-like form, however, predominated, and hence they were δρακόντες in Greek (Eth. En. xx. 7), and Seraphim (שרפים) in Hebrew. How the peculiar name Chalkidri (= Χαλκύδραι brazen serpents ?) arose I cannot say, as it is by no means appropriate. The main objection to identifying the Chalkidri with the Seraphim of the Old Testament is the fact that our author only mentions them here in connexion with the sun, xii. 1 ; xv. 1 ; and speaks directly of Seraphim elsewhere, xx. 1. However this may be, the passage in the Eth. Enoch xx. 7 is conclusive as to the serpent-like forms of the Seraphim. By this interpretation the word receives the meaning which it naturally has in the Hebrew.

5. *On the intercession of Saints*, see liii. 1 (note).

6. *The seven Heavens—an early Jewish and Christian belief.*

Various conceptions of the seven heavens prevailed largely in the ancient world, alike in the far east and in the west. With these we shall deal only in so far as they influenced or were in any degree akin to the views that prevailed on this subject among the Jews and early Christians.

---

[1] Variously spelt in the MSS. as Chalkadri, Chalkidri, Chalkedry.

For the sake of clearness it may be well to indicate the direction our investigations will take. We shall first set forth or merely mention the beliefs of this nature that prevailed among the Babylonians and the followers of Zoroaster in the East and the speculations of certain Greek philosophers in the West. We shall next touch briefly on certain indications in the Old Testament that point in the direction of a plurality of the heavens, and show that Israel was not unaffected by the prevailing traditions of the ancient world.

That we have not misinterpreted such phenomena in the Old Testament, we are assured, when we descend to Jewish Apocalyptic writings, such as the Testaments of the XII Patriarchs, the Slavonic Enoch, 4 Ezra, and to the Talmud, and the Mandaic Religion. Having thus shown that speculations or definitely formulated views on the plurality of the heavens were rife in the very cradle of Christendom and throughout its entire environment, we have next to consider whether Christian conceptions of heaven were shaped or in any degree modified by already existing ideas on this subject. We shall find that there is undoubted evidence of the belief in the plurality or sevenfold division of the heavens in the Pauline Epistles, in Hebrews, and in the Apocalypse.

In early Christian literature such ideas soon gained clearer utterance in Christian Apocalypses, such as the Ascension of Isaiah, the Apocalypses of Moses, Ezra, John, Isaac, Jacob, and the Acts of Callistratus. Such writers also as Clement of Alexandria and Origen are more or less favourably inclined to such conceptions. But shortly after this date these views fell into the background, discredited undoubtedly by the exaggerations and imbecilities with which they were accompanied. And thus though a Philastrius declares disbelief in a plurality of the heavens a heresy, Chrysostom is so violently affected against such a conception that he denies any such plurality at all. Finally such conceptions, failing in the course of the next few centuries to find a home in Christian lands, betook themselves to Mohammedan countries, where they found a ready welcome and a place of authority in the temple of Moslem theology. We shall now proceed as we have above indicated.

Among the Babylonians we find that hell was divided into seven parts by seven concentric walls (see Sayce, *Babylonian Religion*, 1887, pp. 221–227; Jensen, *Die Kosmologie der Babylonier*, Strasburg, 1890, pp. 232–3[1]). Hence, we may here observe, this view passed over into the Talmud (Feuchtwang, *Zeitschr. f. Assyr.*, iv. 42, 43).

This sevenfold division of things in general was a familiar one among this people[2]. Thus the cities, Erech and Ecbatana, were each surrounded by seven walls, modelled, no doubt, as Jensen conjectures, on their conception of the seven world-zones (*op. cit.* 172). For the world was held to be divided in this fashion according to the *Gudia* (*op. cit.* 173). This division was due either to the overwhelming importance of the sacred number seven, or else specifically to the number of the planets (*op. cit.* 174). We should observe also that the temple of Erech was called the temple of the seven divisions. Since, therefore, both earth and hell were divided into seven zones, it is only reasonable to infer that a similar conception was entertained regarding the heavens. Jensen, indeed, says that he can find no trace of such a division in the inscriptions. But since the sevenfold division of the planets gave birth to the sevenfold division of earth and hell, it is next to impossible to avoid the inference with Sayce and Jeremias that this same division must have been applied to the heavens through which the planets moved.

In Parseeism we find the doctrine of the seven heavens. This does not appear in the earliest writings, but in the Ardâi-virâf-nâme there is an account of the seven heavens

---

[1] See also Jeremias, *Die babyl.-assur. Vorstellungen vom Leben nach dem Tode*, 1887, pp. 34–45.

[2] Cf. Sayce, *Babylonian Religion*, p. 82 note.

through which Sosiash made a progress in seven days. In the first heaven are men who feel heat and cold simultaneously. (If we might infer from corresponding ideas in the Slavonic Enoch, and other apocalypses, we should conclude this heaven to be an abode of the wicked, and not of the good. There is, however, a hell independently of this.) The inhabitants of the second heaven shine as the stars; of the third as the moon; of the fourth as the sun. The blessedness of endless light is reserved for heroes, lawgivers, and the preeminently pious. In the seventh heaven Zarathustra sits on a golden throne. As we have already remarked, there is only one hell mentioned in the Ardâi-virâf-nâme. On the influence which such ideas had on the Talmud see Kohut, *Zeitschrift D M G*, xxi. 562.

If we now turn from the East to the West, we meet first of all with the Pythagorean tenfold division of the universe. In the centre there was the central fire around which revolved from west to east the ten heavenly bodies. Furthest off was the heaven of fixed stars; next came the five planets; then the sun, the moon, the earth, and finally the counter earth [1]. According to the *Timaeus* of Plato the universe is shaped as a sphere at the centre of which is placed the earth. Next follow the sun, the moon, and the five other planets, revolving round the earth in orbits separated from each other by distances corresponding to the intervals of the harmonic system. The outermost circle is formed of the heaven of fixed stars.

When we turn to the Stoics we find kindred conceptions; in the centre of the universe the earth is placed in a state of repose. Nearest to the earth revolves the moon, and next in their appropriate orbits the Sun, Venus, Mercury, Mars, Jupiter, Saturn.

We have thus seen that speculations were rife throughout

---

[1] For further details see the English translation of Zeller's *Pre-Socratic Philosophy*, i. 444-5.

the ancient world on the plurality of the heavens. It is clear further that these speculations were based mainly on astronomical considerations. That ancient·Judaism· was not un-affected by such views we may reasonably conclude from certain passages in the Old Testament. The plural form of the word· for 'heaven' in Hebrew probably points to a plurality of heavens. Such phrases as 'the heaven of heavens,' Deut. x. 14; 1 Kings viii. 27; Ps. cxlviii. 4, cannot be adequately interpreted unless in reference to such a belief. In Job i. 6, 7; ii. 1, 2, 7 we find a further peculiar feature in the ancient conception of heaven. Satan there presents himself along with the angels in the presence of God. The place indicated by the context is heaven. Similarly in 1 Kings xxii. 19–22 an evil spirit presents himself among the heavenly hosts before the throne of God. The presence of evil in heaven, though offensive to the conscience of later times, seems to have caused no offence in early Semitic thought.

We shall find in the course of our investigations that this peculiar idea reasserted itself from time to time in Judaism and Christianity till finally it was expelled from both.

The probability of an Old Testament belief in the plurality of the heavens is heightened, if we consider the fact that the Jews were familiar with and attached names to the planets. Thus Kronos, Aphrodite, Ares, Zeus, Hermes are mentioned respectively in Amos v. 26; Is. xiv. 12; 2 Kings xvii. 30; Is. lxv. 11; xlvi. 1. The Jews were acquainted also with the signs of the Zodiac (Job xxxviii. 32), and offered them an idolatrous worship (2 Kings xxiii. 5).

Since, therefore, we have seen that in the East astronomical considerations, i. e. the sevenfold division of the planets led in due course to a similar division of the heavens, it is not unlikely that this knowledge gave birth to a like result among the Jews.

However this may be, the reasonable probability we have

already arrived at is converted into a certainty when we come down to the Apocalyptic and other writings of the Jews. Of these, the Slavonic Enoch and the Apocalyptic sections of the Testaments of the XII Patriarchs were written about or before the beginning of the Christian Era. As the description of the seven heavens in the latter is very brief we shall deal with it first. The rendering that follows presupposes an emendation of Dr. Sinker's text, which I cannot justify here, but hope to do so later in an edition of this work.

The third chapter of the Testament of Levi runs : ' Hear then concerning the seven heavens. The lowest is the gloomiest, because it witnesses every iniquity of men. The second has fire, snow, ice, ready against the day of the ordinance of the Lord, in the righteous judgement of God. In it are all the spirits of the lawless ones which are confined for punishment. (Cf. Slav. Enoch vii.) In the third are the hosts of the armies (cf. Slav. Enoch xvii) which are appointed against the day of judgement to execute vengeance on the spirits of deceit and of Beliar. . . . In the highest of all the Great Glory dwells, in the holy of holies. . . . In the heaven next to it (i. e. the sixth) are the angels of the presence of the Lord, who minister and make propitiation to the Lord for all the sins of ignorance of the righteous. . . . And in the heaven below this (i. e. the fifth) are the angels who bear the answers to the angels of the presence of the Lord. And in the heaven next to this (i. e. the fourth) are thrones, authorities, in which hymns are ever offered to God.' In chapter ii of the same Testament there is a short reference to the first three heavens: ' And I entered from the first heaven into the second, and I saw there water hanging between the two. And I saw a third heaven brighter than these two.'

We cannot pause here to deal with the details of the above account. We shall only draw attention to the description of the denizens of the second heaven. These are the fallen angels who are reserved for punishment. Although the

description of the seven heavens just given is short, it is too
definitely conceived to have appeared thus for the first time
in Judaism. In the Slavonic Enoch, whose evidence we shall
presently briefly summarize, we have, so far as I am aware, the
most elaborate account of the seven heavens that exists in
any writing or in any language. 'The Book of the Secrets
of Enoch,' as it is named in the Slavonic MSS. in which
it is alone preserved, but which for the sake of brevity I call
'the Slavonic Enoch,' was written in the main in Greek,
at Alexandria, although portions of it are merely reproductions
of a Hebrew original. In the first heaven there is 'a very
great sea, greater than any earthly sea.' (Cf. Rev. iv. 6.)
This sea seems to be described in the Testaments of the XII
Patriarchs as 'water hanging between the first and second
heavens.' (See above.) In this heaven also are 'the elders
and the rulers of the orders of the stars.' Although the
number of these is not given, it is either twelve (and then
we have here an account related to Eth. En. lxxxii. 9–18,
20) or possibly it is twenty-four, and thus there may be
a remote connexion on the one hand between this class of
'elders and rulers . . . of the stars' and the twenty-four
elders in Rev. iv. 4, and on the other between it and the
Babylonian idea set forth in Diodorus Siculus, ii. 31 μετὰ δὲ
τὸν ζωδιακὸν κύκλον εἴκοσιν καὶ τέτταρας ἀφορίζουσιν ἀστέρας,
ὧν τοὺς μὲν ἡμίσεις ἐν τοῖς βορείοις μέρεσι, τοὺς δὲ ἡμίσεις ἐν
τοῖς νοτίοις τετάχθαι φασί, καὶ τούτων τοὺς μὲν ὁρωμένους τῶν
ζώντων εἶναι καταριθμοῦσι, τοὺς δ' ἀφανεῖς τοῖς τετελευτηκόσι
προσωρίσθαι νομίζουσιν, οὓς δικαστὰς τῶν ὅλων προσαγορεύουσιν
(quoted by Gunkel, *Schöpfung und Chaos*, p. 308, who establishes
a connexion between Rev. iv. 4 and this Babylonian idea).
The first heaven, further, contains treasuries of snow, ice,
clouds, and dew.

In the second heaven (chap. vii) Enoch saw the prisoners
suspended reserved for and awaiting the eternal judgement.
'And these angels were gloomy in appearance, . . . they

had apostatized from the Lord and transgressed together with their prince.' For a similar account see Test. Levi, above.

In the third heaven (chap. viii) we have the garden of Eden and the tree of life, and likewise 'an olive tree always distilling oil,' i. e. the *arbor misericordiae* (cf. Evang. Nicodemi, ii. 3). We should observe that the location of Paradise in this heaven agrees with the Pauline account 2 Cor. xii. 2, 3.

But (chap. x) in the northern region of this heaven Enoch sees the place of the damned. 'That place has fire on all sides and on all sides cold and ice, thus it burns and freezes.' When Enoch exclaims, 'Woe, woe! how terrible is this place!' his escort replies: 'This place, Enoch, is prepared for those who did not honour God; who commit evil deeds on earth, sodomy, witchcraft, enchantments, . . . stealing, lying, calumnies, envy, evil thoughts, fornication, murder. (Chap. x. 4.)

In the fourth heaven (chap. xi–xv) Enoch sees the course of the sun and moon, and the angels and the wonderful creatures, the phoenixes and the chalkidri, which wait upon the sun. In the midst of this heaven (chap. xvii) are 'the armed host serving the Lord with cymbals and organs and unceasing voice.' Cf. Test. Levi on third and fourth heavens above.

In the fifth heaven (chap. xviii) are the watchers whose fallen brethren Enoch had already seen undergoing torments in the second heaven. These are troubled and silent on account of their brethren.

In the sixth heaven (chap. xix) are 'seven bands of angels, very bright and glorious,' who arrange and study the revolutions of the stars and the changes of the moon and the revolutions of the sun, &c.; 'And the angels over all the souls of men who write down all their works and their lives before the face of the Lord. In their midst are seven phoenixes and seven cherubim and seven six-winged creatures.'

In the seventh heaven (chap. xx) Enoch sees all the heavenly hosts, the ten great orders of angels standing before the Lord in the order of their rank, and the Lord sitting on His lofty throne.

With regard to this scheme, I will content myself with calling attention to the fact that a preliminary Tartarus is situated in the second heaven (cf. second heaven in the Test. Levi); and that hell is placed in the north of the third heaven, and that evil in various forms is found in the second and third heavens, and dissatisfaction and trouble in the fifth.

In 4 Ezra (vi. 55–74) there is a detailed description of the seven ways of the wicked and the seven ways of the righteous. These ways are represented in a form so essentially abstract, that as Gunkel rightly remarks (*op. cit.* p. 309), they must be derived from what were originally concrete conceptions such as the seven heavens and the seven hells. To the latter conception there is no reference in the Slavonic Enoch: yet see xl. 12 (note).

Passing onward we come to the Talmud. In the Talmud the views of the Rabbis waver. Some thought as the Rabbi Jehuda that there were two heavens, *Chagiga* 12^b, but Rabbi Simeon ben Lakish enumerated seven. This latter view was the usual one. In the *Beresh. rabba* c. 6 and the *Chagiga* 12^b, the seven heavens are as follows. The lowest which is called *vilun* is empty. In the second, named *rakía*, are the sun, moon, and stars. In the third, named *shechaqim*, are the mills which grind the manna for the righteous. In the fourth heaven, *zebul*, are the heavenly Jerusalem, the temple, the altar, and Michael. In the fifth, *maon*, are the angels who sing by night, but are silent by day in order that God may hear the praises of Israel. In the sixth, *machon*, are the treasuries of the snow, hail, rain, and dew. In the seventh, *aravoth*, are judgement and righteousness, the treasures of life, peace, and blessing, the souls of the departed pious as

well as the spirits and souls yet to be born, and the dew
wherewith God will awake the dead. Finally there are the
seraphim, ophannim, chayyoth and other angels of service,
and God Himself sitting on a throne. See Weber, *Die Lehren
des Talmud*, pp. 197–8; Eisenmenger, *Entdecktes Judenthum*,
i. 467; Wetstein on 2 Cor. xii.

It is well to observe here that, though the Talmudic
description of the seven heavens is puerile in the extreme,
its character attests the influence of a growing ethical consciousness.

To such a consciousness the presence of evil in heaven
could not but seem incongruous. In banishing evil, however,
from the precincts of the heavens, the Rabbis weakened the
vigour of the old conceptions; for they were not masters of
sufficient imagination to fill up adequately the gaps brought
about by their righteous zeal. In connexion with Jewish
evidence on this subject, we might point out that the same
division of the heavens probably prevailed in the Mandaic
Religion, since at all events one of its dogmas was the
sevenfold division of hell (Brandt, *Die Mandäische Religion*,
p. 182).

We have now found that among the Babylonians, the
later followers of Zoroaster, the Greeks, in all probability in
ancient Judaism, and certainly in Judaism generally from
before the Christian Era onward, speculations, and as a rule
clearly defined conceptions, were rife on the plurality of the
heavens. We have seen also that the prevailing view was
that of the sevenfold division of the heavens, and we have
observed further that a feature impossible in modern conceptions of heaven shows itself from time to time in pre-
Christian religious conceptions, i.e. the belief in the presence
of evil in the heavens.

We have now to consider whether Christian conceptions
of heaven were shaped, or in any degree influenced, by already
existing views of that nature. A knowledge of ancient

thought on this subject would naturally lead us to expect
such an influence at work, and we find on examination that
our expectations are in certain respects fully realized.   First
from 2 Cor. xii. 2, 3 we learn that St. Paul believed in a
plurality of the heavens. 'I know a man in Christ fourteen
years ago ... such a one caught up even to the third heaven.
And I know such a man ... how that he was caught up into
Paradise.'

Heretofore exegetes have been divided as to whether
St. Paul believed in the existence of three heavens or of seven.
Owing to the fresh evidence on the subject furnished by the
Slavonic Enoch there is no longer room for reasonable doubt
on the question.   In the Slavonic Enoch we have presented
to us a scheme of the seven heavens which in some of its
prominent features agrees with that conceived by St. Paul.
Thus in the Slavonic Enoch Paradise is situated in the third
heaven as in 2 Cor. xii. 2, 3, whereas according to later Judaism
it belonged to the fourth heaven (see above).   In the next
place the presence of evil in some part of the heavens is
recognized.   Thus in Eph. vi. 12 we meet with the peculiar
statement ' Against the spiritual hosts of wickedness in the
heavens,' πρὸς τὰ πνευματικὰ τῆς πονηρίας ἐν τοῖς ἐπουρανίοις.
The phrase ἐν τοῖς ἐπουρανίοις occurs only in Ephesians of the
Pauline Epistles.   It is found five times i. 3, 20 ; ii. 6 ; iii.
10 ; and vi. 12, and always in a local sense.   It is thus in
fact = ἐν τοῖς οὐρανοῖς.

This phrase is then capable of two interpretations.   The
' hosts ' in question are the fallen angels in the second
heaven, or else the powers of Satan, the prince of the air (cf.
Eph. ii. 2).   For the latter interpretation the Slavonic Enoch
xxix. 4, 5 might be quoted as a parallel: 'One of the ranks
of the archangels, having turned away with the rank below
him, entertained an impossible idea, that he should make
his throne higher than the clouds over the earth, and should
be equal in rank to My power.   And I hurled him from the

heights with his angels. And he was flying in the air continually above the abyss.' The latter explanation of ἐν τοῖς ἐπουρανίοις is probably right. In Col. i. 20, however, we must, if we deal honestly with the context, suppose some such a view of the heavens as that given in the Slavonic Enoch to underlie the words: 'To reconcile all things unto Himself, whether things upon the earth or things in the heavens.' That 'things upon earth' need to be reconciled to God is universally intelligible; but so far as I am aware no exegete has hitherto recognized any such necessity on the part of 'things in the heavens.' Yet this is the obvious meaning of the words. Hence 'the things in the heavens' that are to be reconciled to God must be either the fallen angels imprisoned in the second heaven, or else the powers of Satan whose domain is the air. Though to some universalistic aspects of Paulinism the conversion of Satan is not impossible, it is nevertheless unlikely to be his thought here. Hence we seem to be restricted to the other interpretation, and thus we have therein an indirect parallel to 1 Pet. iii. 19, 'He went and preached to the spirits in prison.' Another statement in Eph. iii. 10 belongs to the same plane of thought: 'To the intent that now unto the principalities and the powers in the heavens (ἐν τοῖς ἐπουρανίοις) might be made known through the church the manifold wisdom of God.' These 'principalities and powers' may also be taken as the fallen angels in the second heaven; but it is more likely that they are the rulers of the various lower heavens which are mentioned in iv. 10: 'He . . . that ascended far above all the heavens.' This thought of the seven heavens through which Christ passed or above which he was exalted twice recurs in Hebrews iv. 14: 'Having then a great high priest, who hath passed through the heavens' (διεληλυθότα τοὺς οὐρανούς); vii. 26: 'Made higher than the heavens' (ὑψηλότερος τῶν οὐρανῶν γενόμενος). Before we pass on to the consideration of the Apocalypse, we should observe that Paul used οὐρανός [1] frequently (cf. Rom. i. 18; x. 6; 1 Cor. viii. 5; xv. 47), though he believed in a plurality of the heavens.

In the twelfth chapter of Revelation we have a record of the war in heaven between Michael and his angels against Satan and his angels, with the subsequent overthrow and expulsion of the latter. These events spiritually interpreted symbolize, it is true, the victory of good over evil, but when studied in reference to their origin, they mark a revolutionizing of the old Semitic conception of heaven. Evil can no longer be conceived as possible in the abode of righteousness, nor can its place be any more found in heaven. And thus Satan and his angels are cast down to the earth. When once evil in all its forms is driven forth from heaven, the rationale of a sevenfold division of it disappears. There are then no longer conflicting elements which must be restricted to certain divisions and kept apart by concrete barriers. The old Semitic doctrine of the seven heavens really presupposes in some respects dualistic influences. Such a conception could not long hold its ground in a monistic faith. It was this dualistic tinge that made it so acceptable with the heretics. We must now follow the subsequent fortunes of this doctrine in the early centuries of Christianity.

First we find in one of the Christian sections (chaps. vi–xi) of the Ascension of Isaiah an elaborate but sinewless account of the seven heavens. Evil has already been expelled, and the inhabitants of one heaven differ from those of another merely in possessing greater degrees of glory and knowledge. This account of the seven heavens is singularly wanting in variety and imaginative power: it is valuable, however, in an historical reference.

---

[1] The singular and plural of this word are used, according to Sir J. C. Hawkins, in the New Testament as follows:—

	Mat.	Mark	Luke	John	Acts	Paul.	Heb.	James	Pet.	Rev.
οὐρανός	27	12	31	18	24	11	3	2	1	51
οὐρανοί	55	5	4	0	2	10	7	0	5	1*

*xii. 12—a quotation from, or reference to Is. xliv. 23 and xlix. 13.

Leaving the Ascension of Isaiah, we shall now give the evidence of Clement of Alexandria and Origen on the prevalence of this doctrine.

In the *Stromata* iv. 25 of Clement there is a reference to the seven heavens which are obviously regarded as a true conception; while in v. 11 we have a quotation from a lost Apocalypse of Zephaniah: ἆρ' οὐχ ὅμοια ταῦτα τοῖς ὑπὸ Σοφονία λεχθεῖσι τοῦ προφήτου; καὶ ἀνέλαβέν με πνεῦμα καὶ ἀνήνεγκέν με ὡς οὐρανὸν πέμπτον καὶ ἐθεώρουν ἀγγέλους καλουμένους κυρίους . . . ὑμνοῦντας θεὸν ἄρρητον ὕψιστον.

This passage seems to be ultimately derived from the Slavonic Enoch xviii.

In the lost Book of Baruch the Prophet, there was some account of the seven heavens according to Origen, *de Princip.* ii. 3, 6: 'Denique etiam Baruch prophetae librum in assertionis huius testimonium vocant, quod ibi de septem mundis vel coelis evidentius indicatur.'

But to proceed to Origen's own views we read in *contra Cels.* vi. 21 as follows: ἑπτὰ δὲ οὐρανούς, ἢ ὅλως περιωρισμένον ἀριθμὸν αὐτῶν, αἱ φερόμεναι ἐν ταῖς ἐκκλησίαις τοῦ θεοῦ οὐκ ἀπαγγέλλουσι γραφαί· ἀλλ' οὐρανούς, εἴτε τὰς σφαίρας τῶν παρ' Ἕλλησι λεγομένων πλανήτων, εἴτε καὶ ἄλλο τι ἀπορρητότερον ἐοίκασι διδάσκειν οἱ λόγοι.

Though Origen says that there is no authoritative teaching as to there being seven heavens, it is clear that he really believes in there being this number; for elsewhere he identifies these heavens with the planets of the Greeks, *de Princip.* ii. 11. 6: 'Si quis sane mundus corde, et purior mente, et exercitatior sensu fuerit, velocius proficiens cito ad aeris locum adscendet, et ad coelorum regna perveniet per locorum singulorum, ut ita dixerim, mansiones, quas Graeci quidem sphaeras, id est globos, appellaverunt, scriptura vero divina coelos nominat: in quibus singulis primo quidem perspiciet ea, quae ibi geruntur, secundo vero etiam rationem quare gerantur agnoscet: et ita per ordinem digredietur singula, sequens eum, qui transgressus est coelos, Iesum filium Dei, dicentem : " Volo, ut ubi sum ego, et isti sint mecum." '

We shall now cite the evidence of Christian Apocalyptic works as attesting the prevalence of this belief in the seven heavens.

In the Apocalypse of Moses, p. 19 (*Apocalypses Apocryphae*, ed. Tischendorf, 1866), Eve is bidden to look up to the seven firmaments : ἀνάβλεψον τοῖς ὀφθαλμοῖς σου καὶ ἴδε τὰ ἑπτὰ στερεώματα ἀνεῳγμένα. On p. 21 Michael is bidden : ἄπελθε εἰς τὸν παράδεισον ἐν τῷ τρίτῳ οὐρανῷ. Thus the writer of this Apocalypse, so far as he touches on the subject of the seven heavens, agrees with the teaching of the Slavonic Enoch. In the Apoc. Esdrae (pp. 29, 30 *op. cit.*) there is mention made of a plurality of the heavens, and of Paradise as lying in the east. In the Apoc. Johannis (p. 84 *op. cit.*) the seven regions of the heavens are spoken of : καὶ γενήσεται κρότος μέγας ἐν τοῖς οὐρανοῖς, καὶ σαλευθήσονται τὰ ἑπτὰ (a. l. ἐννέα) πέταλα τοῦ οὐρανοῦ.

In our account of the third heaven according to the Slavonic Enoch, we showed that hell was situated in the north of that heaven. Similarly in the Testament of Isaac (*Testament of Abraham*, ed. James, pp. 146–8) hell is understood to be in one of the heavens. The same holds true of the Testament of Jacob (*op. cit.* p. 153), and of the Apoc. Esdrae, p. 29.

Finally in the Acts of Callistratus (ed. Conybeare), pp. 311–12, the seven circles of the heavens are mentioned.

Speculations about the seven heavens prevailed largely among the heretics. Thus according to Irenaeus, *contra Haer.* i. 5, 2, the Valentinians taught : ἑπτὰ γὰρ οὐρανοὺς κατεσκευακέναι, ὧν ἐπάνω τὸν δημιουργὸν εἶναι λέγουσι. Καὶ διὰ τοῦτο Ἑβδομάδα καλοῦσιν αὐτόν, τὴν δὲ μητέρα τὴν Ἀχαμὼθ Ὀγδοάδα . . . τοὺς δὲ ἑπτὰ οὐρανοὺς οὐκ (?) εἶναι νοητούς φασιν, ἀγγέλους δὲ αὐτοὺς ὑποτίθενται . . . ὡς καὶ τὸν παράδεισον ὑπὲρ τρίτον οὐρανὸν ὄντα, τέταρτον ἄγγελον λέγουσι δυνάμει ὑπάρχειν.

In Tertullian, *Adv. Valent.* xx, practically the same account is given : ' Tum ipsam caelorum septemplicem scenam solio desuper suo finit. Unde et Sabbatum dictus ab hebdomade sedis suae ... Caelos autem noeros deputant, et interdum angelos eos faciunt . . . sicut et Paradisum Archangelum quartum, quoniam et hunc supra caelum tertium pangunt.'

The heretic Marcus taught according to Hippolytus a similar doctrine of the heavens, but according to Irenaeus, *adv. Haer.* i. 17, 1, he reckoned eight heavens in addition to the sun and moon.

Basilides' view as to their being 365 heavens is well known (Augustine, *de Haer.* i. 4).

The Ophites (Irenaeus, *adv. Haer.* i. 30. 4, 5) believed in seven heavens ruled over by seven potentates, named Jaldabaoth, Jao, Sabaoth, Adoneus, Eloeus, Horeus, Astaphaeus—a Hebdomad which with their mother Sophia formed a Ogdoad. A fuller account of this Hebdomad will be found in Origen, *contra Celsum*, vi. 31, and in Epiphanius *Haer.* xxvi. 10.

In the mysteries of Mithras described by Origen, *contra Celsum*, vi. 22, there are certain speculations akin to the doctrine of the seven heavens.

A fragment of Theodotus preserved by Clement is found regarding the creation of man : ὅθεν ἐν τῷ παραδείσῳ τῷ τετάρτῳ οὐρανῷ δημιουργεῖται [1].

The doctrine of the seven heavens, therefore, being associated with so many grotesque and incongruous features even in the thoughts of the orthodox, became in due time an offensive conception to the sounder minds in the Church, and this offensiveness was naturally aggravated by the important role it played in heretical theology. Augustine, though he expounds a peculiar doctrine of his own which asserts the existence of three heavens (*de Gen. ad Litt.* xii. 67), feels himself beset with abundant difficulties on this question. On the subject in general he writes : ' Si autem sic accipimus tertium coelum quo Apostolus raptus est, ut quartum etiam, et aliquot ultra

---

[1] The Valentinians also placed Paradise in the fourth heaven.

superius coelos esse credamus, infra quos et hoc tertium coelum, sicut eos alii septem, alii octo, alii novem vel decem perhibent ... de quorum ratione sive opinione nunc disserere longum est' (*de Gen. ad Litt.* xii. 57). In the fourth century of the Christian era, Churchmen were required according to the clear tenor of Scripture to believe in the plurality of the heavens, but as to the number of these heavens they were at liberty to decide for themselves without prejudicing their orthodoxy. Thus Philastrius, Bishop of Brescia, at the close of the fourth century holds it a heresy to doubt the plurality of the heavens, but a man may without offence believe in seven, three, or two. ' De caelorum diversitate est haeresis quae ambigat. Scriptura enim in primo die caelum et terram facta declarat duo haec elementa, secundo firmamentum aquae factum, et nihilominus ipsum firmamentum caelum appellatum fuisse testatur. David autem dicit de caelis ita : *Laudate dominum caeli caelorum et aquae quae super caelos sunt.* Sive ergo sex caelos, secundum David, et septimum hoc firmamentum accipere quis voluerit, non errat; nam Solomon tres caelos dicit, ita: *Caelum et caelum caeli.* Paulus aeque apostolus usque ad tertium caelum se raptum fatetur. Sive ergo septem quis acceperit, ut David, sive tres, sive duos, non errat, quia et Dominus ait: *Pater qui in caelis est.*' (*De Haeres. Liber* xciv.)

But these and the like speculations had become so objectionable to the master mind of Chrysostom, that despite 2 Cor. xii. 2, 3 he declares the doctrine of a plurality of the heavens to be a mere device of man and contrary to holy scripture : τίς ἂν οὖν λοιπὸν μετὰ τὴν τοσαύτην διδασκαλίαν ἀνέχοιτο τῶν ἁπλῶς ἐξ οἰκείας διανοίας φθέγγεσθαι βουλομένων, καὶ ἀπεναντίως τῇ θείᾳ γραφῇ πολλοῖς οὐρανοῖς λέγειν ἐπιχειρούντων (*Hom. in Gen.* iv. 3). And again, in order to discredit the last traces of this view he maintains that the heaven neither revolves nor is spherical (*In Epist. ad Hebraeos, Hom.* xiv. 1).

Our task is now nearly done. It only remains for us to

point out that this doctrine, on its rejection by the Christian Church, passed over with many similar ones into Mohammedanism. In fact, Mohammedanism formed in many respects the *cloaca maxima* into which much of the refuse of Christianity discharged itself.

Thus in the Koran xxiii it is written: 'And we have created over you seven heavens, and we are not negligent of what we have created.' And again in xli: 'And he formed them into seven heavens in two days, and revealed unto every heaven its office.'

Into a detailed representation of these heavens by later Mohammedan writers it is not necessary for us to enter.

So far as I am aware every detail is borrowed from Jewish and Christian Apocalypses. Some form of the Slavonic Enoch seems to have been in Mohammed's hands [1].

---

[1] The four streams of Paradise (Slav. En. viii. 5) which pour honey and milk and oil and wine, reappear in the Koran xlvii. Again, irrational animals are to be restored to life at the resurrection, to receive the recompense due to them, and then to return to the dust, with the exception of Ezra's ass and the dog of the seven sleepers (cf. Koran iii; xviii; Sale's note on vi; Slav. Enoch lviii. 4-6).

THE

BOOK OF THE SECRETS OF ENOCH

THE SON OF ARED; A MAN WISE AND
BELOVED OF GOD [1].

———•◆•———

[*Concerning the Life and the Dream of Enoch [2].]

THERE was a very [3] wise man and a worker of great things :
God loved him, and received him, so that he should see the
heavenly abodes, the kingdoms of the wise, great, incon-
ceivable and never-changing God, the Lord of all, the
wonderful and glorious, and bright and all-beholding station
of the servants of the Lord, and the unapproachable throne
of the Lord, and the degrees and manifestations of the incorporeal hosts, and should be an eye-witness of the unspeakable ministrations of the multitude of creatures, and of the
varying appearance, and indescribable singing of the host of
Cherubim, and of the immeasurable world.

I. 1. At that time he said : ' Hardly had I accomplished
*165 years, when I begat my son Methusal : after that I lived
200 years and accomplished all the years of my life [4], 365

———————————

years.   2. *On the first day of the first month[1] I was alone in my house, *and I rested on my bed and slept.   3. And as I slept a great grief came upon my heart, and I wept with mine eyes[2] *in my dream, and I could not understand what this grief meant, or what would happen to me[3].   4. And there appeared to me two men very tall, such as I have never seen on earth.   5. And their faces *shone like the sun[4], and their eyes *were like burning lamps[5]; and fire came forth from their lips. *Their dress had the appearance of feathers: their feet were purple[6], *their wings were brighter than gold[7]; *their hands whiter than snow[3]. They stood at the head of my bed and called me by my name.   6. I awoke from my sleep and *saw clearly these men standing in front of me[8].   7. I *hastened and[9] made obeisance to them and *was terrified, and the appearance of my countenance was changed[10] from fear.   8. And these[11] men said to me: " Be of good cheer, Enoch, be not afraid; the everlasting[12] God hath sent us to thee, and lo! to-day thou shalt ascend with us into heaven.

---

[1] In the second month on an appointed day, B; Sok. is conflate.
[2] I had made myself melancholy weeping with my eyes, and I lay down on my bed to sleep, B.   [3] B om.; Sok. supports text.   [4] Were like the shining sun, Sok.   [5] Burnt like lamps, A.   [6] So Sok. A reads there was a conspicuousness in their raiment and singing, in appearance purple; B, their dress and singing were wonderful.   [7] And on their shoulders as it were golden wings, B.   [8] So Sok.; standing up quickly (?), B; A om.   [9] A B om.   [10] Veiled my face, B.   [11] The two, Sok.   [12] Almighty, B.

I. With verses 2, 3, cf. Eth. En. lxxxiii. 3, 5.   5. Faces shone like the sun: cf. xix. 1; Rev. i. 16; 4 Ezra [vi. 71]. Eyes were like burning lamps, from Dan. x. 6 עֵינָיו כְּלַפִּידֵי אֵשׁ: cf. Ezek. i. 13; Rev. i. 14; xix. 12. Fire came forth from their lips: cf. for language Rev. ix. 17; xi. 5. Their dress ... purple: the text is corrupt. Their hands whiter than snow; cf. Eth. En. cvi. 2, 10 'his body was

whiter than snow': Apoc. Petri τὰ μὲν γὰρ σώματα αὐτῶν ἦν λευκότερα πάσης χιόνος.   7. Countenance was changed: Dan. v. 6, 9, 10.   8. Be of good cheer: Matt. ix. 2 θάρσει; xiv. 27; Mark vi. 50; x. 29; Acts xxiii. 11; xxvii. 22, 25. In LXX Gen. xxxv. 17; Exod. xiv. 13, &c. θάρσει is a rendering of אַל־תִּירָא Be not afraid: cf. 2 Kings i. 15; Ezek. ii. 6, &c.; Eth. En. xv. 1. The conjunction of Be of good cheer and

9. And tell thy sons and thy servants, all [1] *who work [2] *in thy house [3], and let no one seek thee, till the Lord bring thee back to them."   10. And I *hastened to obey [4] them, and went out *of my house [5]. And I called my sons Methusal, Regim [*and Gaidal [6]], and told them what wonderful [7] things *the two men [8] had said to me.'

[*The Instruction: how Enoch taught his Sons.*]

II. 1. 'Hear me, my children, for I do not know whither I am going, or what awaits me.   2. Now, my children, I say unto you : turn not aside from God : *walk before the face of the Lord and keep his judgements [9] *and do not worship vain gods [10], who did not make heaven and earth [11] , for these

---

[1] That they are to do without thee on the earth A.   [2] A and Sok. om.   [3] Sok. om.   [4] **Obeyed**, B.   [5] B omits; A adds and shut the doors as was ordered me.   [6] B om.; Sok. supports text. See exegetical note *in loc.*   [7] B om.   [8] **They**, A ; these men, Sok.

II. A om.   [9] Sok. adds do not defile the prayers offered for) your salvation, that the Lord may not shorten the work of your hands, and ye may not be deprived of the gifts of the Lord, and the Lord may not deprive you of the attainment of His gifts in your treasuries. Bless the Lord with the firstlings of your flocks and the firstlings of your children, and blessings shall be upon you for ever; and do not depart from the Lord.   [10] **To vain creatures**, A.   [11] Sok. adds nor any other creature.

Be not afraid is found in Matt. xiv. 27.   10. Sons : these are mentioned though not named in Eth. En. lxxxi. 5, 6 ; xci. 1. **Regim**: see lvii. 2. **Gaidal**: this name is derived from LXX Gen. iv. 18 ἐγεννήθη δὲ τῷ 'Ενὼχ Γαϊδάδ. For Γαϊδάδ Mass. gives Irad (עִירָד) and Syriac Idar (ܥܝܕܪ), which more nearly approaches LXX. Observe that this Gaidal is the son of Enoch who is the *grandson of Cain*, and therefore wrongly appears here. As however B omits it both here and in lvii. 2, it is probably spurious. A confusion of Enoch, son of Lamech, and Enos, son of Seth, is to be found in the Clementine Recognitions iv. 12.

II. 1. Know whither I am going, &c.: cf. vii. 5.   2. Turn not aside from God : 1 Sam. xii. 20. Walk before the face of the Lord : Ps. lvi. 13; cxvi. 9. Keep his judgements : Lev. xviii. 5 ; Ezek. xxxvi. 27. Worship vain gods : Deut. viii. 19 ; cf. 1 Sam. (LXX, Syr., Vulg.) xii. 21. Vain gods who did not make heaven and earth, for these will perish, from Jer. x. 11 ; cf. Ps. xcvi. 5 ; Is. ii. 18 ; Acts xiv. 15 'Ye should turn from these vain things unto the living God, who made the heaven and the earth.' Jub. xii. 2, 3, 4 'What help . . . have we from those idols which thou dost worship . . . worship them not. Worship the God of heaven.'

will perish, * and also those who worship them [1].   3. * But
may God make confident your hearts in the fear of Him [2].
4. And now, my children, let no one seek me till the Lord
brings me back to you.'

[*Of the taking up of Enoch ; how the Angels took him up
into the first heaven.*]

III. 1. It came to pass when I [3] had spoken to my sons,
* these men [4] * summoned me and [5] took me on their wings [6]
and placed me * on the clouds [7]. * And lo! the clouds moved [8].
2. *And again (going) higher I saw the air and (going still)
higher I saw the ether [9], and they placed me in the first
heaven.   3. * And they showed me a very great sea, greater
than the earthly sea [10].

[*Of the Angels who rule the Stars.*]

IV. 1. And they brought * before my face the elders, and
the rulers of the orders of the stars [11], and they showed me the

---

[1] B om.   [2] But keep your hearts in the fear of God, B. For the
fear of Him A reads His own paths.
III. Instead of 'Of the taking up of Enoch, &c.' B reads ' The entry of
Enoch into the first heaven.'   [3] Throughout this verse A speaks of Enoch in the
third person.   [4] The angels, A.   [5] A om.   [6] A B add and brought
me (him A) to the first heaven, which should be read at end of verse 2.
[7] There B.   [8] A B om.   [9] And there I gazed, and as I gazed higher
I saw the air, A.   [10] B trans. after the 200 angels, iv. 1.
IV. [11] Me before the face of the elder, the ruler of the orders of the
stars; and showed me their goings and comings from year to year, B.

---

3. Make confident your hearts in
the fear of Him: Prov. xiv. 26.
III. 1. Placed me on the clouds.
And lo! the clouds moved : cf. Eth.
En. xiv. 8 ' the clouds invited me . . .
and the winds gave me wings and
drove me.'   The air . . . and the
ether. This corresponds to the firmament in Asc. Is. vii. 9 ' Ascendimus
in firmamentum et ibi vidi Sammaelem ejusque potestates . . . 13. et
postea me ascendere fecit supra firma-

mentum : hoc jam est (primum)
coelum.'   3. A very great sea : cf.
Rev. iv. 6 ; xv. 2 ' sea of glass.' In
Test. xii. Patriarch. Levi 2 this sea
lies between the first and second
heavens, ὕδωρ κρεμάμενον ἀνάμεσον
τούτου κἀκείνου.
IV. 1. Rulers of the orders of the
stars, &c. For a full but divergent
account of these see Eth. En. lxxxii.
9-18, 20. The 200 angels. In the
Eth. En. Uriel is the sole ruler of the

two hundred angels * who rule the stars and their heavenly service [1] ; 2. * And they fly with their wings [2] * and go round all (the stars) as they float [1].

[*How the Angels guard the Habitations of the Snow.*]

V. 1. And * then I looked and saw [3] the treasuries of the snow * and ice [4] and the angels [5] who guard their terrible [6] store-places ; 2. And the treasuries of the clouds from which they come forth and into which they enter.

[*Concerning the Dew and the Oil, and different Colours.*]

VI. And they showed me the treasuries of the dew, like * oil for anointing [7], * and its form was in appearance like that of [8] all earthly colours [9] : also many [10] angels keeping their treasuries, * and they shut and open them [10].

[*How Enoch was taken into the second Heaven [11].*]

VII. 1. And the men took me and brought me to the

---

[1] B om. [2] B reads immediately after earthly sea, iii. 3. Sok. om.
V. [3] They showed me, B. There I saw, Sok. [4] A om. [5] Terrible angels, B. [6] B om.
VI. [7] The balm of the olive tree, Sok. [8] And the appearance of it as also of, A. And their robes are like, B. [9] May be rendered *flowers*.
[10] B om.
VII. [11] The Entry of Enoch into the second Heaven, B; Sok. om.

---

stars : cf. lxxii. 1 ; lxxx. 1. In Eth. En. vi. 5 this is the number of angels that apostatized.

V. 1. **Treasuries of the snow and ice** : Job xxxviii. 22 ; cf. Eth. En. lx. 17, 18. These treasuries are placed in the second heaven by the Test. xii. Patriarch. Levi 3 ὁ δεύτερος (οὐρανὸς) ἔχει πῦρ χιόνα κρύσταλλον. 2. Treasuries of the clouds : cf. Eth. En. lx. 19.

VI. 1. **Treasuries of the dew** : cf. Eth. En. lx. 20. In the *Beresch. rabba* c. 6, *Bammidbar rabba*, c. 17, and the *Chagiga* 12[b], there is an enumeration of the seven heavens. The lowest of these which is called יְלוֹן (Lat. velum) is empty. According to some, it appears in the morning and disappears in the evening (see Weber, p. 197) : according to Berachoth 58[b] the Wîlôn is rolled up in order that the light of the second heaven, the Rakîa, may be seen. This heaven seems also to be empty according to the Test. xii. Patr. Levi 3 ὁ κατώτερος διὰ τοῦτο στυγνότερός ἐστιν ἐπειδὴ οὗτος ὁρᾷ πάσας ἀδικίας ἀνθρώπων

second heaven, and showed me [1] * the darkness, and there I saw [2] the prisoners suspended [3], reserved for (and) awaiting [3] the eternal [4] judgement.   2. * And these angels were gloomy in appearance, more than the darkness of the earth [3].   * And they unceasingly wept every hour [5], and I said to the men who were with me: 'Why are these men continually [3] tortured?'   3. * And the men [6] answered me: 'These are they who apostatized from * the Lord [7]: who obeyed not the commandments of God, and took counsel of their own will * and transgressed together with their prince and have been already confined to the second heaven [8].   4. And I felt great pity for them.   * And lo! the angels [9] made obeisance to me, and said to me: "O man of God! * pray for us to the Lord [10]."   5. And I answered [11] them: "Who am I, a mortal

---

[1] Sok. adds and I saw.   [2] B om.; after darkness, A adds greater than the darkness on earth.   [3] B om.   [4] Great and immeasurable, A; immeasurable, Sok.   [5] And I saw those who were condemned weeping, B.   [6] And they, A; The men, Sok.   [7] God, A.   [8] B om. For second A Sok. read fifth.   [9] They, A; and these angels, Sok.   [10] Oh! that thou wouldst pray to God for us! B.   [11] Sok. adds and said unto.

VII. 1. The darkness and . . . the prisoners . . . reserved for . . . judgement: cf. 2 Pet. ii. 4 'Committed them (the angels that sinned as here) to pits of darkness to be reserved unto judgement.' These prisoners are the angels that 'kept not their first estate' and are 'reserved . . . under darkness unto the judgement of the great day,' Jude 6. They appear to be referred to also in Test. xii. Patr. Levi 3 ἐν αὐτῷ (τῷ δευτέρῳ οὐρανῷ) εἰσὶ πάντα τὰ πνεύματα τῶν ἐπαγωγῶν εἰς ἐκδίκησιν τῶν ἀνόμων, where ἐπαγωγῶν seems corrupt. Observe that the angels who sinned with women are imprisoned *under the earth* in the Eth. En. x as also in our text xviii. 7. On the other hand the angels who sinned through lust

for empire are prisoners in the second heaven.   3. Took counsel of their own will. For phraseology cf. Eph. i. 11; Is. xlvi. 10. These angels wished to form a kingdom of their own. Cf. Weber, p. 244. Their prince Satanail: xviii. 3. Second heaven. This emendation is necessary. When the angels of the fifth heaven rebelled they were cast down to the second heaven and imprisoned there.   4. The angels ask Enoch to intercede for them, exactly as in Eth. En. xiii. 4. 'They besought me to draw up a petition that they might find forgiveness.' Man of God: Deut. xxxiii. 1; 1 Tim. vi. 11; 2 Tim. iii. 17.   5. Cf. Eth. En. xv. 2 'Say to the watchers of heaven . . . you should intercede for men and not men

man, that I should pray for angels? Who knows whither I go,
or what awaits me: or who prays * for me [1] ? ".'

[* *Of the taking of Enoch to the third Heaven* [2].]

VIII. 1. And these men took me from thence, and brought
me to the third heaven, and placed me * in the midst of
a garden [3]—* a place [4] such as has never been known for * the
goodliness of its appearance [5].   2. And * I saw [6] all the
trees of beautiful colours and [7] their fruits ripe * and fragrant [6],
and all kinds of * food which they produced [8], springing up with
delightful fragrance [9].   3. And in the midst (there is) the
tree of life, in that place, on which God rests, when He comes
into Paradise. And this tree cannot be described for its
* excellence and sweet odour [10].   4. And it is beautiful
more than any created thing. And on all sides in appearance
it is like gold and crimson and transparent as fire, and
it covers everything [11].   5. * From its root in the

---

[1] B om.

VIII. [2] Entry into the third Heaven, B.   [3] So B and Sok. A reads There,
I looked below and I saw gardens.   [4] I looked below and saw that place,
Sok.   [5] Their goodliness, A and Sok.   [6] B om.   [7] And I beheld, A.   [8] Agree-
able food, B.   [9] B adds and four rivers flowing with soft course and every
kind of thing good that grows for food. These words belong to verse 6.   [10] The
excellence of its sweet odour, B.   [11] The whole garden, Sok. After this
A adds and the gardens have all kinds of fruits; Sok. adds and the garden
has all kinds of trees planted and all fruits.   B OMITS VERSE 4.

---

for you. Who knows whither I go,
&c.: cf. ii. 1.

VIII. 1. A garden: as in 2 Cor. xii.
2, 4 Paradise is placed in the third
heaven.   2. All the trees ... fragrant: cf. Gen. ii. 9; Eth. En. xxix. 2;
Apoc. Mosis (p. 20) . . . All kinds
of food which they produced: cf.
Rev. xxii. 2 'Bearing twelve manner
of fruits.'   3. In the midst the
tree of life: Gen. ii. 9. This is a
familiar feature in Jewish Apocalypses. Cp. Eth. En. xxv. 4, 5; Rev.
ii. 7; xxii. 2, 14; 4 Ezra vii. 53; viii.
52; Test. Levi 18. See also Iren.
i. 5, 2. When we come to Epiphanius

we find it denounced as a Mani-
chaean doctrine, *Haer.* 66, p. 278.
The tree of life . . . on which
God rests. This is reproduced in
a modified form in the Apoc. Pauli
(ed. Tischend. p. 64) δένδρον παμμεγέθη
ὡραῖον, ἐν ᾧ ἐπανεπαύετο τὸ πνεῦμα
ἅγιον. There is a modification of this
idea in Apoc. Mosis (ed. Tischend.
p. 12) καὶ ὁ θρόνος τοῦ θεοῦ ὅπου ἦν τὸ
ξύλον τῆς ζωῆς ἐντρεπίζετο.   5. From
its root, &c. This is the source of
the words in Apoc. Pauli (ed. Tischend.
p. 64) καὶ ἐκ τῆς ῥίζης ·αὐτοῦ ἐξήρχετο πᾶν εὐωδέστατον ὕδωρ, μεριζόμενον εἰς τέσσαρα ὀρύγματα.   The

garden[1] there go forth four[2] streams which pour honey and milk[3], oil and wine, and are separated in four directions, and go about with a soft course.   6. And they go down to the Paradise of Eden, between corruptibility and incorruptibility. And thence[4] they go along the earth, and have a revolution in their circle like also the other elements[5].   7. * And there is another tree, an olive tree always distilling oil[6]. And there is no tree there without fruit, and every tree[7] is blessed[8]. 8. And there are * three hundred angels very glorious, who keep the garden[9], and with never ceasing voices and blessed singing, they serve the Lord * every day[10]. And I said[11] : ' What a very[12] blessed place is this ! ' And those men spake unto me :

[*The showing to Enoch of the Righteous, and the Place of Prayers.*]

IX. ' This place, O Enoch, is prepared for the righteous

---

[1] Emended with Apoc. Pauli from its root ; B omits ; A and Sok. add in the going out towards earth Paradise is between corruptibility and incorruptibility. This is clearly a corrupt addition. See quotation from Apoc. Pauli in explanatory notes.   [2] Two, A and Sok. See note 9 on p. 7 for text of B.   [3] A adds and the streams pour.   [4] Sok. adds they go forth and are divided into forty (four ?) and ; B omits verse 6.   [5] Sok. adds of the air.   [6] A Sok. om.   [7] Place, A.   [8] Sok. adds in its fruit and every place is blessed.   [9] Angels guarding them, very bright in appearance, B.   [10] Every day and hour, A ; the whole day, Sok.   [11] A adds lo !   [12] B om.

---

writer has tried to reduce to one organic conception the two originally different conceptions of the heavenly and the earthly Paradise. The latter seems to have been the older : Gen. ii. 8-17 ; Eth. En. xxxii. 3-6 ; lxxvii. 3. The heavenly Paradise is referred to in Eth. En. lx. 8 ; lxi. 12 ; lxx. 3. Four streams which pour honey and milk and oil and wine. Cf. Apoc. Pauli (ed. Tischend. p. 52) ποταμοὶ τέσσαρες ἐκύκλουν αὐτήν, ῥέοντες μέλι καὶ γάλα καὶ ἔλαιον καὶ οἶνον. These four streams are taken over into the Koran xlvii, save that

instead of a river of oil there is a river of incorruptible water. The earthly Paradise is said to be between corruptibility and incorruptibility, because existence in it was a probation and might issue either in corruptibility or incorruptibility : or because it lay on the confines of the regions of corruptibility and incorruptibility.   7. Another tree . . . distilling oil : Cf. xxi. 7. These are the *arbor misericordiae* and the *oleum misericordiae* of Evang. Nicodemi ii. 3 : cf. ch. xxii. 8.

IX. 1. **Prepared for the righteous:**

who endure * every kind of attack [1] * in their lives [2] * from those who [3] afflict their souls : who turn away their eyes from unrighteousness, and accomplish a righteous judgement, and also give bread to the hungry, and clothe the naked, and raise the fallen, and assist the * orphans who are [4] oppressed, and who walk * without blame [4] before the face of the Lord, and serve him only.   For them this place is prepared as an eternal inheritance.'

[*Here they showed Enoch the terrible Places, and various Tortures.*]

X. 1. And the men then [5] led me to the Northern region [6], and showed me there [7] a very terrible place.   2. And there are all sorts of tortures in that place.   Savage [7] darkness and impenetrable [7] gloom ; and there is no light there [7], * but

---

IX. [1] Attacks, B.   [2] A om.   [3] Who, B.   [4] B om.
X. [5] Removed me from thence and, B.   [6] Part of the heavens, B.
[7] B om.

---

cf. Matt. xxv. 34. See note on Eth. En. lx. 8.   **Turn away their eyes from unrighteousness**: Ps. cxix. 37; cf. Is. xxxiii. 15.   **Execute righteous judgement**: Ezek. xviii. 8.   **Give bread to the hungry, and clothe the naked**: Ezek. xviii. 7: cf. Tob. iv. 16; 4 Ezra ii. 20; Or. Sibyll. ii. 83; viii. 404-405.   **Assist the orphans who are oppressed**: cf. Is. i. 17; Jer. xxii. 3, 16.   **Walk without blame before . . . the Lord**: cf. Luke i. 6.   **Eternal inheritance**: cf. Heb. ix. 15.   .

X. 1. Northern region. To the modern mind it may seem strange that a division of heaven should be assigned to the wicked, but this idea presented no difficulty to the Jews and early Christians. Thus in the O. T. Satan can present himself in heaven, Job i. 7, 8 ; while in the N. T. evil may not only appear, but can also have a settled habitation there : Eph. vi. 12 ' the spiritual hosts of wickedness in the heavens ' (ἐν τοῖς ἐπουρανίοις).   In Rev. xii. 7, 8, 9 this condition of things is represented as being at an end. Satan is cast out of heaven with his angels, and the sphere of his activity and residence is now limited to the earth, Rev. xii. 12. The old idea of wickedness being in heaven reappears in Test. Levi 3, where however it is limited to the second heaven (see also Test. Isaac 146, 147; Test. Jacob 153); but it was subsequently banished from Christian and Jewish thought.   See Introduction.   **2. Darkness and . . . gloom**: Apoc. Petri 12 τόπῳ σκοτεινῷ: Apoc. Pauli, p. 62, where one region of

a gloomy fire is always burning¹, *and a fiery river goes
forth². * And all that place has fire on all sides, and on all
sides³ cold and ice, * thus it burns and freezes⁴.   3. *And
the prisoners are very savage². And the angels terrible and
without pity, carrying savage² weapons, and their torture was
unmerciful. 4. And I said : *'Woe, woe²! How terrible
is this place⁵!' And the men said to me : 'This place,

---

¹ Neither fire nor flame and a gloom is over that place, B.   ² B. om.
³ In that place; on both sides fire and on both sides, Sok.; B om.   ⁴ So
Sok. A reads thirst and freezing, B; and murkiness.   ⁵ What a
terrible place is this ! A.

Hades is said σκότους καὶ ζόφους πεπλη-
ρωμένον. There is no light there:
quoted by Apoc. Pauli (p. 57) οὐκ
ἦν ἐκεῖ φῶς. Fiery river. This
idea appears first in Eth. En. xiv. 19 ;
Dan. vii. 10, but not there as an
instrument of punishment. It seems
however to have been applied early
to that purpose, as here, and in the
form of a lake of fire in Rev. xix. 20 ;
xx. 10, 14, 15 ; xxi. 8. Or. Sibyll.
ii. 196–200, 252–253, 286; iii. 84;
viii. 411 : cf. Apoc. Petri 8 λίμνη τις ἦν
μεγάλη πεπληρωμένη βορβόρου φλεγο-
μένου. Apoc. Pauli (ed. Tischend.
p. 57) ἔνθα ἐπέρρεεν ποταμὸς πύρινος.
In Clem. Alex. *Exc. Theod.* 38 the
two ideas are combined : ποταμὸς
ἐκπορεύεται πυρὸς ὑποκάτω τοῦ θρόνου
τοῦ τόπου, καὶ ῥεῖ εἰς τὸ κενὸν τοῦ
ἐκτισμένου, ὅ ἐστιν ἡ γέεννα (quoted
by James, *Test. Abraham*, p. 160).
Fire on all sides, and on all
sides cold and ice. This seems
to be drawn from Eth. En. xiv. 13,
where God's dwelling in heaven
is said to be 'hot as fire and
cold as ice.' 3. Angels terrible
and without pity, carrying savage
weapons. Angels of destruction are

mentioned in the O. T. 2 Sam. xxiv.
16 ; 2 Kings xix. 35 ; 1 Chron. xxi.
15. A class of destroying angels may
be referred to in Ecclus. xxxix. 28
πνεύματα, ἃ εἰς ἐκδίκησιν ἔκτισται. In
Eth. En. liii. 3, 4 ; lvi. 1 ; lxii. 11 ; lxiii.
1, a class of evil angels whose sole function is to punish is mentioned and the
conception is evidently a familiar one,
though here found for the first time
in Jewish literature. This idea
appears in the N. T. Rev. ix. 11, 15 ;
xvi. Of these the angel mentioned in
ix. 11 is Ἀπολλύων. In Matt. xiii. 49
good angels cast the wicked into
the furnace of fire. These angels of
destruction or punishment are frequently referred to in Latin literature.
Test. Levi 3 αἱ δυνάμεις... οἱ ταχθέντες
εἰς ἡμέραν κρίσεως, ποιῆσαι ἐκδίκησιν
ἐν τοῖς πνεύμασι τῆς πλανῆς. These
angels of punishment are placed in
the third heaven as in our text. Cf.
Apoc. Petri 6 οἱ κολάζοντες ἄγγελοι :
8 ἄγγελοι βασανισταί. The words
angels terrible and without pity,
carrying savage weapons seem to
have been before the writer of
Test. Abraham A. xii ἄγγελοι . . .
ἀνηλεεῖς τῇ γνώμῃ καὶ ἀπότομοι τῷ

Enoch, is prepared for * those who do not honour God ; who
commit evil deeds on earth, vitium sodomiticum, witchcraft [1],
enchantments, devilish [2] magic ; and who boast of their evil [2]
deeds, * stealing, lying, calumnies, envy, evil thoughts, fornication, and murder [2].   5. Who steal [3] the souls of wretched [2]
men [4], oppressing [5] * the poor and spoiling them of their possessions [2], and themselves grow rich * by the taking of other men's
possessions [6], * injuring them [7]. Who when they might feed
the hungry, allow them to die of famine ; who when they
might clothe them, strip them naked.   6. Who do not
know their Creator and have worshipped * gods without life ;
who can neither see nor hear, being [2] vain gods, * and have
fashioned the forms of idols, and bow down to a contemptible
thing, made with hands [2] ; for all these this place is prepared
for an eternal inheritance.

[* *Here they took Enoch to the fourth Heaven, where is the
Course of the Sun and Moon* [8].]

XI. 1. And the men took me and conducted me to the
fourth heaven, and showed me all * the comings and [9] goings
forth and all the rays of the light of the sun and moon.

---

[1] The impure who have done godlessness on the earth, who practise,
B.   [2] B om.   [3] B adds secretly.   [4] B adds who bind them with
a galling yoke.   [5] Who see, A ; B om.   [6] And in order to
acquire the goods of strangers, A.   [7] Oppress them, A ; B om.
 XI. [8] Entry of Enoch into the fourth Heaven, B.   [9] A om.

βλέμματι ... ἀνηλέως τύπτοντες αὐτοὺς
ἐν πυρίναις χαρζαναῖς. 4. Prepared
for those who do not honour God.
Contrast Matt. xxv. 41. *Vitium sodomiticum*. Cf. Apoc. Petri 17 : Test.
Isaac (James' ed.), p. 148.   6. Cf.
Lev. xix. 4 ; xxvi. 1 ; Or. Sibyll.
v. 77–85 ; viii. 378–81 ; 395–98 ;
Fragm. i. 20–22 ; iii. 21–45.

 XI. 1. Fourth heaven. According

to the Rabbinic tradition *Chagiga* 12 [b]
the fourth heaven was called זבול
and it was said to contain the heavenly
Jerusalem, the temple, the altar, and
Michael who offered daily sacrifice.
The following quotation (ἐκ τῶν Θεο-
δότου ... 'Επιτομαί) seems to agree
with the Rabbinic view : ὅθεν ἐν τῷ
παραδείσῳ τῷ τετάρτῳ οὐρανῷ δημιουργεῖται. Comings and goings . . .

* And I measured[1] their goings, * and computed their light.
2. And I saw that[2] the sun has a light * seven times[3] greater
than the moon. * I beheld their circle, and their chariot[4] on
which * each goes[5] like a wind * advancing with astonishing
swiftness[6], and * they have[7] no rest day or night coming or
going.   3. There are four great stars ; * each star has
under it a thousand stars[6] at the right of the chariot of the
sun ; and four at the left[8], * each having under it a thousand
stars, altogether eight thousand[6].   4. * Fifteen myriads
of[9] angels go * out with the sun and attend him during the
day, and by night one thousand[6]. * Each angel has six
wings. They go[10] before the chariot of the sun[11].   5. And
a hundred angels * keep warm and light up the sun[12].

[*Of the wonderful Creatures of the Sun.*]

XII. 1. * And I looked and saw other flying creatures,
their names phoenixes and chalkadri wonderful and strange

---

[1] Their dimensions, B.   [2] And I saw their goings, B.   [3] A om.
[4] His circle and his chariot, A ; and around them is a chariot, B.   [5] They
go always, A.   [6] B om.   [7] He has, A.   [8] B adds always going
with the sun.   [9] Fifteen, A ; B om.   [10] Six winged creatures
go with the angels, A ; B om.   [11] A adds in a fiery flame.   [12] Minister
unto him fire, Sok. ; B om. verse 5.

---

of the sun and moon : cf. Eth. En.
lxxii–lxxviii. 2. The sun has a light
seven times, &c. : Eth. En. lxxii.
37. Their chariot on which each
goes like a wind : Eth. En. lxxii. 5
' the chariots on which he (the sun)
ascends are driven by the wind' : so
also of the moon in Eth. En. lxxiii. 2
and of both in lxxv. 3 ; lxxxii. 8.
Have no rest day or night : Eth.
En. xli. 7 ' (the sun and moon) rest
not' : lxxii. 37 'rests not . . . day
and night.' Sibyllines iii. 21 'Ἥλιόν
τ' ἀκάμαντα.   3, 4. There is nothing
corresponding to these verses in Eth.
En.   5. Cf. Eth. En. lxxv. 4.

XII. 1. Phoenixes and chalkadri. This seems to be the only
reference to such creatures in literature. The phoenix, which according
to all ancient writers was solitary and
unique (' unus in terris,' Tac. *Ann.* vi.
28 ; cf. Mart. v. 7 ; Ovid, *Met.* xv.
392) in its kind, is here represented as
one of a class. The phoenix is mentioned in Job xxix. 18 according to
Jewish authorities, where for ' I shall
multiply my days as the sand' they
render ' as the phoenix' כחול. There
are many references to it among
the Greeks and Romans : Herod. ii.
73 ; Tac. *Ann.* vi. 28 ; Ovid, *Met.* xv.

in appearance, with the feet and tails of lions, and the heads
of crocodiles¹; *their appearance was of a purple colour, like

---

XII. ¹ And the flying creatures are in form like two birds, one like
a phoenix and the other like a chalkedry. And in their shape they
resemble a lion in their feet and tail and in the head a crocodile, Sok.;
B om.

392; Mart. *Epigr.* v. 7, 1; Stat.
Sylv. ii. 4, 37; Plin. *N. H.* x. 2. The
fable regarding it is recounted as sober
fact by 1 Clem. *ad Corinth.* xxv;
Tertullian, *de Resurrect. Carn.* xiii;
Ambrose, *Hexaem.* v. 23; Epiphanius,
Ancorat. lxxxiv; and the *Apostolic
Constitutions* v. 7. Origen, *contra
Celsum* iv. 98, doubts it: so also Greg.
Naz. *Orat.* xxxi, 10, and among the
later Greeks Maximus and Photius,
and among the Latins Augustine *de
Anima* iv. 33. To those who believed
the fable we should add Rufinus
Comment. in Symb. Apost. xi. and the
Pseudo-Lactantius, from whose poem
De Phoenice we draw the following
references, which seem to be derived
either directly or indirectly from our
text. The phoenix in that poem is an
attendant of the sun, 'satelles phoebi'
ver. 33, as in xii. 2 are the phoenixes:
when the sun appears it greets him
with strains of sacred song (verses
43-50) and claps its wings (verses
51-54) exactly as the phoenixes in
xv. 1. This poem belongs probably to the fourth century. The
voice of the phoenix was celebrated
for its sweetness: cf. the Jewish poet
Ezekiel v. 10 φωνὴν δὲ πάντων εἶχεν
εὐπρεπεστάτην: Pseudo-Lactantius,
de Phoenice 46 'miram vocem': 56
'innarrabilibus sonis.' Its colour
was purple—purpureus (Pliny); κυά-
νεός ἐστιν ῥόδοις ἐμφερής (Achil.
Tat.), cf. xv. 1 and xii 1. On
the two different legends in the
Talmud about the origin of the
phoenix see Hamburger, *R. E.*

für Talmud 908-9. On the question generally see Lightfoot, and
Gebhardt and Harnack on 1 *Clem.*
xxv. 1; Eckermann in *Ersch und
Grueber* sect.iii.xxiv.310-16; Creuzer,
Symbol. und Mythol. ii. 163 (third
ed.); Piper, *Mythol. und Symbol. der
Christl. Kunst* i. 446, 471; Ebert,
*Allgemeine Geschichte der Litera-
tur des Mittelalters* i. 93-98; Seyf-
farth, *Z. D. M. G.* 1849, 63-89;
Gundert, *Z. f. luth. Theol.* 1854,
451-54. Chalkadri. This may be
a transliteration of Χαλκύδραι, brazen
hydras, or serpents. They are classed
with the Cherubim in Eth. En. xx. 7
'Gabriel . . . who is over Paradise
and the Serpents (τῶν δρακόντων in
the Greek) and the Cherubim.' Hence
they seem to have been a class of
heavenly creatures, i.e. the Seraphim
שְׂרָפִים. The idea of flying serpents
was a familiar one from the O.T. Is.
xiv. 29; xxx. 6 שָׂרָף מְעוֹפֵף. It was
not unfamiliar to the rest of the
ancient world: cf. Herod. ii. 75;
Lucan ix. 729-30; Ovid, *Met.* v.
642-4; *Fast.* iv. 562; also Claudian,
Valerius Flaccus, Ammianus,
Aelian, Apollonius. In the O.T.
these flying serpents are venomous in
such passages as Num. xxi. 6; Deut.
viii. 15; Is. xiv. 29; xxx. 6. What
relation these seraphim bear to those
in Is. vi. 2, 6 it is hard to determine.
That these latter were winged dragons
we must assume according to Delitzsch
(*Das Buch Jesaia*, pp. 124, 5). The
analogy of the animal-like forms of
the Cherubim in Ezek. i. 5-11 is

the rainbow; their size nine hundred measures [1].   2. * Their wings were like those of angels, each with twelve, and they attend the chariot of the sun, and go with him [2], bringing heat and dew * as they are ordered by God [3].   3. * So the sun makes his revolutions, and goes [4] * under the heavens,

---

[1] B om.   [2] So A and Sok., but that the former omits chariot of the. Twelve flying spirits and twelve wings to each angel who accompanies the chariot, B.   [3] And as he is ordered by God, Sok.   [4] B om.; A adds and proceeds.

---

certainly in favour of this view. The serpent was anciently a symbol of wisdom and healing among the Greeks, the Egyptians (Brugsch, *Rel. und Myth.* pp. 103, 4), and the Hebrews, Num. xxi. 8, 9; 2 Kings xviii. 4 : Matt. x. 16; John iii. 14. Hezekiah's destruction of the 'brazen serpent' as associated with idolatry may have caused the symbol to bear almost without exception an evil significance in later times, so that at last it became a designation of Satan : cf. Rev. xii. 9. We are therefore inclined to identify these Chalkadri with the Seraphim or heavenly creatures of Isaiah vi. These Chalkadri, we should add, sing in xv. 1 as do the Seraphim in Is. vi. 3, though their functions in the main are different. The idea here appears in a developed form and is no doubt indebted for its enlargement to Egyptian mythology. The Seraphim first appear in conjunction with other orders of angels in Eth. En. lxi. 10. Here their original character seems already to have been forgotten almost as wholly as in modern days, and they are regarded merely as a special class of angels ; whereas in Eth. En. xx. 7 their true nature is still borne in mind. In the N. T. neither Cherubim nor Seraphim appear, but the character-

istics of both reappear, fused together in the 'four living creatures' of Rev. iv. 6–8. However, though the N. T. takes no notice of the Seraphim save the indirect one of Rev. iv. 6–8, the conception obtained in later times the recognition of the Church through Dionysius the Areopagite's scheme of the nine heavenly orders. See Cheyne's *Prophecies of Isaiah*, i. 36, 42 ; ii. 283–6. Feet and tails of lions. The feet of the Cherubim in Ezek. i. 7 are like calves' feet. **Their size nine hundred measures.** In Bochart's *Hierozoicon* iii. 225–227 we find by citations from Strabo, Aelian, Valerius, Philostorgius, Diodorus, &c., that the ancients were ready to believe in monstrous dragons or serpents. Aelian, for instance, speaks of one 210 feet long, while an Arabian writer describes one of 8,000 paces in length. In the Talmud there is frequent mention of angels and creatures of a like monstrous size. **2. Each with twelve.** As the ordinary angels in xi. 4 have six wings each, these creatures are assigned twelve each. It would seem more natural to read this verse immediately after xi. 5 ; xii. 1 however must in some form and in some place appear in the text, as we see from xv. 1. **Bringing heat and dew.** Contrast

and goes under [1] the earth with the light * of his beams unceasingly [2].

[*The Angels took Enoch, and placed him on the East at the Gates of the Sun.*]

XIII. 1. These men brought me to the East [3] and * showed me the gates [4] by which the sun * goes forth [5] at the appointed seasons, and according to the revolution of the months * of the whole year [6], and * according to the number of the hours, day and night [7].   2. And I saw the six great [8] gates * open, each gate having sixty-one stadia and a quarter of one stadium [6]; * and I truly measured them and understood their size to be so much [9], by which the sun goes forth; and he goes to the west * and makes his course correspond. And he proceeds through all the months [6].   3. * And by the first gates he goes out forty-two days; by the second gates thirty-five days; by the fourth gates thirty-five; by the fifth gates thirty-five; by the sixth gates [8] forty-five [10].   4. * And so he returns [11] * from the sixth gates in the course of time [6] : * and he enters by the fifth gates during thirty-five days, by the fourth gates thirty-five, by the third gates during thirty-five days; by the second gates thirty-five [10].   5. * And so the

---

[1] To descend upon, B; under the heaven and under, Sok.   [2] The rays of the sun, B ; Of his beams, Sok.

XIII. [3] B adds of the heavens.   [4] Placed me at the gates of the sun, A.   [5] Enters, B.   [6] B om.   [7] At the shortening up to the lengthening of the days and nights, B.   [8] A om.   [9] And I measured their size, and I could not comprehend their size, B.   [10] A B om.   [11] B om. A adds to rest.

---

the conception in Æth. En. lx. 20. 3. **Goes under the earth.** This is undoubtedly corrupt, as the sun does not go under the earth but through the fourth heaven when he sets in the west. See xiv. 2 (note). **Unceasingly :** cf. xi. 2 (note).

XIII. 1. The gates by which the sun goes forth. These are the six gates mentioned in the next verse. For an account of the sun's six eastern gates and six western see Eth. En. lxxii. 2-4. **Six gates :** Eth. En. lxxii. 3. The rest of the chapter is hopelessly corrupt. The account seems to be derived originally from Eth. En.

days of the whole year[1] are finished according to the alterna-
tion of the four[2] seasons.

[*They took Enoch to the West.*]

XIV. 1. And *then these[3] men took me to the *West of
the heavens[4] and showed me six great gates open, *corresponding to the Eastern gates[5], opposite *to which the sun
goes out by the Eastern gates[6], according to the number of
the days *three hundred and sixty-five, and the quarter of
a day[7].   2. *So he sets by the Western gates[8]. When
he goes out by the Western gates[9] *four hundred angels

---

[1] By his regular departure the years, B.   And so the whole year, A.
[2] B om.
XIV. [3] The, B.   [4] Western regions, A.   [5] Corresponding to the
Eastern entrance, B.   Opposite to the circuit of the Eastern gates, Sok.
[6] Where the sun retires, A.   By which the sun passes, Sok.   [7] B om.
[8] A om.   [9] A adds he conceals his light under the earth and the
glories of his luminary.

---

lxxii. 2–37.   5. Four seasons : cf.
xl. 6.   The account of two of these
seasons is found in Eth. En. lxxii.
15–20 : that of the remaining two is
lost.

XIV. 1.   Three hundred and
sixty-five, and the quarter of a
day.   I have shown in my edition
of the Eth. En. pp. 190–91 that the
writer of chs. lxxii-lxxxii. was
familiar with the solar year of 365¼
days, but that owing to national
prejudices he refused to acknowledge
it.   2. According to the Eth. En.
lxxii. 5 the sun returns after sunset
through the north in order to reach
the east.   In our text, however, the
sun revolves through the fourth
heaven, xi ; xxx. 3, and when he
rises in the east goes under the
heavens and appears to men.   During the night while he passes through

the fourth heaven he is *without light*,
or in the words of the text *his crown
is taken from him* : when he is about
to reappear in the east his crown, or
in other words his light, is restored to
him.   The reason why the sun is
obliged to surrender his crown in
passing through the fourth heaven
before God is presumably that which
is given in the Apoc. Mosis (ed. Tischend. p. 19) : the sun cannot shine
before the Light of the Universe
(ἐνώπιον τοῦ φωτὸς τῶν ὅλων).   The
passage in this Apocalypse appears
undoubtedly to be founded on the
present text.   Eve is there represented
as seeing the sun and moon praying
for Adam before God but *without
their light*.   She thereupon asks : ποῦ
ἐστὶν τὸ φῶς αὐτῶν, καὶ διὰ τί γεγό-
νασιν μελανοειδεῖς ; καὶ λέγει αὐτῇ Σήθ.
οὐ δύνανται φαίνειν ἐνώπιον τοῦ φωτὸς

take his crown and bring it to the Lord[1].   3. And the sun revolves[2] in his chariot *and goes without light[3] *for seven complete hours in the night[4]. *And when he comes near the East[5] *at the eighth hour of the night[6], *the four hundred angels bring his crown and crown him[7].

[*The Creatures of the Sun; the Phoenixes and Chalkidri sang.*]

XV. 1. Then sang the creatures[8] called the Phoenixes and the Chalkidri. On this account every bird claps its wings, rejoicing at the giver of light, *and they sang a song at the command of the Lord[9].   2. The giver of light comes to give his brightness to *the whole world[10].   3. *And they showed me the calculation of the going of the sun. And the gates by which he enters and goes out are great gates, which God made for the computation of the year[11].   4. *On this account the sun is great[12].

---

[1] So B and Sok., but that the former reads four instead of four hundred. A reads but the crown of his splendour is in heaven before the Lord: and there are four hundred angels attending Him.   [2] Revolves, B Sok. Goes under the earth, A.   [3] And rests, A.   [4] B om.; A Sok. support text, but that Sok. omits complete. After night A adds and reaches half his course under the earth.   [5] At the Eastern gates, B; Sok. om.   [6] B om.   [7] He brings forth his luminary and his shining crown, and the sun is lighted up more than fire, A. And places on it again the crown, B.

XV. [8] A adds of the sun; B OMITS VERSES 1, 2.   [9] Singing with their voices, Sok.   [10] His creation, Sok.; A adds and there will be the guards of the morning, which are the rays of the sun and the earthly sun will go out and will receive his brightness to light up all the face of the earth.   [11] So A and Sok. B reads this arrangement of the gates by which he enters and goes out the two angels showed me; these gates the Lord made for the computation and his yearly record of the sun.   [12] B om.; A adds its revolutions extend to twenty-eight years, and so it was from the beginning.

τῶν ὅλων, καὶ τούτου χάριν ἐκρύβη τὸ φῶς ἀπ' αὐτῶν. 3. **Seven complete hours in the night.** This is corrupt. The writer must have known that the length of the night varied with the season. In the Eth. En. a chapter (lxxii) is devoted to the explanation of the varying lengths of the day and night.

XV. 1. See xii. 1 (note). **Every bird.** We should expect 'all these winged creatures,' i. e. the Phoenixes and Chalkidri. Or are we to take it that the early song of birds at sunrise is here referred to? but this is unlikely.

[The Men took Enoch and placed him at the East, at the Course of the Moon.]

XVI. 1. *The other, the computation of the moon these men showed me[1]; *all the goings and revolutions[2]. *And they pointed out the gates to me[3], twelve great[4] gates extending *from the West to the East[5], by which the moon enters *and goes out[6] at the customary times.   2. She enters *the first gate when the sun is in the West thirty-one days exactly[7]; by the second gate thirty-one[8] days exactly; by the third gate thirty days exactly; by the fourth gate thirty days exactly; by the fifth gate thirty-one days exactly; by the sixth gate thirty-one days exactly; by the seventh gate thirty days exactly; by the eighth gate thirty-one days exactly; by the ninth gate thirty-one[9] days exactly; by the tenth gate thirty[10] exactly; by the eleventh gate thirty-one days exactly; by the twelfth gate twenty-eight days[11] exactly.   3. And so by the Western gates in her revolutions, and corresponding to the number of the Eastern gates she goes, and accomplishes the year[12].   4. *And unto the sun there are three hundred and sixty-five days and a quarter

---

XVI. [1] They also showed me the other arrangement, that of the moon, B.   [2] And all its course. And the men showed me all the movements of these two, B; A om.   [3] A Sok. om.   [4] Eternal, B.   [5] Towards the East, B.   [6] B om.   [7] B OMITS ENTIRE VERSE. Sok. reads the first gates (western place of the sun) 31 days to the place of the sun exactly. For 31 A reads 1.   [8] Emended from 35 A Sok.   [9] 35, A.   [10] 31, Sok.   [11] 22, Sok.   [12] Sok. adds in the days.

XVI. 1. **Twelve great gates.** These are the same as the gates of the sun in xiii.   2–3. It is obvious that the text is here corrupt, as this account cannot possibly apply to the moon. In order to correct it we have only to read 'sun' instead of 'moon' wherever it occurs. We have thus a description of the Solar year. The numbers when added together = 365. Hence in ver. 4 we are told that a Solar year = 365¼ days. Then in ver. 5 we proceed to consider the lunar year which amounts not to 365 but to 354 days, there being a difference of eleven days, or more exactly eleven and a quarter days.

of one day [1].   5. But in the lunar year there are three
hundred and fifty-four days, making twelve months of twenty-
nine days; and * there remain eleven days over, which belong
to the solar circle of the whole year [2], and are * lunar epacts
of the whole year [3]. [Thus the great circle has five hundred
and thirty-two years.]   6. The fourth part (of one day) is
neglected during three years and the fourth year completes it
exactly.   * On account of this they are omitted from the
heavens during three years, and are not added to the number
of the days [4], on which account these change the seasons of
the year * in two new months, to make the number complete
and there are two others to diminish [5].   7. And when she
has gone through the Western gates, she returns and goes to
the Eastern, with her light, * and so she goes day and night
in the heavenly circles, below all the circles more quickly than

---

[1] So she sets by the western gates and finishes the year in 364
days that are accomplished, B. This may be the original text, or 364 may
be an error for 354. B OMITS VERSE 5.   [2] Eleven days of the solar
circle are wanting, Sok.   [3] Epacts of the lunar year, A.   [4] She
goes through the year on this account and therefore the computation
is made apart from the heavens, and in the years the days are not
reckoned, B.   [5] B om.

XVI. 5. Twenty-nine days. This
should be 'twenty-nine and a half
days.' [Thus the great circle has
532 years.] I have bracketed these
words as they have no real connexion
with the context. They arose obviously
from a marginal gloss. The writer in
this chapter does not get beyond
the Metonic cycle, whereas the great
cycle of 532 years is produced by
multiplying together the Metonic
cycle of nineteen years, and the Solar
cycle of twenty-eight years. This
great cycle is called the Dionysian or
Great Paschal Period. As it includes
all the variations in respect of the
new moons and the dominical letters,
it is consequently a period in which
Easter and all the movable and un-
movable feasts would occur on the
same day of the week and month as
in the corresponding year of the preceding cycle. This cycle was first
proposed by Victorius of Aquitaine,
circ. 457 A.D. It is obvious that any
reference to such a cycle here is an
intrusion.   6. The fourth part,
&c. Explanation of leap year. On
which account these change the
seasons of the year, &c. Hopelessly corrupt.   7. With her
light. This seems to imply that her
light is not borrowed from the sun
as it is taught in the Eth. En. lxxiii.

the winds of the heavens, and there are spirits and creatures, and angels flying [1], with six wings to each of the angels [2]. 8. * And seven (months) are computed to the circle of the moon during a revolution of nineteen years [3].

[*Of the singing of the Angels, which cannot be described.*]

XVII. 1. In the middle of the heavens I saw an armed host serving the Lord with cymbals, and organs, and unceasing voice [4]. I was delighted at hearing it.

[*Of the taking up of Enoch into the fifth Heaven.*]

XVIII. 1. The men took * and brought [5] me up into the fifth heaven [6], and I saw there many hosts * not to be counted

---

[1] So Sok. but that it omits of the heavens and of the angels. B reads, So their circle goes as it were round the heavens and their chariot. The wind goes with it, urging its course and the flying spirits draw on the chariots.   [2] B adds and such is the arrangement of the moon.   [3] So Sok.; and its course is in seven different directions for nineteen years, A; B om.

XVII. [4] A adds and noble and continuous and varied singing, which it is not possible to describe. And so wonderful and strange is the singing of these angels that it amazes every mind. Sok. adds and with noble singing.

XVIII. [5] A B om.   A [6] adds and placed me there.

Spirits ... with six wings. The moon has its attendant *six-winged* spirits as the sun has its *twelve-winged* attendants (xii. 2).   **8.** This verse deals with the Metonic cycle. This cycle consists of a period of nineteen solar years, after which the new moons happen on the same days of the year. As nineteen solar years = 6,939·1860 days = 235 lunar months = nineteen lunar years and seven months, the solar and lunar years can be reconciled by intercalating seven lunar months at the close of the 3rd, 5th, 8th, 11th, 13th, 16th, and 19th years of the cycle.

XVII. An armed host. The purpose for which they are armed is given in Test. Levi 3, though in this Testament they are placed in the third heaven: ἐν τῷ τρίτῳ εἰσὶν αἱ δυνάμεις τῶν παρεμβολῶν, οἱ ταχθέντες εἰς ἡμέραν κρίσεως, ποιῆσαι ἐκδίκησιν ἐν τοῖς πνεύμασι τῆς πλάνης καὶ τοῦ Βελίαρ.   **Serving the Lord with cymbals ... and unceasing voice.** This is exactly the conception which Test. Levi 3 gives of the functions of the inhabitants of the fourth heaven: ἐν δὲ τῷ μετ' αὐτὸν εἰσὶ θρόνοι, ἐξουσίαι, ἐν ᾧ ὕμνοι ἀεὶ τῷ θεῷ προσφέρονται.

XVIII. 1. Fifth heaven. Our text and Test. Levi 3 differ absolutely

called Grigori [1]; and their appearance was like men, and their
size was * greater than that of the giants [2].   2. And their
countenances were withered, and their lips are always silent.
And there was no service in * the fifth [3] heaven.   And I said
to the men who were with me : ' Why are these men very
withered, and their faces melancholy, and their lips silent, and
there is no service in this heaven ? '   3. And they said to
me : ' These are the Grigori, who, with their prince Satanail,

---

[1] B om.   [2] Greater than great wonders, B. Great and they were
huge limbed, A.   B OM. REST OF CHAPTER.   [3] This, Sok.

---

as to the inhabitants of the fifth
heaven. According to the latter the
inhabitants are οἱ ἄγγελοι οἱ φέροντες
τὰς ἀποκρίσεις τοῖς ἀγγέλοις τοῦ προσώπου κυρίου. This view, however,
seems limited to the Test. of Levi,
whereas we find in *Chag.* 12ᵇ the
same view expressed as here: i.e.
in מעון the fifth heaven are to be
found ' hosts of angels praising God by
night, but keeping silent by day that
God may hear the praises of Israel.'
The latter clause is a late Rabbinic
idea. Again, in Clem. Alex. *Strom.*
v. 11. 77, we find a fragment of the
Apocalypse of Zephaniah which supports, and in all probability is based
on, our text : ἄρ' οὐχ ὅμοια ταῦτα τοῖς
ὑπὸ Σοφονία λεχθεῖσι τοῦ προφήτου ;
καὶ ἀνέλαβέν με πνεῦμα καὶ ἀνήνεγκέν
με εἰς οὐρανὸν πέμπτον καὶ ἐθεώρουν
ἀγγέλους καλουμένους κυρίους . . .
ὑμνοῦντας θεὸν ἄρρητον ὕψιστον. This
Apocalypse is extant in Thebaic in
a fragmentary condition, but these
fragments do not contain the passage
just quoted.   Grigori. These are
the Watchers, the Ἐγρήγοροι, or עירים,
of whom we have so full accounts in
the Eth. En. vi-xvi.; xix.; lxxxvi.
3. The Grigori. These are the
angels whose brethren rebelled and

were confined in the second heaven.
See vi. 3 (note). These Watchers
rebelled against God before the angels
were tempted to sin with the daughters of men. In other words, we
have here the agents of the original
revolt in heaven, the Satans ; and
their leader is naturally named Satanail. These existed as evil agencies
before the fall of the angels ; for in
Eth. En. liv. 6 the guilt of the latter
consisted in becoming subject to Satan.
See Eth. En. xl. 7 (note). The myth
here, however, varies somewhat from
that in Eth. En. vi-xvi. The leaders
in the Eth. En. vi-xvi. are not Satans,
but ' watchers,' like their followers.
In Eth. En. lxix, however, we have
an account which harmonizes with
our text. There we see that the
superior angels had rebelled before
the creation of Adam ; that they had
tempted Eve and brought about the
fall of the angels in the days of Jared.
Thus, in Eth. En. lxix. and here, the
leaders of the angels who fell in
Jared's days are Satans. This is
practically the view of portions of the
Talmud. See Weber, pp. 211, 243,
244.   Who with their prince
Satanail. Quoted in Test. Dan. 5 . .
τῶν πνευμάτων τῆς πλάνης. Ἀνέγνων

rejected the holy[1] Lord[2].   4. And *in consequence of these
things[3] they are kept in great darkness in the second heaven ;
* and of them there went three[4] to the earth from the throne
of God to the place Ermon ; and they entered into dealings
on the side of Mount Iermon, and they saw the daughters
of men, that they were fair, and took unto themselves wives.
5. And they made the earth foul with their deeds[5]. And
they acted lawlessly in all times of this age, and wrought
confusion, and the giants were born, and the strangely tall
men, and there was much wickedness.   6. And on account
of this God judged them with a mighty judgement. And
they lament for their brethren, and they will be punished at
the great day of the Lord.   7. And I said to the Grigori :
' I have seen your brethren and their works, and their great[1]

---

[1] Sok. om.   [2] Sok. adds to the number of twenty millions.   [3] Those
who followed them are the prisoners who, Sok.   [4] Who went, Sok.
[5] Sok. adds And the wives of men continue to do evil.

γὰρ ἐν βίβλῳ 'Ενὼχ τοῦ δικαίου, ὅτι
ὁ ἄρχων ὑμῶν ἐστὶν ὁ Σατανᾶς. ὑμῶν
is here corrupt for αὐτῶν. The text
cannot mean that all the watchers
rebelled, but only that it was from
the class of the watchers that the
rebels proceeded. It is, of course,
just possible that the writers' scheme
may differ from the conception we
have given above, and be as follows.
The rebellious watchers, with their
prince Satanail, are confined to the
fifth heaven. The subordinate angels
who followed them are imprisoned
in the second heaven, whereas the
watchers who went down to earth and
sinned with women are imprisoned
under the earth. This view is very
attractive, but is open to more difficulties of interpretation than the one
we have followed. The MSS. reading
fifth in vii. 3 is indeed in its favour,
but then for ' prince and ' in the

same verse we must read ' prince and
leaders who.' The main objections
to this interpretation, however, lie
in xviii. 8, 9, and in vii. 3, where the
prisoners of the second heaven are
clearly identified with the watchers.
In xxx. 1–3 Satanail with his angels
is cast down from heaven.   4.
Kept ... in the second heaven :
see vii. 3.   **Three.** According to
Eth. En. ix. 6 Azazel, or vi. 3, ix. 7
Semjaza : according to *Jalkut* Schim.,
Beresch 44 Assael and Semjaza.
Ermon : see Eth. En. vi. 2–6 (notes).
**Entered into dealings on . . .
Mount Iermon :** Eth. En. vi. 5.
5. Eth. En. x. 8 ; vii. 2.   **6.** Eth.
En. x. 4–15. **They will be punished :**
i. e. the lustful watchers.   **7.** There
is a confusion in this verse. In vii.
Enoch has seen the rebellious
watchers being tortured in the second
heaven ; whereas he says here that he

torments[1]. And I have prayed for them, but God has condemned them (to be) under the earth, till the heaven and
earth are ended for ever.'   . 8. And I said : ' Why do ye
* wait, brethren [2], and not serve before the face of the Lord ?
and perform your duties [3] before the face of the Lord, and do
not anger your Lord [4] to the end.'   9. And they listened
to my rebuke. And they * stood in the four orders in this [5]
heaven, and lo ! as I was standing with these men, four
trumpets resounded together with a loud voice, and the
Grigori sang with one voice, and their voices went forth
before the Lord [6] with sadness and tenderness.

[The taking up of Enoch into the sixth Heaven.]

XIX. 1. And these men took me thence and brought me
to the sixth heaven, and I saw there seven bands of angels,
very bright and glorious, and their faces shining more than
* the rays of [7] the sun. * They are resplendent [7], and there
is no difference * in their countenances, or their manner, or
the style of their clothing [8].   2. *And these orders [9] arrange
and study * the revolutions of the stars, and the changes

---

[1] Sok. adds and their great entreaties.   [2] Await your brethren,
Sok.   [3] Sok. adds and serve.   [4] Sok. adds your God.   [5] Spoke to
the four orders in, A.   [6] Sok. adds God.
  XIX. [7] B om.   [8] Of form between them nor in the fashion of their
raiment, Sok.   [9] Some of these angels, B.

---

has seen the lustful watchers who are
punished under the earth. I have
prayed for them: cf. vii. 5 (note).
8, 9. The watchers are silent out
of sympathy with their brethren
who are punished in the second
heaven and under the earth, but at
Enoch's rebuke they resume the worship they had left off. Even so their
singing is still marked with sadness.

  XIX. 1. The account of the sixth
heaven disagrees more or less with
that of Test. Levi 3, with that of

Chag. 12[b], and with the colourless
account in the Asc. Is. There is no
difference in their countenances,
&c. : Asc. Is. viii. 16 ' Omnium una
species et gloria aequalis,' seems to be
derived from our text, as it emphasizes the differences in glory between
the angelic orders in each of the first
five heavens, and emphasizes no less
the equality in glory of all the angels
of the sixth heaven (cf. Asc. Is. viii.
5-7).   2. The heavenly bodies are
under Uriel in Eth. En. lxxii–lxxxii.

of the moon, and revolutions of the sun, and superintend the good or evil condition of the world [1].   3. *And they [2] arrange teachings, and instructions, and sweet * speaking, and [3] singing, and all * kinds of glorious [4] praise.   * These are the archangels who are appointed over the angels ! They hold in subjection all living things both in heaven and earth [5]. 4. And there are the angels who are over seasons and years, and the angels who are over rivers and the sea, and those who are over the fruits * of the earth, and the angels over every herb, giving all kinds of nourishment to every living thing [6].   5. And the angels over all souls of men, who write down all their works and their lives [7] before the face of the Lord.   6. In the midst of them are seven phoenixes and seven cherubims, and seven six-winged creatures, * being as one voice and singing with one voice [8]; and it is not possible to describe their singing, and * they rejoice before the Lord [9] at His footstool.

[Thence Enoch is taken into the seventh Heaven [10].]

XX. 1. And these men took me thence *and brought me [11]

---

[1] The peaceful order of the world, and the revolutions of the sun, moon, and stars.   [2] Other heavenly angels, B.   [3] And clear, A ; voiced, Sok.   [4] Things concerned with, A.   [5] So A Sok.; but that A reads measure for hold in subjection, B om.   [6] So A Sok.; but that A reads all those who give nourishment for giving all kinds of nourishment; B reads and grass and all things that grow.   [7] And the angels who write down all the souls of men and all their works and their lives, A ; Other angels arrange the things of all men and all living things, and write, B.   [8] With one voice they sing in harmony, A ; Each uttering words by himself, and singing by himself things in harmony, B. [9] The Lord rejoices with them, B.

XX. [10] Entry of Enoch into the seventh heaven, B.   [11] A om.

---

4. In Eth. En. lx. it is subordinate spirits that are over these natural objects. Cf. Eth. En. lxxxii. 13 ; Rev. ix. 14 ; xvi. 5.   5. It is Raphael in Eth. En. xx. 3.   6. Six-winged creatures : i. e. seraphim. Cf. xii. 1 (notes). Observe that both cherubim and seraphim are also in the seventh heaven. *Chag.* 12[b] places the Sera-

phim, Ophannim, and Chajjoth, and other angels of service in the seventh heaven. Test. Levi 3 in agreement with this verse represents the inhabitants of the sixth heaven as οἱ ἄγγελοί εἰσι τοῦ προσώπου κυρίου, οἱ λειτουργοῦντες.

XX. 1. With this description of the heavenly hosts cf. Is. vi ; Ezek.

to the seventh heaven, and I saw there a very [1] great light and
*all the fiery hosts of great archangels, and incorporeal powers [2]
*and lordships, and principalities, and powers; cherubim
and seraphim, thrones [1] *and the watchfulness of many eyes.
There were ten troops, a station of brightness [3], and I was
afraid, and trembled * with a great terror [1].   2. And those
men *took hold of me and brought me into their midst [4]
and said to me: ‘Be of good cheer, Enoch, be not afraid.’
3. And they showed me the Lord from afar sitting on His
lofty [5] throne [6]. And all the heavenly hosts having approached
stood [1] on the ten [1] steps, *according to their rank: and [1] made

---

[1] B om.   [2] A fiery host of great archangels of spiritual forms, A.
All the fiery and bright host of the incorporeal archangels, B.   [3] And
the ten many-eyed bands of bright station, Sok.; B om. After brightness
A Sok. add the gloss like the followers of John. For nine (A) I have
read ten with Sok.   [4] Placed me in their midst, B. For unto their
midst A reads after them.   [5] Very lofty, Sok., B om.   [6] A adds for
it is that upon which God rests. In the tenth heaven, in the tenth
heaven is God. In the Hebrew language it is called Avarat.

---

i; Eth. En. xiv. 9–17; lxxi. 7-9;
Rev. iv. For *Chag.* 12ᵇ see xix. 6
(note). But this account can well
compare for grandeur with any of the
above. Lordships, and principalities, and powers . . . thrones. So
exactly Col. i. 16 εἴτε θρόνοι εἴτε κυριότητες εἴτε ἀρχαὶ εἴτε ἐξουσίαι. Cf.
Eph. i. 21 ἀρχῆς καὶ ἐξουσίας καὶ δυνά-
μεως καὶ κυριότητος: also Rom. viii.
38; Eph. iii. 10, 15; 1 Pet. iii. 22;
Eth. En. lxi. 10. Watchfulness of
many eyes seems to be derived from
Ezek. x. 12. These are the Ophannim, Eth. En. lxi. 10. Ten . . .
brightness. These are the ten orders
of angels mentioned in ver. 3. Was
afraid and trembled: Eth. En. xiv.
14.   2. Be of good cheer, &c.:
cf. i. 8.   3. The Lord . . . on
His lofty throne: Is. vi. 1; Eth.
En. xiv. 20; Rev. xix. 4. All the
heavenly hosts . . . on the ten
steps according to their rank.

These hosts consist of the ten troops
mentioned in ver. 1, arranged in the
order of their rank. According to
Maimonides in the *Mishne Thora*
S. 1; Jesode Thora C. 2, they are:
Chajjoth, Ophannim, Arellim, Chash-
mallim, Seraphim, Mal’achim, Elohim,
Bene Elohim, Kerubim, Ishim (Weber, p. 163). In the *Berith menucha*
the list is different: Arellim, Ishim,
Bene Elohim, Mal’achim, Chashmal-
lim, Tarshishim, Shina’nim, Kerubim,
Ophannim, Seraphim (Eisenmenger,
ii. 374). But the nearest parallel is
to be found in the nine orders of Dionysius the Areopagite, i.e. Σεραφίμ,
Χερουβίμ, Θρόνοι, Κυριότητες, Δυνάμεις, Ἐξουσίαι, Ἀρχαί, Ἀρχάγγελοι,
Ἄγγελοι. These are reproduced in
Dante, *Par.* c. xxviii, where the
slightly differing arrangement of
Gregory the Great (*Hom.* xxxiv. 7)
is censured.

obeisance to the Lord.   4. And so they proceeded to their places in joy and mirth, and in boundless light *singing songs with low and gentle voices [1], *and gloriously serving Him [2].

[*How the Angels placed Enoch there at the limits of the seventh Heaven, and departed from him invisibly.*]

XXI. 1. They leave not *nor depart day or night [3] standing before the face of the Lord, working His will [4], cherubim and seraphim, standing round His throne.   *And the six-winged creatures [5] overshadow all [6] His throne, singing *with a soft voice [6] before the face of the Lord: *'Holy, Holy, Holy: Lord God of Sabaoth! heaven and earth are full of Thy glory [6]!'   2. When I had seen all these things, *these men said unto me: 'Enoch, up to this time we have been ordered to accompany thee.'   And [6] those men departed from me, and I saw them no more.   And I remained alone at the extremity of the heaven [7], and was afraid, and fell on my face, *and said within myself: 'Woe is me! what has come upon me![8].'   3. And the Lord sent one of His glorious archangels [6], Gabriel, and he said to me: 'Be of good cheer, Enoch, *be not afraid [9], *stand up, come with me [10], and stand up before the face of the Lord for ever.   4. And I answered him, *and said [11]: 'Oh! Lord, my spirit has departed from me with fear *and trembling [6]! *call to me the men [12] who have brought me to this place: upon them

[1] B om.   [2] The glorious ones seeing Him, Suk.
XXI. [3] A om.   [4] B adds and the whole host of.   [5] With six wings and many eyes, A.   [6] B om.   [7] Seventh heaven, A.   [8] B om.   [9] Fear not thou these hosts, B.   [10] Come unto me, B. A transposes these words after for ever.   [11] B om.; A adds within myself.   B adds Woe is me, O Lord![12] I called the men, A B.

XXI. 1. Leave not nor depart day or night. This is derived from Eth. En. xiv. 23 'The holy ones of the holy—leave not by night nor depart.'   'Six-winged creatures . . . Holy, holy, holy, &c.,' Is. vi. 2, 3.   **3. Be of good cheer, be not afraid.** See i. 8; xx. 2; xxi. 5; Eth. En.

I have relied, and with them I would go before the face of the Lord.' 5. And Gabriel hurried me away like a leaf carried off by the wind, * and he took me [1] and set me before the face of the Lord [2].

XXII. 4. I fell down [3] and worshipped the Lord. 5. And the Lord spake with His lips to me: 'Be of good cheer,

---

[1] Having taken me, Sok., A om. [2] A adds 6. And I saw the eighth heaven, which is called in the Hebrew language, Muzaloth, changing in its season in dryness and moisture, with the twelve signs of the zodiac, which are above the seventh heaven. And I saw the ninth heaven, which in the Hebrew is called Kukhavim, where are the heavenly homes of the twelve signs of the zodiac.

Michael the Archangel led Enoch into the tenth heaven before the face of the Lord.

XXII. 1. In the tenth heaven Aravoth, I saw the vision of the face of the Lord, like iron burnt in the fire, and brought forth and emitting sparks, and it burns. So I saw the face of the Lord; but the face of the Lord cannot be told. It is wonderful and awful, and very terrible. 2. And who am I that I should tell of the unspeakable being of God, and His wonderful face? And it is not for me to tell of His wonderful knowledge and various utterances ; and the very great throne of the Lord not made with hands. And how many stand around Him, hosts of cherubim and seraphim. 3. And moreover their never-ceasing songs, and their unchanging beauty, and the unspeakable greatness of His beauty, who can tell?

In Sok. a duplicate, but somewhat different, version of XXII. 1–3 is given :—

I also saw the Lord face to face. And His face was very glorious, marvellous and terrible, threatening, and strange. 2. Who am I to tell of the incomprehensible existence of the Lord, and His face wonderful, and not to be spoken of: and the choir with much instruction, and loud sound, and the throne of the Lord very great, and not made with hands: and the choir standing around Him of the hosts of cherubim and seraphim !

[3] B adds and could not see the Lord God.

---

xv. 1. 5. Cf. ver. 3. [6. This verse is clearly an interpolation. It is not found either in B or Sok. Furthermore, throughout the rest of the book only seven heavens are mentioned or implied. The term Muzaloth is the Hebrew name for the twelve signs of the Zodiac מַזָּלוֹת. Kukhavim is merely a transliteration of כּוֹכָבִים. Some ground for this conception may be found in Eth. En.

xiv. 17, where the path of the stars is above the throne of God, and as the throne of God according to this book is in the seventh heaven, the signs and stars might be regarded as in the eighth or ninth.]

XXII. [1–3. Aravoth a transliteration of עֲרָבוֹת, which according to *Chagig* 12[b] was really the seventh heaven. The rest of ver. 1 and verses 2, 3, may in some form have belonged

Enoch, be not afraid: rise up and stand before my face for
ever.'   6. And Michael, the chief captain, * lifted me up,
and [1] brought me before the face of the Lord, and the Lord
said to His servants making trial of them : ' Let Enoch come
to stand before My face for ever ! '   7. And the glorious
ones made obeisance * to the Lord, and said: ' Let Enoch
proceed according to Thy word [2] ! '   8. And the Lord said
to Michael : ' * Go and take from Enoch his earthly robe,
and anoint him with My holy [3] oil, and clothe him with the
raiment of My glory.'   9. And so Michael * did as the
Lord spake unto him. He [4] anointed me [5] and clothed me,
and the appearance of that oil was more than a great light,
and its anointing was like excellent dew ; and its fragrance
like myrrh, shining like a ray of the sun.   10. * And
I gazed upon myself, and I was like one of His glorious
ones [6].   * And there was no difference, and fear and
trembling departed from me [7].   11. And the Lord called
one of His archangels, by name Vretil [8], who * was more wise
than the other archangels, and [9] wrote down all the doings of
the Lord.   12. And the Lord said to Vretil [8], ' Bring forth

---

[1] B om. and transposes verses 8-10 before 5.   [2] And told me to come
forth, B.   [3] Take Enoch and strip from him all earthly things and
anoint him with fine, B.   [4] Stripped me of my clothes and, B.
[5] With blessed oil, B.   [6] Sok. om.   [7] A Sok. om.   [8] Pravuil, A ;
Vrevoil, Sok.   [9] With wisdom, B.

---

to the text. I have with some hesi-
tation rejected them].   6. **Michael.**
Cf. Eth. En. lxxi. 13, 14, where
Michael takes charge of Enoch. He
is likewise the chief of the archangels,
Eth. En. xl. 9.   As being the angel
set over Israel, Eth. En. xx. 5, he is
naturally the chief captain.   8.
This is τὸ ἔλαιον τοῦ ἐλέου of *Apoc.
Mosis* ed. Tischend. p. 6.   **Holy oil.**
See viii. 7 : Evang. Nicod. ii. 3.
This oil is described in ver. 9, and its
effects in ver. 10.   **Raiment of my
glory.** These are the garments of

the blessed. Cf. Eth. En. lxii. 15 ;
cviii. 12 ; 2 Cor. v. 3, 4 ; Rev. iii. 4,
5, 18 ; iv. 4 ; vi. 11 ; vii. 9, 13, 14 ;
4 Ezra ii. 39, 45 ; Herm. *Sim.* viii.
2 ; Asc. Is. ix. 9.   11. **Vretil.** I
cannot find this name anywhere else.
12. **Give a reed to Enoch.** These
words are drawn upon in *Liber S.
Joannis Apocryphus* (Thilo, *Cod.
Apocr.* N. T. vol. i. p. 890) ' Ele-
vavit Henoc super firmamentum . . .
et praecepit ei dari calamum . . .
et sedens scripsit sexaginta septem
libros.

the books from my store-places, *and give a reed to Enoch [1],
*and interpret to him the books [2].' *And Vretil made
haste and brought me the books, fragrant with myrrh, and
gave me a reed from his hand [3].

[*Of the Writing of Enoch how he wrote about his wonderful Goings
and the heavenly Visions, and he himself wrote 366 Books.*]

XXIII. 1. And he told me all the works of *the heaven
and [4] the earth and the sea, *and their goings and comings [5],
*the noise of the thunder; the sun and moon and the
movement of the stars; their changings; the seasons and
years; days and hours [6]; and [7] goings of the winds; and
the numbers of the angels; *the songs of the armed
hosts [8].   2. And everything relating to man, and every
language of their songs, and the lives of men, and the
precepts [9] and instructions, and sweet-voiced singings, and all
which it is suitable to be instructed in.   3. *And Vretil
instructed me thirty days and thirty nights, and his lips
never ceased speaking; and I did not cease thirty days and
thirty nights writing all the remarks [10].   4. And Vretil [11] said
to me: *'All the things which I have told thee, thou hast
written down.   Sit [12] down and *write all about [13] the souls

---

[1] And take a reed for speedy writing and give it to Enoch, A Sok.
[2] A om.   [3] And show him the books wonderful and fragrant with
myrrh from thy hand, A; Sok. agrees with text, save that he adds wonderful
before books, and adds for speedy writing after reed.
   XXIII. [4] B om.   [5] The movements of all the elements, B; A om.
[6] The living things and the seasons of the year, and the course of his
days and their changings, and the teaching of the commandments, B;
Sok. supports text, save that for movement of the stars he reads stars and
their goings.   After hours Sok. adds and the coming forth of the clouds.
[7] B OMITS from and goings to end of ver. 2.   [8] The fashion of their
songs, A.   [9] Narratives, A.   [10] A om.; Sok. supports text, but that for
remarks he reads marks of every creature.   After creature Sok. adds and
when I had finished the thirty days and nights.   [11] Právuil, A;
Vrevoil, Sok.   So a'so in previous verse.   [12] Lo! what things I have
instructed thee in and what thou hast written: and now sit, Sok.
[13] Write down all, Sok.

XXIII. 1. This verse would not
unsuitably describe the Book of Celes-

tial Physics in Eth. En. lxxii–lxxxii.
Songs of the armed hosts: see xvii.

of men, those of them which are not born, and the places prepared for them for ever.   5. For every soul was created eternally [1] before the foundation of the world.'   6. And I * wrote all out continuously [2] during thirty days and thirty nights, * and I copied all out accurately, and I wrote 366 books [3].

---

[1] For eternity, Sok.   [2] Sat, Sok.   [3] And so I ceased and I had written 360 books, B.

---

5. Every soul was created . . . before the foundation of the world. The Platonic doctrine of the pre-existence of the soul is here taught. We find that it had already made its way into Jewish thought in Egypt; cf. *Wisdom of Solomon*, viii. 19, 20 παῖς δὲ ἤμην εὐφυής, ψυχῆς τε ἔλαχον ἀγαθῆς, μᾶλλον δὲ ἀγαθὸς ὢν ἦλθον εἰς σῶμα ἀμίαντον. This doctrine was accepted and further developed by Philo. According to him the whole atmosphere is filled with souls. Among these, those who are nearer the earth and are attracted by the body descend into mortal bodies (τούτων τῶν ψυχῶν αἱ μὲν κατίασιν ἐνδεθησόμεναι σώμασι θνητοῖς, ὅσαι προσγειότατοι καὶ φιλοσώματοι, *De Somn*. i. 22). When they have entered the body they are swept off by it as by a river and swallowed up in its eddies (ἐκεῖναι δὲ ὥσπερ εἰς ποταμὸν τὸ σῶμα καταβᾶσαι τοτὲ μὲν ὑπὸ συρμοῦ δίνης βιαιοτάτης ἁρπασθεῖσαι κατεπόθησαν, *De Gigant*. 3). Only a few escape by obedience to a spiritual philosophy and come to share in the incorporeal and imperishable life that is with God (*De Gigant*. 3). But there were other souls, called demons in philosophy and angels in Scripture, who dwelling in the higher parts were never entangled by love of the earthly (μηδενὸς μὲν τῶν περιγείων ποτὲ ὀρεχθεῖσαι τὸ παράπαν, *De Somn*. i. 22), and who reported the commands of the Father to the children, and the needs of the children to the Father (τὰς τοῦ πατρὸς ἐπικελεύσεις τοῖς ἐκγόνοις καὶ τὰς τῶν ἐκγόνων χρείας τῷ πατρὶ διαγγέλλουσι, *De Somn*. i. 22; cf. *De Gigant*. 4). This doctrine of the preexistence of the soul was according to Josephus, *Bell. Jud*. ii. 8. 11, held by the Essenes: καὶ γὰρ ἔρρωται παρ' αὐτοῖς ἥδε ἡ δόξα, φθαρτὰ μὲν εἶναι τὰ σώματα καὶ τὴν ὕλην οὐ μόνιμον αὐτοῖς, τὰς δὲ ψυχὰς ἀθανάτους ἀεὶ διαμένειν, καὶ συμπλέκεσθαι μέν, ἐκ τοῦ λεπτοτάτου φοιτώσας αἰθέρος, ὥσπερ εἰρκταῖς τοῖς σώμασιν ἴυγγί τινι φυσικῇ κατασπωμένας, ἐπειδὰν δὲ ἀνεθῶσι τῶν κατὰ σάρκα δεσμῶν, οἷα δὴ μακρᾶς δουλείας ἀπηλλαγμένας, τότε χαίρειν καὶ μετεώρους φέρεσθαι. It became a prevailing dogma in later Judaism. All souls which were to enter human bodies existed before the creation of the world in the Garden of Eden (*Tanchuma*, Pikkude 3) or in the seventh heaven (*Chagig* 12[b]) or in a certain chamber (אוצר) (*Sifre* 143[b]) whence God called them forth to enter human bodies. These souls were conceived of as actually living beings. According to *Bereshith rabba* c. 8, God takes counsel with the souls of the righteous before He creates the earth (cf. Weber, pp. 204, 205, 217–220). See xxx. 16 (note).

[*Of the great Secrets of God, which God revealed and told to Enoch, and spoke with him Face to Face.*]

XXIV. 1. And the Lord called me *and said to me: 'Enoch, sit thou on My[1] left hand with Gabriel.' And I made obeisance to the Lord.   2. And the Lord spake to me: 'Enoch[2], * the things which thou seest at rest and in motion were completed by me[3]. I will tell thee * now, even[4] from the first, what things I created from the non-existent, and what visible things from the invisible[5].   3. Not even to My angels have I told My secrets, nor have I informed them of * their origin, nor have they understood My infinite creation[6] which I tell thee of to-day.   4. * For before anything which is visible existed[7], * I alone held my course among the invisible things[8], like the sun from the east to the west, * and from the west to the east.   5. But even the sun has rest in himself, but I did not find rest,

---

XXIV. [1] And placed me on His, B.   [2] Beloved Enoch, A.   [3] Thou seest the things which are now completed, A.   [4] All, Sok.   [5] A adds Listen Enoch and pay attention to these words, for.   [6] Their origin nor of My infinite empire, nor have they understood the creation made by Me, A. My mysteries nor their explanations nor My boundless and inexplicable plans in creation, B.   [7] B om.   [8] I revealed the light: I went about in the light as one of the invisible.

XXIV. 2. **From the non-existent.** Here creation *ex nihilo* seems to be taught. In Philo, on the other hand, the world was not created, but only formed from pre-existent chaotic elements. In one passage, however, where the absolute creation of the world is taught, we have an actual and almost verbal agreement with our text—ὡς ἥλιος ἀνατείλας τὰ κεκρυμμένα τῶν σωμάτων ἐπιδείκνυται, οὕτω καὶ ὁ θεὸς τὰ πάντα γεννήσας οὐ μόνον εἰς τὸ ἐμφανὲς ἤγαγεν, ἀλλὰ καὶ ἃ πρότερον οὐκ ἦν ἐποίησεν, οὐ δημιουργὸς μόνον, ἀλλὰ καὶ κτίστης αὐτὸς ὤν (*De Somn.* i. 13). Probably, however, from the non-existent is a

rendering of ἐκ τῶν μὴ ὄντων. This will harmonize with xxv. 1. Visible things from the invisible: cf. passage just quoted from Philo; also Heb. xi. 3 'The worlds have been formed by the word of God, so that what is seen hath not been made out of things which do appear.' These words from *Hebrews* do not necessarily imply creation, but can naturally be interpreted after Philo's conceptions. In Gen. i. 2 LXX we find the idea of invisible elements introduced, as it gives ἡ δὲ γῆ ἦν ἀόρατος as a rendering of what we translate with 'the earth was waste.'   3. **Not even to My angels**: cf. xl. 3; 1 Pet. i. 12.

because I was creating every thing[1]. And I planned to lay the foundations and to make the visible creation.

[God tells Enoch how out of the lowest Darkness, there comes forth the visible and the invisible.]

XXV. 1. '*And I commanded in the depths that visible things should come out of invisible. And out came Adoil very great[2], *and I gazed upon him. And lo! his colour was red, of great brightness[3].   2. And I said unto him : "Burst asunder, Adoil[4], and let that which comes from thee be visible."   3. And he burst asunder, and there came forth a great light[5], and *I was in the midst of a great light, and as the light came forth from the light[6], there came forth the great world, *revealing all the creation[3], which I had purposed to make, and I saw that it was good.   4. And I made for Myself a throne, and sat upon it, and I said to the light:

---

[1] B om.
XXV. [2] I summoned from the regions below the great Idoil to come forth who had in his belly a great stone, B.   [3] B om.   [4] A om.
[5] Stone, B.   [6] I was in the midst of light, and the light thus appearing out of it, Sok. ; B om.

XXV. 1. Here the formation of the world from pre-existing elements is taught, as in the Book of Wisdom xi. 17 ἐξ ἀμόρφου ὕλης. Cf. also Philo, *De Justitia* 7 Μηνύει δὲ ἡ τοῦ Κόσμου γένεσις . . . τὰ γὰρ μὴ ὄντα ἐκάλεσεν εἰς τὸ εἶναι. This is in the main the teaching of the Talmud. See Weber, 193–196. Adoil. Is this from יד אל, the hand of God ? The word does not occur elsewhere that I am aware of. In this and the two subsequent verses we have an adaptation of an Egyptian myth.   2. We have here a modification of the egg theory of the universe. See Clem. *Recog.* x. 17, 30. In Brugsch, *Rel. u. Myth. d. alten Aegypter*, p. 101, we find a very close parallel. According to the monuments: 'der erste Schöpfungsaact began

mit der Bildung eines Eies aus dem Urgewässer, aus dem das Tageslicht, die unmittelbare Ursache des Lebens in dem Bereiche der irdischen Welt herausbrach.'   3. There came forth a great light. This exactly agrees with the ancient Egyptian myth as described in preceding note. Cf. also Brugsch, *Rel. u. Myth.* pp. 160, 161 on *Die Geburt des Lichtes.* There came forth the great world. This should refer to the world of the heavens, as the earth is dealt with in the next chapter.   4. I made for Myself a throne. This throne was created before the world according to *Bereshith rabba* c. 1 as here. This idea may have found support in the LXX of Prov. viii. 27, where wisdom declares that she was with

" Go forth * on high [1] and be established above My throne [2], and be the foundation for things on high.'   5. And there was nothing higher than the light, and as I reclined, I saw it from My throne.

[*God again calls from the Depths and there came forth Arkhas, Tazhis [3], and one who is very red.*]

XXVI. 1. And I summoned a second time from the depths, * and said: ' Let the solid thing which is visible come forth from the invisible [4].'   And Arkhas * came forth [5] firm [6] and heavy [3] and * very red [7].   2. And I said : ' Be thou divided, O Arkhas, and let * that be seen which is [8] produced from thee.'   And when he was divided, the world came forth, very dark and great, * bringing the creation of all things below [9].   3. And I saw that it [10] was good.   And I said to him: '* Go thou down [11] and be thou established. * And be a foundation for things below'; and it was so. And it came forth and was established [12], and was a foundation for things below.   * And there was nothing else below the darkness [12].

[*How God established the Water, and surrounded it with Light, and established upon it Seven Islands.*]

XXVII. 1. * And I ordered that there should be a separation between the light and the darkness, and I said : ' Let

---

[1] Above My throne, Sok.   [2] Sok. om.
XXVI. [3] Corrupt in A, from ТАЖЕСТЬ = heaviness (Old Slav.).   [4] I told him to come forth from the unseen into that which is fixed and visible, B ; and said : ' let the strong Arkhas come forth,' and he came forth strong from the invisible, A.   [5] A om.   [6] Very firm, B.
[7] Black, B.   [8] The thing, A; B OMITS ENTIRE VERSE.   [9] Bearer of the created things from all things below, A.   [10] All, B.   [11] Come forth from below, A Sok.   [12] B om.

God at the creation when he established His throne upon the winds (ὅτε ἀφώριζεν τὸν ἑαυτοῦ θρόνον ἐπ' ἀνέμων).
XXVI. 1. Formation, but not creation, of the earth. Arkhas may be from קֶרַח or even from ἀρχή.

XXVII. The title is very corrupt.
1. Separation between the light and the darkness: Gen. i. 4. I do

there be a thick substance,' and it was so [1].　　2. * And I spread this out and there was water, and I spread it over the darkness [2], below the light.　　3. And thus I made firm the waters, that is, the depths, and I surrounded the waters with light, and I created seven circles and I fashioned them like crystal, moist and dry, that is to say, like glass and ice, and as for the waters, and also the other elements, I showed each of them their paths, (viz.) to the seven stars, each of them in their heaven, how they should go ; and I saw that it was good.　　4. And I separated between the light and the darkness ; that is to say, between the waters here and there. And I said to the light : ' Let it be day [3] '; and to the darkness , ' Let it be night.' And the evening and the morning were the first day [4].

XXVIII. 1. [5] And thus I * made firm the circles of the heavens, and caused the waters * below, which are under the heavens to be gathered into one place, and that the waves should be dried up, and it was so.　　2. Out of the waves I made firm and great stones, and out of the stones I heaped together a dry substance, and I called the dry substance earth.　　3. And in the midst of the earth I appointed a pit, that is to say an abyss.　　4. I gathered the sea into one place, and I restrained it with a yoke. And I said to

---

XXVII. [1] And I ordered that they should take from the light and the darkness and I said : ' Let it be thick and covered with light,' Sok. ; B om.　　[2] So A Sok., but that A adds with light after out. B reads And having clothed (spread out P) certain things with light, I made broad and stretched out the path of the waters above the darkness.　　B OMITS THE REST OF THE CHAPTER.　　[3] Be thou day, Sok.　　[4] A adds as title of XXVIII, Sunday. On it God showed to Enoch all His wisdom and power : during all the seven days how He created the powers of the heaven and earth and all moving things and at last man.

XXVIII. [5] A and Sok. agree in this chapter. B is fragmentary and transposed, and reads : (2) And I made the great stones firm, (1) and ordered

---

not pretend to understand what follows.　　3. Seven stars : see xxx. 5.　　4. Gen. i. 4, 5.

XXVIII. 1. Gen. i. 9.　　2. I called the dry substance earth.

An exact rendering of Gen. i. 10.　　3. This may be Sheol, or Tartarus (cf. xxix. 5), or it may be the abysses of the waters : cf. Gen. vii. 11 ; viii. 2 ; Eth. En. lxxxix. 7, 8 ; Jubilees ii.

the sea: 'Lo! I give thee an eternal portion and thou shalt not move from thy established position.' So I made fast the firmament and fixed it above the water.   5. This I called the first day of the creation. Then it was evening, and again morning, and it was the second day [1].

XXIX. 1. And for all the heavenly hosts I fashioned [2] a nature like that of fire, and My eye gazed on the very firm and hard stone. And from the brightness of My eye the lightning received its wonderful nature.   2. And fire is in the water and water in the fire, and neither is the one quenched, nor the other dried up. On this account lightning is brighter than the sun, and soft water is stronger than hard stone [3].   3. And from the stone I cut the mighty fire. *And from the fire I made the ranks of the spiritual hosts, ten thousand angels [4], *and their weapons are fiery, and

---

the waters of the abysses to dry up, (4) and having collected into rivers the overflowings of the abysses and the seas into one place, I bound them with a yoke. I made an everlasting separation between the earth and the sea, and the waters cannot burst forth. And I made fast the firmament, and fixed it above the waters.   [1] A adds as title of the next three verses : The day is Monday, the fiery creations.

XXIX. [2] B adds the sun of a great light and placed it in the heavens that it might give light upon earth.   [3] So A and Sok., but that Sok. adds keener and before brighter. B omits a nature . . . hard stone. [4] And from stones I created the hosts of spirits, B. A supports text, but that for ten thousand it read of the ten. B adds and all the starry hosts, and the Cherubim, and the Seraphim, and the Ophannim, I cut out of fire.

---

2.   4. Cf. Job xxvi. 10 ; Ps. civ. 9 ; Prov. viii. 29 ; Jer. v. 22. **Firmament** : Gen. i. 7, 8.   5. This verse should be read immediately after xxix, and together with that chapter should be restored before xxviii. This is clear from the analogy of xxx. 1, 2, 7, 8. It is impossible in its present position.

XXIX. This chap. is clearly dislocated from its original position before xxviii. There is no mark of time attached to it. The work of the first day is given in xxv-xxvii ; that

of the second day in xxviii. 1-4 ; that of the third in xxx. 1. xxviii. 5, as we have already seen, must have been differently placed originally. Hence, if we recall the fact that in Jubilees ii. 2, and occasionally in patristic tradition, the creation of the angels is assigned to the first day—evidently on the ground of Job xxxviii. 7.—we can restore the text to perfect harmony with itself and Jewish tradition by placing xxix, followed immediately by xxviii. 5, after xxvii.

their garment is a burning flame, and I ordered them to stand each in their ranks [1].

[*Here Satanail was hurled from the Heights with his Angels.*]

4. *One of these in the ranks of the Archangels, having turned away with the rank below him, entertained an impossible idea, that he should make his throne higher than the clouds over the earth, and should be equal in rank to My power.   5. And I hurled him from the heights with his angels.   And he was flying in the air continually, above the abyss [1].

XXX. 1. *And so I created all the heavens, and it was the

---

[1] B om.

---

3. **From the fire I made the . . . angels.** So Pesikta 3ᵃ : see Weber L. d. J. 161.   4. **One of these . . . with the rank below him.** This is clearly Satan.   The rank below him is probably the watchers.   But however we interpret the text we are beset with difficulties.   There are conflicting elements in the text.   See xii. and xviii. with notes: vii ; xix ; xxxi. 3-7 (notes).   **Make his throne higher than the clouds.**   If this is genuine we must take *clouds* in the sense of heavens.   Satan was one of the highest angels before his fall : cf. xviii. 4.   Satan and Sammael can not be distinguished in Rabbinic writings.   On the attempt of Sammael to found a kingdom see Weber, 244.   The following passage from the *Book of Adam and Eve*, I. vi. is evidently derived from our text : 'The wicked Satan . . . set me at naught and sought the Godhead, so that I hurled him down from heaven.'   5. **He was flying in the air continu-** ally.   This view seems to have been generally received amongst the Jews.   Cf. Eph. ii. 2 'The prince of the power of the air '; vi. 12 ; Test. Benj. 3 τοῦ ἀερίου πνεύματος τοῦ Βελίαρ : Asc. Is. iv. 2 'Berial angelus magnus res huius mundi . . . descendet e firmamento suo '; vii. 9 'Et ascendimus in firmamentum, ego et ille, et ibi vidi Sammaelem eiusque potestates'; x. 29 'descendit in firmamentum ubi princeps huius mundi habitat.'   Tuf. haarez, f. 9. 2 'Under the sphere of the moon, which is the last under all, is a firmament . . . and there the souls of the demons are.'   Cf. Eisenmenger, ii. 411.   According to the Stoics, on the other hand, the abode of the blessed was under the moon.   Cf. Tertull. *De An.* 54 ; Lucan ix. 5 sq.   For other authorities see Meyer on Eph. ii. 2 ; Eisenmenger, ii. 456.   It is hard to get a consistent view of the demonology of this book ; it seems to be as follows : Satan, one of the archangels (xviii. 4 ; xxix. 4), seduced the watchers of the

third day. On the third day[1] I ordered the earth to produce *great trees, such as bear fruit, and mountains[2], and *every sort of herb and every[3] seed that is sown[4], *and I planted Paradise, and enclosed it, and placed fiery angels armed, and so I made a renewing. 2. Then it was evening, and it was morning, being the fourth day[5]. On the fourth day[6] I ordered that there should be great lights in the circles of the heavens. 3. In the first and highest circle I placed the star Kruno; and on the second[7] Aphrodite; on the third

---

XXX. [1] B om. ˙ In verse 1 A adds **Tuesday** as title before On the third day. [2] All sorts of trees and high mountains, B. [3] A om. [4] B adds before I produced living things and prepared food for them. [5] B om. Sok. supports text; but adds of the earth after renewing. A adds **Wednesday** as title of 2ᵇ-7. [6] B OMITS VERSES 2-7^. [7] Sok. adds **lower I placed.**

---

fifth heaven into revolt, in order to establish a counter kingdom to God, xxix. 4. Therefore Satan, or the Satans (for it is the name of a class) (Weber, 244), were cast down from heaven, xxix. 5; xxxi. 4, and given the air for their habitation, xxix. 5. As for his followers, the watchers of the fifth heaven, they were cast down to the second and there kept imprisoned and tortured, vii. 3; xviii. 4. Some, however, of the Satans or Watchers went down to earth and married the daughters of men, xviii. 4. From these were born giants, xviii. 5. Thereupon these watchers were imprisoned under the earth, xviii. 6, 7, and the souls of the giants, their children, became subjects of Satan. To return to the Satans, however, when man was created, Satan envied him and wished to make another world, xxxi. 3. Out of envy he tempted Eve to her fall, xxxi. 6.

XXX. 1. Cf. Gen. i. 10, 11. **Mountains.** This is corrupt. We should have a reference here probably to non-fruit-bearing trees, as in Jub. ii. 7 τὰ ξύλα

τὰ κάρπιμά τε καὶ ἄκαρπα. Every seed that is sown. This phrase is found in Jubilees, ii. 7, as one of the third day creations. Paradise. Also in Jub. ii. 7, among the creations of the third day. 2. Circles of the heavens. In Philo, *De Mundi Op.* 38, we find seven circles as here, though with a different meaning: τὸν οὐρανόν φασιν ἑπτὰ διεζῶσθαι κύκλοις. 3. Gen. i. 14-19. In the *Chronography of Joel,* circ. 1200 A. D., p. 34 (ed. Bekker, 1836), the discovery of the signs of the Zodiac, the solstices and the seasons, and the naming of the planets, are assigned to Seth; but as such discoveries were anciently assigned to Enoch, and were only in later tradition ascribed to Seth, we may not unreasonably regard the mention in Joel of the five planets, Kronos, Zeus, Ares, Aphrodite, Hermes, as ultimately derived from the Enoch literature. The statement in Joel is, ὁ δὲ Σὴθ πρῶτος ἐξεῦρε . . . τὰ σημεῖα τοῦ οὐρανοῦ καὶ τὰς τροπὰς τῶν ἐνιαυτῶν . . . καὶ τοῖς ἄστροις ἐπέθηκεν ὀνόματα καὶ τοῖς πέντε πλανήταις εἰς τὸ

Ares; * on the fourth the Sun [1]; on the fifth Zeus; on the sixth Hermes; on the seventh [2] the moon.   4. And * the lower air I adorned with the lesser stars.·   5. And [3] I placed the sun to give light to the day, and the moon and the stars to give light to the night; the sun that he should go * according to each sign of the Zodiac [4]; and the course of * the moon through the twelve signs of the Zodiac [5]. 6. And I fixed their names * and existence, the thunders, and the revolutions of the hours, how they take place [6].   7. Then it was evening and the morning, the fifth day. * On the fifth day [7] * I commanded the sea to produce [8] fish, * and

---

[1] A om.   [2] A adds the lesser.   [3] And I adorned it with the lesser stars, and on the lower, A.   [4] To every living thing, A.   [5] The twelve months, A.   [6] And their reverberations, and new births, and making of the hours as they go, Sok.   [7] B om. After fifth day A adds Thursday, and after sixth day it adds Friday.   [8] B adds and multiply.

γνωρίζεσθαι ὑπὸ τῶν ἀνθρώπων καὶ μόνον· καὶ τὸν μὲν πρῶτον πλανήτην ἐκάλεσε Κρόνον, τὸν δὲ δεύτερον Δία, τὸν τρίτον Ἄρεα, τὸν τέταρτον Ἀφροδίτην καὶ τὸν πέμπτον Ἑρμῆν. In the mysteries of Mithras, described in Origen, *Contra Celsum* vi. 22, the five planets and the sun and moon are said to be connected by a heavenly ladder. From the first words of the preceding ch. we see that these heavenly bodies had some connexion with the seven heavens, as in our text. The order in which the planets and the sun and moon are mentioned in *Contra Celsum* differs from that given above, and is as follows: Kronos, Aphrodite, Zeus, Hermes, Ares, Selene, Helios. The five planets are first referred to by Philolaus, a Pythagorean, and later by Plato in his *Timaeus*, but not by their individual names (ἥλιος καὶ σελήνη καὶ πέντε ἄλλα ἄστρα ἐπίκλην ἔχοντα πλανήται). These names, which are not found till we come

down to the *Epinomis*, the work of a disciple of Plato, are enumerated as follows, each with an appellation derived from a god: τὸν τοῦ Κρόνου, τὸν τοῦ Διός, τὸν τοῦ Ἄρεος, τὴν τῆς Ἀφροδίτης, τὸν τοῦ Ἑρμοῦ. According to Archimedes (Macrob. *in Somn. Scip.* i. 19. 2) the order of the planets was as follows: Saturn, Jupiter, Mars, the Sun, Venus, Mercury, the Moon, and this order was generally adopted by Cicero (*de Div.* ii. 43), Manilius (i. 803, 6), Pliny, *H. N.* ii. 6. The five planets were known to Israel in O. T. times: Kronos as כּיּוּן Amos v. 26; Aphrodite as הילל Is. xiv. 12; Ares as נרגל 2 Kings xvii. 30; Zeus as גד Is. lxv. 11; Hermes as נבו Is. xlvi. 1.   5. The Sun . . . according to each sign of the Zodiac. See ch. xiii–xiv. and Eth. En. lxxii. The moon, &c. See lvi. and Eth. En. lxxiii–lxxiv.   7. Cf. Gen. i. 20–26. Observe that most of the creations of the sixth day, Gen.

winged fowls of all kinds[1], and all things that creep upon
the earth, and four-footed things that go about the earth, and
the things that fly in the air, *male and female, and every
living thing breathing with life.   8. And it was evening
and morning the sixth day[1]. *On the sixth day [1] *I ordered
My Wisdom to make man[2] of seven substances. (1) His
flesh from the earth; (2) his blood *from the dew; (3) his
eyes from the sun[3]; (4) his bones from the stones; (5) his
thoughts from the swiftness of the angels, and the clouds;
(6) his veins[4] and hair from the grass of the earth[5]; (7) his

---

[1] B om.   [2] And when I had finished all I ordered My Wisdom
to make man, B.   B OMITS THE REST OF THE CHAPTER.   [3] From
the dew and the sun (3) his eyes form the abysses of the seas,
Sok.   [4] For veins we should probably read nails. See quotation from
Philo in the Commentary on this verse.   [5] A Sok. add and from the wind
—a manifest dittography.

---

i. 24-26, are here assigned to the
fifth.   8. Ordered my Wisdom. Wisdom is here hypostatized
as in Prov. viii. 30 'Then I was
by him as a master workman.' In
the Book of Wisdom, Wisdom is the
assessor on God's throne, ix. 4; was
with Him when He made the world,
ix. 9; was the instrument by which
all things were created, viii. 5; is the
ruler and renewer of all things, viii.
1; vii. 27. Compare further this
conception of Wisdom with that of the
Logos of Philo, which was the instrument by which God created the world.
Cf. *Leg. All.* iii. 31 σκιὰ θεοῦ δὲ ὁ
λόγος αὐτοῦ ἐστιν, ᾧ καθάπερ ὀργάνῳ
προσχρησάμενος ἐκοσμοποίει : *De
Cherubim* 35 εὑρήσεις γὰρ αἴτιον μὲν
αὐτοῦ τὸν θεόν, ὑφ' οὗ γέγονεν, ὕλην
δὲ τέσσαρα στοιχεῖα, ἐξ ὧν συνεκράθη,
ὄργανον δὲ λόγον θεοῦ, δι' οὗ κατε-
σκευάσθη.   Of seven substances.
The list of these substances is corrupt.
See Critical Notes.   It seems to have
some connexion with the speculations

of the Stoics (G. Sext. *Math.* ix. 81) and
of Philo. Thus, as in our text, man's
body is derived (1) from the earth,
De Mundi Op. 51. Again, whilst in
(4) his bones are derived from stones,
in Philo, *Leg. All.* ii. 7, he is said at
the lowest stage to have a nature in
common with the stones and trees (ἡ
μὲν ἕξις κοινὴ καὶ τῶν ἀψύχων ἐστὶ
λίθων καὶ ξύλων, ἧς μετέχει καὶ τὰ ἐν
ἡμῖν ἐοικότα λίθοις ὀστέα) : again
whilst in our text (6) his veins (?)
and hair are from the grass of the
earth, in Philo, *Leg. All.* ii. 7, he is
said in the next higher stage to be
allied to plant-nature, such as the
nails and hair (ἡ δὲ φύσις διατείνει καὶ
ἐπὶ τὰ φυτά· καὶ ἐν ἡμῖν δέ εἰσιν ἐοικότα
φυτοῖς, ὄνυχές τε καὶ τρίχες) : finally,
(7) agrees with Philo's doctrine:
cf. *De Mundi Op.* 46. If we could
restore the text as it stood originally
the resemblance would probably be
closer. Philo's view of man's nature
is well summed up in *De Mundi Op.*
51 πᾶς ἄνθρωπος κατὰ μὲν τὴν διάνοιαν

spirit from My spirit and from the wind.   9. And I gave him seven natures: hearing to his body, sight to his eyes, smell to the perception, touch to the veins, taste to the blood, the bones for endurance, sweetness for thought.   10. *I purposed a subtle thing[1]: from the invisible and visible nature I made man. From both are his death and life, *and his form[2]; *and the word was like a deed[3] *both small in a great thing[4], and great in a small thing.   11. And I placed him upon the earth; like a second angel, in an honourable, great, and glorious way.   12. And I made him a ruler *to rule upon the earth, and to have My wisdom[5].

---

[1] Lo! I purposed to say a subtle word, Sok.   [2] Sok. om.   [3] A word is a message as it were something created, Sok.   [4] Both in great things and in little things, A.   [5] Upon the earth having rule by My wisdom, Sok.

ᾠκείωται θείῳ λόγῳ, τῆς μακαρίας φύσεως . . . ἀπαύγασμα γεγονώς, κατὰ δὲ τὴν τοῦ σώματος κατασκευὴν ἅπαντι τῷ κόσμῳ· συγκέκριται γὰρ ἐκ τῶν αὐτῶν, γῆς καὶ ὕδατος καὶ ἀέρος καὶ πυρός, ἑκάστου τῶν στοιχείων εἰσενεγκόντος τὸ ἐπιβάλλον μέρος πρὸς ἐκπλήρωσιν αὐταρκεστάτης ὕλης, ἣν ἔδει λαβεῖν τὸν δημιουργόν, ἵνα τεχνιτεύσηται τὴν ὁρατὴν ταύτην εἰκόνα. For the later Talmudic views cf. Weber, 202-204; Malan's *Book of Adam and Eve,* pp. 209-15. In the Anglo-Saxon Ritual (circ. 950), to which Dr. Murray has called my attention, man is said to be made out of eight substances: 'Octo pondera de quibus factus est Adam. Pondus limi, inde factus est caro; pondus ignis, inde rubeus est sanguis et calidus; pondus salis, inde sunt salsae lacrimae; pondus roris, inde factus est sudor; pondus floris, inde est varietas oculorum; pondus nubis, inde est instabilitas mentium; pondus venti, inde est anhela frigida; pondus gratiae, inde est sensus hominis.'   9. Seven natures. Here again the text is very untrustworthy and the follow-

ing words seem corrupt: body, veins, blood, whilst the clauses the bones . . . thought are quite irrelevant. Here we should possibly follow Philo, *De Mundi Op.* 40 τῆς ἡμετέρας ψυχῆς τὸ δίχα τοῦ ἡγεμονικοῦ μέρος ἐπταχῆ σχίζεται, πρὸς πέντε αἰσθήσεις καὶ τὸ φωνητήριον ὄργανον καὶ ἐπὶ πᾶσι τὸ γόνιμον, and thus for the corrupt clauses read the vocal organ and the generative power. Cp. Test. Napht. 2. Philo's division of man's nature is derived from the Stoics: cf. Plut. *Plac.* iv. 4 οἱ Στωικοὶ ἐξ ὀκτὼ μερῶν φασὶ συνιστάναι (τὴν ψυχήν), πέντε μὲν τῶν αἰσθητικῶν, ὁρατικοῦ, ἀκουστικοῦ, ὀσφρητικοῦ, γευστικοῦ, ἀπτικοῦ, ἕκτου δὲ φωνητικοῦ, ἑβδόμου σπερματικοῦ, ὀγδόου αὐτοῦ τοῦ ἡγεμονικοῦ. Cf. also Plut. *Plac.* iv. 21. 10. Man's spiritual and material nature.   11. Like a second angel. According to the *Beresh. Rab.* fol. 17, Adam, when first created, reached from the earth to the firmament. In the *Book of Adam and Eve,* i. 10, Adam is called a 'bright angel.'   12. Gen. i. 26, 28.   13. This verse may

And there was no one like him upon the earth of all My creations.   13. And I gave him a name from the four substances: the East, the West, *the North, and the South[1].   14. And I appointed for him four special stars, and I gave him the name Adam.   15. *And I gave him his will[2], and I showed him the two ways, the light and the

---

[1] A transposes.   [2] A om.

---

either be the source of or may be derived from the Sibylline Oracles, iii. 24–26

Αὐτὸς δὴ θεός ἐσθ' ὁ πλάσας τετρα-
γράμματον 'Αδάμ,

Τὸν πρῶτον πλασθέντα, καὶ οὔνομα
πληρώσαντα

'Αντολίην τε δύσιν τε μεσημβρίην τε
καὶ ἄρκτον.

The third line is used frequently, though with a different application, in the Oracles, i. e. ii. 195; viii. 321; xi. 3. It will be observed that this arrangement gives the initials A d m a in the wrong order. This etymology is next found in the anonymous writing *De Montibus Sina et Sion,* 4, formerly ascribed to Cyprian: 'Nomen accepit a Deo. Hebreicum Adam in Latino interpretat "terra caro facta," eo quod ex quattuor cardinibus orbis terrarum pugno conprehendit, sicut scriptum est: "palmo mensus sum caelum et pugno conprehendi terram et confinxi hominem ex omni limo terrae; ad imaginem Dei feci illum." Oportuit illum ex his quattuor cardinibus orbis terrae nomen in se portare Adam; invenimus in Scripturis, per singulos cardines orbis terrae esse a conditore mundi quattuor stellas constitutas in singulis cardinibus. Prima stella orientalis dicitur anatole, secunda occidentalis dysia, tertia stella aquilonis arctus, quarta stella meridiana dicitur mesembrion. Ex nomi-nibus stellarum numero quattuor de singulis stellarum nominibus tollo singulas litteras principales, de stella

anatole *a,* de stella dysis *δ,* de stella arctos *a,* de stella mesembrion *μ;* in his quattuor litteris cardinalibus habes nomen αδαμ.' This etymology is given with approval by Bede, *In Genesim Expositio* iv. 'Hae quattuor literae nominis Adam propria habent nomina in partium nominibus, id est anatole, disis, arctus, mesembria; id est oriens occidens, septentrio, meridies. Et haec proprietas significat dominatu-rum Adam in quattuor supradictis partibus mundi.' It is found also in the *Chronikon* of Glycas (circ. 1150), p. 143: κατὰ τοῦτο δὲ τῷ τοῦ 'Αδὰμ ὀνόματι προσηγόρευσεν αὐτὸν ... καὶ ὅρα τὰ τοῦ τοιούτου ὀνόματος γράμματα· τὰ τέσσαρα γὰρ ὑπεμφαίνουσι κλίματα· ἄλφα ἀνατολή, δέλτα δύσις, ἄλφα ἄρκτος, μῦ μεσημβρία.   See Jubilees iii. 28 (notes); Targ.-Jon. on Gen. ii. 7.

14. Four special stars. These stars are named from the four quar-ters of the earth, and Adam's name is formed from their initial letters. See citation from *De Montibus Sina et Sion,* which seems to be derived from our text. *Stars* may here mean 'angels.' According to the Jalk. Rub. fol. 13; Jalk. Shim. fol. 4 (see *Book of Adam and Eve,* p. 215) certain ministering angels were appointed to wait on Adam.   15. I gave him his will: cf. Tanchuma Pikkude 3 (quoted by Weber, p. 208), 'God does not determine beforehand whether a man shall be righteous or wicked, but puts this in the hands of the man

darkness. And I said unto him: 'This is good and this is evil'; that I should know whether he has love for Me or hate: that he should appear in his race as loving Me. 16. I knew his nature, he did not know his nature. Therefore his ignorance is *a woe to him that he should sin, and

---

only.' In the text free-will is conceded to man, but this is prejudicially affected by his ignorance (ver. 16): cf. Ecclus. xv. 14, 15 αὐτὸς ἐξ ἀρχῆς ἐποίησεν ἄνθρωπον καὶ ἀφῆκεν αὐτὸν ἐν χειρὶ διαβουλίου αὐτοῦ. ἐὰν θέλῃς συντηρήσεις ἐντολὰς καὶ πίστιν ποιῆσαι εὐδοκίας. On the question generally see Joseph. *B. J.* ii. 8. 14; *Antt.* xiii. 5. 9; xviii. 1. 3; *Psalms of Solomon*, ed. by Ryle and James, pp. 95, 96. **15. The two ways, the light and the darkness.** This popular figure of the Two Ways was suggested by Jer. xxi. 8 'Thus saith the Lord: Behold, I set before you the way of life and the way of death'; by Deut. xxx. 15 'I have set before thee this day life and good and death and evil'; Ecclus. xv. 17 ἔναντι ἀνθρώπων ἡ ζωὴ καὶ ὁ θάνατος, καὶ ὁ ἐὰν εὐδοκήσῃ δοθήσεται αὐτῷ: xvii. 6 καὶ ἀγαθὰ καὶ κακὰ ὑπέδειξεν αὐτοῖς. For parallel N. T. expressions cf. Mt. vii. 13, 14; 2 Pet. ii. 2. Of the two great post-apostolic descriptions of the Two Ways, in the *Didachè* and in the *Ep. of Barnabas*, that of the latter presents the nearest parallel to our text: chap. xviii. 1 ὁδοὶ δύο εἰσὶν διδαχῆς καὶ ἐξουσίας, ἥ τε τοῦ φωτὸς καὶ ἡ τοῦ σκότους. In the *Didachè* i. 1 we have ὁδοὶ δύο εἰσί, μία τῆς ζωῆς καὶ μία τοῦ θανάτου: cf. *Test.* Asher 1 δύο ὁδοὺς ἔδωκεν ὁ θεὸς τοῖς υἱοῖς ἀνθρώπων ... ὁδοὶ δύο, καλοῦ καὶ κακοῦ: Sibyll. Or. viii. 399, 400 αὐτὸς ὁδοὺς προέθηκα δύο, ζωῆς θανάτου τε Καὶ γνώμην προέθηκ' ἀγαθὴν ζωὴν προελέσθαι: cf. also Pastor Hermae

Mand. vi. 1, 2; Clem. Alex. *Strom.* v. 5; *Apost. Church Order*, iv; *Apost. Constitutions*, vii. 1; *Clem. Homilies* v. 7. **I said unto him:** 'This is good and this is evil,' &c. This does not harmonize with the account in Gen., where the knowledge of good and evil follows on eating the forbidden fruit. **That I should know whether he has love for Me or hate.** Deut. xiii. 3 'Your God proveth you to know whether ye love the Lord your God.' **16. Ignorance is a woe to him that he should sin.** This ignorance, as we see from the preceding verse, is not first and directly an ignorance of moral distinctions, but of his nature with its good and evil impulses (יצר הרע and יצר הטוב). Ignorance is thus regarded here as an evil in itself. This is probably the result of Platonic thought, which had gained great influence over Hellenistic Judaism, and the idea of the text seems related, however distantly, to that ethical system which may be summed up in the words πᾶς δ' ἄδικος οὐχ ἑκὼν ἄδικος (Plato, *Legg.* 731 c): οὐδένα ἀνθρώπων ἑκόντα ἐξαμαρτάνειν (*Prot.* 345 D): κακὸς μὲν γὰρ ἑκὼν οὐδείς (*Tim.* 86 D). See also *Legg.* 734 B; *Rep.* ix. 589 c; *Hipp. Maj.* 296 c. Herein it is taught that no man wilfully chooses evil in preference to good; but in every act of moral judgement the determining motive is to be found in the real or seeming preponderance of good in the course adopted: and that, should this course

I appointed death on account of his sin[1]. 17. And[2]
I caused him to sleep, and he slumbered. And I took from

[1] Worse than sinning, and for sin there is nothing else but death,
Sok. [2] Sok. adds I cast upon him a shadow and.

be the worse one, the error of judgement is due either to physical incapacities or faulty education, or to
a combination of both. This view of
sin as an involuntary affection of the
soul follows logically from another
Platonic principle already enunciated by our author (see xxiii. 5, note).
This principle is the pre-existence of
the soul. The soul, as such, according to Platonic teaching, is wholly
good. Evil, therefore, cannot arise
from its voluntary preferences, but
from its limitations, i. e. from its
physical and moral environment,
from its relation to the body and
from wrong education. In the Book
of Wisdom this view is widely diverged from. There the body is not
held to be irredeemably evil, but souls
are already good and bad on their
entrance into this life (viii. 19, 20).
In Philo, on the other hand, there is
in the main a return to the Platonic
and Stoic doctrine. The body is
irredeemably evil; it is in fact the
tomb of the soul ($\sigma\hat{\omega}\mu\alpha = \sigma\hat{\eta}\mu\alpha$); and
only the sensuously-inclined souls are
incorporated with bodies (see above,
xxiii. 5, note). The views adopted
by our author on these and kindred
points stand in some degree in a closer
relation to the Platonic principles
than do those of Philo or the author
of the Book of Wisdom. Thus he
held: (1) That the soul was created
originally good. (2) That it was not
predetermined either to good or ill
by God, but left to mould its own
destiny (see **xxx.** 15). (3) That its
incorporation in a body, however,
with its necessary limitations served

to bias its preferences in the direction
of evil. (4) That faithful souls will
hereafter live as blessed incorporeal
spirits, or at all events clothed only
in God's glory (xxii. 7); for there is
no resurrection of the body. Death
on account of his sin. So Ecclus.
xxv. 24 ἀπὸ γυναικὸς ἀρχὴ ἁμαρτίας,
καὶ δι' αὐτὴν ἀποθνήσκομεν πάντες;
for 'man was created exactly
like the angels,' Eth. En. lxix. 11,
righteous and immortal, but death
came through sin, Book of Wisdom,
ii. 23, 24; Eth. En. xcviii. 4. The
same teaching is found in the Talmud:
see Weber, 208, 214, 239. This doctrine of man's conditional immortality and of death entering the world
through sin does not belong to O.T.
literature; for Gen. ii. 17, when
studied in its context, implies nothing
more than a premature death; for
the law of man's being is enunciated
in Gen. iii. 19 'Dust thou art, and
unto dust shalt thou return,' and his
expulsion from Eden was due first
and principally to the need of guarding against his eating of the tree of
life and living for ever. Furthermore, even in Ecclus., where the idea
of death as brought about by sin is
first enunciated, the doctrine appears
in complete isolation and in open
contradiction to the main statements
and tendencies of the book; for it
elsewhere teaches that man's mortality is the law from everlasting (ἡ
γὰρ διαθήκη ἀπ' αἰῶνος Ecclus. xiv. 17):
and that being formed from earth
unto earth must he return, xvii. 1, 2;
xl. 11. Nor again is this doctrine
a controlling principle in the system

him a rib[1], and I made him a wife. ·   18. And by his
wife death came, and I received his last word.   And I called
her by a name, the mother; that is Eve.

[*God gives Paradise to Adam, and gives him Knowledge, so
as to see the Heavens open, and that he should see the
Angels singing a Song of Triumph.*]

XXXI. 1. Adam had a life on earth[2], . . . and I made
a garden in Eden in the East, and (I ordained) that he should
observe the law and keep * the instruction[3].   2. I made
for him the heavens open that he should perceive the angels
singing the song of triumph.   And there was light * without
any[4] darkness continually in Paradise.   3. And the devil
took thought, as if wishing to make another world, because
things were subservient to Adam on earth, to rule it and
have lordship over it.   4. The devil is to be the evil spirit
of the lowest places[5]; * he became Satan, after he left the
heavens.   His name was formerly Satanail[6].   5. And
then, * though he became different from the angels in nature,
he did not change his understanding of just and sinful

---

[1] Sok. adds as he slept.
XXXI. [2] There is evidently a lacuna here.   [3] It, Sok.   B OMITS
ENTIRE CHAPTER.   [4] That never knew, Sok.   [5] A adds as he wrought
devilish things.   [6] As flying from the heavens he became Satan,
since his name was Satanail, Sok.

---

of the writers of the Book of Wisdom.
When, however, we come down to
N. T. times we find it the current
view in the Pauline Epistles : cf.
Rom. v. 12 ; 1 Cor. xv. 21 ; 2 Cor.
xi. 3.   On various views on sin and
death and their causes see Eth. En.
vi–viii ; x. 8 ; xxxii. 6 ; lxix. 6, 11 ;
xcviii. 4, with notes.   18. By his
wife death came : cf. Ecclus. xxv.
23 ; 1 Tim. ii. 14.   See preceding note.
I received his last word.   Corrupt.
XXXI. 2. This verse is almost
quoted in the *Book of Adam and*

Eve I. viii. 'When we dwelt in the
garden . . . we saw the angels that
sang praises in heaven.'   According
to S. Ephrem, i. 139, Adam and Eve
lost the angelic vision on their fall
(Malan). Philo, *Quaest.* xxxii. *in
Gen.*, believes 'oculis illos praeditos
esse quibus potuerunt etiam eas quae
in coelo sunt.' For the continual light
in Paradise see *Book of Adam and Eve*,
I. xii ; xiii; xiv.   3. On the envy
of Satan see Wisdom, ii. 24 ; Joseph.
Antt. i. 1. 4 ; Weber, 211, 244.   4.
See notes on xviii. 3 and xxix. 4.

thoughts[1]. He understood the judgement upon him, and the former sin which he had sinned. 6. And on account of this, he conceived designs against Adam; in such a manner he entered[2] and deceived Eve. But he did not touch Adam. 7. * But I cursed him for (his) ignorance[3]: but those I previously blessed, them I did not curse[4], 8. nor man did I curse, nor the earth, nor any other things created, but the evil fruit of man, and then his works.

[*On account of the Sin of Adam, God sends him to the Earth, 'From which I took thee,' but He does not wish to destroy him in the Life to come.*]

XXXII. 1. I said to him: 'Earth thou art, and to earth also from whence I took thee shalt thou return. I will not destroy thee, but will send thee whence I took thee. Then I can also take thee in My second coming'; and I have blessed all My creation, visible and invisible[5]. 2. And I blessed the seventh day, * which is the Sabbath[6], for in it I rested from all My labours.

[*God shows Enoch the Duration of this World, 7000 Years, and the eighth Thousand is the End. (There will be) no Years, no Months, no Weeks, no Days.*]

XXXIII. 1. Then also I established the eighth day. Let

---

[1] Though he was changed from the angels, he did not change his nature, but he had thought, as is the mind of just men and sinners, Sok. [2] Sok. adds into Paradise. [3] Sok. om. [4] Sok. adds and those whom before I had not blessed, them also I did not curse.

XXXII. [5] A adds (against B Sok.) And Adam was five and a half hours in Paradise. B OMITS ENTIRE CHAPTER. [6] Sok. om.

---

6. See xxx. 18, note; Weber, 211, 244.

7. Cursed him for (his) ignorance. This ought to refer to the Serpent or to Satan.

XXXII. 1. My second coming. God's coming to judge the earth, to bless His people, and to punish their enemies. This is called καιρὸς ἐπισκοπῆς

and ἡμέρα διαγνώσεως in the Book of Wisdom, iii. 7, 18. It is referred to again in xlii. 5 of our text. God's first coming to the earth was for the sake of Adam and to bless all that He had made, lviii. 1.

XXXIII. 1, 2. From the fact that Adam did not live to be 1000 years

the eighth be the first * after My work [1], and let * the days [2] be after the fashion of seven thousand.   2. * Let there be at the beginning of the eighth thousand a time when there is no computation, and no end; neither years, nor months, nor weeks, nor days, nor hours [3].   3. And now Enoch, what

---

XXXIII. [1] Of my rest, Sok. . B OMITS VERSES I, 2.   [2] A om.   [3] And let the eighth day be for a beginning in the likeness of eight thousand. So concerning the first day of My rest, and also the eighth day of My rest, let them return continually, Sok.   Margin of Sok.'s MS. reads: the beginning of unrighteousness, the time without end, neither years, nor months, nor weeks, nor days, nor hours.

---

old, the author of the Book of Jubilees, iv. 30, concludes that the words of Gen. ii. 17 'In the day thou eatest thereof thou shalt surely die' were actually fulfilled. It is hence obvious that already before the Christian era 1000 years had come to be regarded as one world-day. To arrive at the conception of a world-week of 7000 years—6000 years from the creation to the judgement, followed by 1000 years, or a millennium of blessedness, and rest—it was necessary to proceed but one step further, and this step we find was taken by the author of our text. In Irenaeus, moreover, *Contra Haer.* v. 28. 3 this reasoning is given explicitly: ὅσαις . . . ἡμέραις ἐγένετο ὁ κόσμος, τοσαύταις χιλιοντάσι συντελεῖται.   Καὶ διὰ τοῦτό φησιν ἡ γραφή. Καὶ συνετέλεσεν ὁ θεὸς τῇ ἡμέρᾳ Ϛʹ τὰ ἔργα αὐτοῦ ἃ ἐποίησε, καὶ κατέπαυσεν ἐν τῇ ἡμέρᾳ τῇ ζʹ ἀπὸ πάντων τῶν ἔργων αὐτοῦ. τοῦτο δʹ ἐστὶ τῶν προγεγονότων διήγησις καὶ τῶν ἐσομένων προφητεία· ἡ γὰρ ἡμέρα κυρίου ὡς ,α ἔτη. ἐν ἓξ οὖν ἡμέραις συντετέλεσται τὰ γεγονότα. φανερὸν οὖν ὅτι ἡ συντέλεια αὐτῶν τὸ ,Ϛ ἔτος ἐστί. Clemens Alex. *Strom.* iv. 25 refers to this conception— possibly to our text. It is not improbable that the statements of Cedrenus on this head are drawn from our text. Thus on p. 9 he writes: τοῦτον χάριν

ηὐλογήθη καὶ αὕτη (ἡ ἡμέρα) ὑπὸ τοῦ θεοῦ καὶ ἡγιάσθη καὶ σάββατον ὡς καταπαύσιμος προσηγορεύθη, καὶ ὡς τύπος τῆς ἑβδόμης χιλιοετηρίδος καὶ τῶν ἁμαρτωλῶν συντελείας, ὡς Ἰωσηππος μαρτυρεῖ καὶ ἡ λεπτὴ Γένεσις ἥν καὶ Μωσέως εἶναί φασί τινες ἀποκάλυψιν. It is, we repeat, not improbable that our text is the original source of Cedrenus' statements, inasmuch as nothing of the kind is found either in Josephus or the Book of Jubilees, from which he professes to derive them. Syncellus, on whom Cedrenus is largely dependent, is frequently wrong in his references in the case of Apocalyptic literature. A most interesting expansion and an adaptation of the text to Christian conceptions are to be found in Augustin, *De Civ.* xxii. 30. 5 'Ipse etiam numerus aetatum, veluti dierum, si secundum eos articulos temporis computetur qui in Scripturis videntur expressi, iste Sabbatismus evidentius apparebit, quoniam septimus invenitur: ut prima aetas tanquam dies primus sit ab Adam usque ad diluvium, secunda inde usque ad Abraham . . . ab Abraham usque ad David una, altera inde usque ad transmigrationem in Babyloniam, tertia inde usque ad Christi carnalem nativitatem. Fiunt itaque omnes quinque. Sexta

things I have told thee, * and what thou hast understood, and what heavenly things thou hast seen [1], and what thou hast seen upon the earth, and what * thou hast.[2] written in books, by My wisdom all these things I devised * so as to create them [3], and I made them from the highest foundation to the lowest, * and to the end [1]. 4. And there is no counsellor [4] * nor inheritor of My works [1]. I am the eternal One, and the One not made with hands : * My thought is without change, My wisdom is My counsellor [5] and My word is reality ; and My eyes see all things, * if I look to all things [3] they * stand fast [6]. If I turn away My face, all are in need of Me. 5. And now pay attention, Enoch, and know thou who is speaking to thee, and do thou take the books which thou thyself hast written. 6. And I give thee * Samuil and Raguil [7] who brought thee * to Me [3]. And go * with them [8] upon the earth, and tell thy sons what things I have said to

---

[1] B om.   [2] I have, A.   [3] A om.   [4] Lamp, B.   [5] My thought is a lamp, B.   [6] Stand and tremble with fear, A Sok.   [7] Semil and Rasuil, B ; B adds and him.   [8] B Sok. om.

---

nunc agitur . . . post hanc tanquam in die septimo requiescet Deus, cum eundem septimum diem, quod nos erimus, in se ipso Deo faciet requiescere. . . . Haec tamen septima erit Sabbatum nostrum, cuius finis non erit vespera, sed dominicus dies velut octavus aeternus. . . . Ecce quod erit in fine sine fine.' For other speculations in reference to the world-week see *Evang. Nicodemi*, ii. 12 ; *Book of Adam and Eve*, I. lii. A time when there is no computation . . . neither years nor months, &c. Sibyll. Or. viii. 424-427 may have been influenced by our text where it speaks of the eternity of blessedness :

Ουκ ετι λοιπον εσει λυπεουμενος.' αθμιον εσται,"

Ουκ " εχθις γεγονεν." ουκ ηματα πολλα μερμηρις,

Ουκ εαρ, ου χειμων, ουτ' αρ θερος, ου μετοπωρον,

Ου δυσις αντολιη· ποιησω γαρ μακρον ημαρ.

3. I made them from the highest foundation to the lowest : cf. Ecclus. xviii. 1 ο ζων εις τον αιωνα εκτισε τα παντα κοινη, where κοινη is a rendering of יַחַד. 4. My thought is without change. Num. xxiii. 19 ; 1 Sam. xv. 29 ; Ezek. xxiv. 14. My wisdom is My counsellor. See xxx. 8 (note). Cf. Ecclus. xlii. 22 και ου προσεδεηθη ουδενος συμβουλου. My word is reality. So Eth. En. xiv. 22 (Gk.) πας λογος αυτου εργον. Cf. Ps. xxxiii. 9 ; Ecclus. xlii. 15 εν λογοις κυριου τα εργα αυτου. My eyes see all things : cf. Ecclus. xxxix. 19. If I turn away My face, &c. Ps. civ. 29 'Thou hidest Thy face, they are

thee, and what thou hast seen from the lowest heaven up to
My throne.   7. For I have created all the hosts, and all the
powers, and there is none that opposes Me, or is disobedient
to Me.   For all are obedient to My sole power, and labour for
My rule alone.   8. Give [1] them the works written out by
thee, *and they shall read them, and know Me to be the
Creator of all; and shall understand that there is no other
God beside Me [2].   9. *They shall distribute the books of
thy writing to their children's children [3], and from generation
to generation, and from nation to nation.   10. *And I will
give thee, Enoch, My messenger, the great captain Michael,
for thy writings and for the writings of thy fathers, Adam,
Seth, Enos, Kainan, Malaleel, and Jared, thy father [4].   11.
*And I shall not require them till the last age, for I have
instructed My two angels, Ariukh and Pariukh, whom I have
put upon the earth as their guardians.   12. And I have ordered
them in time to guard them that the account of what I shall
do in thy family may not be lost in the deluge to come [5].

---

[1] I will give, A.   [2] B om.   [3] Let the children give them to
the children, B.   [4] As being the messenger Enoch of my captain
Michael.   Because that thy writings and the writings of thy fathers,
Adam and Sit, B.   [5] (Because these) will not be required till
the last age, I have ordered my angels, Oriokh and Mariokh, to give
orders to guard in season the writings which I have placed upon
the earth, and that they should guard the writings of thy fathers, so
that what I have wrought in thy family may not be lost, B; A om.   In
the text I have followed Sok., but that for to punish them I have read to
guard them with B.

---

troubled.'   6. Cf. Eth. En. lxxxi.
5, 6. Samuil. This is either from
שָׁמַע אֵל = heard of God, 1 Sam. i.
20, or from שְׁמוֹ and אֵל = name of
God. Raguil is a transliteration of
רְעוּאֵל = friend of God.   9. Cf.
xlvii. 2, 3; xlviii. 7–9; liv; lxv. 5;
Eth. En. lxxxii. 1, 2, where, exactly
as here, the books are to be trans-
mitted straightway to the generations
of the world, whereas in i. 2; xciii.
10; civ. 12 the method and times
of the disclosure of the books are
different.   Though the writings are

committed to the keeping of men,
they are under the guardianship of
special angels until the time for their
complete disclosure and understanding has come.   See verses 11, 12.
10. Michael was the guardian angel
of Israel: Dan. x. 13, 21; xii. 1.
See Eth. En. ix. 1; x. 11; xx. 5
(note); xl. 4, &c.; Weber, 165.   11.
Till the last age.   At last the time
for the due comprehension of these
books will arrive: see ver. 9, note;
xxxv. 2, 3; (liv); Eth. En. xciii.
10; civ. 12. Ariukh. This proper

[*God accuses the Idolators ; the Workers of Iniquity, such as Sodom, and on this account He brings the Deluge upon them.*]

XXXIV. 1. * For I know the wickedness of men that they will not bear the yoke which I have put upon them, nor sow the seeds which I have given them, but will cast off My yoke and accept another, and sow vain seeds and bow to vain gods, and deny Me the only God[1].   2. And they will fill all the world with * wickedness and iniquity, and foul impurities with one another, sodomy and all other impure practices, which it is foul to speak about[2].   3. And on this account I will bring a deluge upon the earth * and I will destroy all[3], and[4] the earth shall be destroyed in great corruption.

[*God leaves one Just Man from the Family of Enoch, with all his House, which pleased God according to His Will.*]

XXXV. 1. And I will leave a righteous man *of thy race[5], with all his house who shall act according to My will.   From

---

XXXIV. [1] Sok. supports text but that it omits nor sow ... given them. A reads: They turned from My law and My yoke and raised up worthless races such as feared not God nor worshipped Me, but began to bow before vain gods, and denied Me, the only God.   [2] Unjust deeds and harlotries and services of idols, B; Sok. adds and evil service.   [3] B Sok. omit.   [4] A adds all.
XXXV. [5] A B om.

---

name is found in Gen. xiv. 1, 9; Dan. ii. 14. The derivation is doubtful, being êri-aku = servant of the moon-god (Delitzsch), or a compound from אַרְיֵה : hence a lionlike man (Gesenius).

XXXIV. 1. Cast off My yoke: cf. for phrase xlviii. 9; Ecclus. xxviii. 19, 20; Matt. xi. 29. **Sow vain seeds.** This is obscure. The words seem to be metaphorical and not to refer to Deut. xxii. 9. **Deny, &c.**: cf. Josh. xxiv. 27.   **2.** It is this verse that is referred to. in Test. Napht. 4, though it is there somewhat

differently applied : ἀνέγνων ἐν γραφῇ ἁγίᾳ Ἐνώχ, ὅτι καίγε καὶ ὑμεῖς ἀποστήσεσθε ἀπὸ κυρίου, πορευόμενοι κατὰ πᾶσαν πονηρίαν ἐθνῶν, καὶ ποιήσετε κατὰ πᾶσαν ἀνομίαν Σοδόμων.   **3.** The words immediately subsequent to those just quoted from Test. Napht. seem to be in part derived from this verse: καὶ ἐπάξει ὑμῖν κύριος αἰχμαλωσίαν . . . ἕως ἂν ἀναλώσῃ κύριος πάντας ὑμᾶς is simply an adaptation of **I will bring a deluge upon the earth, and I will destroy all.**

XXXV. 1. Righteous man, i. e.

their seed * after some time ¹ will be raised up a numerous ²
generation, but * of these, many will be ¹ very insatiable.
2. Then on the extinction of that family, I will show them the
books of thy writings, and of thy fathers, and the guardians of
them on earth will show them to the men who are true, * and
please Me, who do not take My name in vain ¹.   3. And
they shall tell to another ³ generation, and these * having
read them ¹, shall be glorified at last more than before.

[*God ordered Enoch to live on the Earth thirty Days, so as to
    teach his Sons, and his Sons' Sons. After thirty Days he
    was thus taken up into Heaven.*]

XXXVI. 1. And now, Enoch, I give thee a period ⁴ of
thirty days to work in thy house.   And tell thou thy sons ⁵,
* and all thy household before Me ; that they may listen to
what is spoken to them by thee ⁹; that they read and understand, how there is no other God beside Me ; * and let them
always keep My commandments, and begin to read and
understand the books written out by thee ⁶.   2. And after
thirty days, I will send My angels ⁷ for thee, and they ⁸ shall
take thee from the earth, and from thy sons, * according to
My will ⁹.

[*Here God summons an Angel.*]

[XXXVII. 1. And God called one of His greatest angels,

---

¹ B om.   ² Another, Sok.   ⁹ That, B.
    XXXVI. ⁴ Sok. adds of preparation.   ⁵ B adds all that thou
guardest in thy heart.   ⁶ B om.   ⁷ Angel, A Sok.   ⁸ He,
A Sok.   ⁹ To Me, A Sok.

Noah.   2. On the extinction of
that family. This seems to refer to
the destruction of the wicked during
the period of the sword. About the
same time the books of Enoch were to
be given to the righteous. See for
the same connexion of ideas Eth. En.
xciii. 9, 10; xci. 12. The guardians.
See xxxiii. 9, 11 (notes).   3. The

period of the sword and the disclosure
of Enoch's books introduces the Messianic age.

    XXXVI. 1. In Eth. En. lxxxi.
6 the period is one year. Read
and understand, &c. : cf. Eth. En.
lxxxii. 1–3.   2. Cf. Eth. En. lxxxi.
6.

    XXXVII. This chapter, which

* terrible and awful [1], and placed him by me, *and the appearance of that angel was like [2] snow, and his hands were like ice ; * he had a very cold appearance [3], and my face was chilled because I could not endure * the fear of the Lord [4]; *just as it is not possible to [5] endure the mighty fire and heat of the sun, and the frost of the air.   2. And the Lord said to me, ' Enoch, if thy face is not chill here, no man can look upon thy face [6].']

[Mathusal had Hope, and awaited his Father Enoch by his Bed, Day and Night.]

XXXVIII. 1 [7]. And the Lord said to those men who first took me : ' Take Enoch with you to the earth, and wait for him till the appointed day.'   2. And at night they placed me upon my bed, and Mathusal, expecting my coming by day and by night, was a guard at my bed.   3. And he was terrified when he heard my coming, and I gave him directions that all my household should come, that I might tell them everything.

[The mournful Admonition of Enoch to his Sons, with Weeping and great Sorrow, speaking to them [8].]

XXXIX. 1. * Listen, my children, what things are according to the will of the Lord. I am sent to-day to you to tell you from the lips of the Lord, what was and what is happening now, and what will be before the day of

---

XXXVII. [1] In a voice like thunder, B.   [2] In appearance he was white as, A.   [3] In appearance having great cold, Sok.; B om.   [4] The great terror and awe, B.   [5] For I could not, A ; B omits just as . . . frost of the air.   [6] B om.
XXXVIII. [7] B OMITS ENTIRE CHAPTER.
XXXIX. [8] The Instructions given by Enoch to his Sons, B.

---

is found in all the MSS., is read in its present position in A Sok., but after xxxix in B. I have bracketed it as

it seems irrelevant to the entire text.
   XXXVIII. 1. Cf. xxxvi.   2. Cf. i. 2–4.   3. Cf. Eth. En. xci. 1.

judgement.　2. Hear, my children, for I do not speak to you to-day from my lips, but from the lips of the Lord who has sent me to you. For you hear[1] *the words of my lips, a mortal man like yourselves[2].　3. *I have seen the face of the Lord as it were iron that is heated in the fire, and when brought out sends forth sparks and burns.　4. Look at the eyes of me[3], *a man laden with a sign for you[4]. *I have seen the eyes of the Lord shining like a ray of the sun and striking with terror human eyes.　5. You, my children, see the right hand of a man[3] *made like yourselves[5] *assisting you. I have seen the right hand of the Lord assisting me, and filling the heavens.　6. You see the *compass of my actions, like to your own[6]. I have seen the measureless and harmonious[7] form of the Lord. To Him there is no end.　7. You therefore hear the words of my lips, but I have heard the words of the Lord, like great thunder, with continual agitation of the clouds.　8. And now, *my children[3], listen to the[8] discourses *of your earthly father[3]. It is terrible and awful to stand before the face of an earthly prince—*terrible and very awful[3] because the will of the prince is death and the will of the prince is life[9]; how much more is it terrible and awful to stand before the face of the *Lord of lords, and of the earthly[10] and the heavenly hosts. Who can endure this never-ending terror?

_____

[1] 1. Hear, my children, my beloved ones, the admonition of your father: how according to the will of God, I am sent to you now. What exists and what was, and what is happening now, and what will be before the day of judgement, I do not now tell you from my own lips, but from the lips of the Lord; for the Lord sent me to you. 2. And do you therefore hear, A. I was sent of late to tell you from the lips of the Lord what things are, and what shall be before the day of judgement. And now, my children, I do not speak to you from my own lips, but from the lips of the Lord, B.　[2] B om.; Sok. adds I have heard from the fiery lips of the Lord: for the lips of the Lord are like a fiery furnace, and his angels [winds] are a flame of fire going forth. You, my children, as that of a man made like yourselves, but.　[3] B om.
[4] A man in his marks just like you, Sok.; B om.　[5] A B om.　[6] So A Sok., but that for actions Sok. reads body; B om.　[7] Incomparable, B. B transposes 6[b] after 7.　[8] My, B.　[9] A om.; B adds or great terrors, and omits the rest of the verse.　[10] Heavenly Ruler, the Lord of the living and the dead, A.

[*Enoch instructs faithfully his Children about all Things from the Mouth of the Lord ; how he saw, and heard and wrote them down.*]

XL. 1. And now, my children, I know all things [1] from the lips of the Lord; for [2] my eyes have seen from the beginning to the end [3].   2. I know all things and have written all things in the books, both the heavens and the end of them, and their fulness, and all the hosts, and I have measured their goings, and written down the stars and their innumerable quantity. 3. What man has seen their alternations and their goings? Not even the angels know their number; I have written down the names of all.   4. And I have measured the circle of the sun, and I have measured his rays ; *and his coming in and going out, through all the months, and all his courses, and their names I have written down.   5. I have measured the circle of the moon, and its waning which occurs during every day, and the secret places in which it hides every day and ascends according to all the hours.   6. I have laid down the four seasons, and from the seasons I made four circles, and in the circles I placed the years; I placed the months, and from the

---

XL. [1] A Sok. add **One thing I have learned.** Throughout this chapter B is transposed in every way imaginable. B OMITS VERSES 2-7.   [2] And another, A Sok.   [3] Sok. adds **and from the end to the return.**

XL. 1. I know all things ... my eyes have seen, &c. This seems to be the passage to which Clem. Alex. *Eclog. Proph.* (Dind. iii. 456) refers : ὁ Δανιὴλ λέγει ὁμοδοξῶν τῷ Ἐνὼχ τῷ εἰρηκότι 'καὶ εἶδον τὰς ὕλας πάσας': and Origen (*de Princ.* iv. 35) 'scriptum namque est in eodem libello dicente Enoch universas materias perspexi.' Cf. Sibyll. Or. viii. 375, where, in a passage recalling several phrases of this chapter, ἀρχὴν καὶ τέλος οἶδα, ὃς οὐρανὸν ἔκτισα καὶ γῆν.   **2. Stars and their innumerable quantity.**

Cf. Eth. En. xliii. 1, 2; xciii. 14.   **3. Not even the Angels, &c.** Cf. xxiv. 3. **4. See xiii, xiv** (notes).   **5. See xvi** (notes).   **Its waning which, &c.** There is not a single reference to this phenomenon in the Slav. Enoch, but there is a complete account of its waxing and waning in Eth. En. lxxiv. **Secret places in which it hides, &c.** Corrupt.   **6. I have laid down the four seasons.** In xiii. 5 we have a reference to the four seasons, but in Eth. En. lxxxii. 11-20 there is an account which, though

months I calculated the days, and from the days[1] I have
* calculated[2] the hours[3].   7. Moreover, I have written
down all things * moving[4] upon the earth[5].   * I have
written down all things that are nourished[6], all seed sown
and unsown, which grows on the earth, and all things
belonging to the garden, and every herb and every flower,
and their fragrance and their names.   8. And the dwellings
of the clouds, * and their conformations and their wings[7],
how they bring rain and * the rain-drops, I investigated all.
9. And I - wrote down the course of the[7] thunder * and
lightning[7], and they[8] showed me the keys, * and their
guardians[9] and their path[10] by which they go.   They are
brought forth in bonds, in measured degree, * and are let go
in bonds[1], lest by their * heavy course and vehemence[11] they
should overload the clouds of wrath and destroy everything
on earth.   10. I have written down the treasuries of the
snow, and the store-houses of the hail, and the cool breezes.
* And I observed the holder of the keys of them during the
season: and how he fills the clouds with them[12], and yet
does not exhaust their treasuries.   11. I * wrote down[13]
the abodes of the winds, * and I observed and saw[7] how those
who hold * their keys[14] bear balances and measures, and in
the first place they put them on a balance, in the second they[15]
let them go in measure * moderately, with care[7] over the
whole earth, so that with their heavy breathing they should

---

[1] A om.   [2] Measured and calculated, Sok.   [3] Sok. adds and written
them down.   [4] That were arranged, Sok.   [5] Sok. adds making
inquiries into them.   [6] Sok. om.   [7] B om.   [8] The angels, B.
[9] Which guarded them, B.   [10] Coming in and going out, Sok.
[11] Grievous vehemence, B. Heavy opening (?) and vehemence, Sok.
[12] I saw at that time how the clouds are restrained by them as a key
does prisoners, B. I watched their seasons: how those that hold the
keys of them fill the clouds with them, Sok.   [13] Saw, B.   [14] Keys
of their prisons, B.   [15] B adds measure and.

---

now defective, was clearly complete
originally. 8. Cf. Eth. En. lx. 19–
22 for an account of these phenomena.
9. Course of the thunder, &c.

This is to be found in Eth. En. lix;
lx. 13-15.   10. Cf. vi. 1, 2; Eth.
En. lx. 17, 18.   11. See Eth. En.
xli. 4.

not shake the whole [1] earth.   12. * For I have measured the whole earth, its mountains and all hills, fields, trees, stones, rivers; all things that exist I have written down, the height from earth to the seventh heaven, and down to the lowest hell [1], * the place of judgement and the mighty hell [2] laid open, and * full of lamentation. And I saw how [1] the prisoners suffer, awaiting the immeasurable judgement.   13. * And I wrote out all of those who are being judged by the judge, and all the judgement they receive, and all their deeds [1].

---

[1] B om.   [2] From thence I was taken to the place of judgement, and I saw hell, B. I append here chapter XL in full, as it appears in B. This chapter in B is manifestly fragmentary and disarranged, and serves to justify the originality of the fuller form as preserved in A Sok. 1. My children, I know all from the lips of the Lord. For mine eyes saw from the beginning to the end, 8. and the dwelling places of the clouds, 9. with those which bring storms and thunder. And the angels showed me the keys which guarded them. 10. I saw the treasure of snow and ice, 9. and the path by which they go: they are brought forth in bonds in measure, and let go in bonds, so that with grievous vehemence they should not oppress the clouds and destroy in the earth, 10. both the air and the cold. I saw at that time how the clouds are restrained by them as a key does prisoners, and they are not allowed to exhaust their treasuries. 11. I saw the abodes of the winds, how those who hold the keys of their prisons bear with them the balances and the measures: in the first place they lay on the balances; in the second they measure, and in measure do they let them go over the whole earth: so that by their powerful breath they should not shake the earth. 12. From thence I was taken to the place of judgement and I saw hell open and the prisoners and the eternal judgement.

---

12. Down to the lowest hell. We come here upon a conception irreconcilable with the general scheme of the author. Hell, according to this scheme, is really located in the third heaven. See x, where the place, its horrors, and the classes it is prepared for, are described at length. But the old Jewish beliefs of an underworld of punishment are too strong to be wholly excluded, and so consistency is here sacrificed to completeness. For an analogous comparison cf. xviii. 7. It is possible, further, that the author may have had some idea of a series of seven hells, as he speaks here of 'the lowest hell,' and as this idea is afterwards found in Rabbinic tradition; see Eisenmenger, ii. 302, 328–330. If, however, we observe how close this hell is to the Garden of Eden, in xlii. 3, we shall be inclined to identify it with the place of punishment described in x. The interpretation, however, of xlii. 3 is difficult. **Awaiting the immeasurable judgement.** These words, which are found also in vii. 1, in reference to the fallen watchers, would seem to imply an intermediate place of punishment, in fact, Sheol or Hades. **13. This was** an ancient belief of the Jews: cf. liii. 2; lxiv. 5; Jubilees iv. 23; x. 17.

[*How Enoch wept for the Sins of Adam.*]

XLI. 1. And I saw * all our forefathers from the beginning with Adam and Eve¹, and I sighed and wept, * and
spake of the ruin (caused by) their wickedness² : * Woe is me
for my infirmity and that of my forefathers¹.   2. And
* I meditated in my heart and said³ : 'Blessed is the man
who was not born, or, having been born, has never sinned
before the face of the Lord, so that he should not come into
this place, to bear the yoke of this place!'

[*How Enoch saw those who keep the Keys, and the Guardians
of the Gates of Hades standing by.*]

XLII. 1. I saw * those who keep the keys, and are the
guardians of the gates of hell, standing⁴, like great serpents,

─────────────

XLI. ¹ B om.   ² The destruction of the unholy, B.   ³ I said in my
heart, B.
XLII. ⁴ The guardians of hell holding the keys, standing opposite to the gates, B. B blends xli and xlii. 1-2 together in this order,
xlii. 1 ; xli; xlii. 2. It will be seen that it omits reference to Adam and Eve.

─────────────

From being the scribe of God's works,
as he is universally in the Eth. and
the Slav. Enoch, the transition was
easy to the conception of Enoch as
a scribe of the deeds of men. Cf. for
later tradition Test. Abraham (ed.
James), p. 115 καὶ εἶπεν 'Αβραὰμ
πρὸς Μιχαήλ· Κύριε, . . . τίς ἐστιν ὁ
ἄλλος ὁ ἐλέγχων τὰς ἁμαρτίας ; καὶ
λέγει Μιχαὴλ πρὸς Ἀβραάμ . . . ὁ ἀπο-
δεικνύμενος οὗτός ἐστιν ὁ διδάσκαλος
τοῦ οὐρανοῦ καὶ τῆς γῆς καὶ γραμματεὺς
τῆς δικαιοσύνης Ἐνώχ· ἀπέστειλεν γὰρ
κύριος αὐτοὺς ἐνταῦθα, ἵνα ἀπογρά-
φωσιν τὰς ἁμαρτίας καὶ τὰς δικαιοσύνας
ἑκάστου.
XLI. 1. It seems to be implied
here that the forefathers of Enoch,
including Adam and Eve, are in the
place of punishment, and that they
are to remain there till God comes to
judge the world (xlii. 5, note). That

Adam and the patriarchs were in
Hades was a prevalent early Christian
belief. Cf. *Descensus ad Inferos*,
viii–ix. 2. Cf. 4 Ezra iv. 12 ' Melius
erat nos non adesse quam advenientes
. . . pati.' Eth. En. xxxviii. 2; Apoc.
Bar. x. 6.

XLII. 1. Who keep the keys.
In Sibyll. Or. viii. 121-2 we have a
strange application of this idea :

αἰὼν κοινὸς ἅπασιν
κλειδοφύλαξ εἱρκτῆς μεγάλης ἐπὶ
βῆμα θεοῖο.

Keys. Cf. Rev. ix. 1 ; xx. 1. Guardians of the gates of hell. According to Emek hammelech, fol. 144,
col. 2, each division of hell is under
the control of a certain angel (Eisenmenger, ii. 332). The Greek word
here may have been τημελοῦχοι. In
the singular number it has become
a proper name in Apoc. Pauli. Like

and their faces were like quenched lamps, and their eyes
were fiery[1], and their teeth were sharp[2].   * And they were
stripped to the waist[3].   2. And I said * before their faces[4],
' Would that I had not seen you, * nor heard of your doings[5],
* and that those of my race had never come to you[6] !   * Now
they have only sinned a little in this life, and always suffer
in the eternal life[7].'   3. * I went out to the East, to the
paradise of Eden, where rest has been prepared for the just,
and it is open to the third heaven, and shut from this world[8].
4. * And guards are placed at the very great gates of the
east of the sun, i. e. fiery angels, singing triumphant songs,
that never cease rejoicing in the presence of the just.
5. At the last coming they will lead forth Adam with
our forefathers, and conduct them there, that they may
rejoice, as a man calls those whom he loves to feast with
him ; and they having come with joy hold converse, before
the dwelling of that man[7], * with joy awaiting his feast,
the enjoyment and the immeasurable wealth, and joy and
merriment in the light, and eternal life[9].   6. * Then

---

[1] **Like a darkened flame, B.**   [2] **B Sok. om.**   [3] **A om.**   [4] **To the
persons (there), B.**   [5] **B om.   A OMITS VERSES 2–14[a].**   [6] **Nor brought
my family to you, Sok.**   [7] **B om.**   [8] **B seems to recall this verse in the
words : And I saw there a blessed place and every created thing blessed.
B introduces this section with the words : Entry of Enoch unto the Paradise
of the Just.**   [9] **And all living there in joy and in boundless happiness
and eternal life, B.**

---

quenched lamps. Contrast the faces
and eyes of the heavenly angels, i. 5.
2. Cf. xli. 2.   3. The expression 'open
to the third heaven' is strange; it
would seem to imply that this is not
the heavenly Paradise in the third
heaven, but the original Garden of
Eden.   On the other hand, as this
Paradise is prepared for the righteous, we are obliged to identify it
with the Paradise of this third heaven
described in viii–ix.   5. The last
coming. See xxxii. 1 (note) ; lviii. 1.
Adam with our forefathers. See

xli. 1 (note).   The idea that the
patriarchs were in hell or hades is at
variance with what is stated or
implied in some parts of the Eth. En.
Cf. lx. 8, 23 ; lxi. 12 ; lxx. 3, 4, where
we find Paradise already peopled with
the righteous ; but it is not incom-
patible with lxxxix. 52 ; xciii. 8,
where apparently Enoch and Elijah
are its only inhabitants.   According
to xxii the patriarchs were to remain
in hades till the final judgement.
This would, in some degree, harmonize with our text.   6–14.   Nine

I said[1], 'I tell you, my children: blessed is he who fears * the name of the Lord. and serves continually before His face, and brings his gifts with fear continually in this life[2], * and lives all his life justly, and dies[3].   7. Blessed is he who executes a just judgement, * not for the sake of recompense, but for the sake of righteousness, expecting nothing in return : a sincere judgement shall afterwards come to him[3].   8. * Blessed is he who clothes the naked with a garment, and gives his bread to the hungry.   9. Blessed is he who gives a just judgement for the orphan and the widow, and assists every one who is wronged[4].   10. Blessed is he who turns from the * unstable path of this vain world[5], and walks by the righteous path * which leads to eternal life[3].   11. Blessed is he who sows just seed,

---

[1] Sok. om.   [2] **And serves the Lord; and do you, my children, learn to bring gifts to the Lord that you may have life, B.**   [3] B om.
[4] **Blessed is he who has given a just judgement, and assists the orphan and the widow, and every one who is oppressed : clothes the naked, and gives bread to the hungry, B.**   [5] **Path of deceit, B.**

---

beatitudes. These are very colourless.   7. **Executes a just judgement.** Cf. ix; Ezek. xviii. 8. This verse recalls in some measure the words of Antigonus of Socho : 'Be not like servants who serve their master for the sake of reward, but be like those who do service without respect to recompense, and live always in the fear of God.' **Expecting nothing in return.** Cf. Luke vi. 35.   **Sincere.** Corrupt. With the entire verse we have a good parallel in Orac. Sibyll. ii. 61, 63

πάντα δίκαια νέμειν, μηδ' εἰς ἄδικον
κρίσιν ἐλθῇς.
ἣν σὺ κακῶς δικάσῃς, σὲ θεὸς μετέ-
πειτα δικάσσει.

8. These words are found in ix. 9. Cf. ix; Ps. x. 18; Is. i. 17; Jer. xxii. 3, 16; Zech. vii. 9, 10.   10.

Walks by the righteous path. Cf. Prov. iv. 11 ; Or Sibyll. iii. 9–10

τίπτε . . . οὐκ εὐθεῖαν ἀταρπὸν
βαίνετε ἀθανάτου κτιστοῦ μεμνημένοι
αἰεί:

also Fragm. i. 23 sq.   11. Is the blessing for those who sow seed that is justly their own? In Orac. Sibyll. ii. 71–72, 'he who steals seed is accursed for ever':

σπέρματα μὴ κλέπτειν· ἐπαράσιμος
ὅς τις ἔληται
ἐς γενεὰς γενεῶν, ἐς σκορπισμὸν
βιότοιο.

On the other hand, the reference may be metaphorical and the sense as follows : 'From your righteous deeds ye will reap sevenfold.' This is probably an adaptation of Ecclus. vii. 3 μὴ σπεῖρε ἐπ' αὔλακας ἀδικίας, καὶ οὐ μὴ θερίσῃς αὐτὰς ἐπταπλασίως.   Cf. Job iv. 8;

he shall reap sevenfold. 12. Blessed is he in whom is the truth, that he may speak the truth to *his neighbour[1]. 13. Blessed is he *who has love upon his lips, and tenderness in his heart[2]. 14. Blessed is he who understands every work of the Lord, *and glorifies the Lord God[3]; *for the works of the Lord are just, and of the works of man some are good, and others evil, and by their works those who have wrought them are known[4].

[*Enoch shows his Children how he measured and wrote out the Judgements of God.*]

XLIII. 1. *Lo! my children, the things which I have gained on the earth and meditated upon from the Lord God I have written down both winter and summer. I have compiled the account of all, and concerning the years I have calculated each hour; I have measured the hours and written out the lists of them and I have ascertained all their differences[5]. 2. As one year is more honourable than another[6], so is one man more honourable than another. This

---

[1] The man who is sincere, Sok. [2] Upon whose lips are tenderness and mercy, B. [3] Accomplished by the Lord and glorifies him, Sok. [4] B om. A reads And I saw all the works of the Lord how righteous they are, and of the works of men some (are righteous) but others wicked. And the impure are known by their deeds.

XLIII. [5] I, my children, have measured and written out every deed and every measure, and every just judgement (weight, Sok.), A Sok. Sok. adds: And have written them out as the Lord ordered me, and in all these I have found diversity. [6] B adds and one day more than another and one hour more than another.

Prov. xxii. 8 ; Hos. x. 13. 12. Cf. Lev. xix. 11 ; Eph. iv. 25 ; Orac. Sibyll. ii. 58 ψεύδεα μὴ βάζειν : 64 μαρτυρίην ψευδῇ φεύγειν, τὰ δίκαι' ἀγορεύειν. 13. Cf. Prov. xxxi. 26. 14. By their works . . . are known. Cf. Mt. vii. 16, 20.

XLIII. 2, 3. As one year, &c. We should expect rather as one day, &c. Cf. Ecclus. xxiii. 7 διὰ τί ἡμέρα ἡμέρας ὑπερέχει ; The main thought of these verses is derived from Ecclus. x. 20, 22, 24 (cf. Jer. ix. 23, 24) : in

fact no one is greater than he who fears God is a direct quotation from x. 24. This passage runs: 20 ἐν μέσῳ ἀδελφῶν ὁ ἡγούμενος αὐτῶν ἔντιμος, καὶ οἱ φοβούμενοι κύριον ἐν ὀφθαλμοῖς αὐτοῦ. 22. πλούσιος καὶ ἔνδοξος καὶ πτωχός, τὸ καύχημα αὐτῶν φόβος κυρίου. 24. μεγιστὰν καὶ κριτὴς καὶ δυνάστης δοξασθήσεται, καὶ οὐκ ἔστιν αὐτῶν τις μείζων τοῦ φοβουμένου τὸν κύριον. . . . 30. πτωχὸς δοξάζεται δι' ἐπιστήμην αὐτοῦ, καὶ πλούσιος δοξάζεται διὰ τὸν πλοῦτον αὐτοῦ. Cf. Orac. Sibyll. ii. 125.

man on account of many possessions, that man on account
of the wisdom[1] of the heart; this man on account of understanding, another on account of cunning ; this man for the
silence of the lips[2] ; * this man on account of purity, that on
account of strength ; this man on account of comeliness,
another on account of youth ; this man on account of sharpness of mind, another on account of quicksightedness of body,
and another for the perception of many things.   3. Let it
be heard everywhere[3] ; there is no one greater than he who
fears God.   He shall be the most glorious for ever.

[Enoch instructs his Sons that they should not revile the Persons
of Men, whether they are great or small.]

XLIV. 1. God[4] made man with His own hands, in the
likeness of His countenance, both small and great the Lord
created him.   He who reviles the countenance of * man,
reviles the countenance of the Lord[5].   2. * He who shows
wrath against another without injury, the great wrath of the
Lord shall consume him.   3. If a man spits at the face of
another[6] * insultingly, he shall be consumed[7] * in the great
judgement of the Lord[8].   4. Blessed is the man who * does
not direct his heart with malice against any[9] man, and who
assists the man who is * injured, and[10] under judgement, and
raises up the oppressed, * and accomplishes the prayer of him
who asks[11] !   5. For in the day of the great judgement,

---

[1] Benevolence, B.   [2] Tongue and lips, B.   [3] B om.
XLIV. [4] B adds fashioned and.   [5] The prince, and loathes the
countenance of the Lord; despises the countenance of the Lord, A.
Man reviles the countenance of the prince and loathes the countenance of the Lord, Sok.   [6] There is the anger of the Lord, and a great
judgement for whoever spits in the face of a man, B.   [7] His insolence
will consume him, Sok. ; B om.   [8] B om.   [9] Puts confidence in, B.
[10] A, Sok. om.   [11] Performs a kindness to him who wants it, Sok. ; B om.

XLIV. 1. He who reviles the
countenance, &c.   We may reasonably compare James iii. 9.   2. Cf.

Matt. v. 22.   4. This beatitude
seems out of place here. It would
come in fittingly at the close of xlii.

every measure and standard and weight, * which is for traffic,
namely, that which is hung on a balance and stands for
traffic [1], knows its own measure, and * shall receive its
reward by measure [2].

[*God shows that He does not wish Sacrifices from Man, nor
Burnt-Offerings, but pure and contrite Hearts.*]

XLV. 1. * He who hastens and brings his offering before
the face of the Lord, then the Lord will hasten the accomplishment of his work, and will execute a just judgement for him [3].
2. He who increases his lamp before the face of the Lord, the
Lord increases greatly his treasure * in the heavenly kingdom [4].
3. God does not require bread, nor a light, * nor an animal,
nor any other sacrifice [5], * for it is as nothing [6]. 4. * But
God requires a pure heart [4], and by means of all this, He tries
the heart of man.

---

[1] Hang as on a balance, that is on the scale and which stands for
traffic, Sok. B OMITS ENTIRE VERSE. [2] Its measure shall receive its
reward, Sok.
XLV. [3] If a man hastens to work folly before the Lord, the Lord
furthers him in the carrying out of his work, and makes his judgement
faulty. So A through a corruption of приносъ into прасно and insertion of
не before сотворить; B om. [4] B om. [5] Nor food of any kind nor
meat, B. Nor an animal, nor an ox, nor any other victim, Sok. [6] That
is not so, Sok.; B om.

XLV. 3. Cf. Ps. xl. 6; li. 16;
Is. i. 11; Mic. vi. 6–8; Eccl. xxxii.
1–3; Orac. Sibyll. viii. 390, 391
οὐ χρήζω θυσίης ἢ σπονδῆς ὑμετέ-
ρηφιν
οὐ κνίσσης μιαρῆς, οὐχ αἵματος ἐχθί-
στοιο:
also ii. 82; Athenag. *Supplic. pro
Christo*, 13. This is not Essenism:
see lix. 1–3. We find the same
spiritual appreciation of sacrifices in

Ecclus. xxxii. 1–5 side by side with
injunctions to offer them: ὁ συντη-
ρῶν νόμον πλεονάζει προσφοράς, θυσιάζων σωτηρίου ὁ προσέχων ἐντολαῖς ἀντα-
ποδιδοὺς χάριν προσφέρων σεμίδαλιν,
καὶ ὁ ποιῶν ἐλεημοσύναν θυσιάζων αἰ-
νέσεως καὶ ἐξιλασμὸς ἀποστῆναι ἀπὸ
πονηρίας. 4. A pure heart. Ps.
li. 10. Tries the heart of man.
Deut. viii. 2; 2 Chron. xxxii. 31;
Ps. xxvi. 2.

[*How an earthly Prince will not receive Gifts from Man which
are contemptible and impure. How much more does God
loath impure Gifts, and rejects them with Wrath, and will
not receive the Gifts of such a Man.*]

XLVI. 1. * Hear, my people, and pay attention to the
words of my lips[1]. If any one brings gifts to an earthly
prince, but having unfaithfulness in his heart: if the prince
knows it, will he not be angry with * him on account of that,
and he will not take[2] his gifts, and will hand him over to
condemnation?　　2. Or if a man flatters another * in his
language, but (plans) evil against him in his heart, will not
the other understand the craft of his heart, and he himself
will be condemned, so that his unrighteousness will be evi-
dent to all[3]?　　3. But when God shall send a great light, by
means of that there will be judgement[4] to the just and
unjust, and nothing will be concealed.

[*Enoch instructs his Sons from the Lips of God, and gives
them the Manuscripts of this Book.*]

XLVII. 1. Now, my children, put my thoughts in your
hearts; pay attention to the words of your father, which
* have come to[5] you from the mouth of the Lord.　　2. Take
these books of the writings of your father, and read them,
* and in them ye shall learn all the works of the Lord.
There have been many books from the beginning of creation,
and shall be to the end of the world, but none shall make

XLVI. [1] Sok. om.　B OMITS ENTIRE CHAPTER.　　[2] Sok. om.　　[3] With
falsehood and is good in his tongue but evil in his heart, will not his
heart perceive this and he will judge by himself so that he is proved not
to be right, Sok.　　[4] Just judgement that is no respecter of persons, Sok.
XLVII. [5] I tell, Sok.　B OMITS ENTIRE CHAPTER.

XLVI. 2. Cf. Orac. Sibyll. ii. 120　　light means is not clear.
μηδ' ἕτερον κεύθοις κραδίῃ νόον ἀλλ'　　**XLVII.** 1. Cf. xxxix. 2.　　2.
ἀγορεύων.　　3. What the great　　None shall make things known

things known to you like my writings [1]. 3. But if you shall preserve [2] my writings, you will not sin against God. For there is no other besides the Lord, neither in heaven nor on earth, nor the depths below, nor the solitary foundations. 4. God established the foundations upon things that are unknown, and stretched out the * visible and invisible heavens [3], and made firm the earth upon the waters, and established the waters on things that are not fixed [4]. Who has created all the innumerable works of creation? 5. * Who has numbered the dust of the earth [5], and the sand of the sea, and the drops of rain, and the dew of the morning, * and the breath of the wind [6]? Who has * bound earth and sea with bonds [7] that cannot be broken up: * and has cut [8] the stars out of fire, * and beautified [9] the heavens [10], and placed * the sun [11] in the midst of them * so that [11].

[*Of the course of the Sun throughout the seven Circles.*]

XLVIII. 1. The sun [12] goes in the seven circles of the

---

[1] For the books are many and in them we shall learn all the words of the Lord. Such as they are from the beginning of creation, so shall they be to the end of the world, A. [2] Keep strictly, Sok. [3] Heavens over the visible things, Sok. [4] A reads And He considered what is the water and the foundation of things that are not stedfast and, and transposes these words to end of verse. [6] Sok. om. [7] Has filled earth and sea and the winter, A. [8] Emended from And I cut, A; and (who) sowed, Sok. [9] And I beautified, A. [10] Sok. adds and placed. [11] A om.
XLVIII. [12] He, Sok.

---

to you like my writings. Cf. Eth. En. xciii. 10. 3. But. . . not sin against God. Cf. xxxiii. 9; xlviii. 7-9. This claim is analogous to that made in the Eth. En. xxxvii. 4; xcii. 1; xciii. 10; c. 6; civ. 12, 13. With this we may contrast Ecclus. xviii. 3 οὐθενὶ ἐξεποίησεν ἐξαγγεῖλαι τὰ ἔργα αὐτοῦ. There is no other besides the Lord. Cf. Is. xlv. 5, 14, 18, 22. This is a favourite sentiment in the Sibylline Oracles. Cf. iii. 69

αὐτὸς γὰρ μόνος ἐστὶ θεὸς κοὐκ
ἔστιν ἔτ' ἄλλος:

also iii. 760; viii. 377; Fragm. i. 7, 15; iii. 3; v. 1. **4. Stretched**

out, &c. Ps. civ. 2; Is. xl. 22; xlii. 5. Made firm the earth upon the waters, 2 Pet. iii. 5. 5. Who has numbered . . . the sand of the sea, and the drops of rain. This is drawn word for word from Ecclus. i. 2 ἄμμον θαλασσῶν καὶ σταγόνας ὑετοῦ . . . τίς ἐξαριθμήσει; Cf. Is. xl. 12, and the oracle in Herod. i. 47 οἶδα δ' ἐγὼ ψάμμου τ' ἀριθμὸν καὶ μέτρα θαλάσσης, and likewise recalls LXX Job xxxvi. 27 ἀριθμηταὶ δὲ αὐτῷ σταγόνες ὑετοῦ. **Beautified the heavens.** Cf. Ecclus. xvi. 27 ἐκόσμησεν εἰς αἰῶνα τὰ ἔργα αὐτοῦ.

XLVIII. 1. The text is corrupt

heavens, * and I gave him¹ 182 thrones when he goes on a short day, and also 182 thrones when he goes on a long day.   2. And he has two great thrones on which he rests, returning hither and thither above the monthly thrones. From the month Tsivan² after³ seventeen days he descends to the month Thevan⁴, and from the seventeenth day of Thevad⁴ he ascends.   3. And so the sun goes through all the courses of the heaven³; when he goes near the earth, then the earth rejoices and produces its fruit; when he departs, then the earth is sad, and the trees and all the fruits have no development.   4. * All this by measure and minute arrangement of time He has arranged by His wisdom⁵, both in the case of things visible and invisible.   5. He has made all things visible out of invisible, Himself being invisible.   6. Thus I tell you, my children, distribute the books to your children, in all your families, and among the nations.   7. Those who are wise let them fear God, and let them receive them * and let them love them more than

---

¹ Which are the support of the, A.   B OMITS ENTIRE CHAPTER.
² Pamorus, Sok.   ³ A om.   ⁴ Thibith, Sok.   ⁵ Hereby he gives a complete measure and with good arrangement of the times and has fixed a measure, A.

---

and unintelligible. According to xi. 1; xxx. 3 the sun is in the fourth circle of the heavens and does not revolve through the seven circles. Again the twice-mentioned 182 thrones are really when added the 364 world-stations of which we have some account in the Eth. En. lxxv. 2, i.e. 'the harmony of the course of the world is brought about through its separate 364 world-stations.' These world-stations or thrones as in our text are the 364 different positions occupied by the sun on the 364 days of the year. Just as in the Eth. En. lxxii–lxxxii and Jubilees iv no attempt is made here to get the complete number of days in the solar

year, i.e. 365¼: contrast xiv. 1. This passage therefore either belongs to or is built upon the oldest literature of Enoch. This reckoning of the year at 364 days may be due partly to opposition to heathen systems and partly to the fact that 364 is divisible by 7, and amounts to 52 weeks exactly. See Eth. En. 190–91.   2. Tsivan . . . Thevad. The text is here corrupt. As apparently the two solstices are meant, we should read either Sivan . . . Kislev or Tamuz . . . Tebet.   5. Cf. xxiv. 2 (note); xlvii. 2 (note). Has made here was no doubt ἔπλασε, not ἐποίησε.   6. See xxxiii. 9 (note).   7. Let them love them more than any kind of food.

any kind of food [1], and read them [2].   8. * But those who are senseless and have no thought of the Lord and do not fear God [3] will not receive them but turn away, and * keep themselves from them [4], * the terrible judgement shall await them [5]. 9. Blessed is the man who bears their yoke, and puts it on, for he shall be set free in the day of the great judgement.

[Enoch instructs his Sons not to swear either by the Heaven or the Earth; and shows the Promise of God to a Man even in the Womb of his Mother.]

XLIX. 1. For [5] I swear to you my children [6], but I will not swear by a single oath, neither by heaven, nor by earth, nor by any other creature which God made.   God [7] said : ' There

---

[1] And the books will be more profitable to them than all good food on earth, Sok. A adds or earthly advantage.   [2] Sok. adds And let them cling to them.   [3] And it shall result to them if they have no thought of God nor fear him, and if they, A.   [4] Do not receive the books, A.   [5] Sok. om.
XLIX. [6] B om. rest of verse.   [7] For the Lord, Sok.

So Eth. En. lxxxii. 3 'this wisdom will please those that eat (thereof) better than good food.' Cf. xlvii. 2 (note).   8. Those who ... will not receive them ... the terrible judgement shall await them. The punishment denounced against those who refuse the disclosures of this book is more severe than anything to be found in the Eth. En. For a perfect parallel we must go to Rev. xxii. 18, 19.   9. The appeal for reception is far wider in this book than in the Eth. En. There only 'the elect of righteousness,' 'the righteous and the wise,' 'those who understand,' receive the revelations of Enoch: cf. lxxxii. 3; xciii. 10; civ. 12.   Bears their yoke, cf. xxxiv. 1.

XLIX. 1. Swear ... neither by heaven, &c. From this passage and

from Philo it is clear that Mt. v. 34–35 was a Jewish commonplace. For in Philo *de Special. Leg.* ii. 1 we find: ὁ γὰρ τοῦ σπουδαίου, φησί, λόγος ὅρκος ἔστω βέβαιος, ἀκλινής, ἀψευδέστατος, ἐρηρεισμένος ἀληθείᾳ ... εἰώθασι γὰρ ἀναφθεγγάμενοι τοσοῦτον μόνον 'νὴ τόν,' ἢ 'μὰ τόν,' μηδὲν παραλαβόντες, ἐμφάσει τῆς ἀποκοπῆς, τρανοῦν ὅρκον οὐ γενόμενον. Ἀλλὰ καὶ παραλαβέτω τις, εἰ βούλοιτο, μὴ μὴν τὸ ἀνωτάτω καὶ πρεσβύτατον εὐθὺς αἴτιον, ἀλλὰ γῆν, ἥλιον, ἀστέρας, οὐρανόν, τὸν σύμπαντα κόσμον: *De decem Orac.* 17 Κάλλιστον δὴ καὶ βιωφελέστατον καὶ ἁρμόττον λογικῇ φύσει τὸ ἀνώμοτον, οὕτως ἀληθεύειν ἐφ᾽ ἑκάστου δεδιδαγμένῃ, ὡς τοὺς λόγους ὅρκους εἶναι νομίζεσθαι. Cp. also *Leg. All.* iii. 72; *De Sac. Abelis et Caini*, 28; *De Plant. Noe* 19; *Quod Omnis Probus Liber*, 12. It was Mr. Conybeare

is no swearing in me, nor injustice, but truth. If there is
no truth in men, let them swear by a word, yea, yea, or nay,
nay. 2. * But I swear to you, yea, yea [1], that * there has
not been even a man in his mother's womb, for whom a place
has not been prepared for every soul [2]; * and a measure is fixed
how long a man shall be tried in this world [3]. * O! my
children. be not deceived [1] * there is a place prepared there
for every soul of man [4].

*[How Nobody born upon the Earth can hide himself, nor are his
Deeds concealed. (God) commands that he should be on the
Earth a short time, endure Temptation, and Annoyance, and
not injure the Widow and Orphan.]*

L. 1. I have laid down in the writings the actions of every
man, * and no one born on the earth can hide himself, nor can
his deeds be concealed ; I see all [5]. 2. Now, therefore, my
children. in patience and meekness accomplish the number
of your days, and ye shall inherit the endless life which is to
come. 3. * Every wound, and every affliction, and every

---

[1] B om. [2] So A Sok. but that for every A reads the rest of
that. B reads Even before man was created a place of judgement was
prepared for him. [3] And a measure and a standard how long a man
shall live in this world, and shall be tried in it, Sok. ; And it was measured out and fixed, and there man will be tried, B. [4] So A Sok. but
that Sok. adds previously after place. B reads As before it was appointed
for him.
L. [5] B om. ; Sok. adds as in a looking-glass.

---

that first called my attention to
these passages in Philo. On the
various forms of swearing usual
among the Jews and censured in
Mt. v. 33–36 and indirectly in the
text, see Lightfoot *in loc.*; Eisenmenger, ii. 490 sqq.

XLIX. 2. A place ... prepared
for every soul. So *Tractat Chagiga,*
fol. 15, col. 1 ; *Torath Adam,* fol. 101,
col. 3 ; *Avodath hakkodesh,* fol. 19,
col. 1, where it is said that a place

is prepared for every man either in
Paradise or Hell (Eisenmenger, ii.
315).

L. 1. **Nor can his deeds be concealed.** Eth. En. ix. 5. 2. In
patience, &c. Cp. Luke xxi. 19
'In your patience ye shall win your
souls.' A blessed immortality for the
righteous is taught in this book, but
apparently no resurrection of the
body. 3. Cp. Ecclus. ii. 4 ; 2 Tim.
iv. 5 ; Heb. x. 32 ; 1 Pet. ii. 19 ;

evil word, and attack[1] endure for the sake of the Lord.
4. And when you might have vengeance [2] do not repay, either
*your neighbour or your enemy [3].   For God [4] will repay as
your avenger in the *day of the great judgement [5].   *Let it
not be for you to take vengeance [6].   5. Whoever of you
shall spend gold or silver for the sake of a brother, shall receive
abundant treasure in *the day of judgement [7] *and stretch
out your hands to [8] the orphan, the widow, and the stranger [9].

[*Enoch instructs his Sons, not to hide their Treasures upon
Earth, but bids them give Alms to the Needy.*]

LI. 1. *Stretch out your hands to the poor man[10] according
to your powers.   2. *Do not hide your silver in the earth [11] :

---

[1] Whatever wound or disease or affliction or evil end shall light
upon you, B. Put away from you every wound and every injury and
every evil word. If an attack and an injury be inflicted upon you for
the sake of the Lord, Sok.   [2] Sok. adds an hundredfold.   [3] Your
neighbour, B; one who is near you or afar off, Sok.   [4] Living
God, B; Lord, Sok.   [5] Great day of, A.   [6] Therefore be not
avenged here from men but then from the Lord, Sok. B om.   [7] That
world, A Sok.   [8] Do not oppress, A.   [9] B om.; A adds lest the
wrath of God should come upon you.
   LI. [10] And assist the poor man, B; Sok. om.   [11] Sok. reads in your
treasures after come upon you, B om.

Jam. i. 12. See li. 3. 4. Cp. Ecclus.
xxviii. 1 ὁ ἐκδικῶν παρὰ Κυρίου
εὑρήσει ἐκδίκησιν, καὶ τὰς ἁμαρτίας
αὐτοῦ διαστηρῶν διαστηρίσει. 2. ἄφες
ἀδίκημα τῷ πλησίον σου, καὶ τότε
δεηθέντος σου αἱ ἁμαρτίαι σου λυθήσον-
ται. See also verses 3-6. God will
repay ... in the day of the great
judgement. These words follow the
LXX of Deut. xxxii. 35 ἐν ἡμέρᾳ
ἐκδικήσεως ἀνταποδώσω. The LXX
thus read ליום נקם אשלם instead of
the Mass. לי נקם ושלם. The
Samaritan likewise reads ליום. Cp.
also Prov. xx. 22; xxiv. 29. In
Rom. xii. 19; Heb. x. 30, the writers
follow a text of Deut. xxxii. 35 agree-
ing partly with the Mass. and partly

with that implied by the LXX. 5.
Whoever, &c. Cp. Prov. xix. 17:
Ecclus. xxix. 10. See LI. 2 (note).
Stretch out your hands to the
orphan, &c. Orac. Sibyll. ii. 75
ὀρφανικοῖς χήραις τ' ἐπιδευομένοις τε
παράσχου. Cf. ix.

   LI. 1. Stretch out your hands
to the poor, &c. This is drawn
from Ecclus. vii. 32 πτωχῷ ἔκτεινον
τὴν χεῖρά σου, which in turn seems
drawn from Prov. xxxi. 20. Cf. Job
vii. 9: Orac. Sibyll. ii. 88. According to your powers. Cf.
Ecclus. xiv. 13; xxix. 20. 2. Do
not hide your silver in the earth.
Cf. Ecclus. xxix. 10 ἀπόλεσον ἀργύριον
δι' ἀδελφὸν καὶ φίλον καὶ μὴ ἰωθήτω ὑπὸ

*assist the honest man in his affliction, and affliction shall not come upon you, in the time of your labour. 3. And whatever violent and grievous yoke shall be put upon you, endure all for the Lord's sake[1], and so you will receive your reward in the day of judgement.   4. Morning, afternoon, and evening, it is good to go into the house of the Lord to glorify *the Creator of all[2].   5. Wherefore[3] let every thing that hath breath glorify Him, and let every creature visible and invisible give forth praise.

[God instructs His faithful Servants how they are to praise His Name.]

LII. 1. Blessed is the man who opens *his lips to praise the God of Sabaoth, and praises the Lord with his heart[4]. 2. Cursed is every man who opens his *lips to abuse and to calumniate his neighbour[5].   3. Blessed[6] is he who opens his lips to the blessing and praise of God!   4. Cursed is he who opens his lips to swearing and blasphemy before the face of the Lord all his days.   5. Blessed is he who

---

[1] B om.   [2] Your Creator, A.   [3] For, Sok.; Sok. also puts the verbs in the indicative; B OMITS VERSE.

LII. [4] Heart and lips to the praise of the Lord, B.   [5] Heart to abuse, abusing the poor and calumniating his neighbour, Sok.; B supports text but that it omits and to calumniate. After neighbour A adds for him shall God rebuke.   [6] B OMITS VERSES 3, 4.

τὸν λίθον. Assist... in his affliction. Cf. Ecclus. iv. 4 ἱκέτην θλιβόμενον μὴ ἀπαναίνου. 3. Ecclus. ii. 4 πᾶν ὃ ἐὰν ἐπαχθῇ σοι ... μακροθύμησον. Cf. 1 Pet. ii. 19; iii. 14. Cf. L. 3. 4. Ps. lv. 17: Cf. Dan. vi. 10. These three Jewish hours of prayer—the *third* (that of morning sacrifice), the *sixth* (noon), the *ninth* (that of evening sacrifice)—are observed in Acts ii. 15; iii. 1; x. 9. See Lightfoot *in loc.* for his Talmudic references. House of the Lord. This means the temple; for though the author is a Jew living in Egypt, he is writing

for Judaism as a whole, and is giving herein the ideal conduct of an inhabitant of Jerusalem. In LIX. 2, 3, he prescribes the right method of sacrifice, and sacrifices could only be offered in Jerusalem. 5. Every thing that, &c. Ps. cl. 6.

LII. With these beatitudes compare xlii. 6–14. Like the latter these are wanting in vigour. They seem to be in the main derived from Ecclesiasticus. 2. Cf. Wisdom i. 11 ἀπὸ καταλαλιᾶς φείσασθε γλώσσης. 4. Swearing and blasphemy. Cf. Ecclus. xxiii. 9–12. 5. Cf. Ecclus.

blesses all the works of the Lord.   6. Cursed is he who speaks ill of[1] the works of the Lord.   7. Blessed is he who * looks to raise his own hand for labour[2].   8. Cursed is he who looks to[3] make use of another man's labour. 9. Blessed is he who preserves the foundations of his fathers * from the beginning[4].   10. Cursed is he who breaks the enactments[5] of his fathers.   11. Blessed is he who * establishes peace and love[6].   12. Cursed is he who troubles those who * are at peace[7].   13. Blessed is he who * does not speak peace with his tongue, but in his heart there is peace to all[8] !   14. Cursed is he who speaks peace with his tongue, but in his heart there is no peace[9].   15. For all these things in measures and in books will be revealed in the day of the great judgement[10].

[Let us not say that our Father is with God, and will plead for us at the Day of Judgement. For I know that a Father cannot help his Son, nor a Son a Father.]

LIII. 1. And now, my children, do not say ; Our father

---

[1] Sok. adds all.   [2] **Looks to the work of his own hands, B.   Looks to raise up the fallen, A.**   [3] A adds and is eager to.   [4] B om.
[5] B adds and ordinances.   [6] Goes to seek peace and leads others to peace, B.   [7] Love their neighbours, A.   [8] Speaks peace, for peace abides with him, B.   Speaks with a humble tongue and heart to all, A.   [9] A adds a sword. B OMITS ENTIRE VERSE.
[10] B adds Therefore, my brethren, preserve your hearts from everything unjust that you may inherit an habitation of light for ever.

---

xxxix. 14 εὐλογήσατε κύριον ἐπὶ πᾶσι τοῖς ἔργοις αὐτοῦ. 7. Cf. Eph. iv. 28. 8. Seems to be derived from Ecclus. xxxi. 26 φονεύων τὸν πλησίον ὁ ἀφαιρούμενος συμβίωσιν, καὶ ἐκχέων αἷμα ὁ ἀποστερῶν μισθὸν μισθίου. Cf. Orac. Sibyll. ii. 56–57 :

μὴ πλουτεῖν ἀδίκως, ἀλλ' ἐξ ὁσίων βιοτεύειν.
ἀρκεῖσθαι παρεοῦσι· καὶ ἀλλοτρίων ἀπέχεσθαι.

10. Cf. Eth. En. xcix. 2, 14 ; Ecclus. xvii. 11. 11. Cf. Mt. v. 9. 12. This is derived from Ecclus. xxviii. 9 ἀνὴρ

ἁμαρτωλὸς ταράξει φίλους καὶ ἀνὰ μέσον εἰρηνευόντων ἐκβάλλει διαβολήν. Cf. also Ecclus. xxviii. 13. 14. Cf. Ps. xxviii. 3 ; lv. 21 ; lxii. 4 ; Orac. Sibyll. ii. 120, 122.

LIII. 1. This idea that departed saints interceded on behalf of the living has been attributed by some scholars to Is. lxiii. 16 (see Ewald, *History of Israel,* i. 296; Cheyne, *Prophecies of Isaiah,* ii. 107–108; 299–300). If, however, the doctrine of a blessed immortality or of the resurrection was a late development

stands before God, and prays * for us (to be released) from sin ¹; * for there is no person there to help any man who has sinned ². 2. You see how I have written down all the works of every man * before his creation ², * which is ³ * done in the case of all men for ever ². 3. And no man * can say or unsay ⁴ what I have written with my hand. For God sees all things, * even the thoughts of wicked men ⁵, * which lie in the storeplaces of the heart ². 4. And now,

---

LIII. ¹ Concerning our sins, A. what things are, Sok.; B om. ⁵ The thoughts of man that they are vain, A; B om.

² B om. ³ And I shall write ⁴ Destroy, B; contradict, Sok.

---

among the Jews, this idea must necessarily have been later still, and accordingly unless we are prepared to bring down considerably the date of Is. lxiii, we shall have some difficulty in justifying such an interpretation. It seems indeed that this idea among the Jews was comparatively late in origin. The first indubitable evidence in its favour is to be found in the Eth. En. xxii. 12 ; xcvii. 3, 5; xcix. 16; and thus we find that it was an accepted Pharisaic belief early in the second century B.C. The next mention of this belief is to be met with in 2 Macc. xv. 14 where Jeremiah, who appears in a vision to Judas Maccabaeus, is described as follows: ὁ φιλάδελφος οὗτός ἐστιν ὁ πολλὰ προσευχόμενος περὶ τοῦ λαοῦ καὶ τῆς ἁγίας πόλεως Ἰερεμίας ὁ τοῦ θεοῦ προφήτης. This was also the teaching of Philo, de Exsecrat. 9 : τρισὶ χρησό-μενοι παρακλήτοις τῶν πρὸς τὸν πατέρα καταλλαγῶν ... δευτέρῳ δὲ τῇ τῶν ἀρχηγετῶν τοῦ ἔθνους ὁσιότητι, ὅτι ταῖς ἀφειμέναις σωμάτων ψυχαῖς ἄπλαστον καὶ γυμνὴν ἐπιδεικνυμέναις πρὸς τὸν ἄρχοντα θεραπείαν τὰς ὑπὲρ υἱῶν καὶ θυγατέρων ἱκετείας οὐκ ἀτελεῖς εἰώθασι ποιεῖσθαι, γέρας αὐτοῖς παρέχοντος τοῦ πατρὸς τὸ ἐπήκοον ἐν εὐχαῖς. The

same view was obviously held by Joseph. Antt. i. 13. 3, where he describes Abraham as saying to Isaac when on the point of sacrificing him : μετ' εὐχῶν δὲ καὶ ἱερουργίας ἐκείνου τὴν ψυχὴν τὴν σὴν προσδεξομένου καὶ παρ' αὐτῷ καθέξοντος ἔσῃ μοὶ εἰς κηδεμόνα καὶ γηροκόμον. And also in Orac. Sibyll. ii. 330–333 :

τοῖς καὶ ὁ παντοκράτωρ θεὸς ἄφθιτος ἄλλο παρέξει
εὐσεβέεσσ', ὁπότ' ἂν θεὸν ἄφθιτον αἰτήσωνται·
ἐκ μαλεροῖο πυρὸς τε καὶ ἀκαμάτων ἀπὸ βρυγμῶν
ἀνθρώπους σῶσαι δώσει· καὶ τοῦτο ποιήσει.

Finally this doctrine is recognized and apparently accepted in certain parts of the N. T.: Matt. xxvii. 47, 49; Luke xvi. 24–31 ; John viii. 56 (?); Heb. xii. 1 ? ; Rev. vi. 9–11. For the prevalence of this belief in later Judaism, see Eisenmenger, ii. 357–9 ; 361. The idea of intercession may be derived from ancestor-worship, and not from the doctrine of a future life as I have implied above ; cf. Cheyne's *Introd. to the Book of Isaiah,* 352, 3. 2. Enoch is the universal scribe. 3. Cf. Ps. xciv. 11 ; Ecclus. xvii. 15. 20.

my children, pay attention to all the words * of your father which I say to you [1] : * that ye may not grieve afterwards and say : Our father for some cause or other, never told them to us, in the time of this folly [2].

[*Enoch admonishes his Sons that they should give the Books to Others.*]

LIV. * Let these books which I have given you be the inheritance of your peace [3] : * do not conceal them [4] but tell [5] them to all desiring them * and admonish them [6] that * they may know the works of the Lord which are very wonderful [7].

[*Here Enoch makes a Declaration to his Sons: and speaks to them with Tears: 'My children, my Hour draws near, that I should go to Heaven. Lo! Angels stand before me!'*]

LV. 1. My children, the appointed day and time [8] have drawn near * and constrain me to depart [9]. The angels * will come and [10] stand before me * on the earth awaiting what has been ordered them [11].   2. In the morning I shall go to the highest [12] heavens [13] to my eternal habitation.   3. Therefore I tell you to do all that is good before the face of the Lord.

[*Methosalem asks a Blessing of his Father; that he may give him Bread to eat.*]

LVI. 1. Methosalem having answered his father Enoch said [14] : 'If it is good in thine eyes, * my father [15], * let me

---

[1] Of the lips of your father, B.   [2] B om.
LIV. [3] That you may have an inheritance of peace and the books which I have given you from God, B.   [4] A om.   [5] Give, A.   [6] Sok. om.   [7] Words cannot make known the works of God, B.
LV. [8] B adds appointed by God.   [9] A reads after stand before me.   [10] Who wish to go with me, A Sok.   [11] So A Sok. but that before on the earth, A adds they now stand; B om.   [12] Upper, B; A om.   [13] A adds to the highest Jerusalem.
LVI. [14] B om.   [15] Enoch, Sok.

LIV. See xxxiii. 9 (note). Works ... wonderful. Job xxxvii. 14, 16; Ps. lxxi. 17, &c.

LV. 1. See xxxvi.   2. Highest heavens. Cf. lxvii. 2.

put food[1] before thy -face and then, having blessed our houses and thy sons, * and all thy family[2], let thy people be glorified by thee; and then afterwards thou wilt depart, * as God hath said[3].'   2. Enoch answered his son * Methosalem and said[4]: 'Hear my child, since God has anointed me with the oil of his glory, there has been no[2] food in me, * and my soul remembers nothing of earthly pleasure[5] nor do I desire * anything earthly[6].

[*Enoch orders his Son Methosalem to call all his Brothers.*]

LVII. 1. But[7] call all[8] thy brothers, and all your[9] families, and the elders of the people, that I may speak to them and depart * as is appointed for me[8].   2. And Methosalem hastened, and called his brethren, Regim, Riman[10], Ukhan[11], Khermion, [Gaidal[8]], and[12] the elders of[13] the people, * and brought them all[14] before the face of his father Enoch[15]. And having blessed them, he spake to them[16].

[*The Instruction of Enoch to his Sons.*]

LVIII. 1. 'Listen to me, my sons. * In those days when the Lord came upon the earth for the sake of Adam, and visited[17] all his creation, which He Himself had made[18]. 2. The[19] Lord[20] called all the cattle of the earth[21], and all

---

[1] Let me do, A : let us put food, Sok. Sok.; B om.   [4] And said, Sok.; B om.   [2] A om.   [3] **As God wishes,** [5] B om.   [6] **Earthly food, B.** LVII. [7] **My son Methosalem, A.**   [8] B om.   [9] **Our, B.**   [10] **Rim,** B.   [11] Azukhan, B.   [12] A adds all.   [13] Sok. adds all.   [14] And called them, Sok.; A om.   [15] Sok. adds **and they bowed before his face,** and Enoch saw them.   [16] Sok. adds **saying.** LVIII. [17] So A and Sok., but that Sok. adds **your father after Adam ;** B reads in the days of our father Adam the Lord came to visit him and. [18] A adds and after all these created Adam : Sok. adds in brackets in the previous thousand years and after all these created Adam.   [19] **And** the, A B Sok.   [20] Lord God, B.   [21] B adds **and all the wild beasts** and all the fourfooted things.

LVI. 2. Cf. xxii. 7, 8.   Khermion are not mentioned in i. 10.

LVII. 1. Cf. xxxvi. 1; Eth. En.   On Gaidal, see i. 10 (note).

xci. 1.   2. Riman, Ukhan, and   LVIII. 1. When the Lord came

creeping things, and all the fowls that fly * in the air¹,
and brought them all¹ before the face of our father
Adam², and he gave names to all living things on the
earth.   3. And the Lord made him lord over all, and
put all things under his hands³, and * subdued (them) to
submission and to all obedience⁴ * to man⁵. So the Lord
created⁶ man as master over all His possessions.   4. The
Lord will not judge any soul of beast on account of man,
* but he will judge the soul of man on account of the souls
of beasts in the world to come⁷.   5. * For as there is
a special place for mankind for all the souls of men according
to their number, so there is also of beasts.   And not one

---

¹ B om.   ² Sok. adds that he should give names to all fourfooted
things.   ³ Made subject to Adam all the newly created things, B.
⁴ Secondly he placed all things under the rule of and made them
obedient, B. Made them dumb and made them deaf to obey, A.
⁵ As unto every man, Sok.   ⁶ A adds every.   ⁷ But the soul
of man shall judge the animals in this world, A ; B gives the sense of the
verse ; but there shall not be a judgement of every living soul but only
of that of man, and (?) in the great life to come.

---

upon the earth . . . and visited.
See xxxii. 1 (note).   5. Special
place . . . for all the souls of men.
See xlix. 2 (note).   So also of
beasts. As the Jews believed at
the beginning of the Christian era
that all animals had spoken one language before the fall, and therefore
in some degree possessed rationality
(Jubilees iii. 28; Joseph. *Antt.* i. 1.4),
it was only natural that they should
proceed to infer a future existence of
the animal world. The O. T. indeed
does not show a single trace of this
belief, though it always displays a
most tender solicitude for their well-
being ; nor do we find it in any pre-
Christian Jewish writing, with the
exception of the present text. Even
here the future life is of a limited
nature. It is ethically motived. This

further term of existence is not conceded for the brute's own sake, but
wholly with a view to the punishment of man. The brute creation is
to live just long enough to bring an
indictment for ill-treatment against
man at the final judgement. Though
this idea of any future life in connexion with the brute creation may
move the wonder of the modern mind,
it is justified by perfectly analogous
ideas in the ancient world. Not to
speak of the doctrine of metempsy-
chosis in Greece and the deification of
animals in Egypt, such conceptions
as those in the text would not
unnaturally flow from the powers
and qualities frequently assigned to
animals by Greek thinkers. Thus,
according to Plut. *Plac.* v. 20, 4, the
souls of brutes were rational though

soul shall perish which God has made till the great judgement. 6. And every soul of beast shall bring a charge against man if he feeds them badly[1].

---

[1] I have followed Sok. in verses 5, 6. B partly preserves the sense there is one place and one fold for the souls of beasts. For every living soul which God has made was not reserved for the great judgement. And every soul of beasts, &c., as in text. A is transposed and corrupt; There is a special place for mankind; as there is every soul of man according to his number, so the beast also shall not perish. And every soul of beast which God has made shall bring a charge against man at (or until) the great judgement if, &c., as in text.

---

incapable of acting rationally on account of their bodies; according to Xenocrates they possessed a consciousness of God, καθόλου γοῦν τὴν περὶ τοῦ θείου ἔννοιαν Ξενοκράτης . . . οὐκ ἀπελπίζει καὶ ἐν τοῖς ἀλόγοις ζῴοις (Clem. *Strom.* v. 590). Chrysippus ascribed reason to brutes (Chalkid in *Tim.* p. 148 b); while Sextus Medicus (ix. 127) maintained that the souls of brutes and of men were alike. Hence it was generally believed that the souls of men could pass into brutes, πρῶτον μὲν ἀθάνατον εἶναί φησι τὴν ψυχήν, εἶτα μεταβάλλουσαν εἰς ἄλλα γένη ζῴων (Porph. *V. P.* 19): while Plato indeed went further and derived the souls of all brutes ultimately from those of men, through a process of deterioration, ὡς γάρ ποτε ἐξ ἀνδρῶν γυναῖκες καὶ τἄλλα θηρία γενήσοιντο, ἠπίσταντο οἱ ξυνιστάντες ἡμᾶς (*Tim.* 76 D). With regard to individual animals, some thinkers believed that bees contained a divine element (Virg. *Georg.* iv. 219-221), while Democritus and Pliny placed religion among the moral virtues of elephants (*H. N.* viii. 1). But the closest parallels are to be found in Zoroastrianism, to which indeed we should probably trace in some measure the ideas of the text. Thus in the Zend-Avesta

Vendidad *Fargard* 13 (Darmesteter) we find an entire chapter dealing with the sacredness of the life of the domesticated dog and the crime of attempting its life—its murderer was to lose his soul to the ninth generation (1-4): with the food that was to be given to it and the penalties entailed by feeding it badly (20-28), which were to range from fifty to two hundred blows with the horse-goad. Nay more, the land, its pastures and crops were to suffer for the unatoned death of the dog, and these plagues were not to be removed till the man who had slain it was slain in turn or had offered sacrifices three days and three nights to the pious soul of the departed dog (54, 55). Finally, the soul of the dog went after death to the source of the waters (51). In the *Midrash Koheleth*, fol. 329, col. 1, we find the following quaint and slightly analogous thought: 'Rabbi Chama, the son of Gorion, said that wolves and unfruitful trees must give account: just as man must give account, so also must unfruitful trees.' Eisenmenger, i. 468. It is noteworthy that the ideas of the text have passed over into the creed of the Mohammedans. Thus, according to Sale's note on the sixth chapter of the Koran, irrational animals will be

*[Enoch teaches all his Sons why they must not touch the
Flesh of Cattle, because of what comes from it.]*

LIX. 1. He, who acts lawlessly with regard to the souls
of beasts, acts lawlessly with regard to his own soul.
2. For a man offers clean animals * and makes his sacrifice
that he may preserve his soul[1]. And if he offer as a sacrifice
from clean * beasts and[2] birds[3], he preserves his soul.
3. Everything that[4] is given you for food, bind by the
four feet: that is an atonement: he acts righteously (therein)
and preserves his soul.   4. But he who kills a beast
without a wound kills his own soul and sins against his

LIX. [1] And then he preserves his soul, B.   [2] B om.   [3] A adds it
is a salvation for man.   [4] A om.; B OMITS VERSES 3, 4, 5.

---

restored to life at the resurrection that
they may be brought to judgement
and have vengeance taken on them
for the injuries they had inflicted on
each other in this life. Then after
they have duly retaliated their several
wrongs, God will turn them again to
dust (Sale's Koran, Prelim. Discourse,
Sect. iv), with the exception of Ezra's
ass and the dog of the seven sleepers
which will enjoy eternal life in Paradise (Koran iii; xviii). Are we to
interpret in this manner Orac. Sibyll.
viii. 415–418!—

καὶ ὕστερον ἐς κρίσιν ἥξω
κρίνων εὐσεβέων καὶ δυσσεβέων βίον
ἀνδρῶν·
καὶ κριὸν κριῷ καὶ ποιμένι ποιμένα θήσω
καὶ μόσχον μόσχῳ πέλας ἀλλήλων ἐς
ἔλεγχον.

Even in Christian times animals were
credited with intelligence, conscience,
responsibility, as well as with the
passions, vices and virtues of mankind (see *Bestie delinquenti*, D'Addo-
sio, 1892, from which the following

facts are taken). They were accordingly solemnly tried, and advocates
were assigned at the public expense
to them to plead their cause. Thus
moles (834 A. D.), a sow (1324), a cock
(1474), snails (1487) were duly tried
and condemned. They were also
occasionally subjected to torture, and
their cries were regarded as a confession of guilt (l. c. p. 46). Even as
late as 1531 a book was written by
Chassauée to discuss the lawfulness of
trying animals judicially, and the
legitimate methods of procedure
(l. c. p. 75).

LIX. 1. He who acts lawlessly,
&c. At first sight this would seem to
refer to the sin of bestiality, and such
was the view of the scribe of A: see
title, but the context is against this,
as verses 2–4 clearly show. Hence
some illegitimate method of sacrificing
or slaughtering animals seems to be
referred to here. 2, 3. These verses
point to a date prior to the destruction of the temple, 70 A.D. 4. Against

own flesh. 5. And if any one does an injury to an animal secretly, it is an evil custom and he sins against his soul.

[*How we ought not to kill a Man, neither with Weapon nor with Tongue* [1].]

LX. 1. If he does an injury to the soul of man, he does an injury to his own soul; and there is no salvation for his flesh, * nor forgiveness [2] for ever [3]. 2. He who kills the soul of a man, kills his own soul, and destroys his own body, and there is no salvation for him for ever. 3. He who prepares a net for another man * will fall into it himself and there is no salvation for him for ever [4]. 4. He, who prepares a weapon against a man, shall not escape punishment in the great judgement for ever. 5. If a man acts crookedly or speaks evil against any soul, he shall have no righteousness for himself for ever.

[*Enoch admonishes his Sons to preserve themselves from Unrighteousness, and to stretch out their hands frequently to the Poor, and to give them something from their Labours.*]

LXI. 1. Now therefore, my children, preserve your hearts from every unrighteousness which the Lord hates. As a man asks his soul from God, so let him do to every living soul [5]. 2. * For in the world to come [2], * I know all things

---

LX. [1] A inserts this title after verse 1. [2] B om. [3] B adds but when a man is in Paradise he is liable to judgement no more. [4] Shall not lose the punishment for it in the day of judgement for ever, Sok. B OMITS VERSES 2–5.
LXI. [5] B adds Even if it be not for eternal life.

---

strangling beasts. 5. Bestiality may be here referred to.

LX. 1. The sin referred to in I Thess. iv. 6. 3. Cf. Pss. ix. 15; xxxv. 8; lvii. 6. In this verse and the next two there is an utter want of proportion between the sin

and its punishment. 5. Cf. Ps. ci. 5.

LXI. 1. Unrighteousness which the Lord hates. Cf. Jud. v. 17; Ecclus. xv. 11, 13. 2. In the world to come ... many mansions. Cf. Eth. En. xxxix. 4, 7, 8; xli. 2; John

how that[1] there are many mansions prepared for men; * good for the good; evil for the evil; many and without number[2]. 3. Blessed are those who shall go to the mansions of the blessed[3]; for in the evil ones there is no rest nor any means of return from them. 4. Listen, my children, both small and great: When a man * conceives a good thought in his heart and brings[4] gifts before the Lord of his labours—if his hands have not wrought them[5] then the Lord turns away His face from the labour of his hands, and * he cannot gain advantage from[6] the work of his hand. 5. But if his hands have wrought, but his heart murmurs * and he does not make an offering of his heart, but murmurs[7] continually, he has no success.

·[*How it is proper to bring one's Gifts with Faith, and how there is no Repentance after Death.*]

LXII. 1. Blessed is the man who in patience shall bring

---

[1] I know that, Sok.; B om. [2] **Numberless abodes for the good and the evil,** B. [3] B OMITS THE REST OF THE CHAPTER. [4] Sets it in his heart to bring, Sok. [5] The labour, Sok. [6] It is impossible for him to find, Sok. [7] The sickness of his heart will not cease and making a murmur, Sok.

---

xiv. 2. Good for the good, evil for the evil. This is adapted from Ecclus. xxxix. 25 ἀγαθὰ τοῖς ἀγαθοῖς ἔκτισται ἀπ᾽ ἀρχῆς, οὕτως τοῖς ἁμαρτωλοῖς κακά. Cf. Or. Sibyll. Fragm. iii. 18-19 τοῖς ἀγαθοῖς ἀγαθὸν προφέρων πολὺ πλείονα μισθόν, τοῖς δὲ κακοῖς ἀδίκοις τε χόλον. 4. The text seems corrupt. The idea is: it is a good thing to offer gifts to God; but if a man sacrifice to God that which is another man's or is gotten wrongfully, God turns away His face from him. Cf. lxvi. 2. The author appears to have had before him Ecclus. xxxi. 21 θυσιάζων ἐξ ἀδίκου, προσφορὰ μεμωκημένη, 22 καὶ οὐκ εἰς εὐδοκίαν μωκήματα ἀνόμων. 23 οὐκ εὐδοκεῖ ὁ ὕψιστος ἐν προσφοραῖς ἀσεβῶν.

Further in ver. 24 ὁ προσάγων θυσίαν ἐκ χρημάτων πενήτων is condemned. Finally with he cannot gain advantage from, &c., compare ver. 28 τί ἀφέλησαν πλείον ἢ κόπου; If his hands have not wrought them. Cf. Or. Sibyll. viii. 403, 406:

τούτῳ μὲν καθαρὴν θὲς ἀναίμακτόν τε τράπεζαν

ἐκ μόχθων ἰδίων πορίσας ἀγναῖς παλάμῃσιν.

5. Men must offer willingly: only those are blessed. Cf. Exod. xxv. 2; xxxv. 5; Prov. xi. 25. But his heart murmurs. Cp. lxiii. 2; Deut. xv. 10 'thine heart shall not be grieved when thou givest unto him.' Ecclus. xxxii. 10, 11 ἐν ἀγαθῷ ὀφθαλμῷ δόξασον τὸν κύριον ... καὶ ἐν εὐφροσύνῃ ἁγίασον δεκάτην.

his gifts[1] before the face of the Lord, for he shall avert the recompense of his sin.   2. *If he speaks words out of season[2] *there is no repentance for him: if he lets the appointed time[3] pass and does not *perform the work, he is not blessed; for[4] there is no repentance after death. 3. For every deed which a man does *unseasonably is[5] an offence before men, and a sin before God.

[*How one must not despise the Humble, but give to them truly, so that thou mayest not be accursed before God.*]

LXIII. 1. When a man clothes the naked and feeds the hungry, he gets a recompense from God.   2. If his heart murmurs, *he works for himself a double evil: he works destruction to that which he gives and there shall be no reward for it[6]:   3. *And the poor man, when his heart is satisfied or his flesh is clothed[7] and he acts contemptuously, he destroys the effect of *all his endurance of poverty[8] and *shall not gain the blessing of a recompense[9].   4. For the Lord hates every contemptuous *and proud-speaking[10] man: *and likewise every lying word: and that which is covered with unrighteousness. And it is cut with the sharpness of a deadly sword, and thrown into the fire, and burns for ever[11].

LXII. [1] A adds with faith.   [2] If he remembers the appointed time to utter his prayer, B.   If before the time he recalls his word, Sok. [3] B omits, AND ALSO THE REST OF THE CHAPTER.   [4] Act righteously, A. [5] Before the time and after the time is altogether, A.

LXIII. [6] He works for himself a double destruction and when he gives anything to a man there shall be no reward for that which he has given, A. B reads He renders his deeds of mercy profitless.   [7] Nay more if food fill his heart to the full or his flesh is clothed, A. If he becomes overfed. B.   [8] His good works, B.   [9] Does not return with gratitude the benefits he has received, A. Gains nothing, B.   [10] B om. [11] And every lying word is sharpened with unrighteousness, and is cut with the sharpness of a deadly sword, and that cutting has no healing for ever, Sok. B om.

LXII. 1. Forgiveness is not the message of this book. For most sins there is no pardon. 2. Words out of season. The text is hopeless here.

LXIII. 1. See ix (notes). 2. See lxi. 5 (note). 4. The Lord hates, &c. Pss. xviii. 27; cf. 5; Prov. vi. 16, 17.

[*How the Lord calls Enoch: the People take Counsel to go
to kiss him in the Place called Achuzan.*]

LXIV. 1. When Enoch said these words to his sons, * and
the princes of the people [1], all the people * far and near [2]
heard how the Lord called Enoch. And [3] they took counsel,
* and they all said [4]: 'Let us go and kiss Enoch!'   2. And
the men assembled to the number of 2000 [5], and came to the
place Achuzan [6], where Enoch was, and his sons.   3. And [7]
the elders of the people [8] *came together and made obeisance
and [9] kissed Enoch, and said to him: '*Enoch, our father [9];
be thou blessed of the Lord, the eternal King!'   4. And
now bless thy * sons, and all the [9] people, that we may be
glorified * before thee to-day.   5. For thou art glorified [8]
before the face of the Lord * for ever [1]; since God has
chosen thee * above all men upon the earth, and has appointed thee [9] as * the scribe of His creation of visible and
invisible things, and [9] an avenger [10] of the sins of men, * and
a succour to thy family [9]!' And Enoch answered all his
people saying [9]:

[*Of the Exhortation of Enoch to his Sons.*]

LXV. 1. 'Listen, my children: before that anything existed
* and all creatures were made, the Lord made [11] all things both
visible and invisible.   2. * When the times of these things

LXIV. [1] A om.   [2] And all his neighbours, B.   For how the Lord,
B reads how the Lord God.   [3] A B om.   [4] Saying, B; A om.
[5] 4000, B.   [6] Asukhan, B.   [7] A adds all the host of.   [8] Sok. adds
and all the host.   [9] B om.   [10] One who removes, A B.
XLV. [11] The Lord made the world and then created, B.   The Lord
made, A.

LXIV. 5. **Scribe of His creation.**
See xl. 13 (note); liii. 2.   **Avenger,**
&c. This may refer to Enoch's office
at the final judgement when he re-
counts all the deeds of men. See
quotation from Test. Abraham given

in note on XL. 13.   The reading,
however, of A B one who removes
may be right. Enoch may be conceived as a mediator. Cf. Philo's
conception of the Logos i. 501.

LXV. 1. **Made.** This must mean

had come and were passed, understand how[1] after all these things He made man in His own image *after His[1] likeness, and placed in him eyes to see; and ears to hear; and a heart to understand, and reason[2] to take counsel.   3. And the Lord *contemplated the world for the sake of man[3], and made all the creation* for his sake[4], and divided* it into times. And from the times He made years, and from the years He made months, and from the months He made days, and of the days He made seven.   4. And in these He made the hours[5] *and divided them into small portions[1], that a man should understand *the seasons, and compute years and months, and hours; their alternations and beginnings and ends: and[6] that he should compute *his life from the beginning till death[7], *and should meditate upon his sin, and should write down his evil and good deeds. 5. For nothing done is concealed before the Lord. Let each man know his deeds, and not transgress the commandments and let him keep My writings securely from generation to generation[1].   6. When *all the creation of visible and invisible things[8] comes to an end which the Lord has made; then every man shall come to the great judgement of the Lord[9].   7. Then[10] the times shall perish, *and

---

[1] B om.   [2] With his mind, A.   [3] Saw all the works of man, A. B om.   [4] A om. B transposes it into next sentence.   [5] Time for the sake of man, and determined the times and the years, and the months and the hours, B.   [6] The changes of the times and the end and the beginning of the years, and the end and the days and hours, B.   [7] The death of his life, B.   [8] The world, B.   [9] A om.   [10] And then all, A.

'devised,' if it is original. 2. Made man in his own image ... understand. This agrees too closely to be accidental with Ecclus. xvii. 3 κατ᾽ εἰκόνα αὐτοῦ ἐποίησεν αὐτούς. 5. ... ὀφθαλμούς, ὦτα καὶ καρδίαν ἔδωκε διανοεῖσθαι αὐτοῖς. 4. Understand the seasons ... beginnings and ends. We have here a close resem-

blance to Wisdom vii. 17–18 αὐτὸς γάρ ἔδωκε ... εἰδέναι ... ἀρχὴν καὶ τέλος καὶ μεσότητα χρόνων, τροπῶν ἀλλαγὰς καὶ μεταβολὰς καιρῶν. 5. See xxxiii. 9 (note). 6. The judgement closes the existence of man on earth. At this judgement all men must appear, but there is nothing to suggest that there is a resurrection of the body. 7. See

there shall be no year, nor month, nor day, and there shall
be no hours nor shall they be reckoned[1].   8. There shall
be one eternity, and all the just *who shall escape the great
judgement of the Lord[2] shall be gathered together in eternal
life *and for ever and ever the just shall be gathered
together and they shall be eternal[3].   9. Moreover there
shall be no labour, nor sickness, nor sorrow, *nor anxiety,
nor need[4], nor night, nor darkness, but a great[5] light.
10. *And there shall be to them a great wall that cannot
be broken down[2]; and bright[6] *and incorruptible[2] paradise
*shall be their protection, and their eternal habitation[7].
*For all corruptible things shall vanish[2], *and there shall
be eternal life[8].

[*Enoch instructs his Sons, and all the Elders of the People: how
with Fear and Trembling they ought to walk before the
Lord, and serve Him alone, and not to worship Idols; for
God made Heaven and Earth and every Creature and its
Form.*]

LXVI. 1. And now, my children, preserve your souls from
all unrighteousness, which the Lord hates[9]. Walk before
His face with fear *and trembling[10], and serve Him alone.

---

[1] And the years moreover shall perish and the months and days
and hours shall be dispersed and moreover shall not be counted, Sok.
For hours . . . counted A reads there shall be no hours nor shall there be
any addition to them or calculation.   [2] B om.   [3] And there shall be one
everlasting time for the just and they shall live for ever, A.   And
there shall be everlasting life for the just, being eternal, Sok.   After
eternal B adds and incorruptible.   [4] A adds nor violence; Sok. reads
nor necessary anxiety nor constraint.   [5] B adds unending and never
disturbed.   [6] Great, B Sok.   [7] B om.   Sok. reads and there shall
be the roof of the eternal habitation, and transposes to end of Chapter.
[8] And incorruptible things shall come, Sok.
LXVI. [9] B OMITS THE REST OF THE CHAPTER.   [10] Sok. om.

---

xxxiii. 2.   0 0. A blessed immortality. 10. **Wall.** This may be the
wall that divides Paradise (see ix)
from the place of punishment (see x).
11. Cp. Ecclus. xiv. 19 πᾶν ἔργον
σηπόμενον ἐκλείπει.

LXVI. 1. **Unrighteousness**
which the Lord hates. Cf. Deut.
xii. 31; Wisdom xiv. 9. **Walk
before His face with fear and
trembling.** Cf. Phil. ii. 12 'work
out your own salvation with fear and

* Worship the true God, and not dumb idols.   2. But pay attention to His command[1], and bring every just offering before the face of the Lord.   But the Lord hates that which is unrighteous.   3. For the Lord sees every thing; whatever man meditates in his heart, * and what counsel he plans[2], and every thought is continually before the Lord. 4. * If ye look at the heavens there is the Lord, as the Lord made the heavens.   If ye look at the earth then the Lord is there since the Lord made firm the earth and established every creature in it[3].   If ye scrutinize the depths of the sea, and every thing under the earth there also is the Lord. For the Lord created all things.   5. Do not bow down to the work of men, * nor to the work of the Lord[4], leaving * the Lord of all creation[5]; for no deed is concealed before the face of the Lord.   6. Walk, my children, in long suffering, in humility[6], in spite of calumny, and insult; in faith, and truth: in the promises, and sickness, in abuse, in wounds, in temptation, * in nakedness, in deprivation[7], loving one another, till ye depart from this world of sickness. Then ye shall be heirs of eternity.   7. Blessed are the just, who shall escape the great judgement[8]!   And they shall be seven times brighter than the sun, for in this age altogether the seventh part is separated.   8. (Now concerning) the light, the darkness, the food, the sweetnesses,

---

[1] Sok. om.   [2] Then his reason counsels, Sok.   [3] So Sok. transposed and defective in A. Who made firm the earth, and established every creature in it. If ye look at the heavens there is the Lord.   [4] A om. [5] The works of the Lord, A.   [6] A adds honour.   [7] Deprivation and nakedness, Sok.   [8] Sok. adds of the Lord.

---

trembling.' For fear and trembling cf. also 2 Cor. vii. 15; Eph. vi. 5. 2. Bring every just offering. See lxi. 4 (note). 3. Sees every thing whatever man meditates, &c. Cf. 1 Chron. xxviii. 9; 2 Chron. vi. 30; Ps. xciv. 11; Prov. xv. 11; Dan. ii. 30. 4. Founded partly on Ps. cxxxix.

8–12. The author has rightly omitted all reference to Sheol as this is already included in his conception of the heavens. 5. No deed is concealed, &c. Cf. Jer. xvi. 17; Ecclus. xvii. 15. 6. Cf. Rom. viii. 35; 2 Cor. xi. 27; 2 Pet. 1. 4. 7. Cf. lxv. 8. 8. Sweetnesses, &c. Eth. En. lxix. 8.

the bitternesses, the paradise, the tortures, * the fires, the frosts and other things[1]; * I have put[2] all this down in writing, that ye may read and understand.

[*The Lord sent a Darkness upon the Earth, and covered the People and Enoch; and he was taken up on high; and there was Light in the Heavens.*]

LXVII. 1. When Enoch had discoursed with the people, the Lord sent a darkness upon the earth, and there was a gloom, and it hid those men standing[3] with Enoch.   2. And * the angels hasted and took Enoch and carried him[4] to the highest heaven where the Lord[5] received him, and set him before * His face[6], and the darkness departed from the earth, and there was light.   3. And the people saw and did not understand, how Enoch was taken, and they glorified God.   And they * who had seen such things[7] departed[8] to their houses[9].

LXVIII. 1. Enoch was born on the sixth day of the month Tsivan[10] | he lived 365 years.   He was taken up into heaven on the first day of the month Tsivan[11], and he was in heaven sixty days.   2. He wrote down the descriptions of all the creation which the Lord had made, and he wrote 366 books, and gave them to his sons.   3. And he was on earth

---

- [1] Sok. om.   [2] Put, A.
LXVII. [3] A. adds and talking.   [4] They took him, A.   [5] A adds is and they.   [6] The face of the Lord, A.   [7] Sok. om. A reads Found the roll in which was the instruction concerning the invisible God and they.   [8] A adds all.   [9] B adds and concludes with to our God be glory for ever, Amen.
LXVIII. [10] Pamorus, Sok.   [11] Nisan, Sok.

LXVII. 2. Highest heaven. This is an exceptional privilege; for Paradise in the third heaven is the eternal abode of the righteous. See

LV. 2. In Asc. Is. ix. 7 the seventh heaven is represented as the future habitation of the righteous.

thirty days[1], and thus he was taken to heaven in the same[2] month Tsivan[3] on the * same day the[2] sixth day; the day on which he was born, and the same hour.   4. As each man has * but a dark existence[4] in this life, so also is his beginning * and birth[5], and departure from this life. In what hour he began; in that he was born, and in that he departs.   5. And Methusalem hasted, and all[5] his brethren[6], the sons of Enoch, and built an altar in the place called Achuzan, * whence and when Enoch[7] was taken up * to heaven[5].   6. And they took[8] cattle, and invited all the people and sacrificed victims[9] before the face of the Lord. 7. * All the people came and the elders of the people; all the host of them to the festivity, and brought their gifts to the sons of Enoch, and made a great festivity, rejoicing and being merry for three days; praising God who had given such a sign by means of Enoch, who had found favour with Him. And that they should hand it down to their son's sons, from generation to generation, for ever. Amen[5].

---

[1] Sok. adds **having spoken with them.**   [2] A om.   [3] **Pamorus,** Sok.
[4] **An equal nature,** Sok.   [5] Sok. om.   [6] Sok. adds **and all.**   [7] **Where,** Sok.
[8] Sok. adds **animals and.**   [9] **Victim,** Sok.

APPENDIX.

THE following fragment of the Melchizedekian literature was found by Professor Sokolov in the chief MS. on which he has based his text. In this MS. it is given as an organic factor of the Slavonic Enoch. This is done by omitting all the words in A lxviii. 7, after 'merry for three days,' and then as we see below immediately proceeding 'And on the third day,' &c. No hint of this large addition is found in A or B, but Sokolov writes that it appears in several MSS. to which he had access. The reader will observe that in many passages it implies the Slavonic Enoch. The text is obviously corrupt in many places.

We have in this fragment a new form of the Melchizedek myth. For the other forms it took see Bible Dictionaries *in loc.* This fragment seems to be the work of an early Christian heretic as we may infer from iii. 34 ; iv. 8.

I. 1. And on the third day at the time of the evening the elders of the people spake to Methusalam saying : 'Stand before the face of the Lord, and before the face of all the people, and before the face of the altar of the Lord, and thou shalt be glorified among the people.' 2. And Methusalam answered his people : 'Wait, O men, until the Lord God of my father Enoch—shall himself raise up to himself, a priest over his people.' 3. And the people waited yet a night to no purpose on the place Akhuzan. 4. And Methusalam was near the altar, and prayed to the Lord and said, 'Oh ! only Lord of all the world, who hast taken my father Enoch, do thou raise up a priest for thy people, and teach their hearts to fear thy glory, and to do all according to thy will. 5. And Methusalam slept, and the Lord appeared to him in a nightly vision, and said to him 'Listen, Methusalam, I am the Lord God of thy father Enoch, hear the voice of this people, and stand before My altar and I will glorify thee before the face of all the people, and thou shalt be glorified all the days of thy life.' 6. And Methusalam arose from his sleep, and blessed the Lord who had appeared to him.   7. And the elders of the people hastened to Methusalam and the Lord God inclined the heart of Methusalam to hear the voice of the people, and he said: 'The Lord God gives His blessing upon all these people before my eyes to-day. (May the Lord your God) do what is a good thing in His eyes to this people.'   8. And Sarsan and Kharmis, and Zazus, the elders of the people hastened and clothed Methusalam in beautiful garments and placed a bright crown on his head.   9. And the people hastened, and brought sheep and cattle and of birds all that was known (to be proper for) Methusalam to sacrifice before the face of the Lord, and in the name (before the face) of the people.   10. And Methusalam went out to the altar of the Lord, and his face shone like the sun, as it is rising in the day, and all the people were following after him.   11. And Methusalam stood before the altar of the Lord, and all the people stood round the altar.   12. And the elders of the people took sheep, and oxen, and bound their four feet, and laid them on the top of the altar, and said to Methusalam ;   13. 'Lift the knife and kill them according to the proper way before the face of the Lord.'   14. And Methusalam stretched out his hands to the heavens and called to the Lord, saying thus: ' Woe is me, O Lord! who am I to stand at the head of Thy altar and at the head of these people.   15. Now, Lord, look down on Thy servant and on all these people. Now let all the things sought for happen and give a blessing to Thy servant before the face of all the people, that they may understand that thou hast appointed a priest over Thy people.   16. And it came to pass that when Methusalam had prayed, the altar shook, and a knife rose from the altar, and leaped into the hand of Methusalam before the face of all the people. And the people trembled, and glorified the Lord.   17. And Methusalam was honoured before the face of the Lord, and before the face of all the people from that day.   18. And Methusalam took the knife, and killed every thing that was brought by the people. And they rejoiced, and were merry before the face of the Lord and before the face of Methusalam on that day.   19. And afterwards the people departed each to his own house.

II. 1. Methusalam began to stand at the altar before the face of the Lord and all the people from that day for ten years, trusting in an eternal inheritance, and having taught well the whole land and all his people ; and no man was found to turn from the Lord in vanity during all the days in which Methusalam lived.   2. And the Lord blessed Methusalam and was pleased with his sacrifices, and his gifts and all his services which he served before the face of the Lord. 3. And when the time of the days of the departure of Methusalam took place, and the Lord appeared to him in a nightly vision, and said to him: 'Listen, Methusalam! I am the Lord God of thy father Enoch, I order thee to see, how the days of thy life are finished, and the day of thy rest has drawn near. 4. Call Nir, the son of thy son Lamech, the second, born after Noah, and clothe him in the robes of thy consecration, and place him by my altar, and tell him all that shall be in his days, because the time of the destruction of the whole earth draws near, and of every man and every living thing upon the earth. 5. For in his days there shall be a very great confusion upon the earth, because a man has been envious of his neighbour, and people have become inflamed against people and nation stirs up war against nation, and all the earth is filled with foulness and blood, and every kind of evil. 6. And moreover in addition they deserted their Maker, and have bowed down to vain gods, and to the firmament of heaven, and the course of the earth and the waves of the sea. And the adversary is multiplied and rejoices in his deeds to My great vexation. 7. And all the earth changes its form, and every tree and every fruit changes its seeds, expecting the time of destruction. And all peoples are changing upon the earth to My grief. 8. Then I shall command the abysses to pour themselves upon the earth, and the great treasuries of the waters of heaven shall come upon the earth in their nature and according to their first nature. 9. And all the stability of the earth shall perish and all the earth shall tremble and shall be deprived of its strength from that day. 10. Then I will preserve the son of thy son Lamech, his first son Noe and from his seed I will raise up another world, and his seed shall exist for ever till the second destruction when also men shall sin before my face. 11. Methusalam leaped up from his sleep and his dream troubled him greatly. And he called all the elders of the people and told them all that the Lord had said to him, and all the vision that had appeared to him from the Lord. 12. And the people were grieved at his vision, and answered him : 'Let the Lord God do according to his will! And now, Methusalam, accomplish thou all things which the Lord enjoined thee.' 13. And Methusalam called Nir, the son of Lamech, the younger brother of Noe, and clothed him in the robes of the priesthood before the face of all the people, and placed him at the head of the altar, and taught him all that he was to do among the people. 14. And

Methusalam called to the people : ' Lo ! Nir will be before your face from to-day as a prince and a leader.' 15. And the people said to Methusalam, ' Let it be unto us according to thy word, and let the voice of the Lord be as He spoke to thee.' 16. And when Methusalam had spoken to the people before the altar, his spirit was confused, and he bent his knees, and stretched out his hands to the heavens, and prayed to God. And as he prayed his spirit went forth to the Lord. 17. And Nir and all the people made haste and made a grave for Methusalam in the place Aruzan. 18. And Nir came in glorious attire in all his priestly robes, with lights, with much pomp, and the people lifted up the body of Methusalam, and having glorified it, laid it in the grave, which they had made for him, and buried him, and said : ' Blessed was Methusalam before the face of the Lord, and before the face of all people.' 19. When they were about to depart to their own households, Nir said to the people : ' Go quickly now, and bring sheep and heifers, and turtle-doves, and pigeons, and let us offer them before the face of the Lord, and then go to your houses.' 20. And the people listened to Nir the priest, and hastened and brought the victims, and bound them to the head of the altar. 21. And Nir took the sacrificial knife, and slew all the [victims] that were brought, and offered them before the face of the Lord. 22. And all the people rejoiced before the face of the Lord, and glorified on that day the Lord of Nir, the ruler of heaven and earth. From that day there was peace and order over the whole earth in the days of Nir, during 202 years. 23. And then the people turned from God and began to be jealous one of another, and people rebelled against people, and tongue arose against tongue, in reviling. 24. And if lips were the same, hearts chose different things. 25. And then the devil began to reign for the third time, the first time before paradise, the second time in paradise, the third time outside of paradise, he continued (doing so) till the deluge. 26. And there arose a great dispute and confusion. And Nir the priest heard it, and was greatly grieved, and said in his heart, ' In truth I have understood that the time has drawn near, and the end which the Lord spake to Methusalam, the father of my father Lamech.

III. 1. And the wife of Nir, named Sopanima, being barren, brought forth no child to Nir. 2. And Sopanima was in the time of her old age, and on the day of her death she conceived in her womb, and Nir the priest did not sleep with her, nor knew her from the day that the Lord appointed him to serve before the face of the people.   3. When Sopanima knew of her conception she was ashamed, and felt humbled, and concealed herself all the days, till she brought forth, and no one of the people knew.   4. And when 282 days were accomplished and the day of birth began to draw near, Nir remembered about his wife, and called her to himself in his house, that he might talk to her.   5. And Sopanima came to Nir, her husband, being with child, and the appointed day of the birth was drawing near.   6. And Nir saw her and was very much ashamed, and said to her: ' What hast thou done, wife, and hast shamed me before the face of these people. And now depart from me, and go where thou didst commence the shame of thy womb, so that I defile not my hand upon thee, and sin before the face of the Lord ! '   7. And Sopanima spake unto Nir, her husband, saying : ' My lord, lo ! the time of my old age, and the day of my death has come (and there was no youth in me) and I do not know when the period of my years is past, and the unfruitfulness of my womb begin.'   8. And Nir did not believe his wife, and said to her a second time: ' Depart from me lest I do thee an injury, and sin before the face of the Lord ! '   9. And it came to pass, when Nir had spoken to his wife, Sopanima fell at the feet of Nir, and died.   10. And Nir was very much grieved, and said in his heart : ' Was this from my voice, since a man by his voice and thought sins before the face of the Lord. 11. Now the Lord is merciful to me ; I know in truth in my heart, that my hand was not upon her.   And so I say : '' Glory to thee, oh ! Lord, since no one on earth knows this deed, which the Lord has wrought ! '' '   12. And Nir hastened and shut the doors of the house, and went to Noe, his brother, and told him all, that had happened concerning his wife.   13. And Noe hastened, and came with Nir, his brother, into the house of Nir, on account of the death of Sopanima, and they talked to themselves (and saw) how her womb was at the time of the birth.   14. And Noe said to Nir : ' Let it not be a subject of sorrow to thee, Nir, my brother, that the Lord has to-day concealed our shame because no one of the people knows this.   15. Now let us go quickly, and bring her secretly, and may the Lord hide the ignominy of our shame. 16. And they laid Sopanima on the bed, and they wrapped her with black robes, and shut her in the house ready for burial, and dug a grave in secret.   17. And then came an infant from the dead Sopanima, and sat on the bed at her right hand.   And Noe, and Nir entered, and saw the infant sitting by the dead Sopanima

and wiping its clothes.   18. And Noe, and Nir were tempted
with a great fear, for the child was complete in its body, like one
of three years old; and spake with its lips, and blessed the Lord.
19. And Noe, and Nir gazed upon it; and lo! the seal of the
priesthood was on its breast, and it was glorious in countenance.
20. And Noe, and Nir said ' See the Lord renews the consecration
according to our blood, as he desires (this is from the Lord, my
brother, and the Lord renews the blood of consecration in us).'
21. And Noe and Nir hastened, and washed the child, and clothed
it in priestly raiment, and gave it the blessed bread. And it
ate. And they called its name Melchizedek.   22. And Noe
and Nir took the body of Sopanima, and stripped from her the
black robes, and clothed her in very bright robes, and built a
church for her (another house—a beautified grave).   23. And
Noe, and Nir, and Melchizedek came and buried her publicly. And
Noe said to his brother Nir : ' Watch this child in secret till the
time, because deceitful people shall arise over all the earth and shall
begin to reject God, and having perceived nothing shall put him
to death. And then Noe went out to his own place.   24. And
great lawlessness began to multiply over the whole earth, in the
days of Nir.   25. And Nir began to be very anxious, especially
about the child, saying : ' Woe is me, eternal Lord. In my days
have begun to multiply all kinds of lawlessness upon the earth, and
I understand, how that the end is near unto us more (than ever), and
upon all the earth for the lawlessness of the people.   26. And now,
Lord, what is the vision, and what is the solution of it, and what
shall I do for (the child) ?—Will it also go with us to destruction ? '
27. And the Lord heard Nir, and appeared to him in a nightly
vision, and said to him : ' Nir, I do not endure the great lawlessness that has been on the earth in many things, and lo! I wish
now to send a great destruction upon the earth, and every earthly
creature shall perish.   28. But do not trouble thyself about the
child, Nir, for in a short time I will send my chief captain Michael,
and he shall take the child and place him in the paradise of Eden,
in the garden where Adam was formerly during a period of seven
years, having the heaven always open until the time of his sin.
29. And this child shall not perish with those who perish in this
generation, as I have shown, but shall be a holy priest in all things,
Melchizedek, and I will appoint him that he may be the chief of
the priests who were before (*alia lectio*—that he may be a priest
of priests for ever, and I will consecrate him, and will appoint
him over the people being made greatly holy).   30. And

Nir rose from his sleep, and blessed the Lord, who had appeared unto him, saying : ' Blessed is the Lord God of my fathers, who has spoken unto me, (*some MSS. add*—who will not allow the depreciation of my priesthood in the priesthood of my fathers, as thy word), who made a great priest in my days in the womb of my wife Sopanima. (*Some MSS. add*—31. Because I had no family and this child shall be to me in the place of my family, and shall be as a son to me, and thou shalt honour him with Thy servants the priests, with Seth, and Enoch, and Tharasidam, Maleleil, and Enos, and thy servant, and thus Melchizedek shall be a priest in another generation. 32. For I know that this generation shall end in confusion, and all shall perish. And Noe, my brother, shall be preserved in that day. 33. And from my race shall rise up many people, and Melchizedek shall be the chief of the priests among the people, ruling alone, serving thee O Lord !) 34. Because I had not another child in this family, who might be a great priest, but this son of mine, and thy servant ; and do thou great Lord, on this account honour him with thy servants, and great priests—with Seth, and Enos, and Rusii, and Almilam, and Prasidam, and Maleleil, and Seroch, and Arusan, and Aleem, and Enoch, and Methusalam, and me, thy servant Nir, and Melchizedek shall be the head over twelve priests who lived before, and at last shall be the head over all, (being) the great high priest, the Word of God, and the power to work great and glorious marvels above all that have been. 35. He, Melchizedek, shall be a priest and king in the place Akhuzan, that is to say, in the middle of the earth where Adam was created : there shall at last be his grave. 36. And concerning that chief priest it has been written that he also shall be buried there, where there is the middle of the earth, as Adam buried his son Abel there whom his brother Cain killed, wherefore he lay three years unburied, till he saw a bird called a jackdaw, burying its fledgling. 37. I know that a great confusion has come and this generation shall end in confusion, and all shall perish except that Noe my brother shall be preserved, and afterwards there shall be a planting from his family, and there shall be other people, and another Melchizedek shall be the head of the priests among the people, ruling, and serving the Lord.'

IV. 1. And when the child had been forty days under the roof of Nir, the Lord said to Michael :- ' Go down upon the earth to Nir, the priest, and take My child Melchizedek, who is with him,

and place him in the paradise of Eden for preservation, because
the time draws nigh, and I will discharge all the water upon the
earth, and all that is upon the earth shall perish.   2. (And I
will establish another race, and Melchizedek shall be the chief of
the priests, in that family, just as Seth is to me in this family[1].')
3. And Michael hastened, and came by night, and Nir was sleeping
in his bed.   And Michael appeared to him, and said to him: ' The
Lord says unto thee, Nir : "Send the child to me ; I entrusted him
to thee." '   4. And Nir did not know that the chief captain
Michael was speaking to him, and his heart was confused, and he
said: ' If the people know about the child, and take him, they will
slay him.   For the heart of this people is crafty before the face of
the Lord.   And Nir said to him who spoke to him ' The child is
not with me, and I do not know who thou art, who art speaking
to me.'   5. And he who was speaking to me answered : 'Be not
afraid, Nir, I am the chief captain of the Lord.   The Lord hath
sent me, and lo! I will take thy child to-day, and will go with
him, and will place him in the paradise of Eden, and there shall
he be for ever.   6. And when the twelfth generation shall be, and
a thousand and seventy years shall be, in that generation a just
man shall be born, and the Lord shall tell him to come out upon
that mountain where the ark of thy brother Noe shall stand, and
he shall find there another Melchizedek who has lived there seven
years, concealing himself from the people who worship idols, so that
they should not slay him, and he shall lead him forth and he shall
be priest, and the first king in the town of Salem after the fashion
of this Melchizedek, the commencement of the priests.   And
3432 years shall be fulfilled till that time from the beginning and
creation of Adam.   7. And from that Melchizedek there shall
be twelve priests in number till the great Igumen, that is to say
leader, who shall bring forth all things visible and invisible.
8. And Nir understood his first dream, and believed it, and having
answered Michael, he said : ' Blessed is the Lord, who has glorified
thee to-day to me, and now bless thy servant Nir, as we are drawing near our departure from this world, and take the child, and do
unto him as the Lord hath spoken unto thee.   . 9. And Michael
took the child on that night on which he came, and took him on
his wings, and placed him in the paradise of Eden.   10. And
Nir having risen on the following day, went to his house, and did
not find the child, and there was instead of joy very great sorrow,
because he had no other son except this (*alia lectio*—because he

---

[1] Clearly a variant of iii. 37.

looked upon this child in the place of a son). 11. So died Nir, and after him there was no priest among the people. And from that time a great confusion arose on the earth.

V. 1. And God called Noe on the mountain of Ararat, between Assyria, and Armenia, in the land of Arabia, by the sea, and said to him: 'Make there an ark of 300 ells in length, and in breadth 50 ells, and in height 30, and two stories in the midst, and the doors about an ell. 2. And of those 300 ells, and of ours 15,000, and so of those 50, and of ours 2000 and 500, and so of those 30, and of ours 900, and of those one ell, and of ours 50.' 3. According to this number the Jews keep this measure of the ark of Noe, as the Lord said to him, and (so) they make each measure, and each rule even up to the present time. 4. The Lord God opened the doors of the heavens, and rain came on the earth 150 days, and all flesh died. 5. Noe was in the 500th year and begat three sons: Shem, Ham, and Japhet. 6. 100 years after the birth of his three sons, he went into the ark in the month according to the Hebrew Itsars, according to the Egyptian Famenoth in eighteen days. 7. And the ark floated forty days. And altogether they were in the ark 120 days. 8. And he went into the ark, being 600 years (old), and in the sixth hundred and first year of his life he went out of the ark in the month Farmut according to the Egyptians, and according to the Hebrews Nisan about twenty-eight days. 9. Then he lived 250 years, and died; he lived altogether 950 years according [to the will of] the Lord our God, to him be glory from the beginning, and now, and to the end of the world. Amen. 10. Enoch was altogether 365 years old.

11. In another way it is written here concerning Noah's ark. Of their 300 ells, and of ours 15,000, of theirs 100, and of ours 5000: of theirs 20, and of ours 1000; of theirs 10, and of ours 500: of theirs 5, and of ours 250: of theirs 1, and of ours 50! This is the truth spoken.

ADDITIONAL NOTE ON THE PHOENIXES.

WHEN I wrote the note on the Phoenixes in XII. 1 I was not aware that mention of a class of these birds was to be found elsewhere. I have, however, since found in Dr. Kohler's article on 'The pre-Talmudic Haggada' (*Jewish Quarterly*, 1893, pp. 399-419) a quotation from an old Essene Mishna—*Massecheth Derech Eretz*—in which it is said that 'the generation of the bird מלחם' went alive into Paradise. This bird Dr. Kohler identifies with the Phoenix. The question is discussed in the *Alphabetum Siracidis* edited by Steinschneider, 1858, p. 28ᵇ.

INDEX I.

PASSAGES FROM THE SCRIPTURES AND ANCIENT WRITERS
CONNECTED OR CLOSELY PARALLEL WITH THE TEXT.

— ✦ —

INDEX II.

NAMES AND SUBJECTS.

———◆———

(When thick type is used in this Index, it is to indicate that the subject in
question is specially dealt with under the reference so given.)

THE END.

THE

APOCALYPSE OF BARUCH

TRANSLATED FROM THE SYRIAC

CHAPTERS I.-LXXVII. FROM THE SIXTH CENT. MS. IN
THE AMBROSIAN LIBRARY OF MILAN

AND

CHAPTERS LXXVIII.-LXXXVII.—THE EPISTLE OF BARUCH
FROM A NEW AND CRITICAL TEXT BASED ON TEN
MSS. AND PUBLISHED HEREWITH

EDITED, WITH INTRODUCTION, NOTES, AND INDICES

BY

R. H. CHARLES, M.A.

TRINITY COLLEGE, DUBLIN, AND EXETER COLLEGE, OXFORD

TO

MY WIFE

PREFACE

THE Apocalypse of Baruch is a composite work written in the latter half of the first century of the Christian era. It is thus contemporaneous with the chief writings of the New Testament. Its authors were orthodox Jews, and it is a good representative of the Judaism against which the Pauline dialectic was directed.

In this Apocalypse we have almost the last noble utterance of Judaism before it plunged into the dark and oppressive years that followed the destruction of Jerusalem. For ages after that epoch its people seem to have been bereft of their immemorial gifts of song and eloquence, and to have had thought and energy only for the study and expansion of the traditions of the Fathers. But when our book was written, that evil and barren era had not yet set in; breathing thought and burning word had still their home in Palestine, and the hand of the Jewish artist was still master of its ancient cunning.

And yet the intrinsic beauty of this book must to a great degree fail to strike the casual reader. Indeed, it could hardly be otherwise. For the present English version is a translation of the Syriac; the Syriac was a translation of the Greek, and the Greek in turn a translation from the Hebrew original. In each translation we may feel assured the original work was shorn in large and growing measure of its ancient vigour, and this is certainly the case in the version now before the reader. For the translator, having the interests of scholars before his eyes, has made it his aim to give a literal reproduction of the Syriac. And yet, even so, much of its native eloquence has survived, so that to be prized it needs only to be known, and our appreciation of its beauty, its tragic power and worth, must grow in the measure of our acquaintance with it.

The Apocalypse of Baruch has had a strange history. Written by Pharisaic Jews as an apology for Judaism, and in part an implicit polemic against Christianity, it gained nevertheless a larger circulation amongst Christians than amongst Jews, and owed its very preservation to the scholarly cares of the Church it assailed. But in the struggle for life its secret animus against Christianity begat an instinctive opposition in Christian circles, and so proved a bar to its popularity. Thus the place it would naturally have filled was taken by the sister work, 4 Ezra. This latter work having been written in some degree under Christian influences, and forming, in fact, an unconscious confession of the failure of Judaism to redeem the world, was naturally more acceptable to Christian readers, and thus, in due course, the Apocalypse of Baruch was elbowed out of recognition by its fitter and sturdier rival.

In this edition of Baruch — which is also the *editio princeps*—no pains have been spared as regards the criticism and emendation of the text, its interpretation, and the determination of its various sources.

As regards the text, the facts are briefly as follows: The first seventy-seven chapters, as appears on the title-page, are found only in one MS., namely, *c*. For the concluding nine chapters—the Epistle of Baruch —I have made use of *c* and nine other MSS. Of these I have collated eight—several of these for the first time. Through the kindness of the publishers I have been enabled to print on pp. 125-167 a critical text of this Epistle based on those MSS. As Ceriani and Lagarde contented themselves each with reproducing a single unamended MS., scholars will, I think, be grateful for this attempt to grapple with all the Syriac MSS. available. By this comparative study of *c* and the remaining nine MSS. in the chapters common to both, I have been able to ascertain the value of *c* in the chapters in which *c* stands alone. The trustworthiness of the MS. *c*, which we have thus established, is further confirmed by a Greek work, which borrows largely from our Apocalypse, the Rest of the Words of Baruch.

There are, of course, corruptions in the text. Some of these that are native to the Syriac have been

removed by Ceriani, others by the editor; others are
provisionally emended, or else reproduced in the
English translation. But many still remain. Of
these some are manifestly peculiar to the Greek,
and have been dealt with accordingly. But the rest
are not so, and are, in fact, incapable of explanation
save on the hypothesis of a Hebrew original. To
this hypothesis, which marks a new departure in the
criticism of this book, I have been irresistibly led in
the course of my study. In many passages I have
by its means been able to reduce chaos to order.
For details the reader should consult the Introduction,
pp. xliv.-liii.

The interpretation of this book has been the
severest task as yet undertaken by the editor.
Insuperable difficulties confronted on every side, till
at last he awoke to the fact that these were due to
plurality of authorship. When once this fact was
recognised and the various sources determined, the
task of interpretation was materially lightened, and
the value of the work for New Testament and Jewish
scholars became every day more manifest. As my
studies in this direction began in 1891, my conclusions
are, save in a few cases, the result of long study and
slowly matured conviction.

A special study of the relations subsisting between
this Apocalypse and 4 Ezra will be found on pp.
lxvii.-lxxvi., where it is shown that whereas 4 Ezra is
in many respects non-Jewish, our Apocalypse is a
faithful exponent of the orthodox Judaism of the

time. To this subject I may return in an edition of the former work.

Scholars are at last coming to recognise that the study of the literature to which this book belongs is indispensable for the interpretation of the New Testament. Thus Dr. Sanday and Mr. Headlam write in their recent work on the Epistle to the Romans (p. vii.): "*It is by a continuous and careful study of such works that any advance in the exegesis of the New Testament will be possible.*"

My knowledge of Talmudic literature, so far as it appears in this book, is derived from Weber's *Lehren des Talmuds*, Edersheim's *Life and Times*, etc., Wunsche's translations of the various treatises of the Babylonian Talmud, Schwab's French translation of the Jerusalem Talmud, and in passages where translations were wanting, I had the ready help of Dr. Neubauer.

My thanks are also due to Mr. Buchanan Gray, for his revision of my proofs of the Hebrew original of Baruch.

17 BRADMORE ROAD, OXFORD,
        September 1896.

CONTENTS

PAGE

tiated from each other by many characteristics. B¹ is the
earliest—soon after 70 A.D., and B³ is probably the latest.
B¹=i.-ix. 1 ; xliii.-xliv. 7 ; xlv.-xlvi. 6 ; lxxvii.-lxxxii. ;
lxxxiv. ; lxxxvi.-lxxxvii. B²=xiii.-xxv. ; xxx. 2-xxxv. ;
xli.-xlii. ; xliv. 8-15 ; xlvii.-lii. ; lxxv.-lxxvi. ; lxxxiii.
B³=lxxxv. x. 6-xii. 4, which I have called S, is probably
from a source distinct from the rest (pp. lviii.-lxv.)—§ 8. The
lost Epistle to the two and a half Tribes, on many grounds
is probably identical with, or is the source of the Greek
Baruch iii. 9-iv. 29 (pp. lxv.-lxvii.)—§ 9. The Relations of
our Apocalypse with 4 Ezra. (a) The composite nature of 4
Ezra. (b) Conflicting characteristics of 4 Ezra and Baruch,
the former to some extent non-Jewish in its teaching on
the Law, Works, Justification, Original Sin and Freewill.
(c) 4 Ezra from a Hebrew Original. (d) Relations of the
respective Constituents of our Apocalypse and 4 Ezra. A¹
is older than E of 4 Ezra, and both A¹ and A² than M. B¹
older than E², and both B¹ and B² than S (pp. lxvii.-lxxvi.)—
§ 10. Relation of this Apocalypse to the New Testament.
Bulk of parallels in these books can be explained as being
drawn independently from pre-existing literature, or as
being commonplaces of the time ; but others may point to
dependence of Baruch on the New Testament (pp. lxxvi.-
lxxix.)—§ 11. Value of our Apocalypse in the Attestation
of the Jewish Theology of 50-100 A.D., and in the Interpretation of Christian Theology for the same Period : The
Resurrection, Original Sin and Freewill, Works and
Justification, Forgiveness (pp. lxxix.-lxxxiv.)

INTRODUCTION

§ 1. Short Account of the Book

This beautiful Apocalypse, with the exception of nine chapters towards its close,[1] was lost sight of for quite 1200 years.

Written originally in Hebrew, it was early translated into Greek, and from Greek into Syriac. Of the Hebrew original every line has perished save a few still surviving in rabbinic writings. Of the Greek Version nothing has come down to us directly, though portions of it are preserved in the Rest of the Words of Baruch, a Greek work of the second century, and in a late Apocalypse of Baruch recently discovered in Greek and in Slavonic. Happily, the Syriac has been preserved almost in its entirety in a sixth century MS., the discovery of which we owe to the distinguished Italian scholar Ceriani. Of this MS., Ceriani published a Latin translation in 1866, the Syriac text in 1871, and the photo-lithographic facsimile in 1883. Though

---

[1] These chapters under the title "The Epistle of Baruch," or a similar one, were incorporated in the later Syriac Bible.

there are no adequate grounds for assuming a Latin
Version, it is demonstrable that our Apocalypse was
the foundation of a Latin Apocalypse of Baruch, a
fragment of which is preserved in Cyprian.

The Apocalypse of Baruch belongs to the first
century of our era. It is a composite work put
together about the close of the century, from at least
five or six independent writings. These writings
belong to various dates between 50 and 90 A.D., and
are thus contemporaneous with the chief New Testament writings. It is this fact that constitutes the
chief value of the work. We have here contemporaneous records of the Jewish doctrines and beliefs, and
of the arguments which prevailed in Judaism in the
latter half of the first century, and with which its
leaders sought to uphold its declining faith and con-
front the attacks of a growing and aggressive Christianity.

Over against many of the Pauline solutions of the
religious problems of the day, Jewish answers are here
propounded which are frequently antagonistic in the
extreme. It was this hidden hostility to Christianity
that no doubt brought it into discredit. As early
as the sixth century it seems to have passed out of
circulation.

§ 2. OTHER BOOKS OF BARUCH

In addition to our Apocalypse, a considerable literature arose and circulated under Baruch's name, some-

time before and after the Christian era. It will be
sufficient for our present purpose to touch briefly
on the different books belonging to it.

1. The Apocryphal Baruch in the LXX.—This book
falls clearly into two parts—i.-iii. 8 being the first part,
and iii. 9-v. constituting the second. The first part
was originally written in Hebrew, the second is generally held to be of Greek origin, but this is doubtful.
The first part of the book is said by Ewald and
Marshall to have been composed three centuries before
the Christian era, by Fritzsche and Schrader in the
Maccabean period, by Kneucker and Schürer after
70 A.D. Most writers agree in assigning the second
half of the book to the last - mentioned date. The
second half, however, may also be composite. Thus
Professor Marshall differentiates iii. 9 - iv. 4 from
iv. 5-v. 9, and regards the former as originally written
in Aramaic, and the latter in Greek. The chief authorities on this book are Fritzsche, *Exeget. Handbuch zu
den Apocryphen,* part i., pp. 165-202, 1851; Kneucker,
Das Buch Baruch, 1879; Gifford, *Speaker's Commentary,
Apocrypha,* ii. 241-286, 1888. On the probability
that i. 1-3 ; iii. 9-iv. 29 of this book are a recast of a
lost portion of our Apocalypse, *i.e.* "the Letter to the
two and a half Tribes," see § 8, pp. lxv.-lxvii. There
is no verbal borrowing between our Apocalypse and
and the Greek Baruch, but in the following passages
there is a similarity of diction or of thought or of both.
This list could be enlarged.

Apoc. of Baruch.	Book of Baruch.
i. 1 (mention of Jeconiah).	i. 3.
x. 16.	iv. 10, 14.
lix. 7.	iii. 12.
lxxvii. 10.	ii. 26.
lxxviii. 7.	iv. 36, 37 (v. 5, 6).
lxxix. 2.	i. 17, 18.
lxxx. 5.	ii. 13.
lxxxiv. 2-5.	i. 19 ; ii. 2.
lxxxvi. 1, 2.	i. 14.

2. The Rest of the Words of Baruch.—This book was written in Greek in the second century of our era. It seems in parts to be a Jewish work recast. The Greek text was ·first printed at Venice in 1609, next by Ceriani in 1868 under the title " Paralipomena Jeremiae" in his *Monumenta Sacra*, v. 11-18, and recently it has been critically edited by Rendel Harris in 1889. This book exists also in the Ethiopic Bible. The Ethiopic Version was edited from three MSS. by Dillmann in his *Chrestomathia aethiopica* in 1866. As these MSS. are inferior, and as no attempt was made by Dillmann to revise his text by means of the Greek, the present writer hopes in due time to edit a critical text from eleven Ethiopic MSS., accompanied with translation and notes. In this edition account will be taken of all the important variations of the Greek text.

This book is deeply indebted to our Apocalypse and attests the accuracy of the Syriac text in the following passages :—

Apoc. Bar.	Rest of the Words.
ii. 1.	i. 1, 3, 7.
ii. 2.	ii. 2.
v. 1.	i. 5 ; ii. 7 ; iii. 6 ; iv. 7.
vi. 1.	iv. 1.
vi. 4, 5, 6, 8, 10.	iii. 2, 5, 8, 14.
viii. 2, 5.	iv. 1, 2, 3, 4.
x. 2, 5, 6, 7, 18.	iv. 3, 4, 6, 9.
xi. 4, 5.	iv. 9.
xxxv. 2.	ii. 4.
lxxvii. 21, 23, 26.	vii. 3, 10, 12.
lxxx. 3.	i. 5 ; iv. 7.
lxxxv. 2.	ii. 3.
lxxxv. 11.	vi. 3.
lxxxvii.	vii. 8, 30.

3. The Gnostic book of Baruch.—Of this book large fragments are found in the *Philosophumena of Hippolytus*, v. 24-27. But these fragments are wholly out of relation with the remaining literature of Baruch.

4. A Latin book of Baruch is quoted in one MS. of Cyprian's *Testimonia*, iii. 29. As this book is clearly based on our Apocalypse, I will give the passage in full. Item in Baruch: "Veniet enim tempus, et quaeretis me et vos et qui post vos venerint, audire verbum sapientiae et intellectus, et non invenietis" (cf. Apoc. Bar. xlviii. 36). "Nationes autem cupient videre sapientem praedicantem, et non obtinget eis: non quia deerit aut deficiet sapientia hujus saeculi terrae, sed neque deerit sermo legis saeculo. Erit enim sapientia in paucis vigilantibus et taciturnis et quietis" (cf. Apoc. Bar. xlviii. 33), "sibi confabulantes et in cordibus suis meditantes

quoniam quidam eos horrebunt et timebunt ut malos.
Alii autem nec credunt verbo legis Altissimi : alii
autem ore stupentes non credent et credentibus erunt
contrarii et impedientes spiritum veritatis. Alii autem
erunt sapientes ad spiritum erroris et pronuntiantes
sicut Altissimi et Fortis edicta" (cf. Apoc. Bar. xlviii.
34 ; lxx. 5 ; observe also that the titles of God here
are characteristic of our Apoc., see vii. 1, note; xxi. 3,
note).   " Alii autem personales fidei.   Alii capaces et
fortes in fide Altissimi et odibiles alieno."

In 5 Ezra xvi. 64, 65 (which James ascribes to
the third century) we have a clear use of our text.
Thus: "Certe Hic novit . . . quae cogitatis in cordibus
vestris. Vae peccantibus et volentibus occultare peccata
sua : propter quod Dominus scrutinando scrutinabit
omnia opera eorum et traducet vos omnes," is based on
lxxxiii. 3, which = " Et scrutinando scrutinabit cogitationes arcanas et quidquid in penetralibus omnium
hominis membrorum positum est et in apertum coram
omnibus cum increpatione educet."   We should observe
that not only is the thought of the two passages the
same, but that the actual diction is borrowed, *i.e.* the
Hebraism " scrutinando scrutinabit " and " traducet,"
which = " in apertum cum increpatione educet " (cf.
also "quae cogitatis in cordibus " with " cogitationes
arcanas ").

5. The Greek Apocalypse of Baruch, or, as Mr.
James names it, *Apocalypsis Baruch Tertia.*—This
book belongs to the second century, for, on the one
hand, it is based largely on the Slavonic Enoch, and on

the other, it is mentioned by Origen, *de Princip.* ii. 3.
6 : " Denique etiam Baruch prophetae librum in assertionis hujus testimonium vocant, quod ibi de septem
mundis vel caelis evidentius indicatur." This Greek
Apocalypse of Baruch was discovered some years ago
by Mr. James in a British Museum MS. Through
his kindness I have been permitted to examine his
copy of this MS. His edition of the text will, we
believe, shortly appear. The Slavonic Version of this
book has been known for some time, and was published
in the *Starine*, vol. xviii. pp. 205-209, 1886, by Nova-
kovic. A German translation, preceded by a helpful
introduction by Professor Bonwetsch, appeared this
year in the *Nachrichten der K. Gesellschaft der
Wissenschaften zu Göttingen*, 1886, Heft i. An English
translation will shortly appear by Mr. Morfill in Mr.
James's Cambridge edition. The Slavonic is less
trustworthy and full than the Greek. This Greek is
dependent in certain respects on the Rest of the
Words of Baruch, and is thus of service in determining the date of the latter. With our Apocalypse
it has only one or two points of contact. Thus with
vi. 2, " I was grieving over Zion and lamenting over
the captivity which had come upon the people," compare the opening words of the Greek Apocalypse,
Ἀποκάλυψις Βαρούχ, ὃς ἔστη . . . κλαίων ὑπὲρ τῆς
αἰχμαλωσίας Ἰερουσαλήμ : and with x. 5, " I, Baruch,
. . . sat before the gates of the temple and I
lamented with that lamentation over Zion," and xxxv.
1, " And I, Baruch, went to the holy place, and sat

b

down upon the ruins and wept," compare the words
already quoted together with καὶ οὕτως ἐκάθητο ἐπὶ
τὰς ὡραίας πόλας, ὅπου ἔκειτο τὰ τῶν ἁγίων ἅγια.
Perhaps liv. 8-9, " Even so I could not give Thee the
meed of praise, or laud Thee as is befitting. . . . For
what am I amongst men . . . that I should have heard
all those marvellous things from the Most High?"
may be the source of the following words towards the
close of the Greek Apocalypse—δόξαν ἔφερον τῷ θεῷ
τῷ ἀξιώσαντί με τοιούτου ἀξιώματος.

6. Finally, another book of Baruch, distinct from
the above, and belonging to the fourth or fifth century
of our era, is mentioned in the *Altercatio Simonis
Judaei et Theophili Christiani*, published by Harnack
(*Texte und Untersuchungen*, Bd. 1, Heft 3, 1883). In
this work Theophilus makes the following quotation
from the book of Baruch: " Quomodo ergo prope
finem libri sui de nativitate ejus et de habitu vestis et
de passione ejus et de resurrectione ejus prophetavit
dicens: Hic unctus meus, electus meus, vulvae incon-
taminatae jaculatus, natus et passus dicitur."

Above all the foregoing works which circulated
under Baruch's name, the Apocalypse of Baruch stands
head and shoulders alike in respect of form or matter
or real worth to the student of Judaism and Christianity.

§ 3. THE SYRIAC MSS.

For chapters i.-lxxvii. of this book we have only
one MS., the famous sixth-century Peshitto MS. which

was found by Ceriani in the library in Milan. For convenience we shall call this MS. *c.* In 1871 Ceriani edited the Syriac text from this MS. in his *Monumenta Sacra et Profana*, vol. v. Fasc. 2, pp. 113-180. Of chapters lxxviii.-lxxxvi., which constitute the Epistle of Baruch, many MSS. were known to exist, and of three of them (i.e. *a, b, d*) Ceriani made collations and inserted these in their appropriate place below the printed text of *c.* He made no attempt, however, to correct the text of *c* by their means. This task was attempted in a haphazard fashion by Fritzsche (*Libri Apocryphi Vet. Test. Graece*, 1871, pp. 690-699) in an emended edition of Ceriani's Latin translation of these chapters.

It is manifest that, if we wish to ascertain the value of *c* in those chapters in which it stands alone, *i.e.* i.-lxxvii., we can do so only by an exhaustive examination of its text in those chapters which it attests in common with *a, b, d, e, f, g, h, i, k,* i.e. lxxviii.-lxxxvi., and by a determination of its critical value in respect to them. When we have discharged this task we shall know the real worth of *c* in i.-lxxvii., and familiar with its strength and its weakness shall approach with some confidence the critical problems it presents. With this end in view I have made use of all the Syriac MSS. of lxxviii.-lxxxvi. attainable. These are ten, and are as follows :—

a called A in Ceriani.

b Add. 17,105 in the Brit. Mus., Fol. 116ᵃ-121ᵃ. Sixth century.

c The Milan MS., Fol. 265^b-267^b.   Sixth century.

d called d in Ceriani.

e No. 1 Syr. MSS., Bodley, Fol. 430-432.   1627.

f Egerton 704 Brit. Mus., Fol. 373^a-374^a.   Seventeenth century.

g Add. 12,172 Brit. Mus., Fol. 192^b-195^b.   Tenth or eleventh century.

h Add. 18,715 Brit. Mus., Fol. 242^b-244^a.   Twelfth century.

i No. 2 Syr. MSS., Bodley, Fol. 492-493.   1614.

k No. 20 Syr. MSS., Bodley, Fol. 37-38.

All these MSS. with the exception of k contain the complete Epistle of Baruch. k has only lxxxiii. 7-lxxxiv. 1.   Of the ten MSS. I have collated directly b, e, f, g, h, i, k. b had already been collated and published by Lagarde. I did it, however, afresh, and found only one important error in his work. For a knowledge of a, d I am indebted to Ceriani's collations. Of c my knowledge is derived directly from the photo-lithographic reproduction of that MS. In addition to the above MSS., I have found excerpts from the Epistle of Baruch in the three following MSS., from which I have drawn various readings.

l Add. 12,178 Brit. Mus., Fol. 111^b.   Ninth or tenth century.

m 14,482 Brit. Mus., Fol. 47^b-48^a.   Eleventh or twelfth century.

n 14,684 Brit. Mus., Fol. 24.   Twelfth century.

W and P stand for the Walton and Paris Polyglots. Of the foregoing MSS. a, b, d, e, f, g, h, i, k, l, m, n represent one type of text as c represents another. But although the former belong to one family they are of very different values.   To the more ancient and trustworthy belong a, b, g, h, k to the latter and less trustworthy d, e, f, i. For convenience' sake we shall denote the parent of a, b, g, h, k by the symbol β, that of d, e, f, i by γ, and the ancestor of both by a. First of all we shall study the general relations of c to a and to the sub-groups β and γ.

c stands frequently alone alike when it is right and when it is wrong. In lxxviii. 1; lxxxi. 4; lxxxii. 7; lxxxv. 1, 7; lxxxvi. 3; lxxxvii., it is right against a, i.e. a, b, d, e, f, g, h, i; and most probably also in lxxix. 2, 3; lxxxiii. 3, 7, 8; lxxxiv. 1, 9; lxxxv. 15. On the other hand, it is frequently wrong. Thus it attests a corrupt text against a in lxxviii. 1, 2, 3, 4, 7 (?); lxxx. 1, 2, 3; lxxxi. 3; lxxxii. 2 (twice), 3, 4, 5; lxxxiii. 2, 3, 4, 5, 8, 13, 15, 16, 18, 19, 21; lxxxiv. 1, 2, 8, 10; lxxxv. 7, 8, 12, 13; lxxxvi. 1. Thus we see that whereas c independently preserves the true text in many passages, a preserves it in thrice as many.

Again, as we have already remarked, the MSS. $a, b, d, e, f, g, h, i, k$ are of very different values. Thus a, b, g, h agree with c in attesting the true text against d, e, f, i in lxxviii. 3, 5; lxxix. 1; lxxx. 3; lxxxi. 4; lxxxiv. 4, 6, 7, 10; lxxxv. 6, 11. In lxxxii. 1 a, b, g, h agree alike against c and d, e, f, i. Only in lxxxiii. 17 do d, e, f, i agree with c against a, b, g, h. In the above passages k is wanting, but where it exists it belongs as a rule to β, and agrees with a more than with any other member of this group. Thus if we represent $a, b, d, e, f, g, h, i, k$ by a, and a, b, g, h, k

by β, and d, e, f, i by γ, as we have already arranged, we arrive at the following genealogy :—

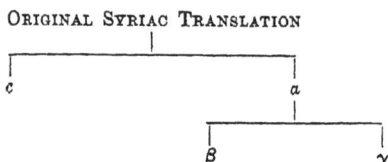

ORIGINAL SYRIAC TRANSLATION

c a

β γ

We have also seen from what precedes that c often agrees with β in giving the true text against γ, but c and γ never agree in attesting the true text against β, except perhaps in lxxxiii. 17.

l, m, n, so far as they exist, support a as against c, and where the attestation of a is divided they generally agree with γ against β, i.e. with d, e, f, i against a, b, g, h, k.

Having now learnt in some measure the relations of the various groups of MSS. to each other, we have still to study those of the individual MSS., so far as our materials admit. The special study of c we reserve till later.

Amongst a, b, g, h, b and g are closely related. They agree against all else in lxxx. 4 ; lxxxi. 3 ; lxxxii. 2, 3 ; lxxxiii. 2, 9, 11 ; lxxxv. 12 ; but this combination is generally wrong. b is never right when it stands alone. a and h are excellent authorities when supported by c. Thus a, c are right in lxxxiii. 4 ; lxxxiv. 6 ; lxxxv. 9. They agree in the wrong in lxxix. 2 ; lxxx. 7 ; lxxxv. 9. a agrees also with b, c, g against all else in lxxxv. 14, and with c, h against all in lxxxiv. 3. h stands alone with c in lxxxi. 4; lxxxiv. 4; lxxxv. 13; but the combination is untrustworthy. From these facts we infer that amongst a, b, g, h, b and g are very closely related, but that no such close relations exist between a and h or between either of these with b, g. Thus the relations of the sub-group to each other might be represented as follows:—

As regards the γ group, we have learnt above that it is quite untrustworthy when it stands alone against c. Yet it is upon two of the members of this group that the text of the Walton and Paris Polyglots is based.

The text of these Polyglots may be shortly described as follows. In all cases where it stands in opposition to c, WP follow a except in lxxxii. 8, lxxxv. 10, where their text is most probably due to conjecture as they here stand alone. Secondly, in cases where γ is opposed to $c\beta$, WP agree with γ. Thirdly, within the group γ, WP are most closely associated with, and in all probability are based upon, e, f. For they agree with e against all other MSS. in lxxx. i., lxxxii. 9 in omitting "and," in lxxx. 2 in giving an impossible form, and in lxxxiii. 14 in omitting half the verse. But WP are not based on e alone; for though e omits a word in lxxxv. 5, it is given in WP. This defect of e was made good from *f ;* for we find that *f* WP stand alone in lxxx. 7. It is of no little interest to have traced the sources of the text in the Polyglots ; for, as their editors have given no information on the subject, scholars have hitherto been quite in the dark in this respect. We are now in a position to give the genealogy of the MSS. dealt with above. This is as follows :—

ORIGINAL SYRIAC TRANSLATION

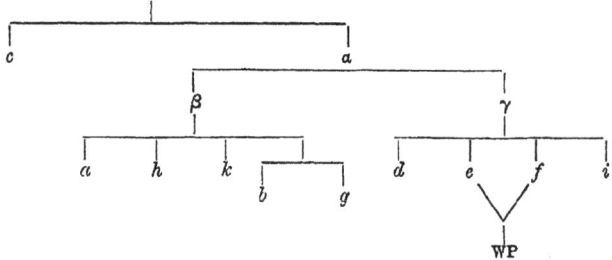

Special Study of c.—It is now time to study the special characteristics of *c.* We have already seen that *c* has independently preserved the true text in many passages against corruptions in *a.* (A list of these passages will be found above, where also it is shown that *a* has preserved the true text much more frequently than *c.*) I have found *c* trustworthy when supported by *a* in lxxxiii. 4 ; lxxxiv. 6 ; lxxxv. 9 ; but not so in lxxix. 2 ; lxxx. 7 ; lxxxv. 9 ; or by *a, b, g* in lxxxv. 14 ; or by *a, h* in lxxxiv. 3 ; or by *b, g* in lxxxv. 1. But the character of *c* appears more clearly in its errors. Thus it is wrong (1) *through omission* in lxxx. 1, 2 (omission due here to an attempted emen-

dation); lxxxii. 2, 3 ; lxxxiii. 4, 5, 16, 18 ; lxxxiv. 1,
10 ; lxxxv. 4 (through homoioteleuton), 12. Cf. li. 16
and lvi. 14 for omissions of the negative. (2) *Through
additions to the text* in lxxviii. 2 ; lxxxiii. 5 ; lxxxv. 8,
9, 15. (3) *Through transposition of words or letters
whereby the sense is generally destroyed. Transposition
of letters* in lxxxii. 4 whereby "drop" becomes "pollution"; lxxxiii. 21 where "by truth" becomes "in
silence." For similar transpositions in the earlier
chapters see xiv. 6 ; lxx. 8. *Transposition of words*
in lxxxi. 3 ; lxxxii. 2, 3 ; lxxxiii. 5 ; lxxxiv. 8. For
similar transpositions see xiv. 11 ; xxi. 16. (4)
Through clerical errors in lxxviii. 3 (for a similar error
see xxiv. 4), 4 ; lxxx. 3 ; lxxxii. 5 ; lxxxiii. 2, 3, 13,
15, 16, 19 ; lxxxiv. 1 (observe that there is the same
erroneous pointing in lxx. 5), 3, 8 ; lxxxv. 12, 13.
In lxxxiv. 2 we have an intentional variation. Cf. in
earlier chapters li. 1.

We have now completed our study of the MSS.
The knowledge which we have thus gained from our
comparative criticism of *c* and the other MSS. helps
to secure us against the characteristic errors of the
former in the chapters where the friendly aid of the
latter cannot be invoked. We can thus address ourselves with a certain degree of confidence and skill to
the obscurities and corruptions that arise in these
chapters. As a further result of this examination, we
have come to feel that so long as we follow its guidance, we can nowhere greatly err from the sense of
the Hebrew original.

Date of the Common Ancestor of c and a.—Since *c*
and *b* are both of the sixth century, we find that
already at that date there existed two distinctly
developed types of text, both of which must have
been for no brief period in existence, owing to the
variety of readings already evolved. Further, though
b belongs to the sixth century, many of its readings
are decidedly later than *c* and even than *a* and *h*. In
fact, *a, h* represent the text at an earlier period than *b*.
The common parent, therefore, of *a, h*, and *b* was probably not later than the fifth century. Such a variety
of related yet different MSS. as *a, b, g, h, k* could not
well have arisen from an MS. of a later date. This
being so, the common progenitor of *c* and *a* can hardly
be sought later than the fourth century.

§ 4. Previous Literature on the Apocalypse of
Baruch

The Syriac Text.—As we have seen in the foregoing section, we have only one MS., i.e. *c*, for chapters
i.-lxxvii. For Ceriani's edition of this MS. see pp. xxii.-
xxiii. Of the text of the remaining chapters, which form
the Epistle of Baruch, many editions have appeared :—
(1) That which is published in the Walton and Paris
Polyglots. This text is, as we have shown above (pp.
xxvii.-xxviii.), founded on two indifferent MSS., *e* and *f*.
(2) Lagarde's edition of *b*, pp. 88-93 of his *Libri Vet.
Test. Apocryphi Syriace*, 1861. This is merely *b* in a
printed form, and not an edition of the Syriac text

based on the Nitrian MSS. in the British Museum, as is everywhere wrongly stated both by German and English writers. Though *b* is a very old and valuable MS., we have now several MSS. at our disposal containing a more ancient text (see pp. xxvi.-xxvii.) (3) Ceriani's published text of *c*, to which he has appended collations of *a, b, d* in his *Monumenta Sacra et Profana*, vol. v. Fasc. 2, pp. 167-180. As we have already remarked, Ceriani has contented himself with printing the text of *c*, and has not sought to correct it by means of *a, b, d*.

Translations.—Only one translation of our Apocalypse has hitherto appeared, *i.e.* the Latin translation of Ceriani in the *Monumenta Sacra et Profana*, vol. i. Fasc. 2, pp. 73-98, 1866. This is certainly a model translation in point of style, and considering the fact that Ceriani was not a specialist in Apocalyptic literature, it is also very accurate. Not quite accurate, indeed, as Ceriani himself was aware in 1871 when he wrote—"Omisi tamen plenam revisionem meae versionis Latinae . . . quia omnino in meis occupationibus tempus me deficit, et quidquid corrigere opus erit, alii ex textu per se poterunt." Some of the errors are as follows :— In xiii. 8 we must expunge " enim est." In verses 4-5 of the same chapter we find the peculiar construction " ut . . . dic." In xv. 6 read " transgressus est " for " fecit." In xix. 1 for " te " read " vos." In xxv. 4 for " terrae " read " terram." In xxxii. 4 for " coronabitur " read " perficietur." In xl. 1 for " qui tunc " read "illius temporis." In xlix. 3 for " vestient " read

"induent." In lv. 1 expunge "ejus." In lx. 1 add
"eorum" after "magiarum." In lxii. 2 add "et"
before "idololatria." In lxxii. 2 for "vivificabit" read
"parcet." In lxxxv. 9 for "veritatem cujuspiam" read
"veritas quodpiam." In lxxxvi. 12 for "viae" read
"recreationis" (= ἀνέσεως); "viae" is a rendering of d
but not of c, Ceriani's text. Although Ceriani made
no critical study of the text of c, he has nevertheless
made some most felicitous emendations in x. 14; xiv.
6; li. 1; lvi. 4, 14; lx. 2; lxix. 1, 4; lxx. 8. A
critical study of the text and matter would have helped
him to deal with the corruptions of the Syriac in xxiv.
4; xlviii. 32; li. 16; lxvii. 2; lxx. 5; lxxii. 1, etc.

As Ceriani did not believe in a Semitic original of
our Apocalypse, he was naturally unable to deal with
corruptions that were not native to the Syriac Version,
but had already appeared in the Hebrew text or had
arisen through the misconceptions of the Greek translator.

Ceriani's Latin translation was republished by
Fritzsche in his *Libri Apocryphi Vet. Test. Graece*,
1871, pp. 654-679. Though Fritzsche introduces
several changes into Ceriani's translation, hardly any
of these can be justified. Sometimes he makes the
change because he has failed to understand the text;
thus in xx. 4; xxi. 9, 10, he has emended Ceriani's
"investigabiles" into "ininvestigabiles"; but "investiga-
bilis" in the Vulgate frequently means "unsearchable."
The change of "omne" into "vanum" in xix. 8 is quite
wanton. The Latin text also is carelessly edited;

thus for "ego" there is "ergo" in lxxxiv. 1 ; for "ibi" there is "tibi" in lxxxv. 13; and "opulus" for "populus" in xlviii. 24. In the critical notes on pp. 690-699 there are many confusions and mis-statements of authorities. It is needless to add that none of Ceriani's actual errors were corrected by Fritzsche, for the Syriac text had not yet been published.

Notwithstanding all these defects, every scholar who has used Fritzsche's book is rightly grateful to him for making Ceriani's translation so generally accessible.

Critical Inquiries.—Langen, *De Apocalypsi Baruch anno superiori primum edita commentatio*, Friburgi in Brisgovia, 1867. This treatise, which consists of twenty-four quarto pages, maintains that our Apocalypse was written in Greek in the reign of Trajan. Although no grounds worthy of consideration are advanced in support of a Greek original, Langen's view has been universally accepted. Only two scholars have expressed a doubt on the subject, Mr. Thomson and Professor Ryle of Cambridge. This fact in itself serves to show how inadequately hitherto this Apocalypse has been studied. In other respects, Langen's work is admirable.

Ewald, *Göttinger Gel. Anzeigen*, 1867, pp. 1706-1717, 1720; *Gesch. des Volkes Israel*, vii. 83-87 (English trans. vol. viii. 57-61). In a short but interesting article Ewald assigns the date of our author to the reign of Domitian. He regards 4 Ezra and this Apocalypse as the work of one and the same author.

Hilgenfeld, *Zeitschrift für wissensch. Theologie*, 1869, pp. 437-440; *Messias Judaeorum*, pp. 63-64. Hilgenfeld ascribes our Apocalypse to the earlier years of Vespasian, possibly to 72 A.D. Vespasian is the leader mentioned in xl. The Baruch Apocalypse is subsequent to 4 Ezra.

Wieseler, "Das Vierte Buch Ezra," *Theol. Stud. und Kritiken*, 1870, p. 288. This writer criticises Hilgenfeld's date. The seven weeks (xxviii. 2) are to be reckoned from the fall of Jerusalem to 119 A.D. The two weeks in that verse point to the years 105-119, *i.e.* to the time of Trajan.

Fritzsche, *Libri Apocryphi Vet. Test.* 1871, pp. xxx.-xxxii. On Fritzsche's reprint of Ceriani's Latin translation see pp. xxxii.-xxxiii.

Stähelin, "Zur paulinischen Eschatologie," *Jahrbücher für Deutsche Theologie*, 1874, pp. 211-214.

Hausrath, *Neutestamentl. Zeitgesch.* 2nd ed. iv. 88-90, 1877.

Renan, "L'Apocalypse de Baruch," *Journal des Savants*, 1877, pp. 223-231; *Les Évangiles*, 1877, pp. 517-530. Renan regards this Apocalypse as an imitation of 4 Ezra and in part designed as a correction of it, as, for instance, on the question of original sin (cf. also Langen). The latter was written in Nerva's reign, the former in the last year of Trajan's. The sombre clouds which obscured the last months of Trajan roused the hopes of the Jews and gave birth to the furious revolt of 117, of which this book is a monument. The fact that this book was accepted amongst the Christians excludes a later date. No

Jewish product later than Hadrian gained currency in Christian circles.

Drummond, *The Jewish Messiah*, 1877, pp. 117-132. Dr. Drummond is of opinion that, " notwithstanding the Hebraic colouring of its thoughts and language, this book may very well have been written in Greek." Its author was a Jew: there is " not a single expression which betrays a Christian hand." It is probably subsequent in date to 4 Ezra, and is divided into the following groups of chapters—i.-ix.; x.-xii.; xiii.-xx.; xxi.-xxx.; xxxi.-xliii.; xliv.-xlvii.; xlviii.-lxxvi.; lxxvii.-lxxxvii.

Kneucker, *Das Buch Baruch*, 1879, pp. 190-196. Kneucker believes that the Apocryphal Book of Baruch is the letter which Baruch undertakes in ch. lxxvii. to send by " three men " to the brethren in Babylon. This view needs to be greatly modified; as it stands, he has found none to follow it. The present book, he holds, is defective.

Dillmann, art. " Pseudepigraphen" in Herzog's *Real-Enc.* 2nd ed. xii. 356-358. Baruch, according to Dillmann, was undoubtedly later than 4 Ezra, and was written under Trajan. The writer was an orthodox Jew and wrote in Greek. Dillmann rightly thinks that parts of the book are lost, but he is wrong in supposing it to be not more truly Jewish than 4 Ezra. He falls also into the same mistake as so many other scholars in supposing Lagarde's edition of MS. *b* to be an edition of the Syriac text, based on the Nitrian MSS.

Edersheim, *The Life and Times of Jesus the Messiah*, 2nd ed. 1884, ii. p. 658.

Rosenthal, *Vier Apocryphische Bücher*, 1885, pp.
72-103. This writer has made a painstaking study of
Ceriani's Latin translation. He has likewise given no
little thought to the subject matter, and discovered many
connections between our book and Talmudic literature.
It cannot, however, be said that he has thrown much
light on the difficult problems of this book. In most
respects Rosenthal follows the traditional lines of interpretation. The work is from the hand of one author.
It was written in Greek in the reign of Trajan. Like
previous writers Rosenthal regards our Apocalypse as
subsequent to 4 Ezra, and as designed in some respects
to correct its statements. He accepts Wieseler's interpretation of xxviii., and reckons the seven weeks there
mentioned as dating from 70 A.D. Hence 70 + 49 = 119
and the two last weeks point to the years 105-119, the
period of the last woes. 119 is the year of the Messiah's
advent. But Rosenthal thinks he can determine the
exact year of the book's publication. Thus the letter to
the Jews in Babylon shows that it was written before
the rebellion of the Jews in Cyrene, Egypt, Cyprus,
Babylon, and their extermination by Quietus in 116.
On the other hand, he believes that the great earthquake in Syria, which did not affect Palestine in
December 115, is referred to in lxx. 8-lxxi. 1. Thus
the book was written in the beginning of 116. With
many of Dr. Rosenthal's statements, in which he departs from the traditional interpretation of this book,
the present writer dissents strongly. Some of these
statements are as follows:—The Messiah, he says, has

a less active *rôle* in 4 Ezra than in Baruch. The real facts are that a passive *rôle* is assigned to the Messiah in xxix. 3 of this Apocalypse and in vii. 28-29 of 4 Ezra, and a highly active *rôle* in xxxix.-xl. and lxx.-lxxii. of this Apocalypse and xii. 32-34 and xiii. 32-50 of 4 Ezra. Rosenthal charges our author with being an ignorant man and unacquainted with Scripture. This is strange, seeing that in every instance save one the quotations from the Old Testament are made from the Hebrew and not from the LXX., and that a large and accurate knowledge of Jewish history is shown throughout the work. Again, he says our author makes the resurrection from the dead depend on faith therein, and then quotes as a proof xxx. 1, which says nothing of the kind, and further adduces lxv. 1, where he alleges Manasseh is reproved for not believing in the future, " dass er an keinen Zukunft glaubte ! " This last assertion rests on a strange misconception of the Latin translation—" cogitabat tempore suo quasi ac futurum non esset ut Fortis inquireret ista." This is, of course, " he thought that in his time the Mighty One would not inquire into these things ! " " Futurum " cannot mean " the future."

Stanton, *The Jewish and Christian Messiah*, 1886, pp. 72-75. This writer ascribes our Apocalypse to the years immediately subsequent to 70 A.D. He divides the book as follows—i.-ix ; x.-xii. ; xiii.-xx. ; xxi.-xxx. ; xxxi.-xliii. ; xliv.-lxxvi. ; lxxvii.-lxxxvii.

Schürer, *A History of the Jewish People in the Time of Jesus Christ* (translated from the second and revised edition of the German), 1886, vol. iii. Div. ii. pp. 83-93. We have here an admirable account of our Apocalypse. Schürer regards it as written shortly after 70 A.D., and argues strongly for its priority to 4 Ezra. After citing passages on the question of original sin from both books, he proceeds: "Here, then, we have not even an actual difference of view, far less a correction of the one writer on the part of the other. Further, such other reasons as have been advanced in favour of the priority of Ezra and the dependent character of Baruch are merely considerations of an extremely general kind which may be met with considerations equally well calculated to prove quite the reverse." " My own opinion is that . . . it is precisely in the case of Baruch that this problem is uppermost, *i.e.* How is the calamity of Israel and the impunity of its oppressors possible and conceivable? while in the case of Ezra, though this problem concerns him too, still there is a question that lies almost yet nearer his heart, *i.e.* Why is it that so many perish and so few are saved? The subordination of the former of these questions to the other, which is a purely theological one, appears to me rather to indicate that Ezra is of a later date than Baruch." It must be admitted that these arguments are as conclusive as are the counter-arguments of Ewald, Langen, Hilgenfeld, Hausrath, Stähelin, Renan, Drummond, and Dillmann for the priority of 4 Ezra. And beyond this *impasse* it is impossible for criticism to advance until it recognises the composite nature of both books. Schürer appends a valuable bibliography.

Baldensperger, *Das Selbstbewüsstsein Jesu,* 1888, pp. 23-24, 32-35. The composition of Baruch is here assigned to a Jew living in Palestine in the reign of Trajan.

Thomson, *Books which Influenced our Lord and His Apostles,* 1891, 253-267, 414-422. This writer believes with Schürer in the priority of Baruch, but his hardihood goes still farther: he assigns the date of its composition to 59 B.C. Such a date of necessity argued a Semitic original, and this Mr. Thomson contends for, and we hold rightly, though his reason may be wrong. This his sole reason is that in v. 5 we find the proper name Jabish ܝܥܒܨ. "This," he says, "almost certainly represents Ἰγαβής of the Septuagint, 1 Chron. iv. 9, 10 (Heb. יעבץ, Syriac ܝܥܒܨ)." There is no ground for this identification; in fact, everything is against it; and even if the identification were right, it would not necessarily prove a Hebrew original. Jabish or Jabesh, for the Syriac is unpunctuated, implies a Greek form Ιαβις or Ιαβης, and this in turn יבש. Here, as elsewhere, I have had occasion to regret that Mr. Thomson acquainted himself inadequately with the facts before he gave loose rein to his vigorous imagination.

Kabisch, "Die Quellen der Apocalypse Baruchs," *Jahrbücher f. Protest. Theol.* 1891, pp. 66-107. With this writer the criticism of Baruch enters on a new stage. So long, indeed, as it pursued the old lines, finality on the question of the chronological relations

of our Apocalypse and 4 Ezra was impossible, and
the champions of the one book with excellent
reasons demolished their rivals, and with reasons just
as excellent were demolished in turn. The explanation is obvious : both books are composite, and if some
parts of 4 Ezra are older than certain parts of Baruch,
no less certainly are some parts of Baruch older than
some of 4 Ezra.

Kabisch emphasises at the outset certain facts
which point to a plurality of authorship. Thus he
shows that we find in Baruch side by side, on the one
hand, a measureless pessimism and world-despair
which look for neither peace nor happiness in this
world ; and, on the other hand, in the same work, a
vigorous optimism and world-joy which look to a
future of sensuous happiness and delight, of perfect
satisfaction and peace.

Kabisch further points out that the same subjects
are treated several times, and often without any fresh
contribution to the subject at issue. Thus the Messianic Kingdom is twice delineated, the advent of the
Messiah twice foretold, and the Messianic woes just
as often depicted. Yet the latter are neither so
identical as to point to the same author, nor are the
novelties so great as to justify the repetition of the
whole complex statement already once given.

On these grounds he shows that the book is derived
from at least three or four authors. Thus he distinguishes i.-xxiii. ; xxxi.-xxxiv. ; lxxv.-lxxxvii. as the
groundwork written subsequently to 70 A.D., since the

destruction of the temple is implied throughout these chapters. Further, these sections are marked by a boundless despair of this world of corruption, which fixes its regards on the afterworld of incorruption. In the remaining sections of the book, however, there is a faith in Israel's ultimate triumph here, and an optimism which looks to an earthly Messianic Kingdom of sensuous delights. In these sections, moreover, the integrity of Jerusalem is throughout assumed. Kabisch, therefore, rightly takes these constituents of the book to be prior to 70 A.D. These sections, however, are not the work of one writer, but of three, two of them being unmutilated productions, *i.e.* the Vine and the Cedar Vision, xxxvi.-xl., and the Cloud Vision, liii.-lxxiv., but the third a fragmentary Apocalypse, xxiv. 3-xxix. Finally, these different writings were incorporated in one book by a Christian contemporary of Papias, and to this editor are probably due xxviii. 5 ; xxx. 1 ; xxxii. 2-4 ; xxxv. ; lxxvi. 1. With the bulk of this criticism I have no reason for variance, as by independent study, and frequently on different grounds, I have arrived at several of these conclusions. But taken as it stands, Kabisch's criticism is only an additional stage on the way. It is far from being final, as a more prolonged study would have convinced this writer. Thus, as we shall presently learn (see pp. liii.-lxiv.), the so-called groundwork of Kabisch is as undoubtedly composite as the whole work is composite, and edited from at least two or three distinct writings. In this and in other respects the criticism of our book is indefinitely more difficult than Kabisch conceives it. But we must not anticipate our conclusions here. Kabisch's work is based on the Latin translation of Ceriani. He follows the traditional views of a Greek original. The possibility of a Semitic original does not seem to have occurred to him.

De Faye, *Les Apocalypses juives*, 1892, pp. 25-28, 76-103, 192-204. It is interesting to find that some of Kabisch's conclusions were reached by this French scholar independently. Thus De Faye, like Kabisch, distinguishes xxxvi.-xl. and liii.-lxxv. as distinct works written before 70 A.D. The rest of his analysis is not likely to gain acceptance. His main conclusions are as follows:—i.-xxxii. 7 constitute an Apocalypse of Baruch written after 70 A.D.; i.-v. and vi.-xxxii. 7, however, were originally derived from two hands (pp. 193-196). Another quite distinct work was the Assumption of Baruch, which consists of xlviii.-lii.; xli.-xliii. 2; lxxvi. 1-4 (p. 97 note). The date of this work is also after 70 A.D. xliii. 3-xlvii. is for the most part the work of the final editor. They are much later in date than the Apocalypse or the Assumption. Thus the following chapters and verses are derived from the final editor: xxxii. 7-xxxv.; xliii. 3-xlvii.; lxxvi. 5-lxxxvii. (pp. 201-202). Much praise is due to M. de Faye for the abundant scholarship and pains he has expended on this book; but his work is unconvincing: a profounder study would have led him to abandon many of the positions which are maintained by him.

Ryle, "The Book of Baruch," *Dictionary of the Bible*, ed. Smith, 1893, vol. i. pp. 361-362. Professor Ryle regards our Apocalypse as written shortly after the destruction of Jerusalem, and possibly in Hebrew. He reverts to Ewald's idea of the common authorship of this book and 4 Ezra as a means of explaining their manifold points of identity and similarity. He divides it into the following sections: i.-xii.; xiii.-xx.; xxi.-xxxiv.; xxxv.-xlvi.; xlvii.-lii.; liii.-lxxvi.; lxxvii.-lxxxv.

§ 5. THE SYRIAC—A TRANSLATION FROM THE GREEK

That the Syriac text is a translation from the Greek is to be concluded on several grounds. 1. It is so stated in the sixth-century MS. *c.* 2. There are certain corruptions in the text which are explicable only on the hypothesis that the translator misinterpreted the Greek, or else found the corruption already existing there. Thus in iii. 7 (see note) the Syrian translator renders " ornament " where the text requires " world." It is obvious here that he followed the wrong sense of κόσμος. The corrupt readings in xxi. 9, 11, 12; xxiv. 1, 2; lxii. 7 are to be explained on this principle (see notes *in loc.*). 3. Imitations of Greek constructions are found. In lxv. 1 we have *hau* = the Greek article in connection with a proper name. 4. We have frequent transliterations of Greek words, as in vi. 4, 7; x. 17; xvii. 4; xxi. 7, etc. It is possible, of course, that these borrowed Greek words may have

xliv   THE APOCALYPSE OF BARUCH

been part of the current language when the translation
was made. In lxxvii. 14, however, we have a Greek
word transliterated which gives no sense in its context.
Hence this word was not written first-hand by a Syriac
writer, but was taken by the Syriac translator from
the Greek text before him. 5. The Rest of the Words
of Baruch is largely based on our Apocalypse, and
frequently reproduces it word for word. This book
was written in Greek by a Christian Palestinian Jew
in the second century. It implies, therefore, the existence of our Apocalypse in a Greek form, and preserves
important fragments of the Greek Version.

§ 6. THE GREEK—A TRANSLATION FROM A
HEBREW ORIGINAL

It is hard to understand how such an unbroken
unanimity has prevailed amongst scholars on the
question of a Greek original. Indeed, it is impossible
to explain it, save on the hypothesis that they gave
the subject the most cursory notice, or more probably
none at all. In fact, since the discovery of the book
not a single serious attempt has been made to grapple
with this problem, and yet, in nearly every instance,
scholars have spoken with an assurance on this subject
that only a personal and thorough study of the subject
could justify. To this strong and unanimous tradition
of the learned world I bowed without hesitation at the
outset of my studies, but with an awakening distrust
and an ever-growing reluctance during the subsequent

years in which the present Translation and Notes were completed. In fact, the feeling grew steadily stronger that only a Hebrew original could account for many of the phenomena of the text. And yet my gathering certainty on this head did not lead to action till the MSS. of the Translation and Notes were partially in type. I then felt that I could no longer stay my hand, and with the kind permission of my publishers I have been enabled to introduce the necessary changes into the Translation and Notes. The facts which have obliged me to maintain a Hebrew original may be summarised as follows:—1. The quotations from the Old Testament agree in all cases but one with the Massoretic text against the LXX. 2. Hebrew idioms survive in the Syriac text. 3. Unintelligible expressions in the Syriac can be explained and the text restored by retranslation into Hebrew. 4. There are many paronomasiae which discover themselves on retranslation into Hebrew. 5. One or two passages of the book have been preserved in Rabbinic writings.

1. *The quotations from the Old Testament agree in all cases but one with the Mass. text against the LXX.*— See vi. 8; xxxviii. 2 ; xli. 4 ; li. 4 ; lviii. 1, with notes *in loc.* In two other passages our text departs alike from the Mass. and LXX.: thus in iv. 2 it agrees with the Syriac Version of Is. xlix. 16 against the Mass., LXX., and Vulg.; and in xxxv. 2 it reproduces Jer. ix. 1, freely and independently. Finally, in lxxxii. 5 only does it agree with the LXX. of Is. xl. 15. It is to be observed, however, that neither does the Vulgate

in that passage agree with the Mass. The Mass. =
כֹּד יִטּוֹל ; the LXX. = ὡς σίελος λογισθήσονται =
כֹּדק נחשבו ; Vulg. = " quasi pulvis exiguus." Here the
Vulg. omits יִטּוֹל and the LXX. replaces it by repeating
a previous verb. Hence this passage is inconclusive,
as the text of Isa. xl. 15 seems to have been uncertain.

2. *Hebrew idioms survive in the Syriac text.*—We
shall treat this section under four heads.

(a) *Survival of the familar Hebrew idiom of the
infinitive absolute combined with the finite verb.*—The
Syriac equivalent of this Hebraism is frequently found
in this Apocalypse : cf. xiii. 3 (note); xxii. 7 ; xli. 6 ;
xlviii. 30 ; l. 2 ; lvi. 2 ; lxxv. 6 ; lxxvi. 2 ; lxxxii. 2 ;
lxxxiii. 1, 2, 3, 6 ; lxxxiv. 2. In this circumstance
alone we have sufficient evidence to establish a Hebrew
original. This idiom is, it is true, also found in
original Syriac, but is comparatively rare. It is not,
however, with original Syriac that we have here to do,
but with a Syriac translation. We shall now proceed
to show that *in a Syriac translation of a Hebrew or a
Greek text this idiom does not appear except as a rendering of the corresponding idiom in the Hebrew or Greek
before it.*

In order to prove this statement we shall examine
the Peshitto Version of Genesis and Exodus. In these
two books I have found fifty-seven instances of the
occurrence of the infinitive absolute with the finite verb
in the Massoretic text.

As we shall require presently to know the usage of
the LXX. in this matter, we shall now give a table

furnishing the facts we are in search of from both versions.

Syriac-Peshitto.	Genesis-Massoretic Text.	LXX.
Noun and verb.	ii. 17.	Noun and verb.
Infinitive and verb.	iii. 4.	,,
,,	iii. 16.	Participle and verb.
,,	xvii. 12.	Noun and verb.
,,	xviii. 18.	Participle and verb.
Finite verb only.	xix. 9.	Noun and verb.
Infinitive and verb.	xxii. 17 (twice).	Participle and verb.
,,	xxvi. 11.	Finite verb only.
,,	xxvi. 13.	Different text followed.
,,	xxvi. 28.	Participle and verb.
Finite verb only.	xxvii. 30.	Finite verb only.
Infinitive and verb.	xxviii. 22.	Noun and verb.
,,	xxx. 16.	Finite verb only.
Finite verb only.	xxxi. 15.	Noun and verb.
Infinite and verb.	xxxi. 30.	,,
,,	,,	Finite verb only.
,,	xxxii. 12.	Adverb and verb.
,,	xxxvii. 8 (twice).	Participle and verb.
,,	xxxvii. 10.	,,
Different text followed.	xxxvii. 33.	Different text followed.
Infinitive and verb.	xl. 15.	Noun and verb.
,,	xliii. 2.	,,
,,	xliii. 6.	Participle and verb.
,,	,,	Finite verb only.
Finite verb only.	xlvi. 4.	Different text followed.
Infinitive and verb.	l. 24 (twice).	Noun and verb.

Thus in Genesis there are twenty-nine instances of this idiom. These are rendered by the Peshitto as follows: twenty-three by the infinitive and verb; one by cognate noun and verb; four by finite verb only; and in one case a different text is followed. In the case of the LXX., eleven by cognate noun and verb; nine by participle and verb; five by finite verb only; while in four a different text is followed.

An examination of Exodus supplies the following evidence :—

Syriac-Peshitto.	Exodus-Massoretic Text.	LXX.
Infinitive and verb.	iii. 7.	Participle and verb.
,,	iii. 16.	Noun and verb.
Different text followed.	xi. 1.	,,
Infinitive and verb.	xiii. 19.	,,
,,	xviii. 18.	,,
Finite verb only.	xix. 12.	,,
Infinitive and verb.	xxi. 12, 15, 16, 17.	,,
Different text followed.	xxi. 19.	Finite verb only.
Infinitive and verb.	xxi. 20, 22, 28.	Noun and verb.
Finite verb only.	xxi. 36.	Finite verb only.
Infinitive and verb.	xxii. 6, 14.	,,
,,	xxii. 16, 19.	Noun and verb.
Finite verb only (twice) } Infinitive and verb }	xxii. 28 (thrice).	{ Noun and verb (twice). Participle and verb.
Infinitive and verb.	xxiii. 4.	Participle and verb.
,,	xxiii. 5.	Finite verb only.
,,	xxiii. 22, 24.	Noun and verb.
,,	xxxi. 14.	,,
,,	xxxi. 15.	Finite verb only.

Thus in Exodus there are twenty-eight instances of this idiom. These are rendered in the Peshitto : twenty-two by the infinitive and verb ; four by finite verb only ; in two cases a different text is followed. In the LXX., nineteen by cognate noun and verb; three by participle and verb; and six by the finite verb only. By combining the facts on both books, we arrive at the following results. The Hebrew idiom occurs fifty-seven times. In the Peshitto forty-five are rendered by infinitive and verb ; one by cognate noun and verb ; eight by finite verb only ; in three cases a different text is followed. In the LXX., thirty are rendered by cognate noun and verb ; twelve by participle and verb ;

eleven by finite verb only; in four cases a different text is followed. Finally, we should mention here that in no case have we found this idiom in the Syriac Version where the same idiom was not also present in the Hebrew from which it was derived, and the same holds true of the LXX. save in one case, *i.e.* Exod. xxiii. 26.

From the above results obtained from the Peshitto Version of Genesis and Exodus we learn that *whereas the Syriac translator on the one hand never inserts this idiom unless as an equivalent of the corresponding Hebrew idiom before him, on the other he has failed to render it in eight cases out of fifty-seven.* In these he gives the finite verb only. Thus the irresistible conclusion is: *if we find this idiom occurring at all in a Syriac translation, it is a presumption that it existed in the language from which the translation was made; whereas if we find it frequently* (as in our Apocalypse) *the presumption changes to a certainty.*

The above conclusions drawn from a study of the Peshitto Version of the Hebrew text of Genesis and Exodus may be further confirmed and extended in their application by a short consideration of the corresponding phenomena in the New Testament. So far as I can discover, the Peshitto Version of the New Testament in no case inserts this idiom where it does not already exist in the Greek. This idiom occurs, as we know, at least six times: see Matt. xiii. 14; xv. 4; Luke vii. 34; xxii. 15; Acts vii. 34; Hebrews vi. 14. Five of these passages are quotations from the LXX., and thus the idiom goes back to the Hebrew. In the remaining one, Luke xxii. 15, it implies undoubtedly an Aramaic or Hebrew original. The Peshitto renders these instances by the infinitive and verb except in Matt. xiii. 14, where it misses the point, and in Luke xxii. 15, where it gives the noun and verb. In both these verses the Sinaitic MS. gives the infinitive and verb.

The Syriac translator therefore is so far from insert-ing this idiom, unless it exists already in the Hebrew or Greek text before him, that, as we found above, *he occasionally fails to do so when he ought.* The bearing of this conclusion on our present investigation is obvious. This idiom is found fifteen times in our Apocalypse; we can therefore conclude with confidence that it occurred at least fifteen times in the Greek, and in all likelihood oftener.

Having now found that this idiom occurred fre-quently in the Greek, we have now to ask, could it have appeared there for the first time, *i.e.* in an original Greek writing?

The answer does not require a long investigation. The idiom is thoroughly Semitic, and is only once found in all Greek literature, and that in Lucian. In the New Testament there is no instance of it unless in a quota-tion from the Old Testament; in the Old Testament only once, Exod. xxiii. 26, without a Semitic background.

Hence we conclude that its frequent occurrence in our Apocalypse is in itself demonstrable evidence of a Hebrew original. Further, it is probable that it occurred in the Hebrew original more frequently than in the Greek translation; for we found above that out of fifty-seven instances of this idiom in Genesis and Exodus, the LXX. failed to render eleven.

(b) *The survival of various Hebraisms.*—In xx. 2 (see note); xxiv. 2, where Syriac for "throughout all generations" = ἐν πάσῃ γενεᾷ καὶ γενεᾷ = בכל־דור ודור; cf. Ps. cxlv. 13; the same idiom is found in xxix. 7, where I render "every morning"; xxxviii. 4, where "from my (earliest) days" is the Hebrew idiom found in 1 Kings i. 6.

(c) *Probable survival of Hebrew order against Syriac idiom.*—In xiii. 12 (see notes); lxiii. 8. In connection with the notes on xiii. 12 it is worth observing that, in Western Aramaic, unlike Syriac, the order of the participle and the substantive verb in the compound past imperfect indicative is indifferent. Thus in Dan. v. 19; vi. 4, 5, 11, 15, etc., the substantive verb precedes, whereas in Dan. ii. 31; iv. 7, 10, 26; vii. 2, 6, 8, etc., the participle.

(d) *Probable survival of syntactical idioms against Syriac idiom.*—For omission of relative see xx. 3, note; imperative used as jussive, xi. 6, note; Hebrew perfect with strong vav in xxi. 21, and the voluntative with weak vav in xlviii. 6, reproduced literally but not idiomatically.

3. *Unintelligible expressions in the Syriac can be explained and the text restored by retranslation into Hebrew.*—In xxi. 9, 11, 12; xxiv. 2; lxii. 7, I have been able to explain and restore an unintelligible

text by retranslation first into Greek and thence
into Hebrew. The Syriac in these verses is the
stock rendering of δικαιοῦσθαι, and this in turn of
צדק. But צדק also = δίκαιος εἶναι, and this is the
meaning required in the above passages (see notes
in loc.), but the Greek translator erroneously adopted
the more usual rendering.

Again in xliv. 12 we have another interesting
restoration through the same means. There we find
in the Syriac " on its beginning " set over anti-
thetically against " to torment." Here the context
requires " to its blessedness." Now the corrupt
text = בראשו, which by the transposition of the
single letter ר gives us the text באשרו = " to its
blessedness." Again in lxxxv. 12 we have another
instance of the Greek translator following the wrong
of two alternative meanings.

Again in xi. 6 ; xx. 3 ; xxi. 21 ; xxix. 5 ; xlviii.
6, we are obliged by the context to translate not the
Syriac text but the Hebrew text presupposed by the
Syriac, but mistranslated by the Greek translator,
and, therefore, of necessity by the Syriac. See notes
in loc.; also 2 (*d*) above, p. xlvii. For other restora-
tions the reader should consult the notes on x. 13 ;
lxx. 6 ; lxxx. 2. Finally in lxxvii. 14 we have a
transliteration of the Greek word ὕλη. ὕλη is either
a corruption or a mistranslation of some Hebrew
word. It could not have been written for the first
time in Greek. I have hazarded a conjecture in the
note on the passage.

4. *Many paronomasiae discover themselves on re-translation into Hebrew.*—We have in xv. 8 (see note) one that is already familiar to us in Isaiah and Ezekiel. As many as three spring into notice in xlviii. 35 (see note), and probably two in lxxxiv. 2. The most interesting perhaps are those on the proper names, Hezekiah and Sennacherib, in lxiii. 3, 4 (see notes). In the case of the former, I had the good fortune to conjecture the existence of the same parono-masia in Ecclus. xlviii. 22, and to restore the Hebrew there as it actually stood before Dr. Neubauer's dis-covery of the Hebrew MS. of Ecclus. xl.-l.

5. *One or two passages of this book have been pre-served in rabbinic writings* (see notes on x. 18; xxxii. 2-4; lxiv. 3).

§ 7. THE DIFFERENT ELEMENTS IN THE APOCALYPSE
      OF BARUCH WITH THEIR RESPECTIVE CHARAC-
      TERISTICS AND DATES.

As we have seen above, the composite nature of this book has already been recognised independently by Kabisch and De Faye. And the more thoroughly we study it, the more conscious we become of the impassable gulf which sunders the world-views which underlie the different parts. In one class of the passages there is everywhere manifest a vigorous optimism as to Israel's ultimate well-being on earth; there is sketched in glowing and sensuous colours the blessedness which awaits the chosen people in the

d

kingdom of the Messiah which is at hand (xxix.;
xxxix.-xl.; lxxiii.-lxxiv.), when healing will descend in
dew, and disease and anguish and lamentation will
flee away; when strife and revenge and hatred will
go into condemnation; when gladness will march
throughout the earth, the reapers not grow weary,
nor they that build toil-worn; when child-birth will
entail no pangs, and none shall die untimely (lxxiii.-
lxxiv. 1); when Israel's enemies shall be destroyed
(xxxix.-xl.; lxx. 7-lxxii.), and to God's chosen people
will be given a world-wide empire with its centre at
Jerusalem (xl. 2; lxxiii.-lxxiv.). Over against these
passages which ring with such assurance of coming
victory and untold blessedness stand others wherein,
alike to Israel's present and its future destiny on
earth, there is written nothing save " lamentation and
mourning and woe." These veritable cries from the
depths give utterance to a hopeless pessimism — a
bottomless despair touching all the things of earth.
This world is a scene of corruption, its evils are
irremediable; it is a never-ceasing toil and strife, but
its end is at hand; its youth is past; its strength
exhausted; the pitcher is near to the cistern, the
ship to the port, the course of the journey to the city,
and life to its consummation (lxxxv.). The advent
of the times is nigh, the corruptible will pass away,
the mortal depart, that that which abides for ever
may come, and the new world which does not turn
to corruption those who depart to its blessedness
(cf. xxi. 19; xliv. 9-15; lxxxv.).

Thus we discover that whereas (1) optimism as to Israel's future on earth is a characteristic of some sections of the book, pessimism in this respect characterises others. The former are the Messiah Apocalypses, xxvii.-xxx. 1 ; xxxvi.-xl. ; liii.-lxxiv. (which for convenience I designate respectively as A¹, A², A³), and a short original Apocalypse of Baruch, B¹. The remaining sections are B², B³. The contents of these we shall determine presently. Again (2), A¹, A², A³, B¹, agree in teaching the advent of the Messianic kingdom, but this doctrine is absolutely relinquished in B², B³.

Thus, A¹, A², A³, B¹, agree in presenting an optimistic view of Israel's future on earth, and in inculcating the hope of a Messianic kingdom ; whereas in B², B³, such expectations are absolutely abandoned, and the hopes of the righteous are directed to the immediate advent of the final judgment and to the spiritual world alone. But at this point a difference between A¹, A², A³, and B¹, emerges. The former look for a Messiah and a Messianic kingdom, the latter for a Messianic kingdom without a Messiah.

As we pursue our study, other features, one by one, disclose themselves which belong to A¹, A², A³, but not to B¹, B², B³, and thus differentiate them from the latter. Some of these are: (1) In A¹, A², A³, Jerusalem is still standing — hence they were written before 70 A.D. ; whereas in B¹, B², B³, it is already destroyed (for details see pp. 49, 61, 87, 101, 111). In B¹, Jerusalem is to be restored ; (2)

in A^1, A^2, A^3, the advent of the Messiah is looked for, but not in B^1, B^2, B^3; (3) in A^1, A^2, A^3, it is only to the actual inhabitants of Palestine that the promise of protection is given in the time of the Messianic woes (see xxix. 2; xl. 2; lxxi. 1)—thus the Jews are still in Palestine; but in B^1, B^2, B^3, the Jews are already carried into exile. In B^1 they are to be ultimately restored.

These conclusions as to the different authorship of A^1, A^2, A^3, and B^1, B^2, B^3, are confirmed by the following facts :—

(1) According to the scheme of the final editor of this book (see v. 7; ix. 2; pp. 36, 61), events proceed in each section in a certain order: first a fast, then a divine disclosure, then an announcement or address to the people based on this disclosure. This being so, it is significant that in the various addresses in v. 5; x. 4; xxxi. 2-xxxiv.; xliv.-xlvi.; lxxvii. 1-17, there is not a single reference to these Messianic Apocalypses, A^1, A^2, A^3. (2) From (1) it follows that A^1, A^2, A^3, have no real organic connection with the rest of the book, B^1, B^2, B^3. And a detailed examination of their immediate contents shows that the removal of A^1 (= xxvii.-xxx. 1), A^2 (= xxxvi.-xl.), A^3 (= liii.-lxxiv.) serves to restore some cohesion to the text (see xxx. 2, note; xli. 1, note; lxxv.-lxxvi., note).

Having thus seen that A^1, A^2, A^3, were written prior to 70 A.D., and are of different authorship to B^1, B^2, B^3, which were written subsequent to that date, we have next to deal with the relations in which A^1, A^2, A^3 stand to each other.

A^1, A^2, A^3; *their relations to each other and dates.* —On pp. 61, 87, we have shown that A^1 is of distinct authorship to A^2 and A^3, on the ground that in A^1 the Messiah pursues an entirely passive *rôle*, and does not appear till the enemies of Israel are destroyed and the kingdom established; whereas, in A^2 and A^3, it is the Messiah that destroys the enemies of Israel and establishes the Messianic kingdom. As regards the date of A^1, all that can be said with safety is that it was composed before 70 A.D.

It is hard to determine with certainty the relation of A^2 and A^3. In many points they are at one: their differences are few. Some of these are: A^2 has more affinities in matter and character with the older Jewish Apocalyptic, *i.e.* that of Daniel; A^3 is more nearly related in form and spirit to later Judaism, to the rabbinic type of thought. Further, whereas in xl. 2, it is the Messiah that defends the inhabitants of the Holy Land, in lxxi. 1, it is the Holy Land itself; and whereas in A^2 ($=$ xxxvi.-xl.) the law is only passingly alluded to, in A^3 ($=$ liii.-lxxiv.) its importance is frequently dwelt upon. The latter difference may partly be due to their diversity in subject and method as well as to the brevity of A^2. On the whole, we are inclined to regard A^2 and A^3 as springing from different authors; but the evidence is not decisive.

As to the date of A^2 we are unable to say any-

thing more definite than that it was composed before
70 A.D. The case of A^3 is different. Like A^1 and
A^2, it was written before 70 A.D., as we have seen
above (see also p. 87 and lxviii. 6, note). The earlier
limit of composition is fixed by lix. 5-11. In the
notes on that passage we have shown that in our
Apocalypse there is a transference of Enoch's functions
to Moses, and an attribution to Moses of revelations
hitherto ascribed to Enoch (see also xiii. 3, note).
This glorification of Moses at Enoch's expense is a
clear sign of Jewish hostility to Christianity, and a
tribute to Enoch's influence in the Christian Church
of the first century. This acceptance of Enoch as a
prophet in Christian circles became the ground of
his rejection by the Jews, and of a hostility which
was unswervingly pursued for several centuries. This
aggressive attitude of Judaism could not have originated
before the open breach of Christianity with the Synagogue, which was brought about by the Pauline controversy. Hence A^3 cannot be earlier than 50 A.D.
Thus the limits of its composition are 50-70 A.D.

B^1, B^2, B^3, *the later constituents of Baruch, their*
characteristics and dates.—We have seen above the
grounds on which we are obliged to ascribe B^1, B^2, B^3,
to a different authorship and later date than A^1, A^2,
A^3. We have now to study the relations which sub-
sist between B^1, B^2, B^3. We shall consider B^3 first, as
it consists of a single chapter.

B^3 = lxxxv. This chapter agrees with B^1, B^2, in
being written after 70 A.D.; but differs from B^1 and

agrees with B^2 in despairing of a national restoration, and in looking only for spiritual blessedness in the world of incorruption.   But, again, it differs from B^2 also, in that B^2 was written in Jerusalem or Judæa, whereas B^3 was written in Babylon or some other land of the Dispersion—in the former most probably; for it was written in Hebrew (cf. lxxxv. 2, 3, 12, notes).   Again, whereas, according to B^2, Jeremiah was with the captivity in Babylon, it is here definitely stated that the righteous and the prophets are dead, and that the exiles have none to intercede for them (see notes on pp. 154, 156). B^3 was thus written after 70 A.D. in Hebrew, and most probably in Babylon.

B^1, B^2.—After the removal of A^1, A^2, A^3, and B^3, the remaining chapters, when submitted to a searching scrutiny, betray underlying suppositions, statements, and facts which are mutually irreconcilable.

Thus certain sections, i.-ix. 1; xliii.-xliv. 7; xlv.-xlvi. 6; lxxvii.-lxxxii.; lxxxiv.; lxxxvi.-lxxxvii., are optimistic and hopeful as to this world, whereas certain others, ix.-xii. (?); xiii.-xxv.; xxx. 2-xxxv.; xli.-xlii.; xliv. 8-15; xlvii.-lii.; lxxv.-lxxvi.; lxxxiii., are decidedly of an opposite character.   The former sections we have named B^1, and the latter B^2.   That B^1 and B^2 are derived from different authors will be clear from the following considerations:—

(1) In B^1 the earthly Jerusalem is to be rebuilt (i. 4, note; vi. 9, note; lxxviii. 7, note), but not so in B^2, where it is said that Jerusalem is removed with a view to usher in the judgment (see xx. 1, 2).

(2) In B¹ the exiles are to be restored, but not in B²; see notes cited in (1).

(3) In B¹ an earthly felicity or a Messianic kingdom is expected (i. 5; xlvi. 6; lxxvii. 12), whereas in B² no earthly consolation of any kind is looked for (xliv. 8-15), and the judgment is close at hand (xlviii. 39; lxxxiii.).

(4) In B² there is a strongly ascetic tone (see xv. 8, note); but this is wholly absent from B¹.

(5) In B¹, Baruch is to die an ordinary death, whereas in B² he is to be taken up or translated and preserved till the last day, to testify against the Gentile oppressors of Israel (see xiii. 3, note).

(6) In B¹, Jeremiah is not sent to Babylon, but in B² he is (see x. 2, note; xxxiii. 2, note; lxxvii. 12, note).

(7) In B¹, Jerusalem is destroyed by angels lest the enemy should boast; this idea seems foreign to B² (see lxvii. 6, note).

(8) In B¹ the main interest of the writer is engaged in dealing with the recent destruction of Jerusalem; in tracing this calamity to the nation's sins; in exhorting to renewed faithfulness; and in inculcating the sure and certain hope of Israel's restoration. In B² the writer has relinquished all hopes of national restoration, and is mainly concerned with theological problems and questions of the schools.

In x. 6-xii. 4 it is not improbable, as we have shown in the notes on the passage, that we have a fragment of a Sadducean writing, which I have marked by the symbol S. It may possibly belong to B²; it

cannot to B^1. Having now recognised that the
groundwork is in the main derived from the two
sources B^1 and B^2, and having already acquainted
ourselves with the leading characteristics of each, it
is next incumbent on us to consider the use made of
these sources.

B^1, *its extent in this book.*—It is not difficult to
ascertain the extent to which B^1 has been put in
requisition by the final editor. Thus i.-ix. 1, with the
exception of the interpolation iv. 2-7, clearly belongs
to it, as it discovers most of the characteristics which
belong to B^1 as over against their contraries in B^2.
B^2 begins clearly with x. 1.-5, for these verses give the
account of Jeremiah's departure to Babylon, which is
peculiar to B^2; ix. 2 and other references to fasts of
seven days are probably due *in their present positions*
to the final editor. The next fragments of B^1 are
xliii.-xliv. 7; xlv.-xlvi. 6 (see pp. 68, 69, for detailed
criticism), and the rest that are drawn from this source
are lxxvii.-lxxxvii., with the exception of lxxxiii. $= B^2$
and lxxxv. $= B^3$ (see pp. 119, 140, 154, 156).

B^2, *its extent in this book.*—Criticism encounters
its chief difficulty in dealing with the source B^2, and
with the use to which it has been put by the final
editor. From B^1 the editor borrowed materials and
used them in a straightforward fashion, but those
from B^2 he mutilated and transposed in every imaginable way. This will be manifest to every serious
student of xiii.-xxv. It was my sheer inability to
write any connected or reasonable commentary on

these chapters in their present order, that led me at
last to recognise the true nature of the case.   Then I
came to see that these chapters could not have been
written originally as they stand at present, and further
study made it clear that we had here a most complete
but instructive example of the perverse ingenuity of a
redactor, by which the original text was dislocated and
transposed, the original development of thought arrested
and inverted, questions frequently recorded after their
specific answers had already been given in full, and
passages torn from their original setting in Baruch's
address to the people and inserted in Baruch's prayers
to God, where they are bereft of all conceivable meaning.

The reader will find a list of these logical *anacoloutha*
and inversions on pp. 20, 21, and likewise an attempt
to restore these chapters to their original order in B².
With the paucity of materials at our disposal, this can
only be partially satisfactory.   The original order
was probably xiii. 1-3*a*; xx.; xxiv. 2-4; xiii. 3*b*-12;
xxv.; xiv.-xix.; xxi.-xxiv. 1.

The next fragment from B² is xxx. 2-5, which
forms a good sequel to xxiv. 1.   Of the intervening
chapters xxvii.-xxx. 1 is an independent Apocalypse,
as we have already found, *i.e.* A¹ and xxvi. is an
addition of the editor; xxxi.-xxxv.; xli.-lii., with the
exception of xliii.-xliv. 7; xlv.-xlvi. 6, which belong
to B¹ and xxxii. 2-4; xlvi. 7, which are due to the
editor, are also fragments of B² (see pp. 57, 58, 66,
68, 69, 74).   These chapters from B² have met with
no better treatment at the hands of the editor than

those already mentioned. Thus we find that xxxi.-
xxxii. 6, which contains an address of Baruch to the
people, presupposes xlii.; xlviii.; lii. to be already in
the background; for the subject of each address is
founded on a previous revelation (see p. 57). Thus
xxxi.-xxxv. was read originally after xlviii.-lii., but not
immediately, for lxxv. intervened (see p. 117), forming
the natural sequel to lii. when A³, *i.e.* liii.-lxxiv. is
removed; xli.-xlii. appear to have followed close on
xxx. (see p. 66). Thus so far the order roughly was:
xxx. 2-5; xli.-xlii.; xlviii.-lii.; lxxv.; xxxi.-xxxv.
But there are grounds for regarding xliv. 8-15;
lxxxiii. as intervening after xxxii. 6. Finally, the
last fragment of B² is found in lxxvi., but this cannot
have formed the end of B². It was probably closed
with an account of the Assumption of Baruch.

For further disarrangements of the text by which
words used originally by Baruch in addressing the
people, are used in their present context in an address
to God, though quite impossible in that connection,
and the probable restoration of these fragments, see
xlviii. 48-50; lii. 5-7; liv. 16-18, notes. The surviving fragments of B², which we have just dealt with,
may be restored as follows to what seems to have
been their original order in their source: xiii. 1-3*a*;
xx.; xxiv. 2-4; xiii. 3*b*-12; xxv.; xiv.-xix.; xxi.-xxiv.
1; xxx. 2-5; xli.-xlii.; xlviii. 1-47; xlix.-lii. 3; lxxv.;
xxxi.-xxxii. 6; liv. 17, 18; xlviii. 48-50; lii. 5-7;
liv. 16; xliv. 8-15; lxxxiii.; xxxii. 7-xxxv.; lxxvi.

S, *its relation to B¹ and B².*—We have adjourned

to the present the treatment of x. 6-xii. 4, which in
the notes on this passage we have assigned to a
Sadducean author, S. However this may be, I cannot but regard it as of different authorship to B¹ and
B². Several grounds for this conclusion will be found
in pp. 14-19. We might further observe that
although, in vividness of grief and the still overwhelming consciousness of national calamity, S has
features in common with B¹, it is sundered from it
as resigning all hope of the restoration of the temple
and its sacrifices, and as presenting the most hopeless
pessimism in the book. And again, whereas S is
related to B² in its world despair, it is no less certainly sundered from it in its complete absorption in
the present wreck of the nation's material interests.
Of this subject as now far distant B² recks little, and
gives its chief energies and affections to religious problems and the conservation of Israel's spiritual interests.

Dates of S, B¹, B², B³.—In respect of date, S
seems to have been written immediately after the fall
of Jerusalem, in 70 A.D.; B¹ soon after this date, when
the destruction of Israel and its hoped-for restoration
were still the supreme subject of interest and speculation.
B² is much later; its interests have passed from the
material to the spiritual world; patriotic aims have
ceased to affect it. B³ is probably still later than B².

Date of editing entire book.—Since the author of
the Rest of the Words of Baruch has used portions of
ii., v., vi., viii., x., xi., xxxv. 2 (?), lxxvii., lxxx., lxxxv.,
lxxxvii. of our Apocalypse, it is clear that he had the

present form of our book before him in Greek.   Thus,
as this Christian Apocalypse was written between
130 and 140 A.D., the date of the Greek translation
of our Apocalypse may be taken as not later than
130.   The editing of the Hebrew may have been one
or more decades earlier.

§ 8. The Lost Epistle to the Two and a Half Tribes

A portion of this letter is probably to be found in
the Apocryphal Book of Baruch, *i.e.* in i. 1-3 ; iii. 9-
iv. 29.   This section corresponds in many respects
with the writings we are in search of.   Thus (1) the
lost Epistle was addressed to Judah and Benjamin in
exile (lxxvii. 12, 17).   Now it is clear that iii. 9-iv. 29
was also addressed *to Judah and Benjamin in exile.*   It
is *Judah and Benjamin* that are addressed ; for throughout iv. 5-29 it is Jerusalem that is represented as
being deprived of her children.   Further, it is Judah
and Benjamin *in exile,* for they are said to be " sold to
the nations and delivered to their enemies " (iv. 6),
and Jerusalem describes herself as robbed of her sons
and daughters (iv. 16), and the writer asks in iii. 10 :
" Why is it, Israel, that thou art in thine enemies'
land, and that thou art waxen feeble (so Kneucker)
in a strange country ? "

(2) The lost Epistle was " an epistle of doctrine
and a scroll of good tidings " (lxxvii. 12).   This
forms an admirable description of iii. 9-iv. 29,

which is essentially a writing of consolation and encouragement.

(3) The lost Epistle was to hold out the promise of return (lxxvii. 6); this is done in iv. 22-24.

(4) The lost Epistle was written by Baruch *to Babylon* (lxxvii. 12, 17).

Now i. 1-3; iii. 9-iv. 29, which purport to have been written by Baruch in Babylon and addressed to the exiles there, appear rather to have been written by Baruch in Jerusalem and addressed to the exiles in Babylon; for (*a*) the speaker does not identify himself with those who are in exile. Cf. iii. 10: " Why is it, Israel, that thou art in thine enemies' land "; and iv. 5, 6, where he calls them the remnant dispersed among the nations; (*b*) the speaker rather identifies himself with Jerusalem; at all events, in iv. 9-29 he personifies Jerusalem, and represents her as addressing the neighbouring peoples, and then her own children as they are being led into captivity, and promising them a safe return to her.

(5) Finally, in B¹, to which the lost Epistle belongs, the blamelessness of Jerusalem over against her children is insisted on (cf. lxxvii. 8). The same thought would naturally recur in some form in the lost Epistle. And so, in fact, we find it underlying iv. 8-29. And as in B¹ it is taught that Israel is punished only as a chastisement (cf. i. 5; lxxix. 2), the same idea would most probably appear in the lost Epistle as an encouragement to the exiles. Now this is emphatically declared to be so in iv. 6.

On the above grounds to which others could be added, I am inclined to regard iii. 9-iv. 29 as a recast of, or, at all events, as based upon the lost Epistle. This Epistle was probably introduced by some form of i. 1-3. These verses are, as Kneucker has shown, corrupt in their present form.

iv. 39-v. 9, which consists of a direct address to Jerusalem, is derived by the final editor from a different source, mainly from the eleventh of the Psalms of Solomon.

§ 9. THE RELATIONS OF THIS APOCALYPSE WITH 4 EZRA

In this section we shall deal with the following questions :—

(a) The composite nature of 4 Ezra.
(b) Conflicting characteristics of 4 Ezra and Baruch, the former to some extent non-Jewish.
(c) 4 Ezra from a Hebrew original.
(d) Relations of the respective constituents of our Apocalypse and 4 Ezra.

(a) *The composite nature of Ezra.* — Into this question this is not the place to enter. I shall content myself with expressing my acceptance in the main of Kabisch's masterly criticism[1] of this work. Though many of his positions cannot be maintained, the greater number of them will, I believe, be ultimately accepted as final. The work is very unequal.

[1] Kabisch, *Das vierte Buch Esra*, 1889, Göttingen.

In it there stand side by side numerous instances of extremely fine insight and not a few gross misapprehensions and bizarre conclusions.   His analysis is as follows :—

> S = an Apocalypse of Salathiel written *circ.* 100 A.D. at Rome, preserved in a fragmentary condition : iii. 1-31 ; iv. 1-51 ; v. 13*b*-vi. 10 ; vi. 30-vii. 25 ; vii. 45-viii. 62 ; ix. 13-x. 57 ; xii. 40-48 ; xiv. 28-35.
>
> E = an Ezra Apocalypse, *circ.* 31 B.C., written in the neighbourhood of Jerusalem : iv. 52-v. 13*a* ; vi. 13-25, 28 ; vii. 26-44 ; viii. 63-ix. 12.
>
> A = Adlergesicht—an Eagle Vision, written 90 A.D. by a Zealot : x. 60-xii. 40.
>
> M = Menschensohn—a Son-of-Man Vision, written in Jerusalem about the time of Pompey : xiii., but much interpolated by R.
>
> E[2] = an Ezra fragment, *circ.* 100 : xiv. 1-17*a*, 18-27, 36-47.
>
> R = the Editor—a Zealot, *circ.* 120 : iii. 1. (*qui et Ezras*), 32-36 ; vi. 11, 12, 26, 27, 29 ; x. 58, 59 ; xii. 9, 34, 37 - 39, 49 - 51 ; xiii. 13*b*-15, 16-24, 26*b*, 29-32, 54-58 ; xiv. 8, 17*b*, 48-50, as well as parts of iv. 52 ; vi. 20, etc.

The above analysis may be taken as a good working hypothesis.   Among other grounds which Kabisch might have pressed to show that the book as it stands has been edited from various independent sources and edited most ignorantly, I will adduce only one.   The title, *Dominator Domine,* which in the Apocalypse of Baruch is used only of God, and rightly so, in 4 Ezra is a designation of God in five instances—iii. 4 ; v. 23 ; vi. 38 (in Syr., Eth., and Arm. Versions) ; xii. 7 ; xiii. 51 ; but of an angel in six—iv. 38 ; v. 38 ; vi. 11 ;

vii. 17, 58, 75. The attribution of this divine title to an angel can only be due to gross confusions or interpolations in the text (see note on iii. 1 of our text). It is to be observed that this phenomenon is found only in the late source S and R.

(b) *Conflicting characteristics of* 4 *Ezra and Baruch, the former to some extent non-Jewish.*—On the following doctrines the teaching of our Apocalypse represents faithfully the ordinary Judaism of the first century, whereas that of 4 Ezra holds an isolated position or is closely related to Christianity.

1. *The Law.*—From an exhaustive comparison of the passages dealing with this subject in the two books (see xv. 5, note) it is clear that the possession of the law by Israel is less a subject of self-gratulation in 4 Ezra than in Baruch. In the latter, especially in B^2, it protects the righteous (xxxii. 1), justifies them (li. 3), is their hope (li. 7) and never-failing stay (xlviii. 22, 24). This is decidedly orthodox Judaism. In 4 Ezra, on the other hand, man trembles before the law; he needs mercy, not the award of the law, for all have sinned (viii. 35); it has served rather unto condemnation; for only a very few are saved through good works (vii. 77) or the divine compassion (vii. 139). It is hardly necessary to point out that this conception of the law approximates to the Pauline view.

2. *Works.*—In my note on xiv. 7 I have contrasted the teaching of the two books on this subject, and arrived at the conclusion that in 4 Ezra the

e

doctrine of works as it is found in Baruch can hardly
be said to exist.   Here again Baruch represents traditional Jewish orthodoxy, but 4 Ezra not.   We should
observe also that the latter guards carefully against the
doctrine of salvation by works by making salvation
depend on works and faith combined (cf. ix. 7; xiii. 23;
cf. St. James ii. 14-26).

3. *Justification, i.e.* by the law or by works.—This
subject might have more logically been treated under
the preceding head.   For my own convenience I have
given it separately.   On p. 39 I have shown that
justification by the law, though taught in Baruch, is
absent from 4 Ezra.   In this respect again the latter
is non-Jewish.

4. *Original Sin and Freewill.* — On pp. 92-93,
from a study of the passages in 4 Ezra bearing on
these subjects, we have found that there was in man to
begin with a wicked element (" granum seminis mali,"
iv. 30); and that through Adam's yielding to this
evil impulse a hereditary tendency to sin was created,
and the *cor malignum* developed (iii. 21-22).   The
evil element having thus gained the mastery over man,
only a very few are saved through mercy (vii. 139;
viii. 3); hence the writer of vii. 118 naturally charges
Adam with being the cause of the final perdition of
man.

In the face of such a hopeless view of man's condition, human freewill cannot be maintained: *practically* man has none, for only a handful out of the
whole human race are saved (vii. 51-61; ix. 16);

theoretically he is said to have it, but this is to justify his final condemnation (see p. 93).

This teaching is practically unique in Judaism between 1-300 A.D.—in fact it is not Jewish but Christian doctrine. In Baruch, on the other hand, conformably to early Rabbinic teaching, it is declared that Adam is not the cause of man's perdition, but that each man is the Adam of his own soul (liv. 19). There is not, moreover, a trace of Ezra's elaborate theory, and the doctrine of original sin is stoutly denied in liv. 15, 19 — not a trace save only in xlviii. 42, where spiritual death is traced to Adam. Elsewhere—xvii. 3; xxiii. 4; liv. 15—it is only physical death that is ascribed to Adam's transgression. But in Ezra, as we might expect from what precedes, both spiritual and physical death are always traced to Adam—iii. 21, 22; iv. 30; vii. 118-121.

Thus on various grounds we see that *whereas Baruch is a pure product of the Judaism of the time, 4 Ezra is the result of two influences at work, first and mainly a Jewish, and secondly a Christian. It was no doubt owing to this Christian element in the latter that it won and preserved a high position in the Christian Church. It constitutes, in fact, a confession of the failure of Judaism.*

The above peculiarities of doctrine in 4 Ezra discover themselves almost universally in S. The author of S was undoubtedly a Jew, but a Jew who had been impressed and imbued to some extent by Christian teaching, probably by Pauline.

(c) 4 *Ezra from a Hebrew Original.*—Though this question could only be settled by an exhaustive study of the text presupposed by the Versions, I am convinced that a Hebrew groundwork underlies at all events the greater part of this book. I might call attention here to the frequent occurrence of the Hebraism—the finite verb combined with the cognate infinitive—as evidence in this direction. Thus in iii. 33 we have "pertransiens pertransivi"; iv. 13, "festinans festinavit"; iv. 26, "proficiscens profectus sum"; v. 30, "odiens odisti"; v. 45, "viventes vivent"; vi. 32, "auditu audita est"; vii. 5 "volens voluerit," and so on in vii. 14, 21, 67, 70, 75; viii. 8, 15, 58; ix. 1; x. 32; xi. 45; xiv. 3, 29. All these appear in the Syriac Version, save five—iv. 26; vii. 5, 14; x. 32; xiv. 29. Still more are omitted in the Ethiopic Version. On the weight to be assigned to this feature of the text as evidence of a Hebrew background, see pp. xliv.-li. I may add that in the late work 5 Ezra xv. 9; xvi. 65, this idiom is found; but in the latter passage it is a quotation from our Apocalypse (see p. xx.), and in the former it is apparently a quotation also.

(d) *Relations of the respective constituents of our Apocalypse and 4 Ezra.*—My present purpose does not call for an exhaustive list of the passages common to the two books. This will be given elsewhere. It will be sufficient to indicate the direction such an inquiry should pursue, and to mention some of the chief grounds for determining the relations in which the various constituents of

Baruch stand to those of 4 Ezra. These determinations must, however, pending further investigation, be regarded as provisional.

Of the multitude of thoughts, phrases, and commonplaces that are common to both books, a large number already occur in previously existing literature; and as these may possibly be drawn independently from such sources by both books, they are not helpful at the outset in determining the priority of either book or of their respective constituents. Again, of many other common passages, the sources, it is true, are no longer found; yet that such did exist in certain cases we have ample grounds for believing; see the note on xxix. 4 for the common original of 4 Ezra vi. 49-52 and of our Baruch xxix. 4. Thus we must be on our guard against tracing relations of dependence where both books have been borrowing independently from the same lost source.

We shall now point out the relations in which A^1, A^2, A^3, B^1, B^2 stand to Ezra. I shall refer to the following constituents of the latter, S, E, E^2, M (according to Kabisch's analysis on p. lxviii.).

A^1.—A^1 and S are apparently related in only one passage: Bar. xxix. 4 and 4 Ezra vi. 49-52. But this relation is not of dependence on either side, but of common derivation from the same lost source; see xxix. 4, note. As regards A^1 and the E constituent of Ezra, xxix. 3b-6 of the former, " *The Messiah will* then *begin to be revealed* . . . and those who hungered will *rejoice;* moreover also they will *behold marvels*,"

and vii. 27*b*-28 of the latter, " Videbit *mirabilia mea ;
revelabitur* enim *filius meus* . . . et *jocundabit* qui
relicti sunt," are certainly connected. If we add to
these connections in thought and diction the fact that
only in A¹ and E in the Baruch and Ezra literature is
the passive *rôle* assigned to the Messiah, we may
reasonably conclude that there is a direct relation of
dependence between them. A¹, I think, is earlier than
E; both are prior to 70 A.D. Finally, A¹ and M may
be connected in xxix. 3 and xiii. 16-20. The thought
seems earlier and more vigorous in A¹. In M it is
threshed out; but such considerations are indecisive.
If there is a relation of dependence between them,
A¹ is probably earlier than M, for in A¹ the Messiah
has a passive *rôle*, in M an active one. The idea of
a passive Messiah conceived as early as 160 B.C. was
not likely to hold its ground in later times when the
needs of the people called for an active leader and
combatant in the Messiah.

A².—A² and M, *i.e.* xiii. of 4 Ezra, are related.
Cf. xl. 2, " My Messiah will convict him of all his
impieties . . . and set before him all the works of his
hosts," with 4 Ezra xiii. 37, " Ipse autem filius meus
arguet quae advenerunt gentes impietates eorum . . .
et improperabit" ("improperabit" is a mistaken rendering; read " ordinabit " with Syr. and Eth.) " coram eis
mala cogitamenta eorum." The connection is manifest.

The first halves of these sentences agree verbally, so
likewise do the second; for "set before him " =
παραστήσει κατὰ πρόσωπον αὐτοῦ = יערך לעיניו; and

"improperabit" (or "ordinabit," Syr. and Eth.) "coram
eis" = ἐπιστοιβάσει κατὰ πρόσωπον αὐτῶν = יערך
לעיניהם; for παριστάναι and ἐπιστοιβάζειν are both
LXX. renderings of ערך. The phrase is derived from
Psalm xlix. 22 (cf. also Leviticus i. 1, 7, 8, 12; vi. 12).

A number of features into which I cannot enter
here show that it is M that is dependent on A², and
not *vice versa*.

The verse just dealt with reappears in xii. 32, in
the Eagle Vision designated A by Kabisch, in a form
which shows it dependent on M. A² is thus earlier
than M and A in 4 Ezra.

A³.—Although there are many points of contact
between A³ and 4 Ezra, there are none that neces-
sitate the theory of dependence on either side save in
liv. 15, 19. These verses which represent the teaching
of orthodox Judaism *circ.* 50-70, were before the writer
of the S element in 4 Ezra (cf. iii. 21-22; iv. 30;
vii. 48), where a non-Jewish turn is given to the
borrowed thoughts and phrases.

B¹.—Although there are many similar and identical
thoughts and phrases in B¹ and 4 Ezra, these are not
sufficiently characteristic or definite to furnish grounds
for determining the dependence of either. This question must be settled on other grounds, *i.e.* chronological.
From the use of like thought or diction, one might
argue, on the one hand, that B¹ is dependent on the E
element of 4 Ezra; compare iii. 7 with vii. 30; on the
other, that B¹ is a source of E² of 4 Ezra; compare
lxxvii. 3-6 with xiv. 30-33, and lxxvii. 14 with xiv.

20; that it is likewise a source of S; compare lxxxiv. 10 with x. 24. In these latter passages a different turn is given to the phrases found first in Baruch.

B². —Between B² and 4 Ezra there are almost innumerable points of contact, but the bulk of them are indecisive for our purposes. With the older elements of 4 Ezra its points of similarity are few and unimportant; but the relations between B² and S are very close. The fact of man's sinning consciously is frequently emphasised in B² and S (cf. Bar. xv. 6; xix. 3; xlviii. 40; and 4 Ezra viii. 56, 58-60; vii. 72). The doctrine that the world was made for man is confined to B² and S; see notes on xiv. 18; xv. 7. Their teaching on the law and on works and justification is allied—*in some particulars identical but as a whole at variance*, owing to Christian influences at work in S; see pp. lxix.-lxx. In B² we have an exposition of the views of orthodox Judaism 70-100 A.D.; in S we find much of the actual teaching in B² recast under Christian influences. S seems to us in every respect to be later than B².

§ 10. RELATION OF THIS APOCALYPSE WITH THE NEW TESTAMENT

The points of contact between this Apocalypse and the New Testament are many in number. The most of these, however, are insufficient to establish a relation of dependence on either side; for the thoughts and expressions in question could be explained from pre-existing literature, or were commonplaces of the time.

Of these a list will be given immediately, followed by another list of passages which seem to show that our text may in a few instances be derived from the New Testament.

New Testament.	Parallels in our Apocalypse.	Probable source of both.
Mt. iii. 16.—Lo, the heavens were opened.	xxii. 1. — Lo, the heavens were opened.	Ezek. i. 1.
Mt. iii. 17 (xvii. 5 ; John xii. 28). — A voice from heaven.	xiii. 1 ; xxii. 1.— A voice from the height.	Dan. iv. 31.
Mt. iv. 8.	lxxvi. 3.	Deut. xxxiv. 1-4.
Mt. xxiv. 7 (Mk. xiii. 8 ; Luke xxi. 11).—Famines . . . and earthquakes.	xxvii. 6, 7.	Commonplaces of Jewish Apocalyptic.
Mt. xxiv. 11, 24. —Many false prophets.	xlviii. 34 (see note).	...
Mt. xxiv. 19 (Luke xxiii. 29).	x. 13, 14 (resemblance slight).	Isa. liv. 1.
Mt. xxvi. 24.— It had been good for that man, etc.	x. 6.—Blessed is he who was not born, etc.	A Jewish Commonplace.
Mt. xxiv. 27.— For as the lightning . . . so shall be the coming of the Son of Man.	liii. 9. — Now that lightning shone exceedingly so as to illuminate the whole earth. (The lightning here symbolises the Messiah.)	A coincidence (?).
Luke xx. 36.— Equal unto the angels.	li. 10.	Eth. En. civ. 4, 6.
Luke xxi. 28 (1 Pet. iv. 7).—Your redemption draweth nigh.	xxiii. 7.—My redemption has drawn nigh.	Eth. En. li. 2. — The day of their redemption has drawn nigh.

New Testament.	Parallels in our Apocalypse.	Probable source of both.
Acts xv. 10 (where the law is spoken of as a "yoke"; cf. Gal. v. 1).	xli. 3.—The yoke of Thy law.	A current expression.
Rom. ii. 14, 15.	xlviii. 40 (see note).	A Jewish Commonplace.
Rom. viii. 18 (2 Cor. iv. 17).—The sufferings of this present time are not worthy to be compared with the glory, etc.	xv. 8. — This world is to them a trouble and a weariness . . . and that which is to come, a crown with great glory.	A Jewish Commonplace (?).
1 Cor. iv. 5 (Heb. iv. 13).	lxxxiii. 3.	(Cf. Eth. En. ix. 5).
2 Cor. iv. 17 (Rom. viii. 18).	xv. 8.	A Jewish Commonplace.
1 Tim. i. 2.— Mercy and peace.	lxxviii. 2. — Mercy and peace.	A coincidence.
2 Peter iii. 9.	xxi. 20.	A coincidence.
2 Peter iii. 13 (Mt. xix. 28; Rev. xxi. 1).—New heavens and a new earth.	xxxii. 6. — Renewed His creation.	Isa. lxv. 17, etc.
Rev. xx. 12.— The books were opened.	xxiv. 1. — The books will be opened.	Dan. vii. 10.

In the following passages our text is dependent on the New Testament, or on some lost common source :—

Mt. xvi. 26.—For what shall a man be profited, if he shall gain the whole world, and forfeit his soul? or what shall a man give in exchange for his soul?

li. 15. — For what then have men lost their life or for what have those who were on the earth exchanged their soul?

Luke i. 42.—Blessed art thou among women, etc.

liv. 10.—Blessed be my mother among those that bear, etc. (probably interpolated).

1 Cor. xv. 19.—If in this life only we have hoped in Christ, we are of all men most miserable.

xxi. 13.—For if there were this life only . . . nothing could be more bitter than this.

1 Cor. xv. 35.—How are the dead raised ? and with what manner of body do they come?

xlix. 2.—In what shape will those live who live in that day ?

James i. 2.—Count it all joy when ye fall into manifold temptations.

lii. 6.—Rejoice ye in the suffering which ye now suffer.

Rev. iv. 6.—In the midst of the throne, and round about the throne, four living creatures.

li. 11.—The living creatures which are beneath the throne.

§ 11. VALUE OF OUR APOCALYPSE IN THE ATTESTATION OF THE JEWISH THEOLOGY OF 50-100 A.D., AND IN THE INTERPRETATION OF CHRISTIAN THEOLOGY FOR THE SAME PERIOD.

This book presents us with a vivid picture of the hopes and beliefs of Judaism during the years 50-100 A.D. As it was written at different dates during this period and by different authors, its composition was thus contemporaneous with that of the New Testament. It is, therefore, of very great value to the New Testament student, as it furnishes him with the historical setting and background of many of the New Testament problems. We are thereby enabled to estimate the contributions made in these respects by Christian thought, as well as to appreciate the world's need of the Pauline dialectic. For the purpose of illustrating our meaning we shall first of all draw attention to the doctrine of the Resurrection in our Apocalypse. Of the Jewish doctrine

here set forth, St. Paul's teaching on this subject
will be seen to be in some respects a development.
Secondly, we shall briefly advert to the doctrines of
Original Sin and Freewill, Works and Justification,
Forgiveness, in which the Jewish teaching and the
Christian stand in strong antagonism.

(a) *The Resurrection.*—In xlix. 2-li. a view of
the resurrection is expounded, which sets forth first
the raising of the dead with their bodies in exactly
the same form in which they had been committed to
the earth with a view to their recognition by those
who knew them, and next their subsequent transformation with a view to a spiritual existence of unending duration. In my notes on pp. 83, 84, I have
shown that the Pauline teaching in 1 Cor. xv. 35-50
is in many respects not an innovation, but a developed
and more spiritual exposition of ideas already current
in Judaism.

(b) *Original Sin and Freewill.*—According to our
Apocalypse,[1] the penalties which man has incurred
through Adam's sin affect only his *physical* existence.
He still preserves his freewill; whether he is saved
or lost, it is his own doing. Adam's sin is limited in

---

[1] Only in B², xlviii. 42, is spiritual death traced to Adam. This
passage may be interpolated; for (1) in all other passages in B² it is only
physical death that is so traced. (2) It conflicts with the presupposition
underlying B² that man can work righteousness and acquire merit as
against God (see xiv. 7, note). (3) In A³ (see liv. 15, 19) original sin is
denied and freewill asserted in the clearest terms. (4) The doctrine of
original sin is unknown to the Talmud (see Weber, 217, 240; Edersheim,
Life and Times, etc., i. 165). We have shown elsewhere (pp. lxix.-lxxi.)
that the teaching of 4 Ezra on this subject is largely non-Jewish.

spiritual consequences to himself; every man is the Adam of his own soul (see pp. 44-45, 93).

St. Paul's doctrine is strongly antagonistic. Both *physical* and *spiritual* death are due to Adam's sin. Owing to that sin man is henceforth dominated by a power (= original sin) which makes his fulfilment of law and therefore his realisation of righteousness impossible. He is not, however, robbed wholly thereby of freewill, but retains it in a degree only sufficient to justify his condemnation.

Works and Justification.—In our Apocalypse the righteous are saved by their works (li. 7), and their righteousness is of the law (lxvii. 6). In the consciousness of their justification by the law (li. 3) they can with confidence approach God and look to Him for the fulfilment of their prayers because of their works wherein they trust (lxiii. 3, 5; lxxxv. 2), and owing to the same ground of confidence they depart from this world full of hope (xiv. 12). But their works are not limited to themselves in their saving influences. So long as the righteous live, their righteousness is a tower of strength to their people (ii. 2), and after their death it remains to their country a lasting ground of merit (xiv. 7; lxxxiv. 10); see notes on xiv. 7; xxi. 9.

With every position here maintained Christianity is at variance, and rabbinic teaching in full accord.

Forgiveness.—How far did this doctrine exist in Pharisaic Judaism, and in what relation does it stand to the Christian doctrine of forgiveness? In Pharisaic Judaism forgiveness was a wholly subordinate conception, and can only be considered in conjunction with its views on merit and demerit. If we wish to discover the Pharisaic doctrine of forgiveness we must have recourse to the Talmud; for that the Pharisaic views of the first century on this subject were those which later prevailed in the Talmud, is to be inferred on these grounds:—(1) In Matt. iii. 9 the words " Think not to say within yourselves, we have Abraham to our father," show that the doctrine of the vicarious righteousness of Abraham was a popular belief. Now this latter doctrine at once presupposes and forms an organic part of the Talmudic doctrine. (2) The teaching on works in our Apocalypse and partially also in 4 Ezra, as well as that of St. Paul's Jewish antagonists, belong also organically to the Talmudic doctrine of works and forgiveness.

The Talmudic doctrine of works may (see Weber, pp. 267-300) be shortly summarised as follows:— Every good work—whether the fulfilment of a command or an act of mercy—established a certain degree of merit with God, while every evil work entailed a corresponding demerit. A man's position with God depended on the relation existing between his merits and demerits, and his salvation on the preponderance of the former over the latter. The relation between his merits and demerits was determined daily by the weighing of his deeds (see Eth. En. xli. 1; lxi. 8; Weber, 272). But as the results of such judgments were necessarily unknown, there could not fail to be much uneasiness, and to allay this the doctrine of the vicarious righteousness of the patriarchs and saints of Israel was developed, not later than the beginning of the Christian era (cf. Matt. iii. 9). A man could thereby summon to his aid the merits of the fathers, and so counterbalance his demerits.

It is obvious that such a system does not admit of forgiveness in any spiritual sense of the term. It can only mean in such a connection a remission of penalty to the offender, on the ground that compensation is furnished, either through his own merit or through that of the righteous fathers. Thus, as Weber vigorously puts it: "Vergebung ohne Bezahlung gibt es nicht." [1] Thus, according to popular Pharisaism, *God never remitted a debt until He was paid in full, and so long as it was paid it mattered not by whom.*

It will be observed that with the Pharisees forgiveness was *an external thing;* it was concerned not with the man himself but with his works—with these indeed as affecting him, but yet as existing independently without him. This was not the view taken by the best thought in the Old Testament. There forgiveness dealt first and chiefly with the direct relation between man's spirit and God; it was essentially a restoration of man to communion with God. When, therefore, Christianity had to deal with these problems, it could not accept the Pharisaic solutions, but had in some measure to return to the Old Testament to

---

[1] In certain extraordinary cases, the divine forgiveness was conceived possible where no merit was at hand, see 4 Ezra viii. 36 ; Weber, 292, 300.

authenticate and develop the highest therein taught, and in the person and life of Christ to give it a world-wide power and comprehensiveness.

We thus see that forgiveness was conceived as (1) *the restoration of man to communion with God;* (2) *the remission of penalty on the receipt of certain equivalents.* Of these two the former alone is taught in the Gospels. In the Pauline Epistles, however, the writer maintains indeed the former as the essential element in forgiveness, but he also incorporates in some degree the latter conception, and not unnaturally as having been originally a Pharisee of the Pharisees. Thus in his doctrine of the Atonement, he introduces the Pharisaic conception by representing the penalty due to man's sin as endured by Christ. This is undoubtedly a more spiritual form of the Pharisaic doctrine, and rightly interpreted it preserves the element of truth which underlies the Pharisaic teaching. It needs, however, to be kept in complete subordination to the former. But that it has not been so kept is obvious from every page of the history of this doctrine since the Christian era. In every age this Pharisaic error has won an evil eminence in the Church—before the eleventh century in representing Christ's death as a debt paid to the devil in lieu of the latter's claim on man, and in the subsequent centuries as a sacrifice to the alleged unforgivingness of God. Wherever or whenever this evil leaven has appeared, it has been followed by shallowness, unreality, and every vice of the unspiritual life.

THE APOCALYPSE OF BARUCH

[TRANSLATED FROM THE GREEK INTO SYRIAC]

I. AND it came to pass in the twenty-fifth year of   I.-IV. 1=B¹.

THE FIRST SECTION

I.-V. 6. These chapters constitute the first of the seven sections
into which, according to the scheme
of the final editor, the book was
originally divided by fasts. These
sections were divided by fasts which
generally lasted seven days (see v. 7,
note; ix., note). In each section there
is a definite movement or order of
events observed. This order briefly
is: first a fast, then a divine command
or revelation, and finally the publication of the command or matter so
revealed. In some cases a prayer
follows the fast, and a lamentation
the publication of the divine disclosure (see notes already referred
to).

It will be observed that iv. 2-7 is
interpolated probably from B².

In this section the word of the
Lord comes to Baruch announcing
the coming, though temporary, destruction of Jerusalem on account
of the wickedness of the two tribes
(i.); with a view to this destruction
Baruch is to bid Jeremiah and the remaining righteous to withdraw (ii.);
Baruch then in his alarm asks, will
this destruction be final? will chaos
return and the number of souls

be completed (iii.)? God replies that
the punishment is only temporary (iv.
1). Yet, rejoins Baruch, even so, the
enemy will, by the pollution and fall
of Zion, glory before their idols over
the nation loved of God (v. 1). Not
so, answers God; judgment must be
executed on Judah, yet the heathen
will have no cause to glory, for it is
not they that will destroy Zion (v.
2, 3). Baruch thereupon assembled
the people in the Cedron valley, and
delivered the divine message; and
the people wept (v. 5, 6).

∴ I. [*Translated from Greek into
Syriac.*] These words are found in
their above position in the Syriac
MS. As they were placed there either
by the Syriac translator or a subsequent scribe, I have bracketed them.
The statement they convey, however,
is borne out by all other evidence.
Thus we find (1) transliterations of
Greek words; (2) renderings explicable only on the hypothesis that
the translator followed the wrong
meaning of the Greek word before
him.

I. 1. *In the twenty-fifth year of
Jeconiah.* Jeconiah was eighteen
years when he began to reign in 599
(2 Kings xxiv. 8). After reigning
three months he was carried into

1

Jeconiah king of Judah, that the word of the Lord
came to Baruch the son of Neriah, and said to him : 2.
" Hast thou seen all that this people are doing to Me,
that the evils which these two tribes which remained
have done are greater than (those of) the ten tribes
which were carried away captive ?   3. For the former
tribes were forced by their kings to commit sin, but these
two of themselves have been forcing and compelling
their kings to commit sin.   4. For this reason, behold
I bring evil upon this city, and upon its inhabitants,
and it will be removed from before Me for a time, and

captivity. Yet during his captivity
he is still called king (2 Kings xxv.
27 ; Jer. xxix. 2 ; Ezek. i. 2). Thus
his twenty-fifth year would be 592,
or two years before the approach of
Nebuchadrezzar. It is no objection
to this that, according to vi. 1, only
one day and not two years should
elapse between the prediction and
its fulfilment ; for in like manner the
siege of Jerusalem, which lasted two
years, is represented as lasting one
day. The unities of time are sacrificed to suit the dramatic purposes
of the writer. Why the writer spoke
of Jeconiah and not of Zedekiah
here, I cannot say. It was not from
ignorance of the latter (cf. viii. 5).

The Lord. This title of God is
found in iii. 1, 4 ; iv. 1 ; v. 2 ; x.
4, 18 ; xi. 3 ; xv. 1 ; xvii. 1 ; xxiv.
3 ; xxviii. 6 ; xlviii. 2 ; liv. 1, 20 ;
lxxv. 1 ; lxxvii. 3. It is, therefore,
not peculiar to any of the different
elements of the book. This, however, may be due in part to the final
editor. See note on iii. 1.

Baruch the son of Neriah.   Cf.
Jer. xxxii. 12 ; xxxvi. 4 ; Bar. i. 1.

2. *The ten tribes.* Elsewhere in
this Apocalypse called " the nine and
a half tribes." See lxxviii. 1, note.

3. *Forced by their kings.*   *I.e.* by
Jeroboam and others of the kings of
Israel.

*These two . . . compelling their
kings to commit sin.* It was in some
instances the princes of Judah, and not
Zedekiah, that resisted the teaching
and prophecy of Jeremiah : cf. Jer.
xxxviii. ; and Josephus, *Ant.* x. 7. 2,
ὁ δὲ Σεδεκίας ἐφ' ὅσον μὲν ἤκουε τοῦ
προφήτου ταῦτα λέγοντος, ἐπείθετο
αὐτῷ, καὶ συνῄδει πᾶσιν ὡς ἀλη-
θεύουσι . . . διέφθειραν δὲ πάλιν
αὐτὸν οἱ φίλοι, καὶ διῆγον ἀπὸ τῶν
τοῦ προφήτου πρὸς ἅπερ ἤθελον.

4. *I bring evil upon this city, and
upon its inhabitants* (2 Kings xxii.
16 ; 2 Chron. xxxiv. 28 ; Jer. vi.
19 ; xix. 3, etc.)

Will be removed from before Me
(2 Kings xxiii. 27 ; xxiv. 3 ; Jer.
xxxii. 31).

For a time. This phrase recurs
in iv. 1 ; vi. 9 ; xxxii. 3. Since we
must on other grounds regard xxxii.
2-4 in its present context as an interpolation, this phrase is peculiar to
i.-viii., *i.e.* to B¹. Although Jerusalem has fallen under the Romans,
the writer of these chapters believes
that its desolation will be but " for
a time." The future restoration of

I will scatter this people among the Gentiles that they may do good to the Gentiles. 5. And My people will be chastened, and the time will come when they will seek for the prosperity of their times.

II. " For I have said these things to thee that thou mayst say (them) to Jeremiah, and to all those who are like you, in order that ye may retire from this city. 2. Because your works are to this city as a firm pillar, and your prayers as a strong wall."

Jerusalem is implied also in lxxvii. 6; lxxviii. 7, where the return of the ten tribes is foretold. In B², *i.e.* ix.-xxvi.; xxxi.-xxxv.; xli.-xliii.; xliv. 9-15; xlvii.-lii.; lxxxiii.; B³, *i.e.* lxxxv., no such restoration is looked for; Jerusalem is removed, xx. 2 (see note *in loc.*), in order to usher in the judgment more speedily; in x. 10 the writer abandons all hope of a restored Jerusalem.

Scatter this people, etc. Jer. xxx. 11; Ezek. xxxvi. 19.

Do good to the Gentiles. This seems to mean to make proselytes of the Gentiles. Cf. xli. 4; xlii. 5; see also xiii. 12.

5. *My people will be chastened.* Cf. xiii. 10; xiv.; lxxix. 2; Pss. Sol. vii. 3; x. 1-3; xiii. 6-8; xviii. 4.

Seek for the prosperity of their times. The writer looks forward to a Messianic kingdom or period of blessedness for Israel on earth.

II. 1. According to Jer. xxxviii. 13, 28, Jeremiah was a prisoner in the court of the guard till the capture of Jerusalem.

Jeremiah is mentioned again in v. 5; ix.; x. 2, 4.

Those who are like you. This phrase is found in three of the sections of this book (cf. xxi. 24;

lvii. 1; lix. 1; lxvi. 7). Cf. 4 Ezra iv. 36; viii. 51, 62; xiv. 9, 49.

Withdraw from the city. This reappears in the Rest of the Words of Baruch i. 1 : "Jeremiah . . . go forth from this city." Cf. also i. 3, 7. The reason for this command appears in the Talmud. Thus, as in *Taanith*, 19, we are told that a house cannot fall so long as a good man is in it; so in *Pesikta*, 115b (Buber's edition, 1868), it is said : "So long as Jeremiah was in Jerusalem, it was not destroyed, but when he went forth from it, it was destroyed."

2. *Your works are to this city as a firm pillar*, etc. We have here quite an illegitimate application of Jer. vi. 27: "I have made thee a tower and a fortress among my people." It is, however, a natural inference from Gen. xviii. 23-33. This verse is reproduced in the Rest of the Words of Baruch i. 2 : αἱ γὰρ προσευχαὶ ὑμῶν ὡς στῦλος ἑδραῖος ἐν μέσῳ αὐτῆς, καὶ ὡς τεῖχος ἀδαμάντινον περικυκλοῦν αὐτήν. It will be remarked that the reference to "works" is omitted by this latter book, as we should naturally expect in a work of Christian authorship.

Your works. On the doctrine of works taught in this book see note on xiv. 7.

III. And I said : " O LORD, my Lord, have I come into the world for this purpose that I might see the evils of my mother ? not (so) my Lord. 2. If I have found grace in Thy sight, first take my spirit that I may go to my fathers and not behold the destruction of my mother. 3. For two things vehemently constrain me : for I cannot resist Thee, and my soul,

III. 1. *O LORD, my Lord.* This title of God is found also in xiv. 8, 16; xvi. 1; xxiii. 1; xxxviii. 1; xlviii. 4, 5, and is thus, except in one instance, confined to B and B¹. It is remarkable that, whereas it is used only of God in the Apocalypse of Baruch, in 4 Ezra it is a designation of God in five instances (iii. 4 ; v. 23 ; vi. 38 (in Syriac, Eth., and Arm. versions); xii. 7 ; xiii. 51), and of an angel in six (iv. 38 ; v. 38 ; vi. 11 ; vii. 17, 58, 75). This fact makes it probable that the introduction of the angel in 4 Ezra is the work of the final editor. The usual titles used in addressing an angel in that book are *dominus meus* (iv. 3, 5 ; v. 33; vii. 3; x. 34). This is applied also to Ezra in ix. 41 ; *domine* (iv. 22, 41 ; v. 34, 35, 41, 56 ; vii. 10, 53, 132 ; viii. 6, 20, 36, 63). These last two titles are probably equivalents of אֲדֹנָי which is employed in Dan. x. 17, 19, in addressing an angel. The words ܡܳܪܝ ܡܳܪܝܳܐ are to be rendered *O LORD, my Lord* as above and not *Dominator Domine*, as we find in Ceriani and Fritzsche. Linguistically indeed either rendering is right, but the frequent occurrence of this phrase in the Syriac Version of 4 Ezra enables us to see that the suffix is not moribund but living ; for it appears in the Ethiopic Version and occasionally in the Armenian. The Syriac is a translation either of δέσποτα κύριέ μου or κύριε κύριέ μου ; these in turn would

point either to אֲדֹנָי יְהֹוִה, as in Gen. xv. 2, 8, or יְהֹוִה אֲדֹנָי. Since such titles could only be used of God, we can with certainty conclude that their attribution to an angel in 4 Ezra is due to gross confusions or interpolations in the text.

My mother. Cf. iii. 2, 3 ; x. 16 ; Baruch iv. 9-16. This was a very natural term for a Jew to apply to Jerusalem. We find the correlative expression in Isa. xlix. 21 ; Matt. xxiii. 37 ; Gal. iv. 25. It is the earthly Jerusalem that is referred to here, for the writer of B¹ looks for a restored earthly Zion (see note on i. 4). Again the same title is applied to the fallen Jerusalem in 4 Ezra x. 7: "Sion mater nostra omnium," though there the writer looks for the restoration of Zion. In Gal. iv. 26 St. Paul uses it of the heavenly Jerusalem ; for he has no further interest in the earthly. The earthly was the mother of Jews, but the heavenly of Christians. The earthly Jerusalem, as we should expect, in Matt. v. 35 is still "the city of the great King."

O Lord. See i. 1, note.

2. *If I have found grace.* xxviii. 6 ; 4 Ezra v. 56 ; vii. 102 ; viii. 42 ; xii. 7.

Take my spirit. An O. T. expression (cf. Ps. xxxi. 13 ; Jer. xv. 15).

Go to my fathers. xliv. 2; cf. also xi. 4 ; lxxxv. 9 ; Gen. xv. 15.

moreover, cannot behold the evils of my mother. 4. But one thing I will say in Thy presence, O Lord. 5. What, therefore, will there be after these things? for if Thou destroyest Thy city, and deliverest up Thy land to those that hate us, how shall the name of Israel be again remembered? 6. Or how shall one speak of Thy praises? or to whom shall that which is in Thy law be explained? 7. Or shall the world return to its nature (of aforetime), and the age revert to primeval silence? 8. And shall the multitude of souls be taken away, and the nature of man not again be named? 9. And where is all that which Thou didst say to Moses regarding us?"

IV. And the Lord said unto me: "This city will be delivered up for a time, and the people will be

4-IV. 1. Baruch asks God if the end of all things will follow on the delivery of Jerusalem into the hands of its enemies; will Israel be blotted out? will there be no longer any students of the law? will all men die and chaos return? In iv. 1 God answers that Jerusalem will again be restored; the chastisement of its people soon be accomplished and chaos will not return. The writer thus looks forward to the returning felicity of Jerusalem.

III. 6. *To whom shall that which is in Thy law be explained?* The real answer to this question is given in Baruch's own words in xlvi. 4.

7. We should observe that the Syriac word |ܢܐܣ̈ܝܐ, here translated "world," really means "ornament." Thus the translator followed a wrong sense of κόσμος here.

Revert to primeval silence. Cf. 4

Ezra vii. 30. In. iv. 1 this is answered in the negative, but in xliv. 9 (*i.e.* B²) in the affirmative.

IV. 2-7. In these verses we have an undoubted interpolation. The earthly Jerusalem, the restoration of which has just been promised, is here derided. This of itself is suspicious. When, however, we turn to vi. 9 and see there that *the very Jerusalem* that is now delivered up to its foes will hereafter be restored, and that for ever, the incongruity of these verses with their present context emerges still more clearly. This incongruity is still further emphasised when we observe that the actual vessels of the earthly temple are committed to the earth by an angel, that they may be preserved for future use in the restored Jerusalem (vi. 7-9). The vessels of the heavenly Jerusalem would naturally be of a heavenly kind, and are in fact already there (iv. 5).

chastened during a time, and the world will not be
IV.2-7 = B²(?). given over to oblivion.   2. [Dost thou think that
this is that city of which I said : 'On the palms of
My hands have I graven thee'?   3. It is not this
building which is now built in your midst; (it is) that
which will be revealed with Me, that which was pre-

2. It is noteworthy that the words "On the palms of My hands," etc., which are taken from Isa. xlix. 16, agree letter for letter with the Syriac Version, which here stands alone against the Mass., LXX., and Vulg., in presupposing יְדִי כַּפּוֹת עַל instead of Mass. כַּפַּיִם עַל. This fuller phrase which the Syriac presupposes is the usual one (cf. 1 Sam. v. 4; 2 Kings ix. 35; Dan. x. 10).

3. *It is not this building . . . (it is) that which will be revealed.* These words represent one of the final stages of a movement which had already its beginnings in the O. T. Throughout the O. T. Jerusalem had always been singled out as the one place on earth in which it had pleased God to dwell, and with which He had inseparably connected His name. But from the growing transcendence and enlargement of the idea of God, combined with the deepened consciousness of sin, and the consequent sense of the unfitness of Jerusalem as God's habitation, the doctrine of a heavenly Jerusalem complete in all its parts came to be evolved.

Of the existence indeed of heavenly antitypes of the Tabernacle and its furniture we are told already in the Priest's Code (Exod. xxv. 9, 40, cf. Heb. viii. 5). It needed only a step further to postulate the existence of the heavenly temple and city. That the earthly copies needed to be purified or even wholly renewed, we are taught in Isa. lx.; Ezek. xl.-xlviii.; but that nothing else could suffice save the actual descent of the heavenly Jerusalem to the earth was not concluded till the revival of religion under the early Maccabees. In Isa. liv. 11 and Tob. xiii. 16, 17, there are highly figurative accounts of the rebuilding of Jerusalem, but it is the earthly. The first actual emergence of the idea of the heavenly seems to be in the Eth. En. xc. 28, 29, where the old Jerusalem is removed and the new is brought and set up by God Himself, though even there a prior existence is not assigned to the latter. This would be about 164 B.C. But the older ideas still held their ground. Thus in the Psalms of Solomon xvii. 25, 33 (*circ.* 70-40 B.C.), as in the oldest part of the Eth. En. x. 16-19; xxv. 1 (*circ.* 180 B.C.), the purification of Jerusalem is all that appears needful to the writers as a preparation for the Messianic kingdom. Even when we come down to the first century of the Christian era, such purification is deemed sufficient for the *temporary* Messianic kingdoms depicted in Apoc. Bar. xxix.; xxxix.-xl.; lxxii.-lxxiv.; Ezra vii. 27-30 (for vii. 26 is an interpolation, as Kabisch points out); xii. 32-34; and possibly in xiii. 32-50, where xiii. 36 seems also an intrusion. In all these passages a Messiah is expected. In B¹ of the Apoc. Bar. *i.e.* vi. 9, Jerusalem is to be restored

pared beforehand here from the time when I took counsel to make Paradise, and showed it to Adam before he sinned, but when he transgressed the commandment, it was removed from him, as also Paradise. 4. And after these things I showed it to My

and to be established for ever, but this is not the new Jerusalem coming down from heaven. The latter is mentioned in xxxii. 2-4. It was indeed a very current conception in the latter half of the first century A.D. Thus we find it in Gal. iv. 26; Heb. xii. 22; Rev. iii. 12; xxi. 2, 10. In Gal. iv. 26 the heavenly Jerusalem is a symbol of the spiritual commonwealth of which the Christian is even now a member. But in Rev. iii. 12; xxi. 2, 10, it is an actual city, the counterpart of the earthly Jerusalem, with its own buildings and vessels. Here we should probably class the passage in Test. Dan. v. This city was to descend from heaven, but this expectation does not apparently lie at the base of Heb. xii. 22. Similar conceptions to that found in Rev. iii. 12; xxi. 2, 10, appear in 4 Ezra viii. 52, 53; x. 44-59; and also in vii. 26 and xiii. 36, though we must regard one or both of the last two as interpolated. With these last we might reckon also the heavenly Jerusalem mentioned in the text. The heavenly Jerusalem is variously described as the νέα (Test. Dan. v.), ἡ ἄνω (Gal. iv. 26), καινή (Rev. iii. 12; xxi. 2), ἐπουράνιος (Heb. xii. 22). It was created in the beginning of creation, and preserved in heaven. It was shown to Adam before he sinned. To Adam indeed the heavens had been open originally (Slav. En. xxxi. 2; Philo, *Quaest.* xxxii. in *Gen.*; Book of Adam and Eve, i. 8); but when he transgressed the commandment the vision of the heavenly Jerusalem

was taken from him and likewise the possession of Paradise. Among the Rabbins the heavenly Jerusalem was called ירושלים של מעלה (= ἡ ἄνω Ἰερουσαλήμ). For the various Rabbinic conceptions regarding it, see Schöttgen, *de Hieros. Coelest.* in his *Horae Hebr.* 1205 *sqq.*; Meuschen, *N.T. ex Talm. ill.* p. 199 *sqq.*; Bertholdt, *Christologia*, 217 - 220; Eisenmenger, *Entdecktes Judenthum*, ii. 839 - 845; Weber, *Lehren d. Talmud*, 356-359, 386.

Took counsel to make Paradise. Which Paradise is this? The context might support either. For we might regard it as the Paradise which is kept in heaven like the heavenly Jerusalem. Adam could see both before his fall, but after it he lost the vision of both. It may, however, be the earthly Paradise in which he was placed at the first. The period to which the creation of the earthly Paradise is assigned varies. In Gen. ii. 8-17 it is apparently one of the last works of the creation. When, however, we come down to the Christian era, its creation was attributed to the third day (Jub. ii. 7; Slav. En. xxx. 1). The heavenly Paradise, on the other hand, is described as already existing before the creation of the world either actually or in the mind of God (see *Pesach.* 54a; *Beresh.* 20 in Weber *L. d. T.* 191).

4. *I showed it to My servant Abraham.* There is naturally no mention of this in Gen. xv. 9-21; but in the *Beresh. rabba* on Gen. xxviii. 17 we are told that this

servant Abraham by night among the portions of
the victims.   5. And again also I showed it to
Moses on Mount Sinai when I showed to him the
likeness of the tabernacle and all its vessels.   6. And
now, behold, it is preserved with Me, as also Paradise.
7. Go, therefore, and do as I command thee."]

V.-IX. 1 = B¹.   V. And I answered and said: "I shall, therefore,
be in great straits in Zion, because Thine enemies will
come to that place and pollute Thy sanctuary, and
lead Thine inheritance into captivity, and will lord it
over those whom Thou hast loved, and they will depart
again to the place of their idols, and will boast before
them.   And what wilt Thou do for Thy great name?"
2. And the Lord said unto me: "My name and My
glory have an eternal duration; My judgment, moreover, will preserve its rights in its own time.   3. And
thou wilt see with thine eyes that the enemy will not
overthrow Zion, nor burn Jerusalem, but be subservient
to the judge for a time.   4. But do thou go and do
whatsoever I have said unto thee."   5. And I went
and took Jeremiah, and Adu, and Seriah, and Jabish,

vision was accorded to Jacob when
sleeping at Bethel.
   5. Cf. Exod. xxv. 9, 40.
   6. See note on verse 3.
   7. *As I command thee.*   A frequently recurring phrase (cf. v. 4;
x. 4; xxi. 1; 4 Ezra v. 20; xii. 51).
   V. 1. *Thine inheritance.*   Deut.
iv. 20; ix. 26, etc.; Rest of Words
of Baruch, ii. 7; iii. 6.
   Whom Thou hast loved. Ephes.
xxi. 20; 4 Ezra iv. 23.
   Boast before them.   Cf. vii. 1;
lxvii. 2, 7; lxxx. 3; Rest of Words
of Baruch, i. 5; iv. 7.

What wilt Thou do, etc.   Joshua
vii. 9; cf. 4 Ezra iv. 25; x. 22.
   2. *My name and My glory*, etc.
Ps. cxxxv. 13.
   *My judgment, moreover, will pre-
serve its rights.*   This phrase in a
slightly different form recurs in
xlviii. 27, and lxxxv. 9.
   3. This is carried out in vi. 5; vii.
   4. This refers to the command
given in ii. 1.
   5. *Adu.*   There is a priest of this
name who went up with Zerubbabel
(Neh. xii. 4).   According to Mass.
he is called Iddo, but both the

and Gedaliah, and all the honourable men of the
people, and I led them to the valley of Cedron, and
I narrated to them all that had been said to me.   6.
And they lifted up their voice, and they all wept.   7.
And we sat there and fasted until the evening.

VI. And it came to pass on the morrow that, lo !

Syriac and Vulgate give Addo. In
Ezra viii. 17 another Iddo is men-
tioned who returned with Ezra from
Babylon.

Seriah. This Seriah was brother
of Baruch and chief chamberlain of
Zedekiah. He went with the latter
to Babylon (see Jer. li. 59, 61).

Jabish. This name has been identified with Ἰγαβής = יַבֵּץ (1 Chron.
iv. 9), but both the form of the name
and the time of Jabez are against
this identification.

Gedaliah. This is Gedaliah the
son of Ahikam (see Jer. xl. 14).
But Gedaliah might also be from
Γοθολίας = עֲתַלְיָה (cf. 1 Chron. viii.
26) a companion of Ezra (see Ezra
viii. 7). Gedaliah is again mentioned in xliv. 1 in a fragment of B[1].

Cedron, i.e. קִדְרוֹן (2 Sam. xv. 23).
The valley of the Cedron is again
the scene of Baruch's fast in xxi. 1,
and of an assembly of the people in
xxxi. 2.

Narrated to them, etc.   After
most of the revelations which Baruch
receives, he makes known their disclosures to his friends and the elders
of the people (see x. 4 ; xxxi. 3-
xxxii. 7 ; xliv.-xlvi. ; lxxvii. 1-17).
There is no need of such a disclosure
in the second section, *i.e.* v. 7-viii.,
and such disclosure is forbidden in
the fourth, *i.e.* xii. 5-xx.

THE SECOND SECTION

V. 7 - VIII.   This is a short
section. First there is the fast of

one day (v. 1). Thereupon to Baruch
in his grief (vi. 2) is disclosed a
vision. In this he sees the sacred
vessels committed to the earth for
a season and the city destroyed
by angels, lest the enemy should
triumph (vi. 3-vii.) The realisation of this vision which follows
thereupon dispenses with the need
of its publication by Baruch (viii.)

7. *Fasted until the evening.* The
other fasts mentioned are of seven
days. Of these there are four
(see ix. 2 ; xii. 5 ; xxi. 1 ; xlvii.
2). The symmetry of the book
would require another such fast
after xxxv. For the scheme of the
final editor is first a fast, then
generally a prayer, then a divine
message or revelation, then an
announcement of this either to an
individual, as in v. 5 ; x. 4, or to
the people (xxxi. 2 - xxxiv. ; xliv.-
xlvi. ; lxxvii. 1-17), followed occasionally by a lamentation. In xx.
5, at the close of the fourth section,
Baruch is bidden to make no announcement.

It will be observed that this
scheme is broken through in the
fifth section only, *i.e.* in xxi.-xlvi.,
where there is a fast, a prayer, an
address to the people followed by a
lament over Zion, a revelation and an
address to the people (see ix. 2, note).
In 4 Ezra there are four fasts of
seven days (see v. 20 ; vi. 35 ; ix.
26, 27 ; xii. 51).

VI. 1. *On the following morning,*
etc. These words are reproduced in
Rest of Words (iv. 1).

the army of the Chaldees surrounded the city, and at the time of the evening I, Baruch, left the people, and I went forth and stood by the oak.   2. And I was grieving over Zion, and lamenting over the captivity which had come upon the people.   3. And, lo! suddenly a strong spirit raised me, and bore me aloft over the wall of Jerusalem.   4. And I beheld, and lo! four angels standing at the four angles of the city, each of them holding a lamp of fire in his hands.   5. And another angel began to descend from heaven, and said unto them: "Hold your lamps, and do not light them till I tell you.   6. For I am first sent to speak a word to the earth, and to place in it what the Lord the Most High has commanded me."   7. And I saw him descend into the Holy of Holies, and take from thence the veil,

By the oak. This oak is outside the city; for in ii. 1 Jeremiah and all that were like him were bidden to leave the city. This they and Baruch did in v. 5, and they fasted in the valley of the Cedron. On the following day the Chaldees surround the city. On that day Baruch left Jeremiah and the rest and went forth (probably from the cavern in the Cedron valley mentioned in xxi. 1) and stood by the oak. The oak thus appears to be near or in the Cedron valley, and thus in the neighbourhood of Jerusalem. This oak is mentioned again in lxxvii. 18. We are not, therefore, to compare this oak with the well-known one at Hebron, as Fritzsche, who compares LXX.; Gen. xiii. 18; xiv. 13; xviii. 1.

It is noteworthy that no mention of this oak appears in B². In B¹ it is found twice (vi. 1 and lxxvii.

18). A tree is referred to in A³ in lv. 1.

3. As the Chaldeans encompassed Jerusalem, Baruch was unable to draw near to the wall. But a strong angel lifts him on high above the wall.

4. Cf. Rev. vii. 1, "I saw four angels standing on the four corners of the earth"; Rest of Words of Bar. iii. 2.

5. Cf. Rev. vii. 2; Rest of Words, iii. 4.

6. The office of the angel here is executed by Jeremiah in Rest of Words, iii. 8.

The Lord the Most High. Occurs here only in this book. It is not found in 4 Ezra.

7. *Take from thence*, etc. According to Josephus, *Bell*, V. 5, 5, the Holy of Holies in Herod's temple was empty.

See Appendix for a similar account

and the holy ephod, and the mercy-seat, and the two tables, and the holy raiment of the priests, and the altar of incense, and the forty-eight precious stones, wherewith the priest was adorned, and all the holy vessels of the tabernacle.   8. And he spake to the earth with a loud voice : " Earth, earth, earth, hear the word of the mighty God, and receive what I commit to thee, and guard them until the last times, so that, when thou art ordered, thou mayst restore them, so that strangers may not get possession of them.   9. For the time comes when Jerusalem also will be delivered up for a time, until it is said, that it is again restored for ever.   10. And the earth opened its mouth and swallowed them up."

VII. And after these things I heard that angel say-

in Macc.   *The veil, i.e.* פָּרֹכֶת (Exod. xxvi. 31). *The ephod, i.e.* אֵפֹר (Exod. xxix. 5).

Mercy-seat, כַּפֹּרֶת (Exod. xxv. 17). *Forty-eight precious stones.* How this number is made up I cannot discover. There were twelve stones on the breastplate (Exod. xxviii. 15-21), and two on the ephod (Exod. xxviii. 9).

The altar of incense. The Syriac implies θυμιατήριον, which in Josephus and Philo = מזבח הקטרה. See Appendix.

According to *Bammidbar rabba,* 15, five things were taken away and preserved on the destruction of Solomon's temple : the candlestick, the ark, the fire, the Holy Spirit, and the cherubim.

8. In the Rest of Words, iii. 8, these words in a greatly altered shape are attributed to Jeremiah.

Earth . . . of the mighty God ; drawn from Jer. xxii. 29. Text agrees with Mass., Syr., Vulg., against LXX., which gives " earth " only twice.

Mighty God. This title recurs in vii. 1, and xiii. 2, 4. It is not found in 4 Ezra.

Guard them until the last times. Cf. Rest of Words, iii. 8, "Preserve the vessels of worship until the coming of the Beloved."

That . . . thou mayst restore them, *i.e.* for use in the temple of the rebuilt Jerusalem.

That strangers may not get possession of them (cf. x. 19). For a slightly different reason see lxxx. 2.

9. *For a time.* See i. 4, note.

Restored for ever. It is not necessary to take the phrase "for ever" literally. In any case a Messianic kingdom of indefinite duration is looked forward to with Jerusalem as its centre, and likewise the temple in which the sacred vessels of the former temple will again be used. During this kingdom the dispersion will again return to Palestine (lxxvii. 6; lxxviii. 7, notes).

ing unto those angels who held the lamps : "Destroy,
therefore, and overthrow its walls to its foundations,
lest the enemy should boast and say : 'We have overthrown the wall of Zion, and we have burnt the place
of the mighty God.'" 2. And the Spirit restored me
to the place where I had been standing before.

VIII. Now the angels did as he had commanded
them, and when they had broken up the angles of the
walls, a voice was heard from the interior of the temple,
after the wall had fallen, saying : 2. "Enter ye enemies,
and come ye adversaries ; for He who kept the house
has forsaken (it)." 3. And I, Baruch, departed. 4.
And it came to pass after these things that the army
of the Chaldees entered and seized the house, and all
that was around it. 5. And they led the people away
captive, and slew some of them, and bound Zedekiah
the king, and sent him to the king of Babylon.

VII. 1. *Destroy, therefore, and
overthrow*, etc. Cf. v. 3 ; lxxx. 1.

Boast. Cf. v. 1 ; lxvii. 2, 7 ; lxxx.
3 ; Rest of Words, i. 5 ; Ps. xxxv.
19 ; xxxviii. 16 ; Ecclus. xxiii. 3 ;
Pss. Sol. xiii. 7, ἐν περιστολῇ
παιδεύεται δίκαιος, ἵνα μὴ ἐπιχαρῇ
ὁ ἁμαρτωλὸς τῷ δικαίῳ.

Mighty God. See vi. 8, note.

2. *And the Spirit restored me.* I
have here made a necessary emendation of the text. Thus I have
emended ܠܐ ܐܘܠܝ ܠܐ ܐܘ ܠܐ ܐ = "and
you have seized it," into ܠܐܘܠܐ
ܠܐ ܠܐ ܐܘ ܠܐ, " And the spirit restored
me." The unamended text gives
no sense, whereas the change just
made restores the harmony of the
context. Thus in vi. 31, "a strong
spirit" carried Baruch aloft in

order to see the vision. After the
vision this spirit restores him to
where he had been before. From
this place Baruch departs in viii. 3.

VIII. 1. Cf. vii. 1 ; lxxx. 1.

2. Cf. Rest of Words, iv. 1. *He
who kept the house has forsaken* (*it*).
Cf. Josephus, *De Bello Jud.* vi. 5. 8 :
μετὰ δὲ ταῦτα (ἀντιλαβέσθαι) καὶ
φωνῆς ἀθρόας μεταβαίνωμεν ἐντεῦθεν.

Tacitus, *Hist.* v. 13, "Et apertae
repente delubri fores et audita major
humana vox, excedere deos."

5. *Led* . . . *away captive.* lxxx.
4 ; Rest of Words, iv. 2.

*Bound Zedekiah the king, and
sent*, etc. Whatever explanation we
give of i. 1, it is clear from these
words that the writer was acquainted
with the history of the kings of
Judah and the captivity of Judah
under Zedekiah.

IX. And I, Baruch, came, and Jeremiah, whose heart was found pure from sins, who had not been captured in the seizure of the city.   2. And we rent our garments, and wept, and mourned, and fasted seven days.

X. And it came to pass after seven days, that the word of the Lord was upon me, and said unto me: " Tell Jeremiah to go and confirm the captivity of the

IX. 2-X. 5 = E and B².

Bound and sent to the king of Babylon. Cf. lxxx. 4.

IX. 1. *Heart . . . pure from sin.* Contrast the "wicked heart" in 4 Ezra iii. 20, 21, 26 ; iv. 4, etc. In Pss. Sol. xvii. 41, the Messiah is said to be καθαρὸς ἀπὸ ἁμαρτίας.

THE THIRD SECTION

IX. 2-XII. 4. We have first the fast of seven days amid the ruins of Zion (ix., cf. x. 3). Then the word of the Lord comes to Baruch and bids him to tell Jeremiah to go to Babylon (x. 2), and promises a revelation of what should be in the end (x. 3). Then follows Baruch's announcement of the divine message to Jeremiah (x. 4). The section closes with Baruch's lament before the gates of the temple over Zion (x. 5-xii. 4).

We have shown below that x. 6-xii. 4 comes probably from the hand of a Sadducean priest.

IX. 2. *Fasted seven days.* See v. 7, note. This is the first fast of seven days. It is observed amid the ruins of Zion (cf. x. 3). There are three others to follow, though, as we have shown in the note just referred to, there should be four. The insertion of the fasts *in their present positions* is the work of the final editor. There seem to have been fasts in his sources (B¹ and B²).

Fasting was the usual preparation for the reception of supernatural communications (cf. Dan. ix. 3, 20-21, and all the instances in this book and 4 Ezra cited in note on v. 7). In Test. Jos. iii. there is likewise a fast of seven days (Armenian Version), and in 2 Macc. xiii. 12, and Ass. Mosis ix. 6, of three days.

The scene of the first and fourth fasts is Cedron ; of the second and sixth, Mount Zion ; of the third, the gates of the temple ; the account of the fourth is lost.

X. 1. *God.* This word is found only twice again, *i.e.* liv. 12 ; lxxxii. 9. Its use is more frequent in 4 Ezra (see vii. 19, 20, 21, 79 ; viii. 58 ; ix. 45 ; x. 16).

2. The divine communication that follows on the fast consists of a command to be given through Baruch to Jeremiah. Jeremiah is bidden to go to Babylon. We have here a violation of historical truth. According to Jer. xliii. 4-7, both Jeremiah and Baruch were carried down into Egypt. In the Apocryphal Baruch i. 1, Baruch is represented as being in Babylon five years after the capture of Jerusalem. In the Rest of Words, iv. 5, Jeremiah was dragged an unwilling captive to Babylon, whereas in our text he goes there at the bidding of God. The words "go and confirm the captivity" recur in xxxiii. 2.

people unto Babylon.   3. But do thou remain here
amid the desolation of Zion, and I will show to thee
after these days what will befall at the end of days."
4. And I said to Jeremiah as the Lord commanded me.
5. And he, indeed, departed with the people, but I,
Baruch, returned and sat before the gates of the temple,
and I lamented with that lamentation over Zion and

X. 6.-XII. 4 =   said: 6. "Blessed is he who was not born, or being
B² or S.

It is probable that the references
to Jeremiah in connection with Babylon belong to B² ; for it is noteworthy that in lxxvii. 17, 19 ; lxxx.
4 ; lxxxv. 6, Baruch always speaks
of writing to the brethren in Babylon,
but never to Jeremiah.   This would
be strange if the writer believed
Jeremiah to be there.   The people
also urge Baruch in lxxvii. 12 to
write to their brethren in Babylon
to confirm them.   Now if Jeremiah
were in charge of the people there,
as x. 2, 5 ; xxxiii. 2, clearly imply,
any letter of Baruch to Babylon
would have been addressed to him.
As a matter of fact, in the Rest
of Words of Baruch, when Baruch
writes to Babylon, he directs the
letter to Jeremiah.
It is probable, therefore, that the
account of B¹ does not conflict with
Jer. xliii., where Johanan takes
Jeremiah with him down into Egypt.
3. Baruch is commanded to remain
among the ruins of Zion, and is
promised a revelation of what will
befall in the last days.   The words
"after these days" show that this
revelation will be accorded on a
future occasion, after a fast, no
doubt.
   At the end of days. Cf. xxv. 1.
5. Before the gates of the temple.
This is the scene of the following
lamentation of Baruch, and probably
of the fast in xii. 5.   It is again the
scene of his lamentation in xxxv. 1.

A passage in the beginning of the
Apoc. Bar. Tert. seems to be derived from our text : οὕτως ἐκάθητο
ἐπὶ τὰς ὡραίας πύλας ὅπου ἔκειτο
τὰ τῶν ἁγίων ἅγια.   Mount Zion,
on the other hand, is the scene
where revelations are accorded to
him (cf. xiii. 1 ; xxi. 2 ; xlvii. 2).
   X. 6-XII. 4.   This fragment appears to be the work of a Sadducee
—probably a Sadducean priest writing just after the fall of the temple.
For (1) in x. 6 and xi. 7 we have
a thoroughly Sadducean sentiment,
i.e. it were best not to be born at
all, or, being born, to die ; for the
dead enjoy a sorrowless rest and a
tranquil sleep (xi. 4) ; they know not
the anguish of the living (xi. 5).   No
resurrection of the individual or of
the nation is looked for, but only
that retribution in due course may
come upon the enemies of Israel (xii.
4).   (2) The conception of Sheol in
xi. 6 is Sadducean.   (3) In x. 6-xii.
4 we have the saddest dirge in the
Jewish literature of the time.   This
might well be ; for for the priesthood
there was no future. As false stewards
they relinquish their charge and
restore the keys of the temple to
God (x. 18).   Never again should
sacrifices be offered in Zion (x. 10).
   X. 6. Blessed is he who was not born,
etc. Similar expressions of pessimism
and despair return time and again
in the later literature of Judaism.
But in this passage and in xi. 7 the

born has died.   7. But as for us who live, woe unto us, because we see the afflictions of Zion, and what has befallen Jerusalem.   8. I will call the Sirens

phrase is used with a significance that severs it from all other instances of its occurrence. For whereas repeatedly elsewhere, as we shall see presently, it is said that it were better man had never been born because of sin and future condemnation, here non-existence or death is said to be preferable to witnessing the present woes of Jerusalem. Lest we should suppose this to be an accidental exaggeration, we should observe that it recurs in an intensified form in xi. 7, where the state of the dead in Sheol is said to be better than that of the living. Such a sentiment was impossible for the Pharisaic author of B², or indeed for any of the authors of this Apocalypse. It is a genuinely Sadducean sentiment, and the conception of Sheol in xi. 6, 7 is likewise Sadducean —practically that of the O. T. or of Hades in the Greek world. To a Pharisee no condition of earthly life could in any way approach the horrors of the existence of the wicked in the after-world.

In 4 Ezra and elsewhere, as we have remarked, quite a different turn is given to the expression in our text. There it is said that it were better man had not been at all than be born and have to face *future torment and judgment*. Thus in vii. 66 the writer declares : "It is much better for them (*i.e.* the beasts of the field) than for us ; for they expect not a judgment and know not of torments." Again in vii. 116, 117, it is urged that "it would have been best not to have given a body to Adam, or, that being done, to have restrained him from sin ; for what profit is there that man should in the present life live in heaviness and

after death look for punishment?" Finally, in iv. 12 the nexus of life, sin and suffering, just referred to is put still more strongly : "It were better we had not been born at all than that we should be born and live in sin and suffer." A perfect parallel to the last passage is found in the Slav. En. xli. 2 : "Blessed is the man who was not born, or, having been born, has never sinned . . . so that he should not come into this place (*i.e.* hell) ;" and to 4 Ezra vii. 116, 117, in the Eth. En. xxxviii. 2, where it is said, in reference to the future destiny of the wicked: "It had been good for them if they had not been born." For a N. T. parallel see Matt. xxvi. 24. It is worth observing that there is a perfect parallelism of thought between the passage in our text and in Sophocles, *Oed. Col.*, 1220—

μὴ φῦναι τὸν ἅπαντα νι-
   κᾷ λόγον · τὸ δ᾽, ἐπεὶ φανῇ,
   βῆναι κεῖθεν ὅθεν περ ἥ-
   κει, πολὺ δεύτερον ὡς τάχιστα,

and in Theognis, 425—

πάντων μὲν μὴ φῦναι ἐπιχθονίοισιν
   ἄριστον,
μὴ ἐσιδεῖν αὐγὰς ὀξέος ἠελίου ·
φῦντα δ᾽ ὅπως ὤκιστα πύλας Ἀΐδαο
   περῆσαι,
καὶ κεῖσθαι πολλὴν γῆν ἐπαμησά-
   μενον.

8.· *Sirens.* These are said in the Eth. En. xix. 2 (Greek Version) to have been the wives of the angels who went astray. It is strange that we have here the Greek conception of the Sirens, Σειρῆνες, *i.e.* that of sea-nymphs. But with the Greek translators of the O. T. it had quite a different meaning. Thus it is a

from the sea, and ye Lilin, come ye from the desert,
and ye Shedim and dragons from the forests: awake
and bind your loins unto mourning, and take up with
me lamentation, and mourn with me.   9. Ye husband-
men, sow not again; and thou, earth, wherefore givest
thou the fruits of thy produce ? keep within thee the
sweets of thy sustenance.   10. And thou, vine, why
further dost thou give thy wine ? for an offering will

rendering of בנות יענה = ostriches in
Isa. xiii. 2I ; Jer. l. 39 ; Mic. i. 8 ;
of חנים or חניך=jackals in Isa. xxxiv.
13 ; xliii. 20. It is similarly used
by Symmachus, Theodotion, and
Aquila in rendering the above words.

Lelioto. These are the Lilin (לִילִין)
from the singular Lilith (לִילִיה). Male
and female demons named Lil and
Lilit belong to Assyrian and Babylonian demonology. They were
thought, as were also the Lilin
(Shabbath, 151b), to attack men and
women in their sleep (Lenormant,
La Magie, p. 36). The Lilith, or
night demon, is mentioned in Isa.
xxxiv. 14, along with the satyr שָׂעִיר.
The Lilin, according to the Talmud,
were female demons corresponding
to the Shedim or male demons.
They were partly the offspring
(*Erub,* 18b ; *Beresh.* 42) of Adam
and Lilith, Adam's first wife, a
demon, and partly were derived from
the generation that God dispersed
(Gen. xi.), for God (*Jalkut Shim.,*
Beresh. 62) transformed that generation into Shedim, Ruchin, and Lilin.
These Lilin inhabited desert places.
They were said to kill children.
They have been compared with the
Lamiæ and Striges ; ὀνοκένταυροι is
the LXX. rendering of the word in
Isa. xxxiv. 14. For further details
on the subject see Weber, *Lehren
d. Talm.,* pp. 245, 246, 248 ; Bochart,

Hierozoicon ; iii. 829-831 ; Eisenmenger, *Entd. Judenthum,* ii. 413-
426, 452.

Shedim. These were male demons
to which various origins were
assigned. Their souls were created
by God, but as the Sabbath intervened before they received bodies
they had to remain without them
(*Beresh. rabba,* c. 7) ; or they were
sprung from Adam and a demon
wife, or from Eve and a demon
husband (*Beresch. rabba,* c. 24) ; or
were originally the generation that
God transformed into Shedim,
Ruchin, and Lilin. Their place of
resort is the wilderness. For an
account of their activities, see Weber,
245, 246.

Dragons. The word ﻣﻌﺟﻮﻥ is
found in the Peshitto of Isa. xiii. 22
as a translation of חנים. Levy (*Neuhebräisches Wörterbuch,* ii. 265) de-
fines it as "Drache oder sonst ein
Thier mit klagendem, heulendem
Tone." The word frequently occurs
in the Targums and later Hebrew
as ירוד (ירוד).

10. The writer of x. 6 - xii. 4
resigns absolutely all hope of the
restoration of Jerusalem. This is
throughout the attitude of B² (see i.
4, note).

With the thought of this verse,
cf. *Kethuboth* 112a : "O land, land,
let thy fruit shrivel : for whom art
thou producing thy fruit ? is it not

not again be made therefrom in Zion, nor will first-fruits
again be offered.   11. And do ye, O heavens, withhold
your dew, and open not the treasuries of rain.   12.
And do thou, O sun, withhold the light of thy rays;
and do thou, O moon, extinguish the multitude of thy
light; for why should light rise again where the light
of Zion is darkened?   13. And you, ye bridegrooms,
enter not in, and let not the brides adorn themselves
with garlands; and, ye women, pray not that ye may
bear.   14. For the barren shall rejoice more, and
those who have no sons shall be glad, and those who
have sons shall have anguish.   15. For why should
they bear in pain and bury in grief?   16. Or wherefore, again, should mankind have sons; or wherefore
should the seed of their nature again be named, where
that mother is desolate, and her sons are led into
captivity?   17. From this time forward speak not of
beauty and discourse not of gracefulness.   18. Moreover,
ye priests, take ye the keys of the sanctuary and cast
them into the height of heaven, and give them to the

for the Gentiles who rose up against
us because of our sins?

13. Cf. Jer. vii. 34; xvi. 9; xxv.
10; Baruch ii. 23.

Brides. Syriac gives "virgins,"
but this idea is out of place in verses
13-16, where everything refers to
marriage. The first right mention
of virgins is in verse 19. The wrong
text may be explained by a corruption of בלוח into בתולות or עלמוח.
In the original Hebrew we should
then have a paronomasia, כלילים
אל תעדינה בלוח. In *Git.* 7a, and in
Shabbath, 59b, bridegrooms are forbidden to use garlands.

14. Cf. Matt. xxiv. 19; Luke
xxiii. 29: "Blessed are the barren,
and the wombs that never bare, and
the breasts that never gave suck"
(cf. Isa. liv. 1).

16. *That mother.* See iii. 1, note

18. The priesthood have proved
faithless to their duty, and the
charge of the temple is no longer
theirs. Cf. Rest of Words, iv. 3, 4,
where another turn is given to the
text: "And thereupon Jeremiah took
the keys of the temple . . . and cast
these keys before the sun, saying:
'I say unto thee, O sun, take the
keys of the house of God and keep

Lord, and say : 'Guard Thy house Thyself, for lo ! we are found false stewards.' 19. And you, ye virgins, who spin fine linen and silk with gold of Ophir, hasten and take all things and cast (them) into the fire, that it may bear them to Him who made them, and the flame send them to Him who created them, lest the enemy get possession of them."

XI. Moreover, I, Baruch, say this against thee, Babylon : " If thou hadst prospered, and Zion had dwelt in her glory, it would have been a great grief to us that thou shouldst be equal to Zion.   2. But now, lo ! the grief is infinite, and the lamentation measure-less, for lo ! thou art prospered and Zion desolate. 3. Who will be judge regarding these things ? or to whom shall we complain regarding that which has befallen us ?   O Lord, how hast Thou borne (it) ?   4. Our fathers went to rest without grief, and lo ! the righteous sleep in the earth in tranquillity.   5. For

them till the days when the Lord shall ask thee concerning them. For we are not worthy to keep them ; for we have been found false stewards.'"

This verse reappears in the *Jalkut Shim.* on Isa. xxi. as follows : "The flower of the priests . . . gathered together . . . the keys of the court and the sanctuary and said before God : 'Lord of the universe, we are not fit to be stewards before Thee (לא זכינו להיות גוברים לפניך).   Behold Thy keys are returned to Thee.' And they cast them aloft " (quoted by Rosenthal).

19. *Fine linen and silk.* Cf. Ezek. xvi. 10.

Lest the enemy get possession. Cf. vi. 8.

XI. 1. *Babylon* stands here for

Rome, as in Rev. xiv. 8 ; xvi. 19 ; xvii. 5 ; xviii. 2.

Prospered. Cf. xii. 1-3.

3. *How hast Thou borne (it)?* Cf. 4 Ezra iii. 30 : "I have seen how Thou dost bear with them that sin." In Pss. Sol. ii. 1 and 4 Ezra iii. 8 the writers complain that God did not prevent such wrong-doing. With the latter cf. Isa. xiv. 6.

4. *Our fathers went to rest.* Cf. lxxxv. 9.

Sleep in the earth. Cf. xxi. 24 ; while the diction corresponds to Dan. xii. 2, "sleep in the dust of the earth," the thought is Sad-ducean and belongs to the earlier sphere of O.T. thought, presupposed in such a phrase as "slept with his fathers" (1 Kings ii. 10 ; xi. 21,

they knew not this anguish, nor yet had they heard of that which had befallen us. 6. Would that thou hadst ears, O earth, and that thou hadst a heart, O dust, that ye might go and announce in Sheol, and say to the dead: 7. 'Blessed are ye more than we who are living.'"

XII. But I will say this as I think, and I will speak against thee, O land, which art prospering. 2. The noonday does not always burn, nor do the constant rays of the sun (always) give light. 3. Do not conclude or expect that thou wilt always be prosperous and rejoicing, and be not greatly uplifted and boastful. 4. For assuredly in its own season wrath will awake against thee, which now in long-suffering is held in as it

etc.) There is no ground for supposing with Kabisch (*Das vierte Buch Ezra*, 68, 69) that this phrase in the mouth of a Pharisee of this period implied a capacity of life as still existing in the body even when interred. That "to sleep in the earth" and "to be in Sheol" are equivalent expressions for a Pharisee, is clear from Eth. En. li. 1 and 4 Ezra vii. 32. The former phrase, "to sleep in the earth," is merely a figure of speech, and must not be pressed. Yet see l. 2, note. These phrases are equivalents in verses 6, 7. Sadducean thought admitted of no resurrection; hence "life in Sheol" or "sleep in the earth" were interchangeable expressions for the same fact.

5. To a Pharisee this would be a trifling pain compared with the torments of the damned. But the Sadducee looked for no retribution in the world to come, but, like most of the writers in the O.T. and in Ecclesiasticus, only for a shadowy existence in Sheol.

6. *That ye might go*, etc. The

Syriac = "and go ye." Here we have a Hebrew idiom, *i.e.* an imperative is used instead of a jussive in order to express the intention signified by the preceding verb (see Driver, *Hebrew Moods and Tenses*, p. 82).

Sheol. We have here the O.T. conception of Sheol—the eternal abode of the shades. This view of Sheol was maintained in N.T. times by the Sadducees. In xxiii. 5; xlviii. 16; lii. 2; lvi. 6, Sheol seems to be the abode of all departed souls prior to the final judgment. This also may be its meaning in xxi. 23 and in 4 Ezra iv. 41. In 4 Ezra viii. 53 it seems to bear the meaning of "hell." For a history of the various meanings borne by this word see Eth. En. lxiii. 10, note.

7. The condition of the shades was for the writer undoubtedly more blessed than that of the living (cf. x. 6, note).

XII. 3. *Boastful.* I have here emended ܠ‍ܡ‍ܒ‍ܟ‍ܡ = "do (not) oppress" into ܠ‍ܡ‍ܒ‍ܪ‍ܗ‍ܬ‍ܡ = "be (not) boastful."

XII. 5 = E.   were by reins.   5. And when I had said these things,
I fasted seven days.

XIII.-XXV. =   XIII. And it came to pass after these things, that
B².

THE FOURTH SECTION

XII. 5-XX. This section begins
with a fast of seven days (xii. 5).
Then follows a long revelation to
Baruch (xiii. 2-xx. 2). (Owing to
the complete disarrangement and
confusion of the text, this revelation
cannot be summarised here. For a
discussion of these chapters see pp.
20-34.) Contrary to the usual procedure, Baruch is bidden not to
publish this revelation (xx. 3).

XII. 5. On the fasts of Baruch
see v. 9, note; ix. 2, note.

XIII.-XXV. The text of these
chapters is inexplicable as it stands.
The difficulties are due not to corruption, though that undoubtedly
exists, but to a recasting of the
original text by the final editor. In
this process many passages were torn
from their original contexts and
placed in settings which are quite un-
suitable. Some of the incongruities
thus produced are as follows: (1) The
words "those prosperous cities" are
represented as speaking in xiii. 4
without a single note of introduction.
(2) In the next verse the words,
"thou and those like thee who have
seen," are similarly unexplained,
and are in fact inexplicable in their
present context; for though Baruch
was to be preserved till the consummation of the times, his contemporaries were not, and hence
they could not see the future
retribution of the Gentiles. If,
however, xxiv. 2 originally preceded
xiii. 3b-5, the words, "thou and
those like thee who have seen,"
would be perfectly intelligible. (3)
Again the retribution of the Gentiles
referred to in xiii. 4, 5 has not been
mentioned before, though the text

presupposes some such mention. It
is intelligible if xxv. or xxiv. 4 precedes where Baruch asks what will
befal the enemies of Israel. (4) In
xiv. 1 Baruch replies that God has
shown him "the method of the
times," whereas in xx. 6 this appears
not to have been yet done, and it
seems that a revelation of "the
method of the times" is still to
come. (5) In xxiv. 4 Baruch asks
what retribution awaits the enemies
of Israel, and when will the judgment be? In xxv. we find the
answer to the latter question, whereas
the answer to the former is already
given in xiii. 4-12. (6) I can discover no adequate explanation of the
"therefore" with which xx. 1 begins
in its present context. If xx. were
read immediately after xiii. the text
would at once become clear. On
these and other grounds we must
attempt to restore the original order
of the chapters before they were
broken up and rearranged, mutilated, and interpolated by the final
editor. Owing to the paucity of
materials the attempt to restore the
original order can only be partially
successful. This order was probably
xiii. 1-3a; xx.; xxiv. 2-4; xiii. 3b-
12; xxv., xiv.-xix.; xxi.-xxiv. 1;
xxx. 2. To reassure Baruch, who is
plunged in grief over Jerusalem
(xiii. 3a), God declares (xx. 1, 2)
that the days and years will speed
more quickly by in order to usher
in the judgment which will right all
wrongs, and that even Jerusalem
was removed with this end in view.
On the "method of the times"
Baruch is then promised disclosures
(xx. 6), and "he and many with
him" will see the mercy of God on
those that sinned and were righteous

I, Baruch, was standing upon Mount Zion, and lo! a voice came from the height and said unto me: 2. 'Stand upon thy feet, Baruch, and hear the word of the mighty God. 3. Because thou hast been astonied at what has befallen Zion, thou shalt therefore be assuredly preserved to the consummation of the times,

(xxiv. 2). Baruch, thereupon, asks two questions (xxiv. 4): (a) what will befal Israel's enemies ? (b) when will God judge the world (of which event He had already spoken, xx. 2)?

The answer to (a) is given in xiii. 3b-12. But the first words of this answer are lost. In these words there was a statement of this nature: "retribution will come upon the prosperous cities of your enemies" (cf. xiii. 4). Baruch, moreover (xiii. 3b-12), will be preserved until those days for the express purpose of testifying the reason of the retribution that has befallen these cities, and the date of its consummation. "He and those like him who have seen" (cf. xxiv. 2) should answer the remonstrances of the tormented Gentiles. And in answer to Baruch's second question, he is informed (xxv. 1, 2) that he shall likewise be preserved till the sign of the last days has come. This sign will be a stupor that shall seize the inhabitants of the earth (xxv. 3, 4). Baruch, thereupon, acknowledges : "Behold Thou hast shown me the method of the times" (xiv. 1). After this the thought advances connectedly through xiv.-xix. ; xxi.-xxiv. 1 ; xxx. 2. For like rearrangements of already existing texts by the final editor, see my edition of the Eth.En. pp. 189, 260, 267, 268, 270, 274.

XIII. 1. *Mount Zion.* Mount Zion is the scene of the revelation in xiii. xx. ; of the prayer in xxi. 4-25 (cf. xiii. 1 ; xx. 6 ; xxi. 2) ; of the revelation in xxii.-xxx. ; of

the seven days' fast in xlvii. 2 ; and of the prayer and revelation that follow xlviii.-lii.

A voice. Cf. xxii. 1, note.

2. *Stand upon thy feet.* Ezek. ii. 1. *The mighty God.* Cf. vi. 8 ; vii. 1 ; xiii. 4.

3. *Thou shalt therefore be assuredly preserved,* etc. This promise recurs twice again in B², *i.e.* in xxv. 1 and lxxvi. 2. Baruch is thus to be preserved as a testimony or a sign against the inhabitants of the earth in the last days (see also xiv. 2). This assumption and preservation of Baruch till the last judgment is the teaching of B². With the above passages compare also xlviii. 30 and xlvi. 7, where the last is due to the final editor. In B¹, on the other hand, Baruch is to die a natural death (lxxviii. 5 ; lxxxiv. 1) ; he is to go the way of all flesh (xliv. 2) and to forget all corruptible things and the affairs of mortals (xliii. 2). Thus we have two conflicting accounts touching the destiny of Baruch. It is noteworthy that we have in the text a transference of a distinct Enochic function to Baruch. For in Jubilees iv. 24 it is stated : "(Enoch) was set as a *sign* there (in Eden), and that he should *testify* against all the children of men ;" and again in x. 17 : "As a *testimony* to the generations of the world the office was ordained for Enoch of recounting all the deeds of generation unto generation till the day of judgment" (see also Slav. En. xl. 13 ; liii. 2 ; lxiv. 5).

that thou mayst be for a testimony.   4. So that, if ever
those prosperous cities say: 'Why hath the mighty
God brought upon us this retribution?'   5. Thou
and those like thee may say to them (even) ye who
have seen: 'This evil and (these) retributions which

This robbing of Enoch to benefit
Baruch is a clear sign of Jewish
hostility to Christianity, and a
tribute to the influence that Enoch
enjoyed in the Christian Church of
the first century. Enoch's acceptance amongst Christians as a Messianic prophet was the ground for
his rejection by the Jews.   So
thoroughgoing, indeed, was this rejection that, although he was the
chief figure next to Daniel in Jewish
Apocalyptic prior to 40 A.D., in
subsequent Jewish literature his
functions and achievements are assigned to others, such as Moses,
Ezra, or Baruch, and, with the exception of two or three passages, his
name in subsequent Jewish literature is henceforth studiously ignored.
The observation of this tendency
of Jewish thought becomes of
practical value to us when we come
to lix. 4-11, as we are thus enabled
to conclude that a document which
on other grounds is prior to 70 A.D.,
is posterior to the rise of Christianity because it manifests clear signs
of this tendency.

Assuredly be preserved. The
Syriac lit. = σωσθείς σωσθήσει, a
familiar Hebraism יִמָּלֵט מַלֵּט. This
idiom recurs frequently in this book
(see xxii. 7; xli. 6; xlviii. 30; l. 2;
lvi. 2; lxxv. 6; lxxvi. 2; lxxxii. 2;
lxxxiii. 1, 2, 3, 6; lxxxiv. 2). That
we have herein indubitable evidence
of a Hebrew original we have shown
in the Introduction.

4. *Those prosperous cities.* The
abruptness with which these cities
are introduced, though not hereto-

fore mentioned, and their complaints
about the retribution that has befallen them, though no such retribution has as yet been recorded,
shows either that the text preceding
these words has been lost, or else
that xiii. 3b-12 should be read
after xxiv. 2-4.   In fact, since
in xiii. 3b-12 we have an answer
to xxiv. 4, we must assume that
xiii. 3b-12 originally followed after
xxiv. 4, and since xiii. 4 presupposes that a statement about the
retribution that is to come upon the
prosperous enemies of Israel has
already been made, and since no
such statement is found, we must
further assume the loss of such
words immediately preceding xiii.
3b (see note on xxiv. 3, 4). It
might be possible to explain xiii.
4 by xxv. 3, and accordingly regard
xiii. 3b-12 as following originally
upon xxiv. 2-xxv. But many difficulties beset this interpretation.
The cities here spoken of are of
course Gentile cities (cf. ver. 11).
Brought upon us this retribution.
The same phrase practically is
applied to Israel in lxxvii. 4, but
here the "us" refers to the "prosperous cities." The *retribution* intended by the editor seems to be
that threatened in xii. 4.

5. *Thou and those like thee who
have seen it.* These words are
hardly capable of interpretation as
they stand.   They clearly mean
Baruch's contemporaries; observe
"ye who have seen"; but as the
time is that of the end, they cannot
be his contemporaries; for only

are coming upon you and upon your people (are sent) in its time that the nations may be perfectly chastened.' 6. And then they will expect.   7. And if they say at that time: 'When?' 8. Thou wilt say to them: 'Ye who have drunk the strained wine, drink ye also of its dregs, the judgment of the Lofty One who has no respect of persons.' 9. On this account He had before no mercy on His own sons, but afflicted them as His enemies, because they sinned.   10. They were therefore chastened then that they might receive mercy. 11. But now, ye peoples and nations, ye are debtors. because all this time ye have trodden down the earth,

---

Baruch is to be preserved till that date. If, however, xiii. 3b-12 was originally preceded by xxiv. 2-4, we can trace the phrase back to xxiv. 2—"thou wilt see and many who are with thee."

That the nations may be perfectly chastened. That this chastisement is vindictive and not corrective is clear from verse 7 ; the nations are to "drink of the dregs, the judgment of the Lofty One" ; and also from verses 10, 11, where the implication obviously is that, whereas Israel is punished with a view to its ultimate pardon, it is otherwise with the Gentiles. The vindictive punishment therefore of the Gentiles is dealt with in this chapter. But so far as I know ܪܕܐ = "chasten" is never used in the sense of vindictive punishment. This difficulty might be surmounted by supposing ܠܕ ܪܕܝܘ = "may be chastened," corrupt for ܠܕ ܪܕܝܘ = "may be dispersed" (cf. Isa. xxxiii. 3). In the next chapter, however, in xiv. 1, the retribution spoken of

by God is to be of service to the Gentiles. But see note *in loc.* On the other hand, it might be possible to understand ܟܢܫܐ = "nations," "peoples," of Israel, as in xlii. 5 (if the text is right there). But in this case it would be better to emend ܙ ܣ̈ into ܟܢܫܐ ܠܕ ܪܕܝܘ = "that the people may be chastened."

6. The Gentiles will wait for or look forward to the consummation of their chastisement. This verse might by a slight change be understood of Israel (cf. xiv. 3).

8. Cf. Ps. lxxv. 7, 8 : "God is the judge. . . . For in the hand of the Lord there is a cup . . . surely all the wicked of the earth . . . shall drink them."

The Lofty One. Here only in this book (see 4 Ezra iv. 34 ; Isa. lvii. 15).

Has no respect of persons. Cf. xliv. 4.

10. *Chastened.* Cf. i. 5.

11. *Trodden down.* I.e. in the sense of oppressing it, a frequent meaning in the O.T.

and used the creation unrighteously.   12. For I have always benefited you, and ye have always denied the beneficence."

XIV. And I answered and said: "Lo! Thou hast shown me the method of the times, and that which will be after these things, and Thou hast said unto me, that the retribution, which has been spoken of by Thee, will be of advantage to the nations.   2. And now I know that those who have sinned are many, and they have lived in prosperity, and departed from the world, but that few

---

12. Cf. i. 4.

I have . . . benefited you. The Syriac is ⏤⏤⏤ ⏤⏤⏤, but this order of the words, with this meaning, is highly irregular; for Syriac idiom all but universally requires the participle before the substantive and not as here, and in lxiii. 8, the converse order. This exceptional order may be due to the survival of the Hebrew order in the Syriac translation, *i.e.* היה סביב. For this seems to be the explanation of two out of the three instances where I have observed this irregularity in the Peshitto O.T., *i.e.* Gen. iv. 17 and 2 Sam. viii. 15. In the third (1 Sam. xviii. 13) I can offer no explanation, and the abnormality is there all the more striking, as three verses later the same phrase recurs in its right order. This irregularity (which is not noticed in Duval's Grammar, and only passingly mentioned in Nöldeke's) is not found, so far as I am aware, in the Peshitto N.T.

Ye have . . . denied. The Syriac is ⏤⏤⏤ ⏤⏤⏤, which, according to Syriac idiom, is an imperative = " deny ye." The converse order = " ye have denied." This irregularity, as in the last instance, I

would trace to a survival of the Hebrew idiom through the Greek.

XIV. 1. The final editor is again greatly to blame here. According to the text Baruch says: "Thou hast shown me the method of the times and that which will be after these things." Now this has not been done. In the preceding chapter instruction has been given as to the reason of the retribution which has come upon the cities of the Gentiles, and likewise as to the date when their chastisement will be consummated. "The method or scheme of the times" would imply such information as we find in xxiv. 2-xxv. taken in conjunction with xiii., or to xxvii.-xxx. In xx. 6 certain disclosures are promised regarding "the method of the times." The phrase is found also in xlviii. 1.

The retribution . . . spoken of by Thee. These words probably refer to xiii. 5, and yet the retribution in question is first mentioned, not by God but by the cities (xiii. 4), unless we suppose xxv. 3 to precede xiv.

Will be of advantage to the nations. In xiii. 5-11 the context is against the idea of a remedial chastisement of the Gentiles, which seems to be asserted here. Here, again something seems wrong.

nations will be left in those times, to whom those words shall be said which Thou didst say. 3. For what advantage is there in this, or what (evil), worse than what we have seen befall us, are we to expect to see? 4. But again I will speak in Thy presence: 5. What have they profited who confessed before Thee, and have not walked in vanity as the rest of the nations, and have not said to the dead: 'Give us life,' but always feared Thee, and have not left Thy ways? 6. And lo! they have been carried off, nor on their account hast Thou had mercy on Zion. 7. And if others did evil, it was

2. *Few nations will be left in those times to whom*, etc. Do these words refer back to xiii. 8? In that case Baruch complains that few of the Gentile nations will be alive to whom the words in xiii. 5, 7-11 are to be addressed.

3. These words seem to point to xiii. 6; cf. "they will expect" and "what . . . are we to expect to see?" But here they undoubtedly refer to Israel, whereas there they naturally refer to the Gentiles.

4-19. Of what profit has been the righteousness of the righteous? Of none; for it has helped neither them nor their city, though the last was at least their due (verses 4-7). Seeing this is so, man cannot understand Thy judgment (verses 8, 9), for he is but a breath; his birth is involuntary, and his end a mystery (verses 10, 11); for that end the righteous indeed may hope, for they have treasures in heaven, but for us there is only woe, here and hereafter (verses 12-14). Hence what Thou hast done on Thy servants' behalf Thou knowest, but we cannot discover. The world indeed Thou didst say was made for man. But how can this be? We pass

away and the world abides (verses 15-19).

5. *Confessed before Thee.* I have here emended ܩܠܝܥ = "knew" into ܩܘܕܝܥ = "confessed."

Walked in vanity. Jer. ii. 5.

Have not said to the dead, etc. Cf. Isa. viii. 19*b*: "On behalf of the living should they seek unto the dead?"

6, 7. In these verses the destruction of Zion seems to be far in the background.

6. *Have been carried off.* Cf. lxxxv. 3. I have here followed Ceriani's emendation of ܐܬܕܒܪܘ into ܐܬܕܒܪܘ, who rightly compares xv. 2.

Nor on their account hast Thou had mercy on Zion. This was a great difficulty to the Jew. The presence of ten righteous men would have preserved Sodom; why then did Zion fall? Moreover, the preservation of the world, according to the Talmud (Weber, 201), depended on Israel. See xiv. 18, note.

7. We have here ideas which in some respects resemble those in Gen. xviii. 23-33. But whereas it

due to Zion, that on account of the works of those
who wrought good works she should be forgiven, and
should not be overwhelmed on account of the works
of those who wrought unrighteousness.   8. But who,
O LORD, my Lord, will comprehend Thy judgment, or
who will find out the profoundness of Thy path ? or
who will think out the gravity of Thy way ?   9. Or
who will be able to think out Thy incomprehensible
counsel ? or who of those that are born has ever found

is taught there that God would
spare a city because of the righteous
persons in it, here and in ii. 2 it is
the works of the righteous considered in themselves that are put
forward as the ground of such
mercy. On the question of good
works the thought of the writers in
this book, *i.e.* between 50 and 80
A.D., is to be described as follows :
(*a*) The righteous are saved by
their works (li. 7) ; they are justified
by the law (li. 3) ; for righteousness
is by the law (lxvii. 6). (*b*) Their
works impart confidence to the
righteous with respect to God when
they pray for themselves or others.
Thus Hezekiah trusted in his works
and was hopeful in his righteousness,
and so God heard him (lxiii. 3, 5) ;
and the prophets also were heard
because they trusted in their works
(lxxxv. 2). (*c*) But the works of the
righteous avail not themselves only ;
they are a defence also to the
unrighteous among whom they
dwell (ii. 2), and even after their
death their works are regarded as a
lasting merit on the ground of which
mercy should be shown to Zion (xiv.
7; lxxxiv. 10). (*d*) Again these works
are conceived as going before them
to the next world, and being there
guarded in the treasure chambers of
God (xiv. 12), where they will be kept

safely till the final judgment (xxiv.
1) ; hence the righteous hope for the
end and leave the world without
fear (xiv. 12). (On the teaching of
this book as to faith, see note on liv.
21.) In 4 Ezra the doctrine of
works as it is found in Baruch can
hardly be said to exist. To (*b*) and
(*c*) we find no parallels and only
seeming parallels to (*a*), such as
men "will be able to escape by
their works or their faith in which
they have believed" (ix. 7), and that
"God will guard those who have
works and faith in the Most
Mighty" (xiii. 23). It will be observed that the doctrine of salvation by works is carefully guarded
against by the addition of the words
"and faith." To (*d*) we have good
parallels in vii. 77, where Ezra is
said to have "a treasury of more
laid up with the Most High,"
and in viii. 33, where "the righteous are those who have many
works laid up with Thee : from
their own works will they receive
their reward."

Though the doctrine of justification as taught in Baruch should
naturally be discussed here, we must
refer the reader to the note on
xxi. 9.

8. O LORD, *my Lord.* See iii. 1,
note.

the beginning or end of Thy wisdom? 10. For we have all been made like a breath. 11. For as the breath ascends from the heart, and returning not is extinguished, such is the nature of men, who depart not according to their own will, and know not what will befall them in the end. 12. For the righteous justly hope for the end, and without fear depart from this habitation, because they have with Thee a store of works preserved in treasuries. 13. On this account also these without fear leave this world, and trusting with joy they hope to receive the world which Thou hast promised them. 14. But unto us there is woe, who also now are shamefully entreated, and at that time look forward

10. See references on next verse.

11. *Ascends from the heart, and returning not is extinguished.* Cf. Ps. lxxviii. 39 : "a wind that passeth away, and cometh not again ; " Ps. cxlvi. 4 ; Job vii. 7 ; James iv. 14. This rendering rests on a slight change of order in the text, *i.e.* ܥܠܝ ܟܕܐ ܡܘ݂ܠ ܘܣܡ instead of ܘܠܢ ܥܠܝ ܟܕܐ ܣܡܘܣ. Ceriani and Fritzsche render the text, "ascendit quin procedat de corde et restinguitur."

Depart not according to their own will. Man does not settle the hour of his departure from this life. Cf. xlviii. 15 ; 4 Ezra viii. 5, "convenisti enim obaudire" (read *nolens* with Syr. for *obaudire*) et profecta es nolens."

Know not what, etc. Cf. Slav. En. ii. 1 ; vii. 5.

12. *The righteous justly hope.* Eth. En. cii. 4.

A store of works, etc. The text reads ܣܡܐ ܘܟܕ݁ |ܣܡܐ = "a force or supply of works." But it also = "a store of works." Cf. 4 Ezra

vii. 77, where we find "a treasure of works." In *Shabbath*, 31b, a man is spoken of as having אוצר וכיות, "a treasure of merits" in heaven. Cf. Matt. vi. 19, 20 ; Pss. Sol. ix. 9, ὁ ποιῶν δικαιοσύνην θησαυρίζει ζωὴν ἑαυτῷ παρὰ κυρίῳ. See note on verse 7.

13. *The world which Thou hast promised.* This is clearly the spiritual world. Thus in li. 3 the righteous after death are to "receive the world which does not die, which is then promised to them;" in xliv. 13, 15 "theirs is the inheritance of the promised time," "for unto them will be given the world to come;" and in xv. 7, 8 "the world which is to come" is said to be on their account. Cf. 4 Ezra ix. 13. It is referred to again in xxi. 25 and lxxxiii. 5 under the general name of something promised. Throughout B² there is no promise of an earthly felicity, but only of spiritual transmundane blessedness.

14. *There is woe.* Cf. for diction lxxxiv. 11 ; 4 Ezra xiii. 16.

(only) to evils. 15. But Thou knowest accurately
what Thou hast made on behalf of Thy servants; for
we are not able to understand by means of any good
thing that Thou art our Creator. 16. But again I
will speak in Thy presence, O LORD, my Lord. 17.
When of old there was no world with its inhabitants,
Thou didst devise and speak with a word, and forthwith the works of creation stood before Thee. 18.
And Thou didst say that Thou wouldst make for Thy
world man as the administrator of Thy works, that it
might be known that he was by no means made on
account of the world, but the world on account of him.

Evils. These words refer back
to xiv. 3, and their subject is again
touched upon in xv. 1. What these
are is given in xliv. 15 ; lxxxv. 13.

15. *What Thou hast made (or
done) on behalf of Thy servants. I.e.*

ܡܕܐ ܕܓ̈ܒ ܡܟ ܕܓ̣ܒ̣ܩ̇ܡ . If
my rendering is right, the entire
verse appears to be in its wrong
place, and should be read after verse
16. The sense then would be excellent : "Thou knowest what good
things Thou hast created on behalf
of Thy servants ; but we know of
none : yet Thou didst say that
Thou didst make the world for man,"
etc. (verses 15, 17, 18). But the
Syriac may be translated, "what
Thou hast made out of Thy servants," or if we neglect the diacritic
point, "what Thou has wrought out
of Thy works." Ceriani translates
the verse : "Tu autem recte nosti
quid feceris de servis tuis : quia
nos non possumus intelligere aliquid
boni, quomodo tu sis fictor noster."
Before *aliquid* we should read "per."

17. *Speak with a word,* etc. Cf.
Gen. i. 6, 7 ; Ps. xxxiii. 6 ; Heb.

xi. 3 ; 2 Peter iii. 5 ; Slav. En.
xxiv. 5 ; xxv. 1 ; 4 Ezra vi. 38.

18. *Thou wouldst make for Thy
world man,* etc. Cf. Gen. i. 26, 28 ;
Ps. viii. 6 ; 4 Ezra vi. 54.

The world on account of him. So
far as I am aware this exalted view
of man's dignity in respect of the
world is not found earlier than the
first century of the Christian era.
It recurs frequently in the literature
of this time : cf. xiv. 19 ; xv. 7 ;
xxi. 24 (this doctrine is thus confined to B[2] in this book) ; Assumpt.
Mosis i. 12 ; 4 Ezra vi. 55, 59 ; vii.
11 ; viii. 44 ; ix. 13. In these
passages the statement of the reason
for the creation of the world assumes three forms : First, the world
was created on account of man
(Apoc. Bar. xiv. 18 ; 4 Ezra viii. 1,
44). But the writers of these books
if pressed, would at once have withdrawn this statement in favour of
two diverging statements : the one,
that the world was created on
account of Israel (4 Ezra vi. 55,
59 ; vii. 11 ; Assumpt. Mosis i. 12) ;
the other that the world was created
on account of the righteous in Israel

19. And now I see that as for the world which was
made on account of us, lo ! it abides, but we, on account
of whom it was made, depart."

XV. And the Lord answered and said unto me :
" Thou art rightly astonied regarding the departure of
man, but thou hast not judged well regarding the evils
which befall those who sin. 2. And as regards what
thou hast said, that the righteous are carried off and
the impious are prospered, 3. And as regards what
thou hast said : ' Man knows not Thy judgment '—
4. On this account hear, and I will speak to thee,
and hearken, and I will cause thee to hear My words.
5. Man would not rightly have understood My judgment, if he had not accepted the law, and if his fear

(Apoc. Bar. xiv. 19 ; xv. 7 ; xxi.
24). Either of the latter forms the
real Jewish view from the Christian
era onwards. Thus in the Talmud,
it is either Israel, or the righteous
in Israel, that were the cause of the
world's creation and its subsequent
preservation. Thus in *Bammidbar
rabba*, ii., "if Israel were not, the
world would not exist" ; in the
Shemoth rabba, xxviii., "The world
was created owing to the merits of
Israel, and upon Israel stands the
world." See Weber, pp. 201, 202,
for other passages of the same
import. See also note on xv. 7.
19. See note on last verse. That
the "us" and the "we" here are
the righteous is clear from xv.
7. This verse shows that the
writer believed in the view that the
safety of the world was bound up
with that of the righteous.
In *Pesikta* 200*b* God is said to
have created the world on account
of Abraham's merit (Weber, p. 295).
XV. 1. *Astonied regarding the de-*

parture of man. These words refer
to xiv. 19. The Syriac noun translated "departure" is derived from
the verb translated "depart" in
xiv. 19. In xiii. 3 Baruch was
"astonied" about the fate of Jerusalem.
*Not judged rightly regarding the
evils*, etc. See xiv. 3, 14.
2. See xiv. 6.
3. See xiv. 8, 9.
5. *The law.* The law was the
centre round which Jewish thought
and life revolved. To a limited
extent the Messianic expectation
was likewise a centre. Frequently
we find that in proportion as the
one is emphasised the other falls
into the background. This will
receive illustration as we proceed to
examine the position assigned to
the law and the Messiah respectively
in the five main constituents of this
book. Thus in B¹ (written after
70 A.D.) *where the restoration of
Jerusalem is looked for, but no
Messiah*, the law is spoken of as

had not been (rooted) in understanding.   6. But now,

follows: God gave the law to Israel (lxxvii. 3) ; for transgressing it they were sent into exile (lxxvii. 4 ; lxxxiv. 2) ; but let not Israel withdraw from the law (xliv. 3), but obey it (xlvi. 5) ; let them remember it (lxxxiv. 8) ; for if they do so, they will see the consolation of Zion (xliv. 7), and a son of the law will never be wanting (xlvi. 4), nor a lamp nor a shepherd (lxxvii. 16) ; for lamps and shepherds are from the law, and though these depart the law stands (lxxvii. 15) ; if they remember it, they will see the consolation of Zion (xliv. 7). In B² *where there is no Messiah and no expectation of the restoration of Jerusalem*, the law is still further glorified. Thus Moses brought the law to Jacob (xvii. 4) ; this conveyed a knowledge of the judgment of God (xv. 5), and entailed retribution on the consciously disobedient (xv. 6 ; xix. 3 ; xlviii. 40) ; it will exact all its rights (xlviii. 27), and repay the transgressor (xlviii. 47) ; apostates from it (xli. 3) will be specially dealt with (xlii. 4). On the other hand it will protect those who receive it in their hearts (xxxii. 1 ; xlviii. 24) ; by it they will be justified (li. 3), and in it will be the hope of the righteous (li. 7) ; the law is with Israel, and so long as they obey it they will not fall (xlviii. 22, 24). They have received one law from One (xlviii. 24). In B³ (which is akin to xiii. 2 in this respect) Israel has nothing save the Mighty One and the law (lxxxv. 3) ; they have one law by one (lxxxv. 14). When, however, we turn to the Messiah Apocalypses A¹ (= xxvii.-xxx. 1), A² (=xxxvi.-xl.), A³ (=liii.-lxxiv.), and to S. (=x. 6-12) which form more than a third of the entire book, we find no mention at all of the law in A¹ and S. In A² there is only one mention of

it, *i.e.* God's law is life (xxxviii. 2). In A³ it naturally becomes more prominent, as A³ gives a brief history of God's dealings with Israel. The law and the tradition were observed by Abraham and his sons (lvii. 2). Thus, through the agency of Moses, its light shone on those in darkness (lix. 2). God imparted to Moses certain studies of the law (lix. 3). Josiah alone was faithful to it in his time (lxvi. 5). Such as loved it not perished (liv. 14). Righteousness comes by the law (lxvii. 6). Thus we observe that in purely eschatological descriptions such as A¹, there is not a single allusion to the law : the Messiah is the entire centre of interest. This is practically true in A² also ; for the reference in xxxviii. 2 does not belong to the account of the last things. In A³ finally, most of the references are to historical incidents, though it is true that in A³ great store is set by the law. The law was the centre of Jewish life, the source of righteousness, and in fact its spiritual schoolmaster, till the advent of the Messiah had arrived. Thenceforward (lxx.-lxxiv.) there is not even an allusion to it. The same phenomena are observable in the various constituents of 4 Ezra. Thus in the three or four distinct Messiah Apocalypses in that book (according to Kabisch's critical analyses) the law is only mentioned two or three times. The only strong expression regarding it is in xiii. 38, and there the text is doubtful. In the groundwork of the book (*circ.* 100 A.D.) however, *where we find no hope of a Messiah nor of a restored Jerusalem*, the law, as might be expected, has a more important rôle to play. Thus God gave the law to Jacob (iii. 19). He sowed it in them that they might keep it (ix. 32), but it bare no fruit owing to

because he transgressed though he knew, yea, on account of this also, he shall be tormented because he knew. 7. And as regards what thou didst say touching the righteous, that on account of them has this world come, nay more, even that which is to come is on their account. 8. For this world is to them

the evil heart (iii. 20); they neglected it (vii. 20), did not keep it (ix. 32), rejected it (vii. 72), despised it (vii. 24; viii. 56), yet the law cannot perish (ix. 37.) Some did try to keep the law perfectly in this life (vii. 89), and God bore testimony to them because they did so (vii. 94); these acquired a store of good works (vii. 77; viii. 33), and from these they received their reward (viii. 33); and yet none can claim heaven purely as the reward of their righteousness, for all men have sinned (viii. 35).

It is obvious at a glance that the possession of the law by Israel is less a subject of self-gratulation in 4 Ezra than in Baruch. In the latter, especially in B² (written, like the groundwork in 4 Ezra, after 70 A.D., and having no expectation of the Messiah or a restored Jerusalem) the law is everything: it protects the righteous (xxxii. 1), justifies them (li. 3), is their hope (li. 7), and so long as it is with Israel, Israel cannot fall (xlviii. 22, 24). In Ezra, on the other hand, the law has begotten in the writer such a sense of sin that he trembles before it. Man needs mercy, not the award of the law; for all have sinned (viii. 35), and all but a very few would perish, but for the divine compassion (vii. 139).

5, 6. *If his fear had not been (rooted) in understanding. But now, because he transgressed though he knew,* etc. Here Ceriani followed by Fritzsche has mistranslated

ܠܒܕ (=transgressus est) by "fecit," thus taking it for ܠܒܕ. This thought partially recurs in xix. 3; xlviii. 40, "Each of the inhabitants of the earth knew when he was committing iniquity" (see note *in loc.*), lv. 2; and almost a perfect parallel is found in 4 Ezra vii. 72: "Qui ergo commorantes sunt in terra hinc cruciabuntur quoniam sensum habentes iniquitatem fecerunt." Cf. Luke xii. 48.

7. *As regards . . . has this world come.* See note on xiv. 18. Nowhere in the present book are these words given as a divine utterance. The same statement is again made in xxi. 24. From a similar statement in 4 Ezra vi. 55, at the close of the short hexæmeron there, it is probable that some such statement was originally included in that hexæmeron in its independent form. On this hexæmeron see xxix. 4, note. Cf. 4 Ezra vi. 55; vii. 11.

Seeing that this world is "a trouble and a weariness" to the righteous, it is hard to understand such a belief unless we suppose that it was designed to be their discipline for the future life. Cf. lii. 6. On *the world which is to come,* see xiv. 13, note.

8. *This world is to them a trouble . . . with much labour.* Cf. xlviii. 50; li. 14; 4 Ezra vii. 3-14; Rom. viii. 18; 2 Cor. iv. 17. This world is evidently regarded by the

a trouble and a weariness with much labour; and that accordingly which is to come, a crown with great glory."

XVI. And I answered and said: "O LORD, my Lord, lo! the years of this time are few and evil, and who is able in this little (space) to acquire that which is measureless?"

XVII. And the Lord answered and said unto me: "With the Most High account is not taken of much time nor of a few years. 2. For what did it profit Adam that he lived nine hundred and thirty years, and transgressed that which he was commanded? 3. Therefore the multitude of time that he lived did not profit him, but brought death and cut off the years of those who were born from him. 4. Or wherein did Moses suffer loss in that he lived only one hundred and twenty years, and, inasmuch as he was subject to Him who formed him, brought the law to the

writer of B² but not of B¹ as a scene of trial and sorrow: a man must give himself to an ascetic life here if he is to attain blessedness hereafter. There is a more ascetic tone about 4 Ezra. In the Eth. En., however, still stronger statements are found. Thus in xlviii. 7 the Messiah "preserveth the lot of the righteous because they have hated and despised this world of un-righteousness," and in cviii. 7 God recompenses "the spirits of the humble and of those who afflict their bodies," and likewise those (cviii. 10) who, though "trodden under foot of wicked men," "loved heaven more than their life in this world."

Crown with great glory. Cf. 1 Pet. v. 4. We should expect " crown

of great glory." Observe that if we retranslate these words into Hebrew, we have a paronomasia already familiar from Isa. lxii. 3; Ezek. xvi. 12; xxiii. 42, *i.e.* עֲטָרָה בתפארה רבה.

XVI. 1. *Years . . . few and evil.* Gen. xlvii. 9.

XVII. 1. *The Most High.* This title belongs to B¹, B², B³, and A³. See xxv. 1; liv. 9, 17; lvi. 1; lxiv. 6, 8; lxvii. 4, 7; lxix. 2; lxx. 7; lxxvi. 1; lxxvii. 4, 21; lxxx. 1, 3; lxxxi. 2, 4; lxxxii. 2, 6; lxxxiii. 1; lxxxv. 8, 12.

3. *Brought death,* etc. See xxiii. 4, note.

4. *Brought the law,* etc. Cf. 4 Ezra iii. 19. " Give the law to the seed of Jacob, and the command-ment to the race of Israel."

seed of Jacob, and lighted a lamp for the nation of Israel."

XVIII. And I answered and said: "He that lighted has taken from the light, and there are but few that have imitated him. 2. But those many whom he has lighted have taken from the darkness of Adam, and have not rejoiced in the light of the lamp."

XIX. And He answered and said unto me: "Wherefore at that time he appointed for them a covenant, and said: 'Behold I have placed before you life and death,' and he called heaven and earth to witness against them. 2. For he knew that his time was but short, but that heaven and earth endure always. 3.

Lighted a lamp. Cf. lix. 2, "lamp of the eternal law." The thought in both phrases is drawn from Ps. cxix. 105, "Thy word is a lamp," etc. Cf. xviii. 2.

XVIII. 1. *Has taken from the light, i.e.* has chosen the light. In the next verse the many are said to have chosen the darkness of Adam.

2. The law and Adam are in this passage symbolical names for the opposing powers of light and darkness. This thought is foreign to the O.T. though Gen. i.-iii. has prepared the way for it. Adam is here, as in the Slav. En., represented as the primary source of human transgression, whereas in the Eth. En. and Jubilees human depravity is traced mainly to the angels that sinned with the daughters of men. Again, as in the Slav. En., the writer does not teach the doctrine of original sin and inherited spiritual incapacities. He implies rather that man is left to determine his own destiny, to choose light or take darkness for his portion, just as in much later

times it was said : "God does not determine beforehand whether a man shall be righteous or wicked, but puts this into the hands of the man himself" (*Tanchuma, Pikkude* 3). See Slav. En. xxx. 15, 16, notes. The same view is enforced in A³, *i.e.* liv. 15, 16. See notes *in loc.*

XIX. 1, 2. Because few chose light and many chose darkness, Moses showed further that their choice of light or darkness was likewise a choice of life or death. xix. 1-3 looks like an addition of the final editor. The answer to xviii. seems to begin with xix. 4.

Behold I have placed, etc., Deut. xxx. 19. *Called heaven,* etc., Deut. iv. 26 ; xxx. 19 ; xxxi. 28. Cf. lxxxiv. 2 ; Ass. Mos. iii. 12.

Later times seem to have drawn from Deut. xxx. 19 the conclusion that the permanence of the law was bound up with that of heaven and earth. Cf. ver. 2 ; Matt. v. 18. Contrast Luke xvi. 17 ; Mark xiii. 31.

For after his death these sinned and transgressed (the covenant), though they knew that they had the law reproving (them), and the light in which nothing could err, also the spheres, which testify, and Me. 4. Now regarding everything that is it is I that judge, but do not thou take counsel in thy soul regarding these things, nor afflict thyself because of those which have been. 5. For now it is the consummation of time that is sought, whether of business, or of prosperity, or of shame, and not the beginning thereof. 6. Because if a man be prospered in his beginnings and shamefully entreated in his old age, he forgets all the prosperity that he had. 7. And again, if a man is shamefully entreated in his beginnings, and at his end is prospered, he remembereth not again his evil entreatment. 8. And again hearken: though each one were prospered all that time—all the time from the day on which death was decreed against those who transgress—and

3. *Transgressed.* This word recurs in the same connection (lxxxiv. 2) where it has as its object "the law." We must supply this or "the covenant" from ver. 1.

4. These words deal with Baruch's difficulties in xviii. 1, 2. Do not distress thyself with such problems ; the end of all things is at hand.

5. Here only the end of all things is looked for—not an earthly felicity in a rebuilt Jerusalem.

6-8. The end of all things is at hand, and the only important question is : How does it find a man ? will it bring him shame or honour ? We are strongly reminded here of the well-known words of Solon in Herodotus i. 32 σκοπέειν δὲ χρὴ

παντὸς χρήματος τὴν τελευτήν, κῇ ἀποβήσεται.   πολλοῖσι γὰρ δὴ ὑποδέξας ὅλβον ὁ θεὸς προρρίζους ἀνέτρεψε.   It was a familiar Hellenic theme. Cf. Soph. *Trach.* 1-3 ; *Oed. Rex*, 1494-97 ; Eurip. *Androm.* 100-103, etc.

8. *Though a man . . . vanity.* This seems the natural rendering of the passage. Ceriani renders: "Omne tempus istud a die quo decreta fuit mors contra eos qui praetereunt in isto tempore, si unusquisque prosperatus esset, et in fine suo in vanitatem corrumperetur, esset omne." Fritzsche quite wrongly writes "vanum" for "omne."

On which death was decreed, etc. See xxiii. 4, note.

in his end was destroyed, in vain would have been everything."

XX. Therefore, behold! the days will come, and the times will hasten more than the former, and the seasons will speed on more than those that are past, and the years will pass more quickly than the present (years). 2. Therefore have I now taken away Zion, in order that I may the more speedily visit the world in its season. 3. Now therefore hold fast in thy heart everything that I command thee, and seal it in the recesses of thy mind. 4. And then I will

XX. 1. *Therefore.* It is not clear that this word follows upon anything in xix. It could be taken closely with xviii. So far as I can see it is best to regard it as following directly on xiii. 3*a.* Jerusalem has fallen, therefore the years intervening before the judgment will be shortened. Cf. liv. 1, "Against the works of the inhabitants of the earth Thou dost hasten the beginnings of the times"; Matt. xxiv. 22. For the probable order of the text originally see pp. 20, 119.

The days will come. Cf. xxiv. 1; xxxi. 5; xxxix. 3; 4 Ezra vi. 18. A familiar O.T. phrase. Cf. Jer. xxiii. 7; xxx. 3, etc.

The times will hasten. Cf. lxxxiii. 1, 6, where almost the same thoughts and diction recur. Cf. liv. 1; 4 Ezra iv. 26.

2. The fall of Jerusalem is one of the steps preparatory for the final judgment. See xxi. 21. There is no hope here of a restored Jerusalem. See i. 4, note.

Speedily visit. The Syriac literally = σπεύσω καὶ ἐπιωκέψωμαι, a Hebraism, אמהר ואפקד,

Visit. Cf. xxiv. 4; lxxxiii. 2.

This word seems to be used in Baruch in a bad sense of the penal visitation of God, as in Exod. xx. 5; Ps. lxxxix. 32; Jer. vi. 15; ix. 25; xi. 22, etc.; also in 4 Ezra v. 56; vi. 18; ix. 2; Pss. Sol. xv. 14. The word (פקד = ἐπισκέπτεσθαι) has generally a good sense in the O.T., as in Gen. xxi. 1; Exod. iv. 31; Job x. 12; Pss. viii. 4; lxxx. 14; also in Ecclus. xlvi. 14; Wisdom vii. 7, 13; Pss. Sol. iii. 14; x. 5 (?); xi. 2, 7; always in the N.T., as in Luke i. 68, 78; vii. 16; xix. 44; Acts xv. 14; 1 Peter ii. 12. It is noteworthy that whereas in the N.T. the thought of God's visitation is one of joy, its associations in 4 Ezra and Baruch are fear and wrath to come.

3. *Everything that I command thee.* The relative is omitted in the Syriac, but both the sense and the Syriac idiom require it. If the text is right, we must take it as a Hebraism; for the Hebrew admits the omission of the relative. We must then suppose this Hebraism misunderstood by the Greek translator; for neither does the Greek allow of the omission of the relative.

show thee the judgment of My might, and My ways which are past finding out. 5. Go therefore and sanctify thyself seven days, and eat no bread, nor drink water, nor speak to any one. 6. And afterwards come to that place, and I will reveal Myself to thee, and speak true things with thee, and I will give thee commandment regarding the method of the times; for they will come and will not tarry.

THE PRAYER OF BARUCH THE SON OF NERIAH

XXI. And I went thence and sat in the valley of Cedron in a cave of the earth, and I sanctified my

4. *Show thee the judgment of My might.* In lxxxiii. 7 we have a nearly related phrase, "The consummation . . . will show the great might of its ruler."

6. *That place.* See xiii. 1, note.

Method of the times. See xiv. 1, note.

Will come and will not tarry. Hab. ii. 3. Cf. xlviii. 39 of text.

THE FIFTH AND SIXTH SECTIONS

XXI.-XLVI. This constitutes the fifth section of the book according to the present text, but in reality the fifth and sixth sections (see v. 7, note). For according to the scheme of the final editor, events proceed in each section in a certain order: thus first we find a fast, then generally a prayer or lamentation, then a divine message or disclosure followed by an announcement to the people. Thus we have here the fast of seven days in Cedron (xxi. 1); the prayer on Mount Zion (xxi. 4-26); the revelation (xxii.-xxx.); address to the

people assembled in Cedron (xxxi.-xxxiv). At the close of xxxiv. there should follow a fast of seven days. The sixth section should open with this fast, but all mention of it has disappeared from the present text. After the fast comes a vision (xxxvi.-xl.) and a revelation regarding apostates and proselytes (xli. xlii.) with some further disclosures (xliii.); then the sixth section duly closes with an address to the people (xliv.-xlvi.)

It will be observed that xxi.-xlvi. embrace material from a variety of sources. Thus xxvi.-xxx. 1 = A¹, and xxxvi.-xl. = A² are independent Messiah apocalypses, and xliii, xliv. 7; xlv. xlvi. are derived from B¹. What remains of B² has been completely rearranged according to the views of the final editor. For what was probably the original order of B² see p. 119, and the Introduction, pp. lxi.-lxiii.

XXI. 1. *Cedron.* See v. 5. On the fasts of Baruch see notes on v. 7 and ix.

Cave. Cf. Assumpt. Mos. ix. 6.

soul there, and I eat no bread, yet I was not hungry, and I drank no water, yet I thirsted not, and I was there till the seventh day, as He had commanded me. 2. And afterwards I came to that place where He had spoken with me. 3. And it came to pass at sunset that my soul took much thought, and I began to speak in the presence of the Mighty One, and said: 4. "O Thou that hast made the earth hear me, that hast fixed the firmament in its fulness, and hast made firm the height of the heaven by the spirit, that hast called from the beginning of the world that which did not yet exist, and they obey Thee. 5. Thou that hast commanded the air by Thy nod, and hast seen those things which are to be as those things

2. *That place.* Probably Mount Zion. Cf. xx. 6 and xiii. 1; otherwise the temple, x. 5. But this and some other such place determinations may be due to the final editor. The scene of the fast, the prayer, and the revelation was probably the same. See xlvii. 1, note.

3. *The Mighty One.* This is the first time this title occurs. It is found in B¹, B², A³, but not in A¹, A². See xxv. 4; xxxii. 1, 6; xxxiv.; xliv. 3, 6; xlvi. 1, 4; xlvii. 1; xlviii. 1, 38; xlix. 1; liv. 1; lv. 6; lvi. 2, 3; lix. 8; lxi. 6; lxiii. 3, 5, 6, 8, 10; lxiv. 3, 4; lxv. 1; lxvi. 1, 5, 6; lxvii. 2; lxx. 2, 5; lxxvii. 11, 26; lxxxi. 4; lxxxii. 5; lxxxiv. 1, 6, 7, 10; lxxxv. 2, 3.

4. *By the spirit.* Have we here a reference to Gen. ii. 1, "The spirit of God," or does the whole phrase, "made firm . . . by the spirit," show a connection partly with the LXX. of Ps. xxxiii. 6, τῷ λόγῳ κυρίῳ οἱ οὐρανοὶ ἐστερεώθησαν καὶ τῷ πνεύματι τοῦ στόματος κτλ.

Hast called . . . that which did not yet exist. Cf. xlviii. 8, "with a word Thou quickenest that which was not." We seem to have here creation *ex nihilo.* On the other hand the words above are found in Philo, *de Justitia,* τὰ γὰρ μὴ ὄντα ἐκάλεσεν εἰς τὸ εἶναι. This may be accidental. At any rate the fundamental principles of the two writers are different; for, except in the *De Somno,* i. 13, Philo taught the formation of the world from pre-existent elements. See Slav. En. xxiv. 2; xxv. 1, notes. Such expressions as that in the text spring from the repeated "and God said," Gen. i. Cf. Ps. cxlviii. 5; Philo, *de sacrif. Abel et Cain,* ὁ γὰρ θεὸς λέγων ἅμα ἐποίει, μηδὲν μεταξὺ ἀμφοῖν τιθείς. In 2 Pet. iii. 5, "There were heavens from of old, and an earth compacted out of water . . . by the word of God," we have the same teaching, with the additional idea that the solid earth was made from the water, as in the Slav. En. xxviii. 2.

which Thou art doing.   6. Thou that rulest with great thought the powers that stand before Thee: (yea) rulest with indignation the holy living creatures, who are without number, which Thou didst make from the beginning, of flame and fire, which stand around Thy throne.   7. To Thee only does this belong that Thou shouldst do forthwith whatsoever Thou dost wish. 8. Who causest the drops of rain to rain by number upon the earth, and alone knowest the consummation of the times before they come: have respect unto my prayer.   9. For Thou alone art able to sustain all who are, and those who pass away, and those who are to be, those who sin, and those who are righteous [as

6. *Powers that stand before Thee.* Cf. xlviii. 10 ; 4 Ezra viii. 21*a*, "cui adstat exercitus angelorum."

Creatures, who are without number. lix. 11.

Which Thou didst make from the beginning. In Jub. ii. 2, the creation of the angels is assigned to the first day—evidently on the ground of Job xxxviii. 7. According to *Targ. Jer. I.* on Gen. i. 26, and *Shemoth rabba*, 15, God created the angels on the second day. So also Slav. En. xxix. 1.

7. Pss. cxv. 3 ; cxxxv. 6 ; Jonah i. 14.

8. *The drops of rain to rain by number.* Cf. lix. 5 ; Ecclus. i. 2 ; Slav. En. xlvii. 5, note.

Alone knowest the end of the times. Cf. liv. 1.

9. *Those who sin, and those who are righteous.* For "who are righteous" the Syriac reads here and in xxiv. 2 ܘܕܙܕܝܩܝܢ = "who are justified" = οἱ δικαιοῦνται, and in xxi. 11, 12 ; lxii. 7, ܐܙܕܕܩܘ = "have

been justified" = δεδικαιωμένοι εἰσιν. In all these passages the Syriac is at fault, but its error is to be traced to the Greek Version ; for the Greek translator mistranslated the Hebrew before him, which was in the former case הצדקים, and in the latter צדקו. The grounds for this conclusion are as follows : (i.) The antithesis to "those who sin" is not "those who are justified," but "those who do righteousness" or "are righteous." (ii.) If "those who are justified" was the true text, then its antithesis would not be "those who sin," as we find it in xxi. 9, 11, 12 ; xxiv. 2, but "those who are condemned," as in li. 1 and 4 Ezra iv. 18.   (iii.) But since "those who sin" is undoubtedly original, the error must lie in the phrase "those who are justified."   (iv.) Now this error is easy to explain. From the LXX. we know that צדק was generally rendered by δικαιοῦσθαι, and only in a few cases by δίκαιος εἶναι (Job ix. 2, 15 ; x. 15 ; xv. 14 ; xxv. 4 ; xxxiii. 12 ; xxxiv. 5 ;

living (and) being past finding out].   10. For Thou
alone dost live immortal and past finding out, and
knowest the number of mankind.   11. And if in
time many have sinned, yet others not a few have been
righteous.   12. Thou knowest where Thou preservest

xxxv. 36). The Greek translator, not appreciating the right meaning of צדק in our Apocalypse, gave it the sense he was most familiar with, and so mistranslated it by δικαιοῦσθαι. (v.) The above conclusions receive confirmation from the fact that the antithesis in our emended text is actually found in Job x. 15 and xxxv. 36, 37. I have emended the text accordingly in xxi. 9, 11, 12; xxiv. 1, 2; lxvii. 2.

The doctrine of justification in this Apocalypse differs from that taught in 4 Ezra.

(1) In Baruch men are justified by the law: thus the text in li. 3 = ἐδικαιώθησαν ἐν τῷ νόμῳ μου (where μου = τοῦ θεοῦ), and in lxvii. 6 it = ἡ δικαιοσύνη ἡ ἐκ τοῦ νόμου, and in lxxxi. 7 it = ἐσώθησαν ἐν τοῖς ἔργοις αὐτῶν. In Ezra, on the other hand, the expression "salvation by works" is qualified by the addition of "and by faith." Cf. ix. 7; xiii. 23. In fact we do not find there either expressed or implied the doctrine of justification by works. (2) Quite in keeping with what precedes is the absolute assurance of salvation on the part of Baruch. He never personally dreads condemnation: he looks forward calmly to a life of future blessedness. Cf. xiii. 3; xxv. 1; xlvi. 7; lxxvi. 2. Ezra, on the other hand, continually assumes his future woe till assured otherwise in viii. 47-49, 51-54. 4 Ezra xiv. does not belong to the rest of the book. There is a pessimistic outlook in Ezra as there is an optimistic one in all Baruch save S (i.e. x. 6-xii.) The note on xiv. 7

of this book will confirm the view above taken.

In 4 Ezra "to justify" preserves its ordinary meaning of "to declare just" in iv. 18 and xii. 7. It is used in this sense also in Ecclus. i. 22; vii. 5; x. 29; xiii. 22; xviii. 22; xxxi. 5; xlii. 2. In 4 Ezra, however, we find another use: thus in x. 16 it = "to vindicate as just." So also in Ps. li. 4; Isa. xlii. 21 (?); Pss. Sol. ii. 16; iii. 5; iv. 9; viii. 7, 27, 31; ix. 3; Luke vii. 29; Apoc. Baruch lxxviii. 5. On the word δικαιοῦν the reader can consult with advantage Sanday and Headlam's *Romans*, pp. 28-31. On the teaching on faith in A[3], i.e. chaps. liii.-lxxiv., see liv. 25, note.

As living . . . out. This I bracket as a dittography. See next line.

10. *Knowest the number of mankind.* Gen. xxiii. 4, 5; xlviii. 4, 6.

11. Men many have sinned, but many also have been justified.

Others not a few have been righteous. This statement differs strongly from that given in 4 Ezra viii. 3, where it is said plainly that whereas "multi quidem creati sunt, pauci autem salvabuntur," and that the ratio of the saved to the lost is as the amount of gold in the earth to that of the clay in it (viii. 2). This optimism which we have observed already (see xxi. 9, note) differentiates Baruch from Ezra. The latter is in the main pessimistic both with regard to his own destiny (till otherwise reassured by God) and that of the vast bulk of mankind.

12, 13. But this life is not all; sin and righteousness have further

the end of those who have sinned, or the consummation of those who have been righteous. 13. For if there were this life only, which here belongs to all men, nothing could be more bitter than this. 14. For of what profit is strength that turns to weakness, or the food of plenty that turns to famine, or beauty that turns to a hateful (thing)? 15. For the nature of man is always changeable. 16. For we have by no means been from the beginning what we now are, and what we now are we shall not afterwards remain. 17. For if a consummation had not been prepared for all, in vain would have been their beginning. 18. But regarding everything that comes from Thee, do Thou inform me, and regarding everything about which I ask Thee, do Thou enlighten me. 19. How long will that which is corruptible remain, and how long will the time of

issues; else the life of the righteous here were a crowning bitterness.

13. This verse may be drawn from 1 Cor. xv. 19, or else both from a common source. Of what worth is life? for (1) it is subject to constant change (xxi. 14, 15); and (2) is likewise mortal (xxi. 16, 17, 22).

14. *Strength that turns*, etc. lxxxiii. 11.

Beauty that turns to a hateful (thing). lxxxiii. 12.

15. There is no fixity in the being of man: he is the creature of change. In ver. 22, which should follow verses 17, 18, man is by appointment mortal.

16. The text is corrupt. The above rendering rests on an emendation of the text. Thus for ܗܘ ܠܐ [Syriac] ܥܕܡܐ ܐܡܪ ܡܕܐ ܘܐܝܟܢܐ ܗܘܐ ܘܡܢ [Syriac] ܐܝܟܢܐ ܗܘ ܡܕܡ . ܨܡܚܐ ܥܟ [Syriac].

I have read ܐܡܪ ܢܡܚܝ ܡܬܝܡ ܠܐ [Syriac] ܡܕܐ ܘܐܡܠܡ ܗܘܐ ܡܢ ܥܟ [Syriac] ܣܡܥܐ This restores, I believe, the original sense (cf. ver. 15). As the text stands it = "aut nihil, sicuti quod sumus, est enim ab initio, nunc non sumus" (Ceriani).

17. Ver. 22 may have originally followed this verse.

19. *How long will that which is corruptible remain?* If this question comes from the final editor, its answer will be found in xl. 8; lxxiv. 3. But if it belongs to B², its answer would naturally be found in xxiii. 7 - xxiv. 1; xxxi. 5. The writers of this book (particularly the writer of B²) are greatly impressed with the corruptibility of the present world. The whole present world, the *olam hazzeh*, belongs

mortals be prospered, and until what time will those who transgress in the world be polluted with much wickedness? 20. Command therefore in mercy, and accomplish all that Thou saidst Thou wouldst bring, that Thy might may be made known to those who think that Thy long-suffering is weakness. 21. And show to those who know not, and let them see that it has befallen us and our city until now according to the long-suffering of Thy power, because on account of Thy name Thou hast called us a beloved people. 22. Every nature therefore from this onward is mortal.

to the sphere of corruption. Even so does the Messianic kingdom if it falls within the *olam hazzeh*, as it does in A¹, A², and A³ in this book. Thus in A² the Messianic reign forms the end of the world of corruption (xl. 3), and in A³, the end of corruption and the beginning of incorruption (lxxiv. 3). In B² all that has been is doomed to corruption (xxxi. 5); all that is corruptible will perish (xliv. 9); the new world that awaits them will not turn them to corruption (xliv. 12). In B³ what the righteous have lost was corruptible, but what they will receive is incorruptible (lxxxv. 5). The only reference to this subject in B¹ is where Baruch is told that he will pass away from the earth and forget all that is corruptible (xliii. 2). As to the remaining passages where this word recurs, the text is doubtful in xlviii. 29, and probably interpolated in xxviii. 5. In 4 Ezra vii. 113, the day of judgment is the end of this period and the beginning of the next immortal period. See also iv. 11; vii. 111.

Who transgress. These words could be rendered "who pass away," as in verse 9.

20. This is a prayer for the hastening of the final judgment (cf. 2 Pet. iii. 4-9).

21. The text is unintelligible as it stands: "Show to those who know not, and they have seen what has befallen us and our city until now according to the longsuffering," etc. Merely by the emendation of ‎ܘܚܙܘ = "and they have seen," into ‎ܘܗܘܐ ‎= "and that it has been," we arrive at a perfectly consistent text. The fall of Jerusalem was brought about in the mercy of God to hasten the final judgment. See verse 23; xx. 2.

But, if the text is correct, it = καὶ ἑωράκασιν = וראו. Have we here an instance of the Hebrew perfect with strong waw used as a continuation of the imperative? In that case the original may have been הודיע . . . וראו את אשר נקרה לנו = "Show . . . and let them see that it has happened to us." I have emended accordingly.

A beloved people. Cf. v. 1.

22. It is obvious that this verse breaks the connection of thought. It should be read after verse 17 as

23. Reprove therefore the angel of death, and let Thy glory appear, and let the might of Thy beauty be known, and let Sheol be sealed so that from this time forward it may not receive the dead, and let the treasuries of souls restore those which are enclosed in them. 24. For there have been many years like those that are desolate from the days of Abraham and Isaac and Jacob, and of all those who are like them, who sleep in the earth, on whose account Thou didst say that Thou hadst created the world. 25. And now quickly show Thy glory, and do not defer

suggested above. It is possible that ܠܐܣ is corrupt for ܠܐܣ. We should then translate, "Every one, therefore, according to this law is mortal" (cf. ver. 15).

23. The writer in 20, 21, urged God to bring on the final judgment, that His power might be made known, and that men might learn that Israel's calamities had befallen them in the mercy of God. With a view to this final judgment the writer prays to God to put an end to death, to let His glory appear, and the dead arise.

23. *The angel of death.* Cf. Rev. vi. 8. On the prominent *rôle* played by this angel in later Jewish writings, see *Testament of Abraham* (ed. James) ; Weber, 239-242, 244, 247 262, 321, 322, 378 ; Eisenmenger, *Entdecktes Jud.* i. 854, 855, 862-879.

Sheol. See xi. 6, note.

Be sealed. Cf. Isa. v. 14.

Treasuries of souls. Only the righteous souls were admitted to these treasuries or chambers. I have preserved the literal meaning of the original word. These are the places in which God *treasures* His righteous ones, or their righteous acts. After

the death of a righteous man his soul was permitted during seven days to behold the seven ways of the righteous and the seven ways of the wicked. After so doing, the soul entered these chambers (4 Ezra vii. 101 ; iv. 35). These chambers were in Sheol (4 Ezra iv. 41) ; only righteous souls could enter them (4 Ezra vii. 80) ; they were guarded by angels, and were full of rest (Eth. En. c. 5 ; 4 Ezra vii. 95) ; at the final judgment they were to restore the souls committed to them (Apoc. Bar. xxi. 3 ; xxx. 2 ; 4 Ezra vii. 32, 80). It is to be observed that as there were treasuries of righteous souls, so there were treasuries of righteous works (see xxiv. 1).

It is strange that only the righteous souls are here mentioned. The reference to the wicked may be lost.

24. This verse should in all probability be read after ver. 19. It would there form a good link between vers. 19 and 20. If this is not so the text seems corrupt.

Sleep in the earth. See xi. 4, note.

On whose account, etc. See xv. 7, note ; xiv. 18, note.

what has been promised by Thee." 26. And it came to pass that when I had completed the words of this prayer that I was greatly weakened.

XXII. And it came to pass after these things that lo! the heavens were opened, and I saw, and power was given to me, and a voice was heard from on high, and it said unto me: 2. "Baruch, Baruch, why art thou troubled? 3. He who travels by a road but does not complete it, or he who departs by sea but does not arrive at the port, can he be comforted? 4. Or he who promises to give a present to another, but does not fulfil it, is it not robbery? 5. Or he who sows the earth, but does not reap its fruit in its season, does he not lose everything? 6. Or he who plants a plant, unless it grows till the time suitable to it, does he who planted it expect to receive fruit from it? 7. Or a woman who has conceived, if she bring forth untimely, does she not assuredly slay her infant? 8. Or he who builds a house, if he does not roof it and com-

---

25. *What has been promised by Thee. I.e.* "the world which Thou hast promised them" (xiv. 13; cf. lxxxiii. 5). The new world would become the dwelling of the righteous after the judgment.

26. *I was greatly weakened.* This weakness follows again on the prayer in xlviii. 25; cf. 4 Ezra v. 14.

XXII. 1. *The heavens were opened and I saw.* Ezek. i. 1; cf. Matt. iii. 16; John i. 52; Rev. iv. 1; Acts vii. 56.

A voice was heard, etc., *i.e.* the *bath-qôl.* Cf. xiii. 1; Matt. iii. 17; xvii. 5; Rev. iv. 1.

3-8. In xxii. 3, 5, God rejoins that no man undertakes a work without hoping to enjoy its results, and that

no work can be duly judged till it is completed (xxii. 8). Thus Baruch's depreciation of this life (xxi. 13-17, 22) is in some fashion answered. Things must be judged in the light of their consummation. Again, in reply to Baruch's request to hasten the period of judgment (xxi. 19, 24, 20, 21, 23, 25), God rejoins that, for the due accomplishment of any work, time is needed (xxii. 6, 7). Finally, to Baruch's plea for the fulfilment of the divine promise (xxi. 25), God acknowledges the obligation of that promise (xxii. 4).

7. *Does . . . assuredly slay.* A Hebraism. Text = הרוג יהרג‎. Cf. xiii. 3; xli. 6; xlviii. 30, etc.

plete it, can it be called a house? Tell me that first."

XXIII. And I answered and said: "Not so, O LORD, my Lord." 2. And He answered and said unto me: "Why therefore art thou troubled about that which thou knowest not, and why art thou ill at ease about things in which thou art ignorant? 3. For as thou hast not forgotten the people who now are and those who have passed away, so I remember those who are remembered, and those who are to come. 4. Because when Adam sinned and death was decreed against those who should be born, then

---

XXIII. 1, 2. Baruch having admitted the justice of the divine reasons, God rejoins in the words of xxii. 3, "Why therefore art thou troubled?" for Baruch thereby acknowledges his ignorance of the things in question.

3. It is hard to see the relevance of this verse to any of Baruch's representations. Baruch has never doubted the ultimate fulfilment of the divine promises.

Who are remembered and those who are to come. The Syriac here ܘܕܡܡܝܢ ܘ ܐ݇ܠܝܢ ܡܬܕܟܪܝܢ ܘܐܠܝܢ seems corrupted from ܘܕܠܡܝܢ ܕܢܐܬܘܢ = "who are appointed to come."

4. *When Adam sinned and death was decreed against*, etc. There are two different conceptions of man's original destiny and of the *physical* effect of Adam's sin upon it in two of the different constituents of this book. (1) Thus in B², *i.e.* in xvii. 3; xix. 8; xxiii. 4, Adam's sin brought in physical death, otherwise man would have been immortal. We find the same view in Ecclus. xxv. 24 ἀπὸ γυναικὸς ἀρχὴ ἁμαρτίας, καὶ δι' αὐτὴν

ἀποθνήσκομεν πάντες, though this view cannot be reconciled with the main teaching and tendencies of that book, which are to the effect that man was mortal from the outset (cf. xiv. 17; xvii. 1, 2; xl. 11). The conditional immortality of man appears next in Eth. En. lxix. 11; Book of Wisdom i. 13, 14; ii. 23, 24; Slav. En. xxx. 16, 17 (see notes *in loc.*); in 4 Ezra iii. 7, "Et huic (*sc.* Adamo) mandasti diligentiam unam tuam: et praeterivit eam, et statim instituisti in eum mortem et in nationibus ejus." It is likewise the Pauline view (cf. Rom. v. 12; 1 Cor. xv. 21). In the Talmud this was the prevailing view; thus, according to the *Beresh. rabba*, c. 9, Adam was not originally destined for death (*Pesikta*, 76a); if Adam had not sinned he would have lived for ever (see Weber, 214, 215, 239). (2) In A³, *i.e.* in liv. 15; lvi. 6, Adam is said to have brought in only *premature* death. This seems to be the view underlying Gen. ii., iii., though many, it is true, take it to be conditional immortality. But such an interpretation is difficult in the face

the multitude of those who should be born was numbered, and for that number a place was prepared where the living might dwell and the dead might be guarded. 5. Unless therefore the number aforesaid is fulfilled, the creature will not live again [for My spirit is the creator of life], and Sheol will receive the dead. 6. And again it is given to thee to hear what things are to come after these times. 7. For truly My redemption has drawn nigh, and is not far distant as aforetime.

of Gen. iii. 19. (3) It may be well to add here that a third view is occasionally taught in the Talmud. Death came into the world in consequence of divine predestination (see Edersheim, *Life and Times, etc.*, i. 166 ; Weber, 238, 239). On the *spiritual* effects of Adam's sin on his posterity, see xlviii. 42, note. On the whole question, see Sanday and Headlam, *Romans*, 136-138.

The multitude of those who should be born was numbered. This was a secret known only to God (xxi. 10 ; xlviii. 46). How this number was fixed upon is not recorded. It could not be added to or diminished ; for the judgment could not come till it was completed (xxiii. 5 ; 4 Ezra iv. 33-43).

For that number a place was prepared. Cf. Slav. En. xlix. 2: "There has not been even a man in his mother's womb, for whom a place has not been prepared for every soul " ; and lviii. 5 : "There is a special place for mankind for all the souls of men according to their number." So in the Tractate *Chagiga*, fol. 15, col. 1 ; *Torath Adam*, fol. 101, col. 3 ; *Avodath hakkodesh*, fol. 19, col. 1, it is said that a place is prepared for every man either in Paradise or hell (Eisenmenger, ii. 315).

The dead might be guarded. The righteous were in " the treasuries of souls " guarded by angels (Eth. En. c. 5 ; 4 Ezra vii. 85, 95) ; the wicked in places of punishment guarded likewise by "those who keep the keys and are the guardians of the gates of hades standing like great serpents, and their faces are like quenched lamps, and their eyes fiery" (Slav. En. xlii. 1).

5. Not till the secret number of mankind is fulfilled can the resurrection take place. In Rev. vi. 11 and 4 Ezra iv. 36 the consummation of the world will follow, not when the number of mankind, but of the saints, is fulfilled. According to the *Shemoth rabba*, c. 39 (cf. *Aboda Sara*, 5a), all the generations of mankind were contained in a register called the ספר תולרות of Adam. And (*Beresh. rabba*, c. 24 ; *Wajjikra rabba*, c. 15) not until all the souls still dwelling in the גוף הנשמות, and included in the above register, had been born in the flesh should the Messiah come (*i.e.* the end of the world). See Weber, 335.

Sheol will receive. Cf. xxi. 23 ; xi. 6, note.

7. Cf. lxxxii. 2 ; Luke xxi. 28 ; 1 Pet. iv. 7.

XXIV. "For behold! the days come and the books
will be opened in which are written the sins of all
those who have sinned, and again also the treasuries
in which the righteousness of all those who have been

XXIV. 1. *Behold! the days come.*
See xx. 1, note.
The books will be opened. Dan.
vii. 10; Eth. En. xc. 20; Rev. xx.
12; 4 Ezra vi. 20. The books mentioned here contain only a record of
the sins of sinners, as in Eth. En. xc.
20. This is probably the case also
in Rev. xx. 12: "And books were
opened." In the last passage the
succeeding words have to do with the
lot of the righteous: "And another
book was opened which (is the book)
of life." This book of life is mentioned also in Eth. En. xlvii. 3;
cviii. 3. The books that are spoken
of in Dan. vii. 10; 4 Ezra vi. 20,
may be records both of the righteous
and the wicked.

The treasuries in which, etc. See
xxi. 23, note. Divine "treasuries"
or "storehouses" are a familiar
idea in the O.T. Thus we have
treasuries of rain (Deut. xxviii. 12),
of snow and hail (Job xxxviii. 22),
of wind (Jer. x. 13; li. 16; Ps.
cxxxv. 7), of the sea (Ps. xxxiii. 7);
see also Eth. En. lx. 11, 19, 20,
21; 4 Ezra vi. 40. Again the
idea of laying up spiritual things in
store is found in the LXX. Thus
in Prov. i. 18 θησαυρίζουσιν ἑαυτοῖς
κακά, and still more clearly in Pss.
Sol. ix. 9 θησαυρίζει ζωὴν ἑαυτῷ
παρὰ κυρίῳ. The last passage
belongs to a time when heaven
had come to be regarded as the
true home and destination of the
righteous. Naturally, when this
was the belief of the faithful, their
highest thoughts, aspirations, and
efforts would be directed thither,
and thus Ezra is assured: "Tibi
thesaurus operum repositus apud

Altissimum" (4 Ezra vii. 77), and
the righteous are those qui
fidem thesaurizaverunt (vi. 5); they
would lay up treasures in heaven
(Matt. vi. 19, 20). By a faithless
life, on the other hand, men "trea-
sured up for themselves wrath
against the day of wrath" (Rom.
ii. 5). Finally, the deeds of the
righteous were regarded as gathered
in "treasuries," as in our text.
The expression is found in another
sense in xliv. 14. We should
observe that אוצר and θησαυρός alike
mean a treasure and the place where
it is stored.

The righteousness of all, etc. As
Dr. Sanday writes (*Romans*, p. 29):
"For a Jew the whole sphere of
righteousness was taken up by the
Mosaic Law. His one idea of
righteousness was that of con-
formity to this law. Righteousness
was for him essentially obedience to
the law." That these words are
true of the conception of righteousness entertained by the writers of
this book will be seen by a perusal
of the note on xiv. 7. But naturally
the conception of righteousness
varied accordingly as it was used
by the legalistic or the prophetical
wing, if I may so speak, of Pharisaism. With the strict Legalists
righteousness meant the fulfilment
first and mainly of ceremonial observances, and secondly, but only
in a very subordinate degree, of
works of mercy. See, for instance,
the Book of Jubilees. With the
prophetical wing, from which eman-
ated most of the Messianic Apocalypses, righteousness was taken in
its large sense as the fulfilment of

righteous in creation is gathered. 2. For it will come to pass at that time that thou shalt see—and many that are with thee—the long-suffering of the Most High, which has been throughout all generations, who has been long-suffering towards all those born that sin and are righteous." 3. And I answered and said: "But, behold! O Lord, no one knows the number of those things which have passed nor yet of those things which are to come. 4. For I know indeed that which has befallen us, but what will happen to our enemies I know not, and when Thou wilt visit Thy works."

moral duties and only in a very secondary degree of ceremonial. The Ethiopic and Slavonic Books of Enoch are illustrations of the latter statement. In some books it is hard to determine the pre-eminence of either tendency.

Who have been righteous. See note on xxi. 9.

2. I have already shown on p. 20 that xxiv. 2-4 probably followed originally on xx.

Thou shalt see—and many, etc. See note on xiii. 5.

Sin and are righteous. Both verbs depend on the same subject.

3, 4. In the preceding verse God had just assured Baruch that he and many with him should ultimately see the long-suffering of God. Baruch rejoins when that time of recompense will be no man knows (ver. 3), but there is one thing he knows well, *i.e.* the present calamities of Israel. Hence he wishes to know (a) what fate is in store for the Gentiles who inflicted these, and (b) when will it take effect. The answer to (a) is given in xiii. 3b-12. Just before xiii. 3b some statement

such as "retribution will come upon your enemies who are now prospering," has been lost. Then follows xiii. 3b-12, in which Baruch is told that a special *rôle* is assigned him in reference to the enemies of Israel. He is to be preserved till the end of the times to testify to these cities, when the threatened retribution has befallen them, the reason of such retribution, the thoroughness with which it will be carried out, and the time of its consummation. Then in xxv. comes the answer to Baruch's second question: "When wilt Thou visit Thy works?" Baruch is to be preserved to play a part in this respect also (xxv. 1).

Befallen us. For ◌◌◌◌ = "what has befallen me," I have read ◌◌◌◌ = "what has befallen us?" The same corruption of the suffix appears in this MS. in lxxviii. 3 over against the right text in nine MSS.

Visit Thy works. xx. 2, note. The reference here is to the final judgment.

XXV. And He answered and said unto me:
"Thou too shalt be kept safely till that time till that
sign which the Most High will work for the inhabitants of the earth in the end of days. 2. This therefore will be the sign. 3. When a stupor shall seize
the inhabitants of the earth, and they shall fall into
many tribulations, and again when they shall fall into
great torments. 4. And it will come to pass when
they will say in their thoughts by reason of their
much tribulation: 'The Mighty One doth no longer
remember the earth'—yea, it will come to pass
when they abandon hope, that the time will then
awake."

XXVI. = E.

XXVI. And I answered and said: "Will that
tribulation which is to be continue a long time, and
will that necessity embrace many years?"

XXVII.-
XXX. 1 = A¹.

XXVII. And He answered and said unto me:

XXV. In this chapter we have
an answer to Baruch's question:
"When wilt Thou visit Thy works?"
XXV. 1. In xiii. 3*b* Baruch was
to be preserved to testify against
the Gentiles. He has also a further
function: observe the "too."
Till that time till that sign which.
The sign is the stupor that will
come on the inhabitants of the earth.
The inhabitants of the earth.
This phrase is always used in a bad
ethical sense in Baruch. Cf. xxv.
2 ; xlviii. 32, 40 ; liv. 1 ; lv. 2 ;
lxx. 2, 10 : generally in 4 Ezra ; cf.
iii. 34, 35 ; iv. 39 ; v. 6 ; vi. 24 ;
vii. 72 ; x. 59 ; xiii. 30 ; but in vi.
18, 26 ; xi. 5, 32, 34 ; xii. 24, the
sense of the phrase is merely geo-
graphical. For the various meanings of this phrase in the Eth. En.
and Rev., see Eth. En. pp. 43, 111.

3, 4. When stupor and despair
have seized the inhabitants of the
earth, the time of the judgment has
come.
3. *Stupor.* Cf. lxx. 2. This is
rendered *excessus mentis* in 4 Ezra
xiii. 30. For the diction, cf. Jer.
viii. 21.
4. At the end of the tribulation
and torments of the inhabitants of
the earth the time of the judgment
has come (cf. xiii. 8). This leaves no
room for the Messianic kingdom in
xxix., which precedes the judgment.
XXVI. This chapter is an addition
of the final editor in order to introduce xxvii.-xxx. 1. xxv. was originally followed by xiv.-xix.
XXVII.-XXX. 1. We have here
a fragment of a Messiah Apocalypse which for convenience of reference we designate A¹. Its (1) chief

" Into twelve parts is that time divided, and each one
of them is reserved for that which is appointed for it.
2. In the first part there will be the beginning of
commotions.   3. And in the second part (there will
be) slayings of the great ones.   4. And in the third
part (there will be) the fall of many by death.   5.
And in the fourth part the sending of desolation.   6.

characteristics, (2) its date, and (3)
its points of divergence from B¹
and B² are as follows :—(1) After a
terrible period of tribulation (*i.e.*
the travel pains of the Messiah)
(xxvii.-xxviii. 1) which should im-
peril the salvation even of the elect
(xxviii. 3), and should prevail over
all the earth (xxviii. 7-xxix. 1), a
glorious kingdom, accompanied with
every possible blessing, was to be
established under the Messiah (xxix.
3-8), who after a reign of indefinite
duration should return in glory into
heaven (xxx. 1*a*). Thereupon the
resurrection was to follow (xxx.
1*b*). The outlook is hopeful and
thoroughly optimistic. (2) The later
limit of composition is easy to determine. (*a*) Since the kingdom is to
be established in Palestine, and only
those Jews who are found there are
to share in it, it is clear that there
has been no dispersion of the Jews ;
for had there been, as it was in the
case of B¹, we should here be told
of a return from exile. Hence this
fragment was written before 70 A.D.
(*b*) Again, since Palestine is the
scene of the kingdom, Jerusalem
must still be standing ; for in case
it had fallen, we should here be told
of its restoration, as in B¹, or of the
setting up of the new Jerusalem, as in
4 Ezra xiii. 36. The Messianic kingdom could not be set up over the
ruins of the holy city. Hence, again,
we conclude that A¹ was written
before 70 A.D. (3) Its points of

divergence from B¹ and B² are
obvious. In the latter, Jerusalem
is destroyed and its people in exile ;
whereas in A¹ Jerusalem is standing and the Jews are in their own
land. Again, whereas the law is
the centre of interest and expectation in B², and in a somewhat less
degree in B¹ (see xv. 5, note), it is the
Messiah that is such in A¹. Further,
whereas there is not a single allusion
to the Messiah in B¹ and B², there is
not a single allusion to the law in
A¹. This, indeed, may be partly due
to the shortness of this fragment.

XXVII. 1. In A³, *i.e.* liii.-lxxiv. and
4 Ezra xiv. 11, 12, there are similar
twelvefold divisions ; but in these it
is the entire history of the world
that is so divided, whereas in our
text it is only the time of troubles
preceding the advent of the Messiah.
These troubles were popularly conceived as the travail pains of the
Messiah חבלי המשיח. We find a
list of such woes (ὠδῖνες, Matt. xxiv.
8) in xlviii. 31-37 ; lxx. 2-10 ; Matt.
xxiv. 6-29, with synoptic parallels ;
2 Tim. iii. 1 ; Jubilees xxiii. 13,
16-25 ; 4 Ezra v. 1-12 ; vi. 14-18,
20-24 ; *Orac. Sibyl.* iii. 796-807 ;
see Weber, 336 ; Schürer, Div. II.,
vol. ii. 154-156. In the Gospels,
however, these woes are to precede
the second coming of Christ or the
end of the world.

5. Cf. 4 Ezra v. 8 ; vi. 22. For
desolation we might also render
"the sword"; cf. 5 Ezra xv. 5.

And in the fifth part famine and the withholding of rain. 7. And in the sixth part earthquakes and terrors. 8. [Wanting.] 9. And in the eighth part a multitude of portents and incursions of the Shedim. 10. And in the ninth part the fall of fire. 11. And in the tenth part rapine and much oppression. 12. And in the eleventh part wickedness and unchastity. 13. And in the twelfth part confusion from the mingling together of all those things aforesaid. 14. For these parts of that time are reserved, and will be mixed one with another and will minister one to another. 15. For some will of themselves be of service, and they will receive from others, and from themselves and others they will be perfected, so that those may not understand who are upon the earth in those days of this consummation of the times.

XXVIII. "Nevertheless, whosoever shall understand will then be wise. 2. For the measure and reckoning of that time are two parts weeks of seven weeks." 3. And I answered and said : " It is good for a man

6. *Famine.* As a sign of the end, cf. lxx. 8; Matt. xxiv. 7; Mark xiii. 8 ; Luke xxi. 11.

7. *Earthquakes.* Cf. lxx. 8 ; Matt. xxiv. 7 ; Mark xiii. 8 ; Luke xxi. 11.

9. *Portents.* Cf. 4 Ezra vi. 21 : " Et anniculi infantes loquentur vocibus suis, et praegnantes immaturos parient infantes, etc." But owing to the next words it would perhaps be better to render $\underline{\ }_{}\Lambda_{}\underline{\ }$ = φαντασίαι as " spectres."

The Shedim. See x. 8, note.

10. *The fall of fire.* Cf. lxx. 8 ; 4 Ezra v. 8. If with the reviser of

the MS. we delete the ܕ before ܢܦܠ we should render "the fire will fall."

15. These verses are obscure. They are possibly corrupt. For " of this . . . times " we can equally well render "that this is the consummation of the times."

XXVIII. 1. This verse recalls Dan. xii. 10 : " the wise shall understand."

2. I cannot interpret this verse.

3. This verse expresses the difficulty of faithfulness in the times just described. Cf. 4 Ezra xiii. 16-20 : " Vae qui derelicti fuerint in diebus illis, et multo plus vae his

to come and behold, but it is better that he should not come lest he fall. 4. [But I will say this also. 5. 'Will he who is incorruptible despise those things which are corruptible, and whatever befalls in the case of those things which are corruptible, so that he might look only to those things which are not corruptible ?'] 6. But if, O Lord, those things shall assuredly come to pass which Thou hast foretold to me; if, moreover, I have found grace in Thy sight, show this also unto me. 7. Is it in one place or in one of the parts of the earth that those things are to come to pass, or will the whole earth experience (them) ? "

XXIX. And He answered and said unto me: " Whatever will then befall will belong to the whole earth; therefore all who live will experience (them). 2. For at that time I will protect only those who are found in those self-same days in this land. 3. And it

qui non sunt derelicti ! Qui enim non sunt derelicti, tristes erunt, intelligentes quae sunt reposita in novissimis diebus et non occurrentes eis . . . adtamen facilius est periclitantem venire in haec quam pertransire . . . et non videre quae contingent in novissimo." Only the righteous, the fittest survive. Cf. xli. 1 ; lxxv. 5 ; 4 Ezra vii. 46, 47 ; Matt. xxiv. 22 ; Mark xiii. 21. This verse looks forward to the blessings described in xxix. 4-8.

4, 5. I have bracketed these verses as an interpolation of the final editor. They break the connection of thought. Further, no account is taken of them either by Baruch to whom they are assigned, or by God to whom they are addressed. They are unreasonable and out of place in the presence of

the sensuous picture of Messianic bliss which meets us in the next chapter. The real answer to Baruch's question here can be gathered from xliii. 2.

6. *If I have found grace*, etc. A familiar O.T. phrase (Gen. vi. 8 ; xix. 19, etc.; 4 Ezra v. 56 ; vii. 102 ; viii. 42 ; xii. 7).

XXIX. 2. *I will protect*, etc. Here God protects His people who are found in the Holy Land, whereas in A² it is the Messiah (xl. 2) in A³ the Holy Land itself (lxxi. 1). In B² it is the law that protects the faithful, irrespective of their place of habitation (xxxii. 1 ; cf. 6 Ezra vii. 122).

Found . . . in this land. Cf. xl. 2 ; lxxi. 1 ; 4 Ezra xiii. 48, 49. A special blessing attached to residence in Palestine. It alone was to escape the woes that should befall

will come to pass when all is accomplished that was to
come to pass in those parts, that the Messiah will then

all the earth besides. But this thought is found only in the sections of this book written prior to 70 A.D. Such ideas as to the sacrosanct and inviolable character of Palestine seem to have disappeared for a time from Jewish speculation with the desecration and destruction of Jerusalem by the Romans, unless where the Messiah was expected. Hence in B² it is the law that protects the faithful (xxxii. 1), and in 4 Ezra vii. 122 it is the glory of God; and this protection avails them irrespective of their place of dwelling. The special privileges attaching to the Holy Land reappear in the Talmud, but in another form. Thus three will inherit the world to come: he who dwells in the land of Israel, he who brings up his sons to the study of the law, and he who repeats the ritual blessing over the appointed cup of wine at the close of the Sabbath (*Pesachim*, fol. 113a). Again the merits of the fathers will not avail a man who leaves the land of Israel for an outside land (*Baba bathra*, fol. 91a). Further, those who died in the Holy Land should rise first in the resurrection (Weber, pp. 64, 352); hence it is called "the land of the living" (*Beresh. rab.* 74); if the righteous died in any other land their bodies would have to roll (מתגלגלים) through underground passages (מחילות) till they came to Palestine before they could be raised (Weber, 352; Eisenmenger, ii. 920, 921). It was for this reason that Jacob and Joseph (Eisenmenger, ii. 925) and the Rabbis, who were specially honoured (Weber, 64), were buried in Canaan. Nay more, residents in the land of Israel could procure the resurrection of their relatives who died among the Gentiles

(Eisenmenger, ii. 900). That the righteous who were buried outside the limits of Palestine should rise is also stated (Weber, 352).

8. The *rôle* here assigned to the Messiah is a passive one like that in Eth. En. xc. 37, 38; 4 Ezra vii. 28, 29. In this respect it differs from that represented in A² and A³, *i.e.* xxxvi.-xl.; lii.-lxxiv.; and in Eth. En. xxxvii.-lxx.; Pss. Sol. xvii., xviii.; 4 Ezra xii. 32-34; xiii. 32-50, where the Messiah fights either with spiritual or material weapons on behalf of Israel, destroys its enemies, and sets up the Messianic kingdom.

The Messiah will then begin to be revealed. The phrase "begin to be revealed" seems corrupt. We should perhaps have "the principate of the Messiah will be revealed," as in xxxix. 7. We can get this by reading [Syriac] instead of [Syriac] Cf. xli. 3. Or by simply reading [Syriac] instead of [Syriac] we have "Messiah the prince will be revealed." In this case the phraseology might be due to Dan. ix. 25. From a comparison of this verse and xxx. 1 the Messiah appears to be in heaven and is to be revealed from thence; but in other passages the implication of such language as "will be revealed" is merely that the Messiah may be already on earth and yet be unknown. This emergence of the Messiah from concealment was a current view. Thus we find it in 4 Ezra vii. 28; xiii. 32; also in John vii. 27: "When the Christ cometh, no man knoweth whence he is." This concealment of the Messiah is mentioned also in Targum Jon. on Zech-

begin to be revealed.   4. And Behemoth will be revealed from his place, and Leviathan will ascend from

ariah iii. 8 ; vi. 12. In the Targum
on Micah iv. 8 it is said to be due
to the sins of the people. From
Justin's *Dial. c. Tryph.* 8, it appears
that though the Messiah may be
already born, yet He may be unknown, and not even know His own
calling till Elijah anoints and re-
veals Him. Χριστὸς δέ, εἰ καὶ γεγένη-
ται καὶ ἔστι που, ἄγνωστός ἐστι καὶ
οὐδὲ αὐτός πω ἑαυτὸν ἐπίσταται
οὐδὲ ἔχει δύναμίν τινα, μέχρις ἂν
ἐλθὼν Ἡλίας χρίσῃ αὐτὸν καὶ φάνε-
ρον πᾶσι ποιήσῃ. Cf. also c. 110.

According to the Talmud, the
Messiah was born at Bethlehem on
the day of the destruction of the
temple, was named Menahem, and
afterwards suddenly carried away
by a storm (*Hieros. Berachoth,* p. 5).
His temporary abode, according to
later writers, was to be Rome
(*Sanhedrin,* 98a). On this subject
see Lightfoot's *Horae* on Matt. ii.
1 ; Oehler's *Messias* in Herzog's
R.E. ix. 668 ; Drummond, *The
Jewish Messiah,* 293, 294 ; Schürer's
N.T. Times, Div. II., vol. ii. 163,
164 ; Weber, 342, 343 ; Wünsche,
Die Leiden des Messias, 57-59.

4. *And Behemoth will be revealed,*
etc. The full form of this myth is
given in 4 Ezra vi. 49-52 : "Et tunc
conservasti duo animalia, nomen
uni vocasti Behemoth et nomen
secundi vocasti Leviathan, Et sepa-
rasti ea ab alterutro, non enim
poterat septima pars ubi erat aqua
congregata capere ea. Et dedisti
Behemoth unam partem quae siccata
est tertio die, ut inhabitet in ea,
ubi sunt montes mille ; Leviathan
autem dedisti septinam partem
humidam : et servasti ea ut fiant
in devorationem quibus vis et
quando vis." From a comparison
of verse 4 with the verses just cited,
it is clear that the words "from his

place" and "from the sea" imply
the account in these verses of Ezra.
This is confirmed by the fact that
not only is the thought the same,
but also almost word for word
the diction in the Syriac Versions
of the two clauses : "Servasti ea ut
fiant in devorationem" (4 Ezra vi.
52) and "kept them until that time
and then they will be for food."
Thus so far 4 Ezra would seem to
be the source of our text. But if
in these respects Baruch presupposes
4 Ezra, 4 Ezra in turn presupposes
Baruch in the clauses : "Quibus vis
et quando vis" (4 Ezra vi. 52) over
against "for all that are left" in
verse 4—the words "those who are
left" being a technical phrase to
express those who should survive to
participate in the Messianic kingdom. We are thus led to assume
that a short hexaemeron, closely
resembling that found in 4 Ezra vi.
38-54, existed at one time independently, and that the writers of Ezra vi.
30-vii. 25 and Bar. xxvii.-xxx. laid
it under contribution for their own
purposes. (For a probable additional
fragment of this hexaemeron, see
xv. 7, note.) This assumption gains
confirmation from the facts (1) that
this hexaemeron cannot originally
have proceeded from the writer of
the Salathiel Apocalypse (*i.e.* the
groundwork of 4 Ezra) ; for the latter
looked for no Messianic kingdom,
whereas the writer of this hexaemeron did as is obvious from vi.
52 compared with xxix. 4 of our
text ; and (2) that whereas A[1] of
Baruch was written prior to the fall
of Jerusalem, the Salathiel Apocalypse was written subsequently to it.

4. *Behemoth . . . and Leviathan.*
In addition to the references in the
preceding note, see Eth. En. lx. 7-
9, 24, notes ; Targ. Jon. on Gen.

the sea, those two great monsters which I created on the fifth day of creation, and I kept them until that time ; and then they will be for food for all that are left. 5. The earth also will yield its fruit ten thousand-fold, and on one vine there will be a thousand branches,

i. 21 : "And God created great beasts Leviathan and his wife which were prepared for the day of consolation ;" see also the Targum on Ps. l. 10 ; Weber, 156, 195, 370, 384 ; Buxtorf, *Lexicon Chald. rabb. Talmud*, and Levy, *Chaldäisches Wörterbuch* and *Neuhebräisches Wörterb. in loc.*

All that are left. This is in fact "the remnant" that survives to share in the Messiah's kingdom. This remnant is frequently referred to in this sense (cf. xl. 2 ; 4 Ezra vi. 25 ; vii. 28 ; ix. 7 ; xii. 34 ; xiii. 48).

5. We have here another fragment of an old Apocalypse, of which we find a Latin version in Irenaeus, v. 33. This Apocalypse Papias, according to Irenaeus, assigned to our Lord. It is recounted in the fourth book of his Λογίων κυριακῶν ἐξήγησις. The passage in question is : "Venient dies, in quibus vineae nascentur, singulae decem millia palmitum habentes, et in uno palmite dena millia brachiorum, et in uno vero palmite dena millia flagellorum, et in unoquoque flagello dena millia botruum, et in unoquoque botro dena millia acinorum et unumquodque acinum expressum dabit vigintiquinque metretas vini. Et quum eorum apprehenderit aliquis sanctorum botrum, alius clamabit : Botrus ego melior sum, me sume, per me Dominum benedic." Scholars have taken our text to be the original of this passage. That this is unlikely, and that both may be derived from the same original source, I will now proceed to show. In the first place, the passage in Irenaeus contains two additional

sentences : "Dena millia brachiorum . . . palmite," and "Et quum eorum . . . benedic." Hence a fuller text is presupposed than we have in Bar. xxix. 5. In the next place, immediately after the words just cited, the text in Irenaeus proceeds : "Similiter et granum tritici decem millia spicarum generaturum, et unamquamque spicam habituram decem millia granorum, et unumquodque granum quinque bilibres similae clarae mundae." With these words compare the Eth. En. x. 19, where, in an account of Messianic bliss, we find "The vine that is planted thereon will yield wine in abundance, and of all the seed which is sown thereon will each measure bear ten thousand." From this we conclude that for a long time prior to Christianity there existed either in tradition or in writing a sensuous description of Messianic felicity. In this description not only the fruitfulness of the vine was dwelt upon, but also of all seeds and fruit-bearing trees. Of this description the largest survival is in Irenaeus, v. 33, preserved through the agency of Papias ; the fragmentary survivals in the Eth. En. x. 19 (see above) and in our text form complimentary portions of this tradition.

Finally, the text presents a syncretistic appearance. In xxix. 4 one description of food—a flesh diet —is provided for the members of the Messianic kingdom ; and in the next verse quite another—a vegetable diet ; and in xxix. 8 a heavenly food, *i.e.* manna. The second is a more ancient view than the first and

and each branch will produce a thousand clusters, and each cluster will produce a thousand grapes, and each grape will produce a cor of wine.   6. And those who have hungered will rejoice : moreover, also, they will behold marvels every day.   7. For winds will go forth from before Me to bring every morning the fragrance of aromatic fruits, and at the close of the day clouds distilling the dew of health.   8. And it will come to pass at that self-same time that the treasury of manna will again descend from on high, and they will eat of it in those years, because these are they who have come to the consummation of time.

the most reasonable, being a return to the food of Adam in Paradise.

As to the origin of the 10,000-fold yield of the corn and wine, etc., Mr. Rendel Harris (*Expositor*, 1895, pp. 448, 449) offers a most ingenious and probable suggestion. He derives it from the blessing of Isaac (Gen. xxvii. 28), where he conjectures that in the statement רֹב דָּגָן וְתִירֹשׁ "plenty of corn and wine," the word רֹב was taken as רִבּוּ = 10,000. He points out that the context in Irenaeus (see above), in which the story of Papias and the elders is given, supports his contention ; for that it follows a discussion of the blessing in question.

Each branch . . . each cluster . . . each grape. Instead of "each" the Syriac in all three cases gives "one." But the sense requires "each," and in the Latin Version of this passage preserved in Irenaeus (see above) "each" is found in the three phrases, *i.e.* "unoquoque flagello, unoquoque botro, unumquodque acinum." The explanation is not far to seek. The Hebrew אחד which = εἶς, one, occasionally

also = ἕκαστος, each. The former meaning was wrongly followed by the Greek translator. Hence the wrong turn in the Syriac.

A cor. This represents κόρος which in turn is a translation of כֹּר or כֹּמֶר. The cor was equal to about 120 gallons. Cf. Joseph. *Ant.* xv. 9, 2 ὁ δὲ κόρος δύναται μεδίμνους ἀττικοὺς δέκα.

6. *Rejoice.* This is a characteristic of the members of the kingdom. Cf. 4 Ezra vii. 28 ; xii. 34.

Behold marvels. The belief that the Messiah would signalise His advent by marvels was general. Cf. 4 Ezra vii. 27 ; xiii. 50 ; Matt. xi. 4-6 ; Luke vii. 22, 23 ; John vii. 31.

8. *The treasury of manna will again descend*, etc. In Ps. lxxviii. 25 manna is called angels' food. In *Or. Sibyl.* vii. 149 it is to be the food of the members of the Messianic kingdom Μάννην τὴν δροσερὴν λευκοῖσιν ὀδοῦσι φάγονται, and in Rev. ii. 17 the idea is spiritualised : the faithful are to receive "hidden manna."

These are they, etc. These are "the remnant" of verse 4.

Consummation of time. This

XXX. "And it will come to pass after these things, when the time of the advent of the Messiah is fulfilled, and He will return in glory, then all who have fallen asleep in hope of Him shall rise again. 2. And it will come to pass at that time that the treasuries will be opened in which is preserved the number of the souls of the righteous, and they will come forth, and a multitude of souls will be seen together in one assemblage of one thought, and the first will rejoice and the last will not be grieved. 3.

XXX. 2-
XXXV. = B².

phrase is found in xxvii. 15. The Messianic age forms the "consummation of the time or times" = ἡ συντελεία τοῦ αἰῶνος or τῶν αἰώνων. We should observe that this phrase has a different meaning in xxx. 3; but there we have the work of B².

XXX. 1. *When the time of the advent of the Messiah is fulfilled,* etc. This can have only one meaning, and this is that, at the close of His reign, the Messiah will return in glory to heaven. The word translated "advent" is]ܢܠܚܠܣܐ which in turn was an ordinary rendering of παρουσία. Now παρουσία can mean not only "coming" or "advent," but also "presence" (cf. 2 Cor. x. 10; 2 Macc. xv. 21, and probably 2 Cor. vii. 6, 7; 2 Thess. ii. 9). Hence we should render: "When the time of the presence of the Messiah is fulfilled."

Return in glory. These words imply that the Messiah pre-existed in heaven before His advent. He returns whither He had come. This is also the teaching of Eth. En. xlvi. 1, 2; xlviii. 3 (see note); lxii. 7; 4 Ezra xii. 32; xiii. 26 (?); xiv. 9. This seems also to be the legitimate interpretation of Pss. Sol. xviii. 6 εἰς ἡμέραν ἐκλογῆς ἐν

ἀνάξει χριστοῦ αὐτοῦ. In 4 Ezra vii. 29, 30, the Messiah and the righteous die at the close of the Messianic kingdom.

Then all who have fallen asleep in hope of Him shall rise again. The resurrection follows immediately on the return of the Messiah into heaven; on his death in 4 Ezra vii. 29, 30. The words "of him" cannot be original. The text was probably "those who have fallen asleep in hope." Cf. LXX. of Ps. xvi. 9 ἡ σάρξ μου κατασκηνώσει ἐπ᾽ ἐλπίδι. The corruption could have arisen easily in the Syriac by a change of]ܟܣܡܪ into ܣܪ݁ܡܣܟ.

Fallen asleep. Cf. xi. 4, note. As A¹ is fragmentary, we are not told what befalls the living righteous. In the following verses of B² only the destinies of *souls* are dealt with. The complementary half of this doctrine is given in l., li. 2. With this verse we return to B², resuming the text that ended with xxiv. 1. We have here an account of the general resurrection (cf. xlii. 8; l. 2).

Treasuries. See xxi. 23, note; xxiv. 1, note.

For he knows that the time has come of which it is said, that it is the consummation of the times.   4. But the souls of the wicked, when they behold all those things, shall then waste away the more.   5. For they will know that their torment has come and their perdition has arrived."

XXXI. And it came to pass after these things that I went to the people and said unto them: "Assemble unto me all your elders and I will speak

---

3. *The consummation of the times.* This phrase means here the final judgment ; in A[1] it means the Messianic age (cf. xxvii. 15 ; xxix. 8).

4. *Waste away.* Cf. li. 5 ; 4 Ezra vii. 87.

5. This verse does not mean that the wicked souls have not hitherto suffered, but that their suffering hitherto is as nothing compared to the torments they shall now endure. Similarly, the righteous have in the treasuries of souls had rest and peace, but they too (cf. ver. 3) know that their real blessedness has now come. See xxxvi. 10.

XXXI.-XXXV. Baruch assembles and addresses the elders of the people (xxxi. 1-8) ; he exhorts them not to forget the anguish of Zion (xxxi. 4), and announces the coming end of all that is corruptible (xxxi. 5) ; and, in case they observe the law, their safety amid the convulsions which will accompany the renewal of the entire creation (xxxii. 1) ; they are not to grieve so much for the past as for the coming time ; for then the strife and stress will exceed all that has been before when God renews creation (xxxii. 1, 5, 6). Thereupon, when Baruch seeks to dismiss the people (xxxii. 7), they remonstrate against his forsaking them (xxxii. 8 - xxxiii.) Baruch rejoins

that he is not forsaking them, but only going to the Holy Place to get light from God (xxxiv.) He then proceeds thither and laments over Zion (xxxv.) A fast of seven days should follow here.

The subject on which Baruch addresses the people is to be found in each instance in the previous divine revelation (see v. 5 ; x. 4) ; but it will be observed that this address (xxxi. 3-xxxii. 6) is wholly out of relation to all that has gone before. There is therefore something wrong. The gist of this address is : (*a*) The end of all things corruptible is at hand ; (*b*) if ye prepare your hearts to obey the law ye will then be safe in this time of crisis ; (*c*) for the entire creation must be shaken, and give place to a new and incorruptible creation. Now these questions are discussed later in the dialogues between God and Baruch. Thus, for (*a*), see xlii. 6-8 ; for (*b*), see xlviii. 22-24, 38-41 ; for (*c*), see xlviii. 49 ; lii. 3, 8-9, 16. We therefore hold that xxxi.-xxxv. was read after lii. originally. Finally, xliv. 8-15 really forms the conclusion of Baruch's address in xxxi., xxxii. ; it should be read immediately after xxxii. 6 (see p. 69).

XXXI. 1. *All your elders.* See xliv. 1, note.

words unto them." 2. And they all assembled in the valley of the Cedron. 3. And I answered and said unto them: "Hear, O Israel, and I will speak to thee, and give ear, O seed of Jacob, and I will instruct thee. 4. Forget not Zion, but hold in remembrance the anguish of Jerusalem. 5. For lo! the days come, when everything that exists will become the prey of corruption and be as though it had not been.

XXXII. "But ye, if ye prepare your hearts, so as to sow in them the fruits of the law, it will protect you in that time in which the Mighty One is to shake XXXII. 2-4 = the whole creation. [2. Because after a little time E. the building of Zion will be shaken in order that it

2. *Cedron.* See v. 5, note.

3. *Hear, O Israel . . . and give ear, O seed of Jacob.* Cf. xvii. 4; xlvi. 4; 4 Ezra ix. 30. For the combination "hear . . . and give ear," see Isa. i. 2.

5. *Will become the prey of.* Literally = "will be taken to corruption." See xxi. 19, note.

XXXII. 1. *Prepare your hearts.* An O.T. phrase (cf. 1 Sam. vii. 3; Job xi. 13; Ps. lxxviii. 8). It is a favourite expression in B[1] and B[2] of this book; cf. xlvi. 5; lii. 7; lxxxiii. 8; lxxv. 9, 11.

The fruits of the law. Cf. 4 Ezra iii. 20; ix. 32; see note on xv. 5.

It will protect. See xxix. 2, note. These words point back to xlviii. 22-24; cf. xliv. 13, 14; xlviii. 38-41.

Shake the whole creation. I.e. with a view to a new heavens and a new earth (see ver. 6). The thought comes originally from Haggai ii. 6; cf. Heb. xii. 26.

2-4. I have bracketed these verses as an interpolation; for in verse 2 it is announced that the temple will be

destroyed after a little time; but, according to all B[2] as well as B[1], the temple has already been destroyed, and this is the presupposition of xxxi. 4. Again, verses 2-4 break the connection of thought in the text. Observe the awkwardness of "Because after a little time," etc., following on verse 1; and, on the other hand, how appropriately verse 5 follows on xxxi. 4-xxxii. 1. We should observe that there is nothing inconsistent in the idea of a heavenly Jerusalem being established on a new and incorruptible earth. Indeed, it is not impossible that iv. 2-7 originally followed xxxii. 6. We have a close parallel to xxxii. 2-4 in *Beresh rab.* 2, and *Pesikta*, 145a, where it is said that the temple was built in glory, destroyed, again rebuilt, but in mean fashion; finally, it should again be rebuilt in glory.

2. *Zion will be shaken. I.e.* in 588 by Nebuchadnezzar; but according to xxxi. 4; xxxii. 5; xxxiii. 2, 3; xxxv. 1, this is already in the past.

may again be built. 3. But that building will not remain, but will again after a time be rooted out, and will remain desolate until the time. 4. And afterwards it must be renewed in glory, and it will be perfected for evermore.] 5. Therefore we should not be distressed so much over the evil which has now come as over that which is still to be. 6. For there will be a greater trial than these two tribulations when the Mighty One will renew His creation. 7. And now do not draw near to me for a few days, nor seek me till I come to you." 8. And it came to pass when I had spoken to them all these words, that I, Baruch, went my way, and when the people saw me setting out, they lifted up their voice and lamented and said:

In order that it may again be built. *I.e.* by Ezra and Nehemiah.

3. *Again . . . be rooted out. I.e.* by the Romans in 70 A.D.

4. On the heavenly Jerusalem. See iv. 3, note.

5. *We should . . . be distressed.* I have here followed Bensly's emendation of ܡܠܝܢ into ܡܠܝܢ. Otherwise, we should render with Ceriani, "Non ergo debet nos contristare hoc omne super malo quod supervenit," etc.

The evil which has now come. The fall of Jerusalem.

6. *Two tribulations. I.e.* those accompanying the destruction of Jerusalem and the renewal of creation. But the more natural rendering is : "For there will be a greater trial than the two tribulations when," etc. If we must accept this, the words "than the two tribulations" are an addition of E, and without them the text would

run : "For the trial will be great when," etc.

Renew His creation. This signifies an incorruptible world which was to take the place of the corruptible (cf. xxxi. 5 ; xliv. 12 ; lvii. 2). It was a current expectation from the times of the captivity (cf. Isa. lxv. 17 ; lxvi. 22 ; Eth. En. xlv. 4, note ; lxxii. 1 ; xci. 15, 16 ; 4 Ezra vii. 75 ; Matt. xix. 28 ; 2 Pet. iii. 13 ; Rev. xxi. 1). This announcement of Baruch is the presupposition of li., lii., and the truth correlative to the renewal and transformation of the righteous in li.

7. *Do not draw near,* etc. 4 Ezra v. 19. This verse was preceded originally by xliv. 8-15 (see p. 69).

For a few days. These words refer to the interval in which the next fast of seven days should take place. The mention of this fast at the beginning or close of xxxv. has through some accident been omitted (see v. 7, note ; ix. 2, note).

9. "Whither departest thou from us, Baruch, and forsakest us as a father who forsakes his orphan children, and departs from them?

XXXIII. "Are these the commands which thy companion, Jeremiah the prophet, commanded thee, and said unto thee: 2. 'Look to this people till I go and confirm the rest of the brethren in Babylon, against whom has gone forth the sentence that they should be led into captivity?' 3. And now if thou also forsakest us, it were good for us all to die before thee, and then that thou shouldst withdraw from us."

XXXIV. And I answered and said unto the people: "Far be it from me to forsake you or to withdraw from you, but I will only go unto the Holy of Holies to enquire of the Mighty One concerning you and concerning Zion, if in some respect I should receive more illumination: and after these things I will return to you."

XXXV. And I, Baruch, went to the holy place, and sat down upon the ruins and wept, and said: 2. "Become ye springs, O mine eyes, and ye, mine eyelids, a fount of tears. 3. For how shall I lament

---

9. Cf. 4 Ezra v. 18.

XXXIII. 1, 2. See x. 2, note, where I have shown that, according to B¹, Jeremiah does not seem to have gone to Babylon.

3. For another form of the same thought, cf. 4 Ezra xii. 44.

XXXIV. *Far be it from me to forsake you.* Cf. 4 Ezra xii. 48: "Si ergo tu nos dereliqueris, quanto erit nobis melius, si essemus succensi et nos in incendio Sion."

Holy of Holies. This is practically the same place as is mentioned in x. 5; in xxxv. 1 it is simply called the holy place. It is where the altar stood. See xxxv. 4.

XXXV. 1. *The holy place, and sat down upon the ruins.* See preceding note, and x. 5, note.

2. From Jer. ix. 1; cf. Eth. En. xcv. 1.

for Zion, and how shall I mourn for Jerusalem ?   4.
Because in that place where I am now prostrate, the
high priest of old used to offer holy sacrifices, and to
place thereon the smoke of the incense of fragrant
odours.   5. But now our glorying has been made
into dust, and the desire of our soul into sand."

XXXVI. And when I had said these things I fell   XXXVI.-XL.
=A².

THE SIXTH SECTION

XXXVI.-XLVI. This in reality
forms the sixth part of this book.
For the symmetry of the book as con-
structed by the final editor requires,
as we have already shown (see v. 7,
note, introduction to the fifth section,
p. 36, and xxxii. 7, note), the insertion of a seven days' fast after xxxv.,
or possibly even before it. The omission of this fast may have been an
original oversight of the editor, or
may have been due to a careless
copyist. The structure of this part
is as follows :—First, the omitted
fast, then a Messiah vision and its interpretation (xxxvi.-xl.), with further
disclosures regarding apostates and
proselytes (xli. 2-xlii. 8), and the
announcement of Baruch's coming
death (xliii.) Finally, Baruch's address to the people (xliv.-xlvi.)

This section is of very composite
origin. Thus xxxvi.-xl. is a Messiah
Apocalypse written prior to 70 A.D. ;
xliii.-xliv. 8; xlv.-xlvi. 6 belongs to
B¹ ; the rest of the section mainly
to B².

XXXVI.-XL. We have here the
second Messiah Apocalypse A². (a)
*Date of A² and its Relation to B¹
and B².* A² is quite distinct in its
world-view and date from B¹ and
B². We shall first establish the
difference of date. Now whereas
we have seen that B¹ and B² were
written subsequent to the fall of
Jerusalem, it is clear that A² was

written prior to that event. For
whereas, in a short historical outline from the rise of Babylon to the
reign of the Messiah (xxxix. 2-xl.
2), the first destruction of Jerusalem is mentioned (xxxix. 3), there
is not even a hint given as to its
destruction by Rome, although the
Roman oppression of Palestine is
clearly indicated (xxxix. 5, 6).
Again the Messiah makes Zion His
capital (xl. 1). If it were in ruins,
its restoration would of necessity be
mentioned. Finally, as there is no
allusion in A² to the second destruction of Jerusalem, so there is
none to the subsequent dispersion
after that event, and none to a
return of the exiles. Consequently,
as we find, the remnant of Israel is
still in Palestine (xl. 2). It is
wholly otherwise in B¹ and B².

As regards their difference of
world-view, it will be sufficient here
to remark that whereas there is no
Messiah in B¹ and B², the Messiah
is the centre of expectation and the
stay of Israel in A². And whereas
B² is pessimistic as regards this
world, A² is optimistic. And
whereas in B², and in a less degree
in B¹, the law is the centre and the
end of life, in A² this place is
occupied by the Messiah.

(b) *Relation of A² to A¹.* The
two writings come from different
authors. In A¹ the Messiah has
only a passive *rôle* assigned to Him ;
He does not appear till the enemies

asleep there, and I saw a vision in the night. 2. And lo! a forest of trees planted on the plain, and lofty mountains surrounded it and precipitous rocks, and that forest occupied much space. 3. And lo! over against it arose a vine, and from under it there went forth a fountain peacefully. 4. Now that fountain came to the forest and was (stirred) into great waves, and those waves submerged that forest, and suddenly they rooted out the multitude of (the trees) of that forest, and overthrew all the mountains which were round about it. 5. And the height of the forest began to be made low, and the top of the mountains was made low, and that fountain prevailed greatly, so that it left nothing of that great forest save one cedar only. 6. Also when it had cast it down and had destroyed and rooted out the multitude of (the trees of) that forest, so that nothing was left of it, nor could its place be recognised, then that vine began to come with the fountain in peace and great tranquillity, and it came to a place which was not far from the cedar, and they brought the cedar which had been cast down to it. 7. And I beheld and lo! that vine opened its mouth and spake and said to that cedar: "Art thou not that cedar which was left of the forest of wickedness, and by whose means wickedness persisted, and was wrought all those years, and goodness never. 8.

of Israel are destroyed. In A², on the other hand, the destruction of the wicked and the vindication of Israel is the sole work of the Messiah.

XXXVI. 1. It will be remarked that these visions are only found in A² and A³. Elsewhere we have direct revelations.

I fell asleep. Cf. lii. 8.

And thou didst keep conquering that which was not thine, and to that which was thine thou didst never show compassion, and thou didst keep extending thy power over those who were far from thee, and those who drew nigh thee thou didst hold fast in the toils of thy wickedness, and thou didst uplift thyself always as one that could not be rooted out!   9. But now thy time has sped and thy hour is come.   10. Do thou also therefore depart, O cedar, after the forest, which departed before thee, and become dust with it, and let your ashes be mingled together.   11. And now recline in anguish and rest in torment till thy last time come, in which thou wilt come again, and be tormented still more."

XXXVII. And after these things I saw that cedar burning, and the vine growing, itself and all around it, the plain full of unfading flowers.   And I indeed awoke and arose.

XXXVIII. And I prayed and said: " O LORD, my Lord, Thou dost always enlighten those who are led by understanding.   2. Thy law is life, and Thy

---

8. *Rooted out.* This phrase is constantly used in the Talmud with reference to the future fate of Rome. The word is עקר.

11. *In anguish,* etc. See xxx. 5, where as here the intermediate state is one involving certain degrees of happiness or pain.

XXXVII. *Unfading flowers.* Cf. Apoc. Pet. τὴν γῆν αὐτὴν ἀνθοῦσαν ἀμαράντοις ἄνθεσι.

XXXVIII. 1. *O LORD, my Lord.* See note on iii. 1. It is God Himself who interprets this vision for

Baruch, but Ramiel who does so in A³ (see lv. 3).

2. *Thy law is life.* Cf. xlv. 2 ; Ecclus. xlv. 5 νόμον ζωῆς καὶ ἐπιστήμης (also xvii. 11).   With this sentiment cf. Hillel's words (*Aboth.* ii. 7): "The more law the more life . . . he who gains a knowledge of the law gains life in the world to come."   As correlative expressions might be cited (John vii. 49), "This people, which knoweth not the law, is accursed," and Hillel's saying: "An unlearned man cannot be

wisdom is right guidance.   3. Make known to me
therefore the interpretation of this vision.   4. For
Thou knowest that my soul hath always walked in
Thy law, and from my (earliest) days I departed not
from Thy wisdom."

XXXIX. And He answered and said unto me:
" This is the interpretation of the vision which thou
hast seen.   2. As thou hast seen a great forest which
lofty and precipitous mountains surrounded, this is the
word.   3. Behold! the days come, and this kingdom
will be destroyed which once destroyed Zion, and it
will be subjected to that which comes after it.   4.
Moreover, that also again after a time will be destroyed,
and another, a third, will arise, and that also will have
dominion for its time, and will be destroyed.   5. And
after these things a fourth kingdom will arise, whose
power will be harsh and evil far beyond those which
were before it, and it will rule many times as the forests
on the plain, and it will hold fast the times, and will

pious" (לא עם הארץ חסיר). He was
even excluded from the resurrection
(see Weber, 42-44). The words in
the text, however, are far from
being as strong as these statements.
So we infer from the parallel, "Thy
wisdom, etc."

Thy wisdom is right guidance.
This is based upon the Massoretic
text of Ecclesiastes x. 10, where the
Versions take directions of their
own.   Thus the Heb. is יתרון הכשיר
הכמה.   The LXX. καὶ περισσεία τοῦ
ἀνδρείου σοφία, and the Syr. = "et
sapientia sollertibus emolumentum."

4. *From my (earliest) days.*
This is the Hebrew idiom מִימַי.

Cf. 1 Kings i. 6 ; 1 Sam. xxv.
28.

XXXIX. 3-5. Of the four world
empires here mentioned there can
be no doubt as to the first and
fourth. The first is of course the
Babylonian, for it is that which
effected the first destruction of
Jerusalem in 588 (see ver. 3). The
fourth (in verses 5-7 ; cf. xxxvi.
5-10) is just as clearly Rome. The
second and third empires are probably the Persian and the Græco-
Egyptian and Syrian. The fourfold
division of world empires in the
text is due no doubt to Dan. vii.
On these four empires, see *Tanchuma, Terumah,* 7.

exalt itself more than the cedars of Lebanon.   6. And by it the truth will be hidden, and all those who are polluted with iniquity will flee to it, as evil beasts flee and creep into the forest.   7. And it will come to pass when the time of his consummation that he should fall has approached, then the principate of My Messiah will be revealed, which is like the fountain and the vine, and when it is revealed it will root out the multitude of his host.   8. And that which thou hast seen, the lofty cedar, which was left of that forest, and with regard to this fact, that the vine spoke those words with it which thou didst hear, this is the word.

XL. " The last leader of that time will be left alive, when the multitude of his hosts will be put to the sword and be bound, and they will take him up to Mount Zion, and My Messiah will convict him of all his impieties, and will gather and set before him all the works of his hosts.   2. And afterwards he will put

---

6. *The truth will be hidden.* Cf. 4 Ezra v. 1, where, in connection with Rome, the same statement is made: "abscondetur veritatis via."

7. *The principate of My Messiah,* etc. See xxix. 3, note.

XL. 1. Who this last leader is we cannot determine ; it may be any emperor or general from 70 A.D. back till Pompey's time. Since the personal wrong-doings of this leader are dwelt upon, it is possible that it is actually Pompey that is here referred to. The words "his impieties" = ܠܘܣܝܳܥܘܳܝ, might favour this view (cf. Pss. Sol. ii. 24-35).

According to the Talmud, a single leader was to "unite in himself all hatred and hostility against God's people. He was to be called Armilus, and to be the אושר שרי κατ' ἐξοχήν." See Weber, 348, 349.

My Messiah. As we have already remarked (pp. 52, 61), the Messiah here plays an active part as compared to the Messiah in A¹, *i.e.* xxvii.-xxx. 1. The protection of the remnant of Israel and the destruction of their enemies, which are here the work of the Messiah, are there assigned to God Himself, and the Messiah does not appear till these tasks are completed (see xxix. 3).

Will convict . . . of . . . impieties. So 4 Ezra xii. 32 ; xiii. 37.

him to death, and protect the rest of My people which shall be found in the place which I have chosen. 3. And his principate will stand for ever, until the world of corruption is at an end, and until the times aforesaid are fulfilled.   4. This is thy vision, and this is its interpretation."

XLI.-XLII.= B².

XLI. And I answered and said: "To whom will these things be, and how many (will they be)? or who will be worthy to live at that time?   2. For I will speak before Thee everything that I think, and I will ask of Thee regarding those things which I meditate.   3. For lo! I see many of Thy people who have withdrawn from Thy covenant, and cast from them the yoke of Thy law.   4. But others again I

2. *Protect the rest*, etc. See xxix. 2, note.

3. *Until the world of corruption is at an end.* The Messianic king-dom is only of temporary duration ; it belongs to the *olam hazzeh* (see xxi. 19, note).

XLI., XLII. These two chapters appear to belong to B², and to have followed originally after xxx. The same world-view is presented as in B². Thus the times (xlii. 6) are hastened, as in xx., in order to usher in the end, when corruption will disappear and the life of incorrup-tion set in through the resurrection (xlii. 7, 8).

The chief topics discussed in these chapters are two: First, the ultimate destiny of the apostates ; and secondly, that of the proselytes.

Thus hitherto the portions of this book derived from B², and their original order, appear to have been ix. 2-xii. (?) ; xiii. 1-3*a* ; xx. ; xxiv. 2-4 ; xiii. 3*b*-12 ; xxv. ; xiv.-xix. ; xxi.-xxiv. 1 ; xxx. 2-5 ; xli.-xlii.

XLI. 1. Baruch's question goes back to xxx. 2-5, with which they originally stood in connection in B². For a similar question, cf. lxxv. 5.

To live. The life referred to here is the spiritual life subsequent to the resurrection (cf. xlix. 2 ; lxxvi. 5 ; 4 Ezra xiv. 22).

3. The apostates here dealt with may be Christians.

Yoke of Thy law. On the "law" see xv. 5, note. The term "yoke" as expressing "obligation" is common in Jewish writings (cf. Ecclus. li. 26), τὸν τράχηλον ὑμῶν ὑπόθετε ὑπὸ ξυγόν (Pss. Sol. vii. 8 ; xvii. 32 ; Acts xv. 10 ; Gal. v. 1). In later Judaism such expressions as "yoke of the law," "yoke of the precept," "yoke of the kingdom of heaven," are frequent. See Schöttgen, *Hor. Hebr.* i. 115-120. Contrast Matt. xi. 29, 30.

4. The proselytes, *i.e.* the נרים. Cf. 4 Ezra vii. 133 : "Et miserator

have seen who have forsaken their vanity, and fled for refuge beneath Thy wings. 5. What therefore will be to them ? or how will the last time receive them ? 6. Or perhaps the time of these will assuredly be weighed, and as the beam inclines will they be judged accordingly ? "

XLII. And He answered and said unto me : " These things also I will show unto thee. 2. As for what thou didst say—'To whom will these things be, and how many (will they be) ?'—to those who have believed there will be the good which was spoken of aforetime, and to those who despise there will be the contrary of these things. 3. And as for what thou didst say regarding those who have drawn near and those who have withdrawn, this is the word. 4. As for those who were before subject, and afterwards withdrew and mingled themselves with the seed of mingled peoples,

in eo quod miseretur illis qui conversionem faciunt in lege ejus."

Their vanity. *I.e.* their idols (cf. Deut. xxxii. 21).

Fled for refuge beneath Thy wings. Exactly the sense of Ps. xxxvi. 8, בצל כנפיך יחסיון ; and of lvii. 1, where in both cases the LXX. renders חסה by ἐλπίζειν and the Syr. by two different words meaning " to hide." This tends to show that the writer used the Hebrew text independently. For other instances of the same metaphor, cf. Ps. xvii. 8 ; lxiii. 8 ; Deut. xxxii. 11.

But in our text the above phrase is technically used of proselytes נרים. This technical sense is derived from Ruth ii. 12, where, in reference to Ruth, it is said · "The God of

Israel under whose wings thou art come to take refuge "(לחסות תחת-כנפיו). In the *Aboda Sara*, 13b, *Shabbat*, 31a, the proselyte is said to have come under the wings of the Shekinah ; and in the *Jer. Sanh.* ii. 20c, it is stated that "Solomon loved many strange women in order to bring them under the wings of the Shekinah."

5. *The last time.* *I.e.* that described in xxx. 2-5.

XLII. 2. *Those who believed.* See liv. 5, note, also xxi. 9, on the doctrine of justification in Baruch.

4. The sense seems to be that the apostates have only this world.

Mingled peoples. This is a rendering of ערֶב (cf. Jer. xxv. 20, 24). The Greek translation of it is found in Pss. Sol. xvii. 17 ἐθνῶν συμμίκτων.

the time of these is the former, and I am meditating deep things. 5. And as for those who before knew not but afterwards knew life, and mingled (only) with the seed of the people which had separated itself, the time of these (is) the former, I am meditating deep things. 6. And time will succeed to time and season to season, and one will receive from another, and then with a view to the consummation will everything be compared according to the measure of the times and the hours of the seasons. 7. For corruption will take those that belong to it, and life those that belong to it. 8. And the dust will be called, and there will be said to it: ' Give back that which is not thine, and raise up all that thou hast kept until its time.'

XLIII.-XLIV.   XLIII. " Moreover, do thou, Baruch, strengthen thy
7=B.¹

5. *Of the people.* The text ܟ݂ܣ݂ܟ݂ܣ݂ **ܕ** = " of the peoples " I have emended into **ܕ** ܟ݂ܣ݂, for it would be strange to speak of Israel as " the peoples " or " the nations."

Which had separated itself. I.e. the legalistic Israel by means of the " fence "of the law (cf. xlviii. 23). The " separatists " are the Pharisees, the פרושׁין.

The former. This seems corrupt, and probably, as Kabisch proposes, we should have " the latter." This would admit the proselytes to all the blessings of the world to come. On the treatment of "proselytes " in the Talmud, see Weber, 55, 73 f., 98,107, 183,254, 257 f.,282 f.,368 f.

6. This verse is obscure. Cf. 4 Ezra iv. 37.

7. Cf. xxxi. 5. See note on xxi. 19.

8. *Give back,* etc. Cf. l. 2. The

earth gives back the body; Sheol gives back the soul.

XLIII.-XLVI. Of these chapters *xliii.-xliv. 7 ; xlv.-xlvi. 6 belong to B¹.* Not to B², for (1) in xliii. 2 ; xliv. 2, as in lxxviii. 5 ; lxxiv. 1, Baruch is to die an ordinary death and go the way of all the earth and forget all the concerns of mortals, whereas in B² he is not to die an ordinary death, but to be taken up and preserved till the last day ; he is not to forget human affairs, for he is in the last days to testify against the Gentile oppressors of Israel (xiii. 3, note ; xxv. 1 ; xlviii. 30). (2) The people are assured of good tidings in store for them (xlvi. 6) just as in lxxvii. 12 ; they are bidden to look for the consolation of Zion (*i.e.* its restoration), as we infer from lxxxi. 1, 4, taken together with i. 4 ; vi. 9, whereas in B² there is no consolation of any kind to be looked for *in this world.* (3) In

heart for that which has been said to thee, and understand those things which have been shown to thee;
for there are many eternal consolations for thee.
2. For thou wilt depart from this place, and thou wilt
pass from the regions which are now seen by thee, and
thou wilt forget whatever is corruptible, and wilt not
again recall those things which happen among mortals.
3. Go therefore and command thy people, and come to
this place, and afterwards fast seven days, and then
I will come to thee and speak with thee."

XLIV. And I, Baruch, went from thence, and

xliv. 7 and xlviii. 38 the same
phrase, *i.e.* as to a "change of the
times," is found ; in the former
with an optimistic, in the latter
with a pessimistic reference. (4)
xliv. 5 vividly recalls the scene depicted in vi.-viii. As all the intervening chapters deal with questions
of the school, xliii.-xlvi. probably
stood originally in close juxtaposi-
tion with vi.-viii.

*The fragment xliv. 8-15 belongs
to B²,* for just as in B² expectation is
fixed not on an earthly felicity but
only on the world to come (xliv. 15),
the inheritance of the promised
time (xliv. 13), the time that passeth
not away (xliv. 11), the new world
which turneth not to corruption
those who enter it (xliv. 12), (2)
the whole present world, the entire
olam hazzeh is hopeless ; it is defiled with evil (xliv. 9), and with
its corruption it will pass away
(xliv. 8). (3) In xliv. 9 the present
world is to be committed to oblivion.
This is in flat contradiction to iv. 1.

The original position of xliv. 8-15.
This seems easy to determine. The
main statements in this address of
Baruch to the people really presup-
pose xlviii.-lii. as their background.

They express shortly some of the
main conclusions of these chapters.
It is not reasonable to suppose that
Baruch makes known to the people
the very truths which, according to
the present order of the book, are
revealed to him later by God. We
have already seen that xxxi.-xxxv.
were originally subsequent to xlviii.-
lii. (see p. 57). Since therefore both
these passages form the address or
part of the address of Baruch that was
based upon previous disclosures of
God, it is obvious that xliv. 8-15
followed originally on xxxii. 6 and
formed the natural sequel to the
closing words of that verse.

XLIII. 1. These words have no
reference to the preceding chapters.
They refer probably to some lost
passage of B¹.

2. *Thou wilt depart.* Both the
context and the word "depart"
point to an ordinary death here.
See xiii. 3, note. The word rendered
"depart" is ✎וֹ|. It is found also
in xiv. 19 ; xv. 1 ; xliv. 2.

Whatever is corruptible. Cf. **xxi.**
19, note.

3. Parts of this verse relating to
the fast, etc., are probably due to
the final editor. See xlvii. 1, note.

came to my people, and I called my first-born son and
the Gedaliahs my friends, and seven of the elders of
the people, and I said unto them : 2. " Behold, I go
unto my fathers according to the way of all the earth.
3. But withdraw ye not from the way of the law, but
guard and admonish the people which remain, lest they
withdraw from the commandments of the Mighty One.
4. For ye see that he whom we serve is just, and our
Creator is no respecter of persons.   5. And see ye
what hath befallen Zion, and what hath happened to
Jerusalem.   6. For the judgment of the Mighty One
will (thereby) be made known, and His ways, which,
though past finding out, are right.   7. For if ye endure
and persevere in His fear, and do not forget His law, the
times will change over you for good, and ye will see
the consolation of Zion.   8. Because whatever is now

XLIV. 8-15 =
B².

XLIV. 1. *My first - born son.*
Elsewhere mentioned only in xlvi. 1.

The Gedaliahs—possibly a corruption for Gedaliah.   Cf. v. 1.   Gedaliah is mentioned only in B¹.

Seven of the elders of the people.
In v. 5 Baruch assembled all the
elders or honourable amongst the
people. This is natural, as it is prior
to the destruction of the city.
That seven should be summoned
now that the bulk of the population
is carried into exile is equally fitting. We must bear in mind that
in xxxii. 1 we have the work of
a different author, else the writer
might seem to have been guilty of
an inconsistency.

2. Cf. iii. 2. See xiii. 3, note.
The text is drawn from Gen. xv. 15
and Joshua xxiii. 14 ; 1 Kings ii. 2.

3. *Way of the law.* See xv. 5,
note.

*Commandments of the Mighty
One.*   Cf. xlviii. 38 ; lxxxiv. 7.

4. *No respecter of persons.* Cf.
xiii. 8.

5. These words as we have observed above (p. 69) vividly recall
vi.-viii., and seem to show that
these chapters followed much more
closely on vi. - viii. than they do
now.

6. *Which, though . . . right.* The
text = *which are past finding out
and right.*

7. *The times will change over you
for good.* Contrast the use of this
phrase in xlviii. 38.

The consolation of Zion. *I.e.* its
restoration ; cf. lxxxi. 1, 4 ; for the
temple was to be rebuilt (i. 4 ; vi.
9) according to B¹. The announcement of this future in store for
Zion is called good tidings in xlvi.
6 ; lxxvii. 12 ; lxxxi. 1.

is nothing, but that which will be is very great. 9. For everything that is corruptible will pass away, and everything that dies will depart, and all the present time will be forgotten, nor will there be any remembrance of the present time, which is defiled with evils. 10. For that which runs now runs unto vanity, and that which prospers will quickly fall and be humiliated. 11. For that which is to be will be the object of desire, and on that which will come afterwards do we place our hope ; for it is a time that will not pass away. 12. And the hour comes which will abide for ever, and the new world which does not turn to corruption those who depart to its blessedness, and has no mercy on those who depart to torment, and will not

8-15. These verses should be read after xxxii. 6 (see p. 69).

8. In xxxii. 6 God has declared His purpose to renew creation ; the reason is given here ; for all things that now are are nothing.

9. *Corruptible.* Cf. xxi. 19, note ; xxxi. 5.

All the present time will be forgotten. In iv. 1 this is denied, but iv. 1 is from B¹ (cf. Isa. lxv. 17).

11. *A time that will not pass away.* This is set over against xlviii. 50 : "this world which passeth away."

12. *The new world,* etc., implied in the new creation (xxxii. 6). In li. 3 it is the world which dies not, nor ages those who come to it (lii. 9, 16).

Who depart to its blessedness. The text here ܪܟܼܡܗ ܐ|ܟܡ܊ = "who depart on its beginning " is corrupt. This clause should describe

the destination of the righteous, as the antithetical clause in the next line, "those who depart to torment," describes that of the wicked. The error thus lies in the words "in its beginning." In the next place, we can reason back to what should stand here instead of these words. For the corresponding phrase in the other clause, *i.e.* "to torment," requires as its antithesis, not the meaningless "on its beginning," but "to blessedness." That is, over against "those who depart to torment," the sense needs "those who depart to blessedness." This conclusion as to the original text is confirmed by the fact that the erroneous text can be explained by the transposition of a single letter in the Hebrew original. Thus "in its beginning" = בראשו, but this arose from a false transcription of באשרו, *i.e.* by wrongly transposing the ר. Now באשרו = "to its blessedness," I have emended accordingly.

lead to perdition those who live in it.   13. For these are
they who shall inherit that time which has been spoken
of, and theirs is the inheritance of the promised time.
14. These are they who have acquired for themselves
treasures of wisdom, and with them are found stores of
understanding, and from mercy have they not withdrawn, and the truth of the law have they preserved.
15. For to them will be given the world to come, but
the dwelling of the rest who are many will be in the fire.

XLV.-XLVI.   XLV. "Do ye therefore so far as ye are able in-
6 = B¹.   struct the people, for that labour is ours.   2. For if
ye teach them, ye will quicken them."

XLVI. And my son and the elders of the people
answered and said unto me : "Has the Mighty One
humiliated us to such a degree as to take thee from us
quickly ?   2. And truly we shall be in darkness, and
there will be no light to the people who are left.   3. For
where again shall we seek the law, or who will dis-
tinguish for us between death and life ? "   4. And I said
unto them : "The throne of the Mighty One I cannot
resist : nevertheless, there shall not be wanting to Israel

13. *The inheritance . . . time*=
"the world to come" in verse
15.
14. This verse presupposes li.
3, 7.   The "treasures" here mentioned differ from those in xxiv. 1.
15. Those described in the preceding verse are to receive the world
to come, just as those who are
similarly described in li. 3 are to
receive the world that dies not.   On
the contrast of this world and the
world to come, see xv. 8, note.
   In the fire. Cf. xlviii. 39, 43 ;
lix. 2 ; lxiv. 7 ; lxxxv. 13.

XLV. B¹ reappears here. The connection with xliv. 7 is all that could
be desired.   There it is said, "If ye
keep faithful to the law ye will see
the consolation of Zion" ; "do ye
therefore . . . instruct the people . . .
for if ye teach them ye will quicken
them."
   2. *If ye teach*, etc. Cf. xxxviii. 2 ;
Ps. cxix. 50, 93.   This is the
work of the true scribe.   Pharisaism
teaches obedience to the law, God
will do the rest (cf. xliv. 7).
   XLVI. 2. For similar diction, cf.
lxxvii. 14 ; 4 Ezra xiv. 20.

a wise man nor a son of the law to the race of Jacob.   5. But only prepare ye your hearts, that ye may hear the law, and be subject to those who in fear are wise and understanding; and prepare your soul that ye may not depart from them.   6. For if ye do these things, good tidings will come unto you, which I before told you of; nor will ye fall into the torment, of which I testified to you before."

[7. But with regard to the word that I was to be taken, XLVI. 7=E. I did not make (it) known to them or to my son.]

XLVII. And when I had gone forth and dismissed XLVII.-LII.= them, I went thence and said unto them : " Behold ! I go B². to Hebron : for thither the Mighty One hath sent me."

4. *There shall not be wanting ... a son of the law.* This is really an answer to the question put in iii. 6. The expression "son of the law" seems to occur here first in existing literature. Its earliest occurrence elsewhere in the Talmud appears to be in *Baba Mezia*, 96a. See Levy, *Neuhebräisches Wörterbuch*, i. 258. The term בר מצוה was used in the Middle Ages as a designation of a full-grown Israelite. See Schürer, Div. II., vol. ii. 51 (note). For the parallelism *Israel ... Jacob*, cf. xvii. 4; xxxi. 3.

5. *Prepare ye your hearts.* See xxxii. 1, note.

Obedience to the law and the Rabbis is here enforced.

6. Here the promise in xliv. 7 is enforced anew.

Good tidings. Cf. lxxvii. 12.

7. This verse is an addition of the final editor in order the better to adapt the fragment of B¹ just given to its new context. It belongs in spirit to B².

I was to be taken. Cf. xiii. 3, note ; xlviii. 30. In lxxxv. 9 the phrase

has a different meaning. ܠܡܣܒ is a rendering of ἀναλαμβάνειν (also of μετατιθέναι in Gen. v. 24). The former is the usual word in the sense of the text. The idea of the ascension into heaven of great heroes in Jewish history was a familiar one. Thus it is told of Elijah in the LXX. of 2 Kings ii. 11, καὶ ἀνελήμφθη ... εἰς τὸν οὐρανόν: Ecclus. xlviii. 9, ὁ ἀναλημφθεὶς ἐν λαίλαπι πυρός: also in Eth. En. lxxxix. 52 ; xciii. 8 ; 1 Macc. ii. 58 ; of Enoch in Ecclus. xliv. 16 ; Eth. En. lxx. 1 ; lxxxvii. 3, 4 ; Slav. En. lxvii. 2 ; Jubilees, iv. 24 ; of Moses, Assumpt. Mos. x. 12 ; of Baruch, Apoc. Bar. xiii. 3 ; xxv. 1; xlvi. 7 ; xlviii. 30 ; lxxvi. 2 ; of Ezra, 4 Ezra viii. 20 ; xiv. 49 ; of many unnamed heroes, 4 Ezra vi. 26. ἀναλαμβάνειν is well-known in the N.T. in this sense (cf. Mark xvi. 19 ; Acts i. 2, 11, 22 ; 1 Tim. iii. 16). The substantive ἀνάλημψις is rare. Ryle and James (Pss. Sol.) take iv. 20 of those Pss. to be the first known instance of its use ; see also Luke ix. 51, and Test. Levi xviii. In the last passage it is a late Christian interpolation.

2. And I came to that place where the word had been spoken to me, and I sat there, and fasted seven days.

PRAYER OF BARUCH

XLVIII. And it came to pass after the seventh day, that I prayed before the Mighty One and said: 2. "O my Lord, Thou summonest the advent of the times, and they stand before Thee; Thou causest the power of the ages to pass away, and they do not resist Thee; Thou arrangest the method of the seasons, and they obey Thee. 3. Thou alone knowest the goal of the generations, and Thou revealest not Thy mysteries to many. 4. Thou makest known the multitude of the fire, and Thou weighest the lightness of the wind.

THE SEVENTH SECTION

XLVII.-LXXVII. First we have Baruch's fast of seven days (xlvii. 2), followed by his prayer (xlviii. 2-24). Then in the dialogue that ensues various revelations are made to Baruch touching the coming woes and the judgment (xlviii. 26-41), and the resurrection (l.-lii.) On these revelations follows a Messiah Apocalypse (liii.-lxxiv. = A³). In lxxvi. Baruch is told of his approaching translation, and in lxxvii. he calls the people together and addresses them.

This section is composite : xlviii.-lii. being derived from B²; liii.-lxxiv. from A³; lxxv., lxxvi. from B² ; and lxxvii. from B¹.

XLVII. 1. The purposeless journey to Hebron spoken of here must be derived from an original source. According to the scheme of the final editor it has no business here. Further, no such command has been given to Baruch in the existing text.

Hence this entire verse must be regarded as drawn from B¹ or B², and the next verse, which conflicts with it, as due to the final editor, as also xliii. 3. It is noteworthy, too, that the words "and dismissed them" must be corrupt ; for "and when I had gone forth and dismissed them, I went thence and said unto them " is absurd. Baruch goes forth from some place (here undefined) and dismisses the people ; then he departs thence and speaks to them. It is possible then that "when I had gone forth" refers to "the cavern in the earth" in xxi. 1. It will be remembered that of chapters xxi.-xlvi., xxi.-xxiv. 1, xxx. 2-5, xli., xlii. belong to B². These form in some sense a whole, and the scene with which they are connected may be the "cavern" in xxi. 1. If this is so, xlvii. 1 belongs to B².

2. Cf. xliii. 3 ; v. 7, note ; ix., note ; xxi. 2, note.

XLVIII. 2. *Method of the seasons.* Cf. xiv. 1, note ; xx. 6.

5. Thou explorest the limit of the heights, and Thou scrutinisest the depths of the darkness. 6. Thou carest for the number which pass away that they may be preserved, and Thou preparest an abode for those that are to be. 7. Thou rememberest the beginning which Thou hast made, and the destruction that is to be Thou forgettest not. 8. With nods of fear and indignation Thou givest commandment to the flames, and they change into spirits, and with a word Thou quickenest that which was not, and with mighty power Thou holdest that which has not yet come. 9. Thou instructest created things in the understanding of Thee, and Thou makest wise the spheres so as to minister in their orders. 10. Armies innumerable stand before Thee and minister in their orders quietly at Thy nod. 11. Hear Thy servant and give ear to my petition. 12. For in a little time are we born, and in a little time do we return. 13. But with Thee hours are as a time, and days as generations. 14. Be not therefore wroth with man; for he is nothing, and take not account of our works. 15. For what are we? for lo! by Thy gift do we come

6. See xxiii. 4, note.

Thou carest . . . preserved. The text which here = "Thou commandest the number which passes away and it is preserved" is nonsense as it stands, but, if retranslated into Hebrew, it supplies us at once with the true text. Retranslated it = אתה פקר את־המספר העובר וישמר. Here clearly the Greek translator followed the wrong meaning of פקר, and mistranslated the weak vav with the voluntative imperfect. The translation required by the context is given above.

8. *With a word . . . which was not.* Cf. xxi. 4, note ; 4 Ezra iv. 37. *Flames . . . spirits.* Cf. Ps. civ. 4 ; Heb. i. 7.

9. *The spheres . . . in their orders.* Cf. Eth. En. ii. 1 ; Slav. En. xxx. 2, 3 ; Pss. Sol. xix. 2, 3.

10. Cf. Slav. En. xvii. ; Test. Levi iii. *In their orders.* There were ten orders of angels according to the Jews ; nine according to the Christians (see Slav. En. xx. 1, 3, note).

13. We should expect rather : "time is as a (few) hours, and generations as days."

into the world, and we depart not of our own will. 16. For we said not to our parents, 'Beget us,' nor did we send to Sheol and say, 'Receive us.' 17. What therefore is our strength that we should bear Thy wrath, or what are we that we should endure Thy judgment? 18. Protect us in Thy compassions, and in Thy mercy help us. 19. Behold the little ones that are subject unto Thee, and save all that draw nigh unto Thee, and destroy not the hope of our people, and cut not short the times of our aid. 20. For this is the nation which Thou hast chosen, and these are the people, to whom Thou findest no equal. 21. But I will speak now before Thee, and I will say as my heart thinketh. 22. In Thee do we trust, for lo! Thy law is with us, and we know that we shall not fall so far as we keep Thy statutes. 23. In this at least we are always blest that we have not mingled with the Gentiles. 24. For we are all named one people, who have received one law from One, and the law which is amongst us will aid us, and the surpassing wisdom which is in us will help us." 25.

15. *Depart not*, etc. In xiv. 11 men are said to "come not of their own will"; in 4 Ezra viii. 5 the two statements are combined.

16. *Sheol.* See xi. 6, note.

18. See lxxv. 6.

19. *That are subject to Thee.* Cf. xlii. 4.

All that draw nigh. Are these proselytes? (see xli. 4; xlii. 3).

20. Cf. xxi. 21; 4 Ezra v. 27. *The nation.* So I have emended by reading ⟩ܠܥܡܐ⟨ for the unmeaning ܚܒܪܟ. This gives a good parallel

to "people" (ܚܒܪ). Ceriani proposes ⟩ܥܒܕ⟨ = "servant."

21. *Say as my heart thinketh.* Cf. xli. 2.

22. See xv. 5, note.

23. Cf. xlii. 5.

24. *One law from One.* lxxxv. 14. This is directed polemically against the Christians.

The law . . . will aid us. Cf. xxix. 2, note; xxxii. 1; xv. 5, note; cf. *De singularitate cler.* 15 (Cyprian, Ed. Hartel. ii. 190), "sicut Esaias ait, legem inquit in adjutorium dedit."

And when I had prayed and said these things, I was greatly weakened.   26. And He answered and said unto me : "Thou hast prayed simply, O Baruch, and all thy words have been heard.   27. But My judgment exacts its own and My law exacts its rights.   28. For from thy words I will answer thee, and from thy prayer I will speak to thee.   29. For this is as follows : he that is corrupted is not at all ; he has both wrought iniquity so far as he could do anything, and has not remembered My goodness, nor been grateful for My long-suffering.   30. Therefore thou shalt surely be taken up, as I before told thee : and the time is coming of which I told thee.   31. For that time will arise which brings affliction ; for it will come and pass by with quick vehemence, and it will be turbulent coming in the heat of indignation.   32. And it will come to pass in those days that all the inhabitants of the earth will be moved one against another, because they know not that My judgment has drawn nigh.   33. For there will not be found many wise at that time, and the intelligent will be but a few : moreover,

25. *I was greatly weakened.* Cf. xxi. 26. The same phenomenon accompanies the visions in Dan. vii. 28 ; viii. 27 ; x. 8, 16.

27. Cf. v. 2 ; lxxxv. 9.

29. *For this ... is not at all.* The text which is unintelligible runs :

ܐܚܕ ܐܚܕ ܡܝ ܕܝܢ ܕܗܐ ܠܐ ܗܘܐ
ܥܡܝܟ ܗܘ ܕܐܬܚܒܠ.

30. See xlvi. 7, note.

31-41. The last woes and the final judgment. Cf. xxvii.-xxix. 1 ; lxx. 2-10.

32. *The inhabitants of the earth.* See xxv. 1, note.

Will be moved one against another. The text ܐܬܬܢܝܚ = "will rest" is meaningless. It seems corrupted from ܐܬܬܙܝܥ or ܐܬܬܢܨܝ, either of which can be rendered as above.

33. Cf. lxx. 5. This verse seems to be the source of the following words which Cyprian (*Testim.* iii. 29) quotes as from Baruch : "erit enim sapientia in paucis vigilantibus et taciturnis."

even those who know will most of all be silent.   34.
And there will be many rumours and tidings not a few,
and the works of portents will be shown, and promises
not a few will be recounted, (and) some of them (will
prove) idle, and some of them will be confirmed.   35.
And honour will be turned into shame, and strength
humiliated into contempt, and probity destroyed, and
beauty will become a scorn.   36. And many will
say to many at that time : ' Where hath the multitude
of intelligence hidden itself, and whither hath the
multitude of wisdom removed itself ? '   37. And whilst
they are meditating these things, then zeal will arise
in those of whom they thought not, and passion will
seize him who is peaceful, and many will be roused in
anger to injure many, and they will rouse up armies
in order to shed blood, and in the end they will perish
together with them.   38. And it will come to pass at the
self-same time, that a change of times will manifestly
appear to every man, by reason of which in all those
times they were polluted and practised oppression, and
walked every man in his own works, and remembered

34. Joseph, *Ant.* xx. 5. 1 ; 8. 6,
tells of many impostors who so
deceived the people (cf. Matt.
xxiv. 11, 24). This verse seems to
be the source of Cyprian's (*Testim.*
iii. 29) quotation from Baruch:
"alii autem sapientes ad spiritum
erroris et pronuntiantes sicut Altissimi et Fortis edicta."

35. Cf. lxx. 3. It is remarkable
that if we retranslate this verse into
Hebrew we have a series of paronomasiae. Thus "honour will be
turned into shame" = כבוד יהפך

לקלון, "strength humiliated into
contempt" = עז יורד אל בוז, and
"beauty will become a scorn" =
יופי יהיה לרפי.

36. Cf. 4 Ezra v. 9-11. This
seems the source of Cyprian's quotation from Baruch (*Testim.* iii. 29) :
"Quaeretis me et vos et qui post vos
venerint audire verbum sapientiae
et intellectus et non invenietis."

37. Cf. lxx. 6.

38. *A change of times.* Cf. xliv. 7.
Walked every man, etc. Cf. 4
Ezra iii. 8.

not the law of the Mighty One. 39. Therefore a fire
will consume their thoughts, and in flame will the
meditations of their reins be tried; for the Judge will
come and will not tarry. 40. Because each of the
inhabitants of the earth knew when he was committing
iniquity, and they have not known My law by reason
of their pride. 41. For many will then assuredly
weep, yea, over the living more than over the dead."
42. And I answered and said : " O Adam, what hast
thou done to all those who are born from thee ?

*Remembered not the law of the
Mighty One.* Cf. xliv. 3, 7; lxxxiv.
7.

39. *A fire will consume*, etc. Cf.
verse 43 ; xliv. 15 ; lix. 2, note.

*The Judge will come and will not
tarry.* Cf. xx. 6, note.

40. *Knew when he was committing*, etc. See xv. 6, note ; lv. 2.
Cf. Ep. Barn. v. 4 δικαίως ἀπο-
λεῖται ἄνθρωπος ὃς ἔχων ὁδοῦ δικαιοσύνης γνῶσιν ἑαυτὸν εἰς ὁδὸν σκότους ἀποσυνέχει. In xv. 6 men are
to be tormented because, though
knowing the law, they transgressed
it. In that passage the words,
therefore, may be limited to
Israel, but here they are obviously descriptive of the Gentiles :
"the inhabitants of the earth"
(see xxv. 2, note). The writer thus
holds that all men alike possessed
a conscience or faculty for moral
judgment. We have, therefore, in
this verse a statement in some degree
parallel to Rom. ii. 14, 15 : "For
when Gentiles, which have no law,
do by nature the things of the law,
these, having no law, are a law unto
themselves : in that they shew the
work of the law written in their
hearts, their conscience bearing witness therewith, etc."

Have not known My law by reason

of their pride. These words seem
to point to the rejection of the law
by the Gentiles ; for according to
an oft-repeated statement in the
Talmud (see Weber, 19, 56, 57, 65),
the law was originally designed
for all nations, but the Gentiles
rejected it (see 4 Ezra vii. 72, 73).

41. Since the sin of the world is
intensified towards its close, so
naturally the sinners then surviving
will meet with severer judgment
than the less guilty of earlier times.

42-50. What havoc Adam and
Eve have wrought by the spiritual
death and torments which they have
brought upon their posterity. Yet
God knows all that is in man, for
He created him ; He knows likewise the number of men that are to
be, and their sins (verses 42-46).
But since the law will give all these
their due in the judgment, let inquiry be made rather after the
blessedness of the righteous ; for
though they have endured much
weariness in this passing world, in
the world to come they shall have
abundant light.

42. Spiritual death is here traced
to Adam and Eve, but in xvii. 8 ;
xxiii. 4 ; liv. 15 it is only physical
death. See notes on xxiii. 4 ; liv.
15-19. In 4 Ezra both spiritual

and what will be said to the first Eve who hearkened to the serpent? 43. For all this multitude are going to corruption, nor is there any numbering of those whom the fire devours. 44. But again I will speak in Thy presence. 45. Thou, O LORD, my Lord, knowest what is in Thy creature. 46. For Thou didst of old command the dust to produce Adam, and Thou knowest the number of those who are born from him, and how far they have sinned before Thee, who have existed and not confessed Thee as their Creator. 47. And as regards all these their end will convict them, and Thy law which they have transgressed will requite them on Thy day. [48. But now let us dismiss the wicked and enquire about the righteous. 49. And I will recount their blessedness and not be silent in celebrating their

death and physical are always traced to Adam (iii. 21, 22 ; iv. 30 ; vii. 118-121).

43. *Fire devours.* Cf. verse 39 ; xliv. 15 ; lxiv. 7.

46. *Command the dust to produce Adam.* 4 Ezra iii. 4, 5 ; vii. 116.

The number of those who are born. See xxiii. 5, note.

47. *Thy law . . . will requite.* See v. 2, note.

48-50. These verses were used originally in B² by Baruch in addressing the people, or by God in addressing Baruch, but not by Baruch in addressing God as the present text implies. That they could not have been addressed by Baruch to God is clear ; for Baruch could not say to God, "In this world . . . in which ye live" (ver. 50). Two facts are in favour of their being God's words to Baruch : (1) The very same contrast between the two worlds is found in God's reply to

Baruch in xv. 7 ; and (2) the very same change of subject is enjoined and the same word "inquire" used in reference to the righteous in 4 Ezra ix. 13 : "tu ergo adhuc noli curiosus esse quomodo impii cruciabuntur sed inquire quomodo justi salvabuntur." But the plural in verse 48 is against this view ; and secondly, the words "I will not be silent in celebrating, etc.," while hardly conceivable on the divine lips, are appropriate on Baruch's. Hence we must regard xlviii. 48-50 as a fragment of an address delivered by Baruch to the people. Another fragment of this same address which originally preceded xlviii. 48-50 is to be found in liv. 16-18, and yet another which followed it in liv. 16-18.

49. *Will not be silent in celebrating.* A Hebrew idiom = לא אחדל לשבח.

glory, which is reserved for them. 50. For assuredly as in a little time in this world which passeth away, in which ye live, ye have endured much labour, so in that world to which there is no end, ye shall receive great light."]

XLIX. "Nevertheless, I will again ask from Thee, O Mighty One, yea, I will ask mercy from Him who made all things. 2. 'In what shape will those live who live in Thy day? or how will the splendour of those who (are) after that time continue? 3. Will they then resume this form of the present, and put on these entrammeling members, which are now involved in evils, and in which evils are consummated, or wilt Thou perchance change these things which have been in the world as also the world?'"

L. And He answered and said unto me: "Hear,

---

50. Cf. xv. 8 for the same contrast and largely the same diction.

Light. This does not seem the right word.

XLIX. 2. *In what shape*, etc. Cf. 1 Cor. xv. 35 : "How are the dead raised? and with what manner of body do they come?"

Live. See xli. 1, note.

The splendour of those who (are) after that time. For "splendour" we might perhaps render "appearance." The text is ‏ܐܡܬ ܘܢܗܪ ‏ ܕܐܝܠܝ̈ܢ ܕ ‏.

3. *Entrammeling members*, lit. members of bonds.

L.-LI. *The nature of the resurrection body.* The teaching here as to the nature of the resurrection proceeds on the line suggested in xlix. 3: "Wilt thou perchance change these things (*i.e.* man's material body)

which have been in the world as also the world?" The world was to be renewed (xxxii. 6), and in this renewal from being transitory and verging to its close (xlviii. 50; lxxv. 10), it becomes undying (li. 3) and everlasting (xlviii. 50); from being a world of corruption (xl. 3; lxxiv. 2; xxi. 19; xxxi. 5, etc.) it becomes incorruptible (lxxiv. 2) and invisible (li. 8). As these conceptions are in germ and principle as old as Isa. lxv. 17-lxvi., the same doctrine of renewal and transformation that was taught touching the world was naturally applied in due course to those destined to live in it. This is done partially in Isa. lxv. 17-25, but the developed form appears in Dan. xii. 2, where the risen righteous are to shine as the stars for ever and ever; in Eth. En. they are to joy as the angels (civ. 4)

6

Baruch, this word, and write in the remembrance of thy heart all that thou shalt learn. 2. For the earth will then assuredly restore the dead, which it now receives, in order to preserve them, making no change in their form, but as it has received, so will it restore them, and as I delivered them unto it, so also shall it raise them. 3. For then it will be necessary to show to the living that the dead have come to life again, and that those who had departed have returned (again). 4. And it will come to pass, when they have severally

and to become angels in heaven (li. 4) and companions of the heavenly hosts (civ. 6), and to be clad in garments of life (lxii. 15, 16) and in raiment of light (cviii. 12) ; see also xc. 38. We thus see that long before the time of the writers of Baruch the Pharisees were familiar with the idea of the spiritual transformation of the body after the resurrection ; and that *to some extent* the Pauline teaching on the resurrection in 1 Cor. xv. 35-50 was not an innovation, but an able and developed exposition of ideas that were current in the Judaism of the time. 1 Cor. xv. 35-50 is in one of its aspects the logical sequel of Isa. lxv. 17.

Over against this spiritual view of the future life we must remember that a materialistic one prevailed not only popularly, but also in Rabbinic circles. According to the latter the blessed should beget children and eat the flesh of the Leviathan. See Weber, 383, 384.

L. 2. Cf. xi. 4, note ; xlii. 8, note ; Eth. En. li. 1, note. In the resurrection soul and body were to be united. On the scene of the resurrection see xxix. 2, note. The soul's abode was Sheol (see xxi. 23 note) ; the body rested in the earth

(xlii. 8). According to the text the body was to be restored in exactly the same form in which it had been committed to the earth. The following speculations of later Judaism on this subject are instructive. According to the *Othioth*, 17c, of R. Akiba (Weber, 352, 353), God was to sound a trumpet seven times at the end of the world. At the first blast the whole world was to be moved, at the second the dust was to be separated, at the third the bones of the dead were to be gathered together, at the fourth their limbs were to be warmed, at the fifth they were to be covered with skin, at the sixth the souls and spirits were to enter their bodies, in the seventh they were to become living and stand upon their feet, clad in their clothes. According to another account (*Beresh. rab.* 28) the resurrection body was built up from a small fragment of the backbone which was in all cases indestructible. This was called נ׳. See Levy, *Neuhebräisches Wörterb.* ii. 481 ; see verse 4, note.

L. 3. Those who are to be judged are the living righteous, and sinners, and the risen dead.

4. The object with which the dead are raised is for common recognition.

recognised those whom they now know, then judgment will grow strong, and those things which before were spoken of will come.

LI. "And it will come to pass, when that appointed day has gone by, that then shall the aspect of those who are condemned be afterwards changed, and the glory of those who are justified. 2. For the aspect of those who now act wickedly will become worse than is that of such as suffer torment. 3. Also (as for) the glory of those who have now been justified in My law, who have had understanding in their life, and who have planted in their heart the root of wisdom, then their splendour will be glorified in changes, and the form of their face will be turned into the light of their beauty, that they may be able to acquire and receive the world which does not die, which is then promised to them. 4. For

There is nothing corresponding to this in the N.T. In later Judaism the resemblance of the risen was to be so carefully preserved that they were to be raised in the same clothes in which they were buried. This was proved *Sanhedrin*, 90*b* (Weber, 353) by the analogy of a grain of corn which comes up from the earth, not naked but clothed. The Rabbis, therefore, on the approach of death, gave careful directions as to their grave-clothes. According to the *Beresh. rab.* 95 (Weber, 353), men were to be raised with all their bodily defects, such as blindness, lameness, etc., in order that their identity might be established. Thereupon, in the case of the righteous these infirmities were healed.

LI. 1. This transformation of the living is mentioned in 1 Cor. xv. 51.

Aspect. I have here followed Ceriani's emendation of ⲟⲥⲁⲗⲥ into ⲟⲥⲗⲁⲥ.

Condemned . . . justified. See xxi. 9, note. The word "justify" has here its ordinary meaning of "to declare righteous."

3. *Justified in My law.* See xv. 5, note ; xxi. 9, note.

Root of wisdom. lix. 7 ; Ecclus. i. 6, 20, ῥίζα σοφίας ; Wisdom iii. 15.

Their splendour, etc. The righteous will undergo successive transformations till their bodies are assimilated to their new environment, or to use the words of the text, "that they may be able . . . to receive the world that does not die."

The world that does not die. Cf. xlviii. 50 ; li. 8 ; lxxiv. 2, for various characteristics of the *olam habba* or future world.

Then promised. See xiv. 13, note.

over this above all will those who come then lament, that they rejected My law, and stopped their ears that they might not hear wisdom or receive understanding. 5. When therefore they see those, over whom they are now exalted, (but) who will then be exalted and glorified more than they, they will respectively be transformed, the latter into the splendour of angels, and the former will mainly waste away in wonder at the visions and in the beholding of the forms. 6. For they will first behold and afterwards depart to be tormented. 7. But those who have been saved by their works, and to whom the law has been now a hope, and understanding an expectation, and wisdom a confidence, to them wonders will appear in their time. 8. For they will behold the world which is now invisible to them, and they will behold the time which is now hidden from them. 9. And again time will not age them. 10. For in the heights of that world shall they dwell, and they shall be made like unto the angels, and be made

4. The wicked here include not only the faithless Israelites, but also the Gentiles.

Stopped their ears that they might not hear. Zech. vii. 11. The LXX. renders differently: τὰ ὦτα αὐτῶν ἐβάρυναν κτλ.

5. *The splendour.* This word ‎ここ here, and in xlix. 2; li. 3, might also be rendered by "appearance."

Will waste away, or *will be dissolved.* Cf. xxx. 4; 4 Ezra vii. 87. The latter reference as well as our text show that the writer here was not thinking of annihilation, though this view is found later. Cf. Weber, 374, 375.

7. *Saved by their works.* See xiv. 7, note.

9. Cf. verse 3, note, and the phrase in verse 16: "The world which ages not those." After this verse we should probably read verses 13 and 14. Verse 12 would then form a fitting close and climax to li. 1-9, 13, 14, 10, 11.

10. The condition of the risen righteous is very spiritually conceived. Thus they have passed from a world of tribulation (li. 14) and enter a world that is everlasting (li. 3), invisible (li. 8); they live in the high places thereof (li. 10); they are made equal to the stars (li. 10),

equal to the stars, and they shall be changed into every form they desire, from beauty into loveliness, and from light into the splendour of glory. 11. For there will be spread before them the extents of Paradise, and there will be shown to them the beauty of the majesty of the living creatures which are beneath the throne, and all the armies of the angels, who [are now held fast by My word, lest they should appear, and] are held fast by a command, that they may stand in their places till their advent comes. 12. Moreover, there will then be excellency in the righteous surpassing that in the angels. 13. For the first will receive the last, those whom they were expecting, and the last those of whom they used to hear that they had passed away. 14. For they have been delivered from this world of tribulation, and laid down the burthen of anguish. 15. For what then have men lost their life, and for what have those who were on the earth exchanged their soul? 16. For then they chose (not) for themselves that time, which, beyond the reach of

and their glory is greater than that of the angels (x. 12).

Made equal to the stars. Cf. 4 Ezra vii. 97, 125.

11. *Living creatures which are beneath the throne.* Cf. Rev. iv. 6.

Armies of the angels who . . . are held fast, etc. These angels are probably the armed host mentioned in lxx. 7 ; Slav. En. xvii. ; and in Test. Lev. 3 : ἐν τῷ τρίτῳ εἰσὶν αἱ δυνάμεις τῶν παρεμβολῶν, οἱ ταχθέντες εἰς ἡμέραν κρίσεως, ποιῆσαι ἐκδίκησιν ἐν τοῖς πνεύμασι τῆς πλάνης καὶ τοῦ Βελίαρ. I have bracketed one of the clauses in this verse as a gloss.

13, 14. These two verses seem to be wrongly transposed from their place after verse 9.

13. Cf. 4 Ezra v. 42 : "Coronae adsimilabo judicium meum ; sicut non novissimorum tarditas, sic nec priorum velocitas " ; also Matt. xix. 30.

14. See xv. 8, note.

15. Cf. Matt. xvi. 26.

16. I have added a negative in the first clause as the sense requires it. In lvi. 14 there is a similar loss of the negative, as Ceriani has already observed. *Whish ages not*, etc. (cf. ver. 9).

anguish, could not pass away, and they chose for themselves that time, whose issues are full of lamentations
and evils, and they denied the world which ages not
those who come to it, and they have rejected the time
and the glory, so that they shall not come to the
honour of which I told thee before."

LII. And I answered and said : " How do those
forget for whom woe is then reserved ?   2. And why
therefore again do we mourn for those who die ? or
why do we weep for those who depart to Sheol ?   3.
Let lamentations be reserved for the beginning of that
coming torment, and let tears be laid up for the advent
of the destruction of that time.   4. But even in the
face of these things I will speak.   [5. And as for the
righteous, what will they do now ?   6. Rejoice ye in
the suffering which ye now suffer : for why do ye look
for the decline of your enemies ?   7. Make ready
your soul for that which is reserved for you, and prepare your souls for the reward which is laid up for
you."]

LIII. And when I had said these things I fell
asleep there, and I saw a vision, and lo ! a cloud was

LII. 1, 2. Considering the terrible
destiny in store for the wicked after
the resurrection, our grief should be
reserved for those who shall suffer
its torments, and not for those who
depart to Sheol. And yet there is
a certain degree of pain and torment
in Sheol as we have seen (cf. xxx.
5 ; xxxvi. 10).

5-7. These verses cannot have been
addressed by Baruch to God. Like
xlviii. 48-50, they are part of his
address to the people. They would

form an appropriate sequel to xlviii.
48-50 (see note on liv. 16-18).

6. Cf. lxxviii. 6. These words recall
James i. 2 : "Count it all joy, my
brethren, when ye fall into manifold
temptations." The sentiment looks
Christian.

7. *Make ready . . . prepare your
souls.* See xxxii. 1, note.   One
half of this verse seems to be a
gloss on the other.

8. Cf. xxxvi. 1.

LIII. - LXXIV. This constitutes

ascending from a very great sea, and I kept gazing
upon it, and lo! it was full of waters white and black,
and there were many colours in those self-same waters,
and as it were the likeness of great lightning was
seen at its summit.   2. And I saw that cloud passing swiftly in quick courses, and it covered all the
earth.   3. And it came to pass after these things

the third Messiah Apocalypse = A³
embodied by the final editor in this
book. It will be sufficient here to
indicate (a) its date ; (b) its relation
to the other constituents of the
book ; and to touch on (c) the question of its integrity ; (d) and of its
author.

(a) *Its date.* It was written prior
to 70 A.D. (see lxviii. 5, note), and
subsequent to 50 A.D. (see lix. 5-11,
note).

(b) *Relations of A³ to B¹, B², A¹,
A².* It is distinct from B¹, and B²
in date, as these were composed subsequently to the fall of the temple.
It is distinct in character from B¹
and B² ; for whereas in the latter
there is no expectation of the Messiah,
in A³ the Messiah is the centre of
interest. Other points of difference
will be dealt with in the notes. A³
is distinct from A¹. In the latter
the Messiah does not appear till the
enemies of Israel are destroyed ; in
A³, on the other hand, the Messiah
is the agent of their destruction. A³
may be distinct from A² ; contrast
lxxi. 1 with xl. 2. If xl. 1, 2 refers
to Pompey, it was written prior to
his death, and A² would in that case
be much earlier than A³, which was
composed between 50 and 70 A.D.

(c) *Integrity.* A³ is handed down
in tolerable preservation. liv. 17, 18
is an interpolation, and possibly lxx.
9. The text has been badly tam-
pered with in lxxii. 1 and lxxxiv. 4
by the final editor.

(d) *The author.* A³ is of extreme
interest, as it is the oldest writing
in which full justice is done alike to
the claims of the Messiah and those
of the law in moulding the world's
history. The author belongs to the
Rabbinical school, and assigns to
certain elements of the law and
tradition (cf. lvii., notes) the pre-
Mosaic origin attributed to them in
Jubilees. On the other hand, he recognises the popular aspiration for
God's kingdom on earth as a legitimate outcome of prophecy, and gives
it complete development in his forecast of history. Thus A³ is the
oldest literary evidence of the fusion
of early Rabbinism and popular
Messianic expectation.

LIII. In this vision a cloud is
seen coming up from the sea and
covering the whole earth with its
summit crowned with lightning.
And soon it began to discharge
black waters, and then clear, and
again black waters, and then clear,
and so on till this succession of
black and bright waters had occurred six times. And at the end
of these twelve showers there was
yet another shower of black waters,
blacker than had been all before.
Thereupon the lightning on the
summit of the cloud flashed forth
and healed the earth, and twelve
streams came up from the sea and
were subject to that lightning.

1. *A very great sea.* Cf. Dan.
vii. 2.

that that cloud began to pour upon the earth the
waters that were in it.   4. And I saw that there was
not one and the same likeness in the waters which
descended from it.   5. For in the first beginning they
were black exceedingly for a time, and afterwards
I saw that the waters became bright, but they were
not many, and after these things again I saw black
(waters), and after these things again bright, and again
black and again bright.   6. Now this was done twelve
times, but the black were always more numerous than
the bright.   7. And it came to pass at the end
of the cloud, that lo! it rained black waters, and
they were darker than had been all those waters that
were before, and fire was mingled with them, and
where those waters descended, they wrought devastation and destruction.   8. And I saw after these things
that lightning which I had seen on the summit of the
cloud, that it held it fast and made it descend to the
earth.   9. Now that lightning shone exceedingly, so
as to illuminate the whole earth, and it healed those
regions where the last waters had descended and
wrought devastation.   10. And it took hold of the

6. For the twelvefold division of
history see 4 Ezra xiv. 11, 12 : "XII
enim partibus divisum est saeculum,
et transierunt ejus X jam et dimi-
dium Xmae partis, Superant autem
ejus duae post medium decimae
partis." Cf. Hilgenfeld, *Mess. Jud.*
104.

7. These black waters are interpreted in lxix., lxx. They symbolise
the travail pains of the Messiah.

8. The lightning on the cloud
symbolises the Messiah. The im-

agery is derived from Dan. vii. 13.
It was from the last passage that
the Messiah was named ענני = "the
cloud-man," or בר נפלי = "the son of
the cloud." See Levi, *Neuhebräisch.
Lex.* iii. 271, 422.

9. *Lightning shone . . . so as to
illuminate the whole earth.* Cf. Matt.
xxiv. 27 : "For as the lightning
cometh forth from the east, and is
seen even unto the west, so shall be
the coming of the Son of man."

whole earth and had dominion over it.   11. And I saw after these things, and lo! twelve rivers were ascending from the sea, and they began to surround that lightning and to become subject to it.   12. And by reason of my fear I awoke.

[PRAYER OF BARUCH]

LIV. And I besought the Mighty One, and said : " Thou alone, O Lord, knowest of aforetime the deep things of the world, and the things which befall in their times Thou bringest about by Thy word, and against the works of the inhabitants of the earth Thou dost hasten the beginnings of the times, and the end of the seasons Thou alone knowest.   2. For whom nothing is too hard, but Thou doest everything easily by a nod.   3. To whom the depths as the heights are accessible, and the beginnings of the ages minister to Thy word.   4. Who revealeth to those who fear Him what is prepared for them, that He may thereby console them.   5. Thou showest great acts to those

---

10. We have here symbolised the Messiah's reign.

11. Do these twelve rivers symbolise the Gentile nations submitting themselves to the Messiah, or the twelve tribes of Israel ?

LIV. 1. *Against the works*, etc. . . . *hasten the beginnings of the times.* See xx. 1, note.

The end of the seasons Thou alone knowest.   Cf. xxi. 8.

2. *For whom nothing is too hard.* This is a rendering of the phrase found in Gen. xviii. 14 ; Jer. xxxii. 17, 27.   By comparing the text

with the Peshitto of Luke i. 37, we see that the Greek was here παρ' ᾧ ῥῆμα οὐκ ἀδυνατεῖ. This is the LXX. of Gen. xviii. 14 μὴ ἀδυνατεῖ παρὰ τῷ θεῷ ῥῆμα, but not of Jer. xxxii. 17, 27, where we find (xxxix. 17, 27 in LXX.) οὐ μὴ ἀποκρυβῇ ἀπὸ σοῦ οὐθέν. This is the rendering of the Peshitto also in Gen. xviii. 14 and Jer. xxxii. 17, 27.   From this verse in itself, therefore, we cannot conclude for or against the influence of the LXX. on the writer.

5. *Great acts* or " wonders."

who know not; Thou breakest up the enclosure of those who are ignorant, and lightest up what is dark, and revealest what is hidden to the pure, who in faith have submitted themselves to Thee and Thy law.   6. Thou hast shown to Thy servant this vision; reveal to me also its interpretation.   7. For I know that as regards those things wherein I besought Thee, I have received a response, and as regards what I besought, Thou didst reveal to me, and didst show me with what voice I should praise Thee, or from what members I should cause praises and hallelujahs to ascend to Thee. 8. For if my members were mouths, and the hairs of my head voices, even so I could not give Thee the meed of praise, or laud Thee as is befitting, nor could I recount Thy praise, nor tell the glory of Thy beauty, 9. For what am I amongst men, or why am I reckoned amongst those who are more excellent than I, that I should have heard all those marvellous things from the Most High, and good tidings numberless from Him who created me?   10. Blessed be my mother amongst those that bear, and praised among women be she that bare me.   11. For I will not be silent in praising the Mighty One, and with the voice of praise I will recount His marvellous deeds. 12. For who doeth like unto Thy marvellous deeds, O God, or who comprehendeth Thy deep thought of

In faith. See note on liv. 21.

8. In the *Shir ha-Shirim rabba*, i. 3 we find the hyperbolic statements of this verse far outdone: " R. Eliezer said: 'if all the seas were ink, and all the reeds were pens, and heaven and earth were rolls, and all men were scribes, yet the law could not be written down which I have taught.'"

10. An interpolation? it breaks

life ?   13. For with Thy counsel Thou dost govern all
the creatures which Thy right hand has created, and
Thou hast established every fountain of light beside
Thee, and the treasures of wisdom beneath Thy throne
hast Thou prepared.   14. And justly do they perish
who have not loved Thy law, and the torment of
judgment will await those who have not submitted
themselves to Thy power.   15. For though Adam

the connection.   Cf. Luke i. 42 ;
xi. 27 ; Judges v. 24.
13. *Thou dost govern.*   Cf. verse
22.
14. A deliberate rejection of the
law of God is here implied as in
xlviii. 40, see note.
15, 19. In xxiii. 4 the *physical*
effects of sin are referred to ; in
xlviii. 42 the *spiritual* effects. The
former consisted according to B²
(see xxiii. 4, note) in man's subjection to physical death.   According
to A³ (see liv. 15 ; lvi. 6), however,
man was already subject to physical
death, and the penalty of sin consisted in premature death.
The main question, however,
which concerns us here is that of
predestination and free will.   In
order to understand the position of
the writers of this book, it will be
helpful to draw attention to the chief
statements which appear on these
subjects in Jewish non - canonical
literature. In Ecclesiasticus these
antinomies are stated uncondition-
ally, not indeed in immediate contrast, but in distinct passages. Thus
in xv. 11, 12, 14, 15, 17, 20, we have the
freewill of man strongly affirmed :
μὴ εἴπῃς ὅτι διὰ κύριον ἀπέστην . . .
μὴ εἴπῃς ὅτι αὐτός με ἐπλάνησεν· οὐ
γὰρ χρείαν ἔχει ἀνδρὸς ἁμαρτωλοῦ
. . . αὐτὸς ἐξ ἀρχῆς ἐποίησεν ἄνθρωπον, καὶ ἀφῆκεν αὐτὸν ἐν χειρὶ διαβουλίου αὐτοῦ. ἐὰν θέλῃς, συντηρήσεις ἐντολάς. . . ἔναντι ἀνθρώπων

ἡ ζωὴ καὶ ὁ θάνατος καὶ ὃ ἐὰν εὐδοκήσῃ δοθήσεται αὐτῷ. . . . καὶ οὐκ
ἐνετείλατο οὐδενὶ ἀσεβεῖν.   Cf. also
xvii. 6.   The doctrine of predestination is absolutely maintained in
xxxvi. 10, 12, 13, καὶ ἄνθρωποι πάντες ἀπὸ ἐδάφους καὶ ἐκ γῆς ἐκτίσθη
'Αδάμ· ἐξ αὐτῶν εὐλόγησεν καὶ ἀν-
ύψωσεν . . . ἀπ' αὐτῶν κατηράσατο
καὶ ἐταπείνωσεν καὶ ἀνέστρεψεν
αὐτοὺς ἀπὸ στάσεως αὐτῶν.   ὡς
πηλὸς κεραμέως ἐν χειρὶ αὐτοῦ,
πᾶσαι αἱ ὁδοὶ αὐτοῦ κατὰ τὴν εὐδοκίαν αὐτοῦ· οὕτως ἄνθρωποι ἐν χειρὶ
τοῦ ποιήσαντος αὐτοὺς ἀποδοῦναι αὐτοῖς κατὰ τὴν κρίσιν αὐτοῦ. Cf. also
xxiii. 20 ; xxxix. 20, 21.   These two
doctrines which are thus separately
affirmed in Ecclus., are given by
Josephus as co-ordinate articles of
the Pharisaic creed.   Thus in *Bell.
Jud.* ii. 8, 14, he says : Φαρισαῖοι
. . . εἱμαρμένῃ τε καὶ θεῷ προσ-
άπτουσι πάντα καὶ τὸ μὲν πράττειν
τὰ δίκαια καὶ μὴ κατὰ τὸ πλεῖστον
ἐπὶ τοῖς ἀνθρώποις κεῖσθαι, βοηθεῖν
δὲ εἰς ἕκαστον καὶ τὴν εἱμαρμένην.
Ant. xiii. 5, 9 : οἱ μὲν οὖν Φαρισαῖοι τινὰ καὶ οὐ πάντα τῆς εἱμαρ-
μένης εἶναι λέγουσιν ἔργον, τινὰ δ'
ἐφ' ἑαυτοῖς ὑπάρχειν, συμβαίνειν τε
καὶ μὴ γίνεσθα (*Ant.* xviii. 1. 3)
πράσσεσθαί τε εἱμαρμένῃ τὰ πάντα
ἀξιοῦντες, οὐδὲ τοῦ ἀνθρωπείου τὸ
βουλόμενον τῆς ἐπ' αὐτοῖς ὁρμῆς ἀφαι-
ροῦνται, δοκῆσαν τῷ θεῷ κρᾶσιν γε-
νέσθαι καὶ τῷ ἐκείνης βουλευτηρίῳ καὶ
τῶν ἀνθρώπων τῷ θελήσαντι προσ-

first sinned and brought untimely death upon all, yet
of those who were born from him each one of them has

χωρεῖν μετ' ἀρετῆς ἢ κακίας. The
same paradoxical creed appears in
the *Pirke Aboth.* iii. 24 (ed. Taylor
p. 73): "Everything is foreseen;
and freewill is given. And the
world is judged by grace: and
everything is according to work";
and possibly also in the Pss. Sol.
ix. 7 τὰ ἔργα ἡμῶν ἐν ἐκλογῇ καὶ
ἐξουσίᾳ τῆς ψυχῆς ἡμῶν τοῦ ποιῆσαι
δικαιοσύνην καὶ ἀδικίαν (see Ryle
and James's edition, pp. 95, 96).

This co-ordination of fate and
freewill as articles of faith was
nothing more or less than an
attempt on the part of the Pharisees to embody in their creed the
two O.T. doctrines of God's omni-
potence and man's responsibility.
That theoretically such a creed was
current may reasonably be concluded
from the passages just cited, as well
as from the attestation it receives
in Pauline teaching in Rom. ix.-xi.
(see Sanday and Headlam's *Romans*,
pp. 347-350). Its acceptance, too,
would, no doubt, be furthered by the
pressure of the rival creeds of the
Sadducees and the Essenes, who
were the champions, respectively,
of freewill and of fate (Joseph. *Bell.
Jud.* ii. 8. 14; *Ant.* xiii. 5. 9).
With the disappearance of Saddu-
ceeism, however, the paradoxical
character of Pharisaic belief seems
to have disappeared also. Henceforth the Rabbinic schools teach
mainly man's freedom of the will
and limit God's predestinating
action to his external lot.

The two doctrines of fate and freewill, though seen to be mutually
exclusive, were, as we have already
remarked, accepted *theoretically* as
equally imperative by the Pharisees.
The only instance where these two
doctrines are developed into irre-

concilable fulness and results and
applied to religious questions in the
first century is to be found in St.
Paul's teaching (see above). In
every other attempt to grapple with
these problems a compromise is
effected which results either in a
vigorous or else in a very attenuated
doctrine of freewill. Of this waver-
ing attitude among the Pharisees in
the first century we have sufficient
evidence. Thus man's freewill is
maintained in the Slav. En. xxx. 15:
"And I gave him his will, and I
showed him the two ways, the light
and the darkness . . . that I should
know whether he has love for Me or
hate"; though in the next verse
it is recognised that his freewill is
hampered by his incorporation in
the body, and his ignorance of its
good and evil impulses. But the
best evidence in this direction is
furnished by the Apocalypse of
Baruch and 4 Ezra. From our
comparative study hitherto of these
two works (see notes on xiv. 7;
xxi. 9; xlviii. 42), we should
expect that man's freewill and
capacity for doing God's will, despite Adam's sin, would be emphasised in the former, and that man's
helplessness and practical incapacity
for righteousness in consequence of
his original defects or Adam's sin
would be conspicuous in the latter,
and this we do find as a matter of
fact. First as to 4 Ezra. In 4 Ezra
the bulk of mankind was predestined
to destruction (viii. 1-3); for from
the beginning there was in man a
wicked element (*i.e.* יצר רע) called
here *granum seminis mali* (4
Ezra iv. 30): "Quoniam granum
seminis mali seminatum est in corde
Adam ab initio, et quantum im-
pietatis generavit usque nunc et

prepared for his own soul torment to come, and again
each one of them has chosen for himself glories to come.

generabit usque cum veniat area";
through Adam's yielding to this
evil element a hereditary tendency
to sin was created and the *cor
malignum* developed (iii. 21, 22).
*Cor enim malignum baiolans primus
Adam transgressus et victus est, sed
et omnes qui ex eo nati sunt. Et
facta est permanens infirmitas, et
lex in corde populi cum malignitate
radicis, et discessit quod bonum est,
et mansit malignum.* We should
observe that *baiolans* in iii. 21
just cited represents φορέσας: for
both the Syriac and Ethiopic Versions = *cum vestivit.* Hence Adam
"clothed himself" with a wicked
heart by yielding to the evil impulse which was in him when
created. Adam was created with
two impulses : "the good impulse "
(יצר הטוב) implied in the words
discessit quod bonum est (iii. 22),
and "the evil impulse" already
referred to. This subject is further
pursued in iii. 25, 26 : "Et deligue-
runt qui habitabant civitatem, In
omnibus facientes sicut fecit Adam et
omnes generationes ejus, utebantur
enim et ipsi cor malignum." As a
result of Adam's transgression, the
evil impulse having been developed
into the *cor malignum*, and having
thus obtained the mastery over man,
the writer of vii. 118 naturally
charges Adam with being the cause
of the final perdition of mankind:
" O tu quid fecisti Adam ? si enim
tu peccasti, non est factum solius
tuus casus sed et nostrum qui ex te
advenimus." Naturally in the face
of such a hopeless view of man's
condition no real doctrine of freewill
could be maintained. In fact, in
4 Ezra only sufficient freewill is
accorded to man to justify his final
condemnation. Cf. 4 Ezra viii. 56,

58-60, "Nam et ipsi accipientes
libertatem spreverunt Altissimum et
legem ejus contempserunt. . . . Et
dixerunt in corde suo non esse
deum, et quidem scientes sciunt
quoniam moriuntur. . . . Non enim
Altissimus voluit hominem disperdi ;
Sed ipsi qui creati sunt coinquina-
verunt nomen ejus qui fecit eos."
vii. 72, "Qui ergo commorantes sunt
in terra hinc cruciabuntur, quoniam
sensum habentes iniquitatem fecerunt et mandata accipientes non ser-
vaverunt ea et legem consecuti frau-
daverunt eam quam acceperunt." ix.
11, Fastidierunt legem meam cum
adhuc erant habentes libertatem.

Turning now to the present
Apocalypse, we find in all its
sections, even in the gloomiest, B²,
a view of man's present capacities
and future destiny that is optimistic when set side by side with 4
Ezra. Whereas in A³, according to liv. 15, 19, the effects of
Adam's sin are limited to physical
results ; his descendants must die
prematurely. On the nature of
these physical results in other
sections see xxiii. 4, note. As to
spiritual results, each man is the
Adam of his own soul, and can
choose for himself either bliss or
torment ; he can work out his own
salvation and even make God his
debtor (see xiv. 7, note). Only in
xlviii. 42 is spiritual death traced
to Adam.

The view set forth in the text as
to man's condition is exactly that
which prevails in the Talmud. In
fact, Weber's summing up on this
question would serve admirably for
an exposition of the text : " Der freie
Wille auch in Bezug auf das Ver-
halten gegen Gott ist dem Menschen
auch nach dem Fall geblieben. Es

LIV. 16-
18 = B².

[16. For assuredly he who believeth will receive reward.   17. But now, as for you, ye wicked that now
are, turn ye to destruction, because ye will speedily be
visited, in that from time to time ye have rejected the
understanding of the Most High.   18. For His works
have not taught you, nor has the skill of His creation
which is at all times persuaded you.]   19. Adam is

gibt eine Erbschuld, aber keine
Erbsünde: der Fall Adam's hat dem
ganzen Geschlecht den Tod, nicht
aber die Sündigkeit im Sinne einer
Nothwendigkeit zu sündigen verur-
sacht ; die Sünde ist das Ergebnis
der Entscheidung jedes Einzelnen,
erfahrungsgemäss allgemein, aber
an sich auch nach dem Fall nicht
schlechthin nothwendig " (*Lehren d.
Talmud*, p. 217).

Only one statement in this
citation seems untrustworthy, *i.e.*
Es gibt eine Erbschuld. I can
see nothing in Weber's learned work
to justify this statement, but everything to show that there was neither
hereditary sin nor hereditary guilt.
Moreover, on p. 240 this statement
is actually made : " Wenn die Sünde
und Schuld nicht erblich ist, kann
dann die Strafe erblich sein ? . . .
Diese Antinomie hat die jüdische
Theologie durch drei Sätze auszu-
gleichen versucht."

15. *Untimely.* See note on xxiii.
4. The phrase rendered "untimely" is ܩܛܝܠ ܒܠܐ. It recurs in lvi. 6 and lxxiii. 3.

16-18. These verses are clearly
an interpolation for the same reasons
as xlviii. 48-50 and lii. 5-7. These
three passages seem to have been
addressed by Baruch to the people,
and to have formed part of one and
the same discourse. The original
order appears to have been: first,
liv. 17, 18, where the wicked are

menaced with the final judgment ;
then xlviii. 48-50, in which the
destiny of the wicked is dismissed
and that of the righteous described ;
next, lii. 5-7, where a line of conduct is prescribed to the righteous
on the ground of that destiny, and a
preparation of their souls for the
reward laid up for them ; and finally,
liv. 16, where the faithful are assured
of that reward.

It will be observed (1) that these
verses break the sense of the context ;
(2) that a direct address to the
wicked could not occur in a prayer
to God.

18. In liv. 14 it is implied that
the wicked there described knew the
law. This is intelligible from the
standpoint of the Jewish belief that
the Gentiles were offered the law but
refused it. But in this verse no
such view is implied. Their knowledge of God could only arise from
reflection on His works in nature.
The same argument is found in Rom.
i. 20. This argument "is as old as
the Psalter, Job, and Isaiah (Pss.
xix. 1 ; xciv. 9 ; cxliii. 5 ; Isa. xli. 5 ;
xlv. 18 ; Job xii. 9 ; xxvi. 14 ; xxxvi.
24 ; Wisdom ii. 23 ; xiii. 1, 5). It is
common to Greek thought as well
as Jewish (Arist. *De Mundo*, 6 ;
Philo, *De Praem. et Poen.* 7 " (Sanday
and Headlam, Rom. p. 43).

19. See note on verse 15. The
real force of this verse is that a
man's guilt and sin are not derived

therefore not the cause, save only of his own soul, but each one of us has been the Adam of his own soul. 20. But do Thou, O Lord, expound to me regarding those things which Thou hast revealed to me, and inform me regarding that which I besought Thee. 21. For at the consummation of the world there will be vengeance taken upon those who have done wickedness according to their wickedness, and Thou wilt glorify the faithful according to their faithfulness. 22. For those who are amongst Thine own Thou rulest, and those who sin Thou blottest out from amongst Thine own."

LV. And it came to pass when I had finished speaking the words of this prayer, that I sat there under a tree, that I might rest in the shade of the branches. 2. And I wondered and was astonied, and pondered in my thoughts regarding the multitude of goodness which sinners who are upon the earth

from Adam, but are due to his own action. The evil impulse (יצר הרע) does not constitute guilt or sin unless man obeys it. As the Talmudists say, it was placed in man to be overcome (Weber, 210).

21. *The faithful according to their faith.* Faith in this passage is contrasted with unrighteousness (ܣܟܠܐ = ἀνομία). Hence we should take it here as equivalent either to "righteousness" or "fidelity to the law." In liv. 16 the verb "believe" may mean "to be faithful." But the context is doubtful. Elsewhere in Baruch faith = "belief." Thus in lix. 2 those who "believe" are opposed to those who "deny"; in xlii. 2 to those who "despise." This is the meaning also in liv. 5; lvii. 2; lxxxiii. 8. In 4 Ezra vi. 5

faith seems to mean "righteousness," the result of fidelity to the law (as in Apoc. Bar. liv. 21); for the righteous are those *qui fidem thesaurizaverunt;* possibly also in v. 1; vi. 28; it means fidelity to the law in vii. 34, as *incredulitas* in vii. 114 = "disloyalty." In ix. 7, 8; xiii. 23, faith and works are combined and appear nearly synonymous. For a most instructive note on the various meanings of "faith," see Sanday and Headlam's *Romans*, pp. 31-34.

Faith in the Talmud is in one of its aspects regarded as a work which as the fulfilment of the law produces merit. In the *Beresh. rabba,* lxxiv. the merit arising from faith and the merit arising from the law are co-ordinated. See Weber, pp. 292, 295, 298.

have rejected, and regarding the great torment which
they have despised, though they knew that they should
be tormented because of the sin they had committed.
3. And when I was pondering on these things and
the like, lo ! the angel Ramiel who presides over true
visions was sent to me, and he said unto me : 4.
" Why does thy heart trouble thee, Baruch, and why
does thy thought disturb thee ? 5. For if by the hear-
say which thou hast only heard of judgment thou art
so moved, what (wilt thou be) when thou shalt see it
manifestly with thine eyes ?   6. And if with the expectation wherewith thou dost expect the day of the
Mighty One thou art so overcome, what (wilt thou be)
when thou shalt come to its advent ?   7. And, if at
the word of the announcement of the torment of those
who have done foolishly thou art so wholly distraught,
how much more when the event will reveal marvellous
things ?   8. And if thou hast heard tidings of the good
and evil things which are then coming and art grieved,
what (wilt thou be) when thou shalt behold what the
majesty will reveal, which will convict these and cause
those to rejoice ?

LV. 2. *Despised, though they knew.* See xv. 6, note ; xlviii. 40, note.

3. *Ramiel.* Cf. lxiii. 6 ; this angel is mentioned in the Eth. En. xx. 7 (Greek) Ῥεμειὴλ ὁ εἶς τῶν ἁγίων ἀγγέλων ὃν ἔταξεν ὁ Θεὸς ἐπὶ τῶν ἀνισταμένων : also in 4 Ezra iv. 36, where the Syriac Version = "And the angel Ramiel answered and said unto them " (*i.e.* the righteous souls in the soul-treasuries) ; for "Ramiel" the Latin gives *Hieremihel.* Finally,

in *Or. Sibyl.* ii. 215-217, Ramiel is one of the five angels appointed by God to bring the souls of men to judgment : ᾽Αρακιὴλ Ῥαμιὴλ Οὑριὴλ Σαμιὴλ ᾽Αζαὴλ τε . . . ἀνθρώπων ψυχὰς . . . ἐς κρίσιν ἄξουσιν πάσας. The function of Ramiel in the text agrees to some extent with that assigned to him in 4 Ezra.

5. *And art so moved.* I have followed Ceriani's suggestion here in supplying ‎ܘ before ‎ܗܢܐ.

LVI. " Nevertheless, because thou hast besought the Most High to reveal to thee the interpretation of the vision which thou hast seen, I have been sent to say to thee. 2. And the Mighty One hath assuredly made known to thee the methods of the times that have passed, and of those that are destined to pass in His world from the beginning of its creations even unto its consummation, of those things which (are) deceit and of those which (are) in truth. 3. For as thou didst see a great cloud which ascended from the sea, and went and covered the earth, this is the duration of the world (= αἰών) which the Mighty One made when He took counsel to make the world. 4. And it came to pass when the word had gone forth from His presence, that the duration of the world had come into being in a small degree, and was established according to the multitude of the intelligence of Him who sent it. 5. And as thou didst previously see on the summit of the cloud black waters which descended previously on the earth, this is the transgression wherewith Adam the first man transgressed. 6. For owing to his transgression untimely death came into being, and grief was named

LVI. 2. *And the Mighty.* We should expect *That the Mighty.*

3. *A great cloud . . . this is the duration of the world.* This cloud is divided into thirteen parts : the first twelve parts of alternate black and bright waters (see liii. 5, 6), and the thirteenth of the blackest waters of all (see liii. 7). These symbolise the thirteen periods into which the history of the world is divided prior to the Messiah's kingdom. This kingdom is foreshadowed by the lightning that shone on the extremity or summit of the cloud.

4. *Was established.* I have followed Ceriani here in reading ⲟⲌⲌⳑⲟ instead of ⲟⲌⳑⲟ.

6. *Owing to his transgression.* The text literally = " when he transgressed."

Untimely. See liv. 15, note.

and anguish was prepared, and pain was created, and
trouble perfected, and boasting began to be established,
and Sheol to demand that it should be renewed in
blood, and the begetting of children was brought
about, and the passion of parents produced, and the
greatness of humanity was humiliated, and goodness
languished.   7. What therefore can be blacker or
darker than these things ?   8. This is the beginning
of the black waters which thou hast seen.   9. And
from these black (waters) again were black derived,
and the darkness of darkness produced.   10. For he
was a danger to his own soul : even to the angels was
he a danger.   11. For, moreover, at that time when
he was created, they enjoyed liberty.   12. And some
of them descended, and mingled with women.   13.
And then those who did so were tormented in chains.
14. But the rest of the multitude of the angels, of
which there is no number, restrained themselves.   15.
And those who dwelt on the earth perished together
(with them) through the waters of the deluge.   16.
These are the black first waters.

Sheol to demand, etc. For this
hunger of Sheol, cf. Prov. xxvii. 20;
Isa. v. 14. On Sheol, see note on
xi. 6.

10. *He was a danger*, etc. This
must mean that man's physical
nature was a danger to his spiritual ;
for it was the physical side of man
that proved a danger to the angels
who fell through lust.   Man's
physical nature was dangerous ; for
in it resided the " evil impulse "
(see note on liv. 15, 19).

11 - 13. *They enjoyed liberty*,

i.e. the   angels.   This   liberty,
according to the ancient myth,
they abused by taking to themselves wives of the daughters of
men (see Eth. En. vi. 2, note ; Slav.
En. xviii. 4-6 ; Jubilees v. 1-11 ;
x. 1-13).

14. *No number*. The MS. omits
the negative, but wrongly, as Ceriani
has already observed (cf. xxi. 6 ;
lix. 11).   For a still more obvious
loss of the negative see li. 16,
though strangely enough it has not
hitherto been remarked.

LVII. "And after these (waters) thou didst see bright waters: this is the fount of Abraham, also his generations and advent of his son, and of his son's son, and of those like them. 2. Because at that time the unwritten law was named amongst them, and the works of the commandments were then fulfilled, and belief in the coming judgment was then generated, and hope of the world that was to be renewed was then built up, and the promise of the life that should come hereafter was implanted. 3. These are the bright waters, which thou hast seen.

LVIII. "And the black third waters which thou

LVII. 1. The first bright period embraces human history from the time of Abraham to that of the twelve sons of Jacob and their righteous ·contemporaries or immediate successors.

2. *The unwritten law.* This statement proceeds from the same spirit which animates the entire Book of Jubilees, and which seeks to trace traditionalism and its observances to the times of the patriarchs. In later Judaism there were manifold attempts of this nature. Thus in the *Avoda-sara*, 36*b*, according to Gen. xxxviii. 24, impurity was forbidden by the Rabbinic tribunal of Shem ; in the *Beresh. rabba*, xciv., Shem and Eber are said to have handed on certain traditions to Jacob ; in the *Joma*, 28*b*, Abraham is said to have observed the whole Torah and the traditional or unwritten law. To Abraham, Isaac, and Jacob the three daily times of prayer are traced back in the *Berachoth*, 26*b*. The above statements are drawn from Herzfeld, *Geschichte Israels*, p. 226. For a detailed description of the traditional law from the

earliest times down to Hillel, see *op. cit.* iii. 226-263 ; Weber, 255.

Works of the commandments were then fulfilled. See preceding note.

Belief. See note on liv. 21.

Hope of the world to be renewed. See note on xxxii. 6. In the earlier Messiah-Apocalypses in this book, *i.e.* in A¹ and A², the renewal of the world is to take place at the close of the Messianic kingdom, for in these writings this kingdom belongs to this world ὁ αἰὼν οὖτος (Matt. xii. 32) = הָעוֹלָם הַזֶּה ; whereas in A³ with which we are at present dealing it is said (lxxiv. 2) to form the close of the present world and the beginning of the next (*i.e. ὁ αἰὼν ὁ μέλλων* or *ὁ ἐρχόμενος* = הָעוֹלָם הַבָּא). If we are to take (lxxiv. 2) literally, then the renewal of the world is to take place during the Messiah's reign. But this is unlikely. In 4 Ezra vii. 28-30 ; xii. 32-34, the Messiah's kingdom belongs to this world. In xiii. 32-50 to the next, if xiii. 36 is genuine. In the older literature the Messianic kingdom belongs to the next world (cf. Eth. En. xxxvii.-lxx.)

hast seen, these are the mingling of all sins, which the nations afterwards wrought after the death of those righteous men, and the wickedness of the land of Egypt, wherein they did wickedly in the service wherewith they made their sons to serve. 2. Nevertheless, these also perished at last.

LIX. "And the bright fourth waters which thou hast seen are the advent of Moses and Aaron and Miriam and Joshua the son of Nun and Caleb and of all those like them. 2. For at that time the lamp of the eternal law shone on all those who sat in darkness, which announced to them that believe the promise of their reward, and to them that deny, the torment of fire which is reserved for them. 3. But also the heavens at that time were shaken from their place, and those who were under the throne of the Mighty One were perturbed, when He was taking Moses unto Himself. 4. For He showed him many admonitions together with the principles of the laws and the consummation of time, as also to thee, and likewise the pattern of Zion and its measures, which was to be

LVIII. 1. *The service where-with they made their sons to serve.* Exod. i. 14 is here closely followed : בל־עבדתם אשר־עבדו בהם. As the LXX. has here πάντα τὰ ἔργα ὧν κατεδου-λοῦντο αὐτούς, it is clear that the original writer had the Hebrew text and not the LXX. before him.

LIX. 2. *The eternal law.* Cf. xvii. 6. See xv. 5, note.

The lamp . . . darkness—a Rabbinic application of Isa. ix. 2. Isa. ix. 2 was a favourite passage in N.T. times (cf. Matt. iv. 16 ; Luke i. 79).

That believe. See liv. 21, note.

Torment of fire. Cf. xliv. 15 ; xlviii. 39 ; lxxxv. 13. It will be observed that these passages suggest a material fire in which the wicked are to be tormented after the resurrection, *i.e.* after they have resumed their bodies.

4. *The pattern of Zion and its measures.* Cf. Exod. xxv. 40 ; xxvi. 30 ; Heb. viii. 5.

Which was to be made, etc. A very slight change in the Syriac would give a good text : "In the

made in the pattern of the sanctuary of the present time. 5. But then also He showed to him the measures of the fire, also the depths of the abyss, and the weight of the winds, and the number of the drops of rain. 6. And the suppression of anger, and the multitude of long-suffering, and the truth of judgment. 7. And the root of wisdom, and the riches of understanding, and the fount of knowledge. 8. And the height of the air, and the greatness of Paradise, and

pattern of which the sanctuary of the present time was to be made."

5-11. It is of importance to observe, with a view to determining the date of A³, that in these verses we have a transference of Enoch's functions to Moses, and that the revelations hitherto attributed to Enoch are here for the first time assigned to Moses. It is noteworthy that another of Enoch's chief functions is ascribed to Ezra in 4 Ezra xiv. 50. This opposition to Enoch is unswervingly pursued in the Talmud. Thus, whereas in pre-Christian Judaism, Enoch, and Enoch only, is described as the scribe of the deeds of men (Jub. iv. 23; x. 17; Slav. En. xl. 13; liii. 2; lxiv. 5), this office is assigned to various Jewish heroes in later Judaism. Thus according to *Ruth rabba*, 33a, it is Elijah; according to *Esther rabba*, 86d, it is the angels; according to *Jalkut Shim., Beresh.* 141, it was formerly the prophets, but now it is only Elijah and the Messiah (Weber, 272). We have already drawn attention to this phenomenon in the note on xiii. 3, and have there pointed out that this hostility to Enoch is the outcome of Jewish hostility to Christianity as a whole; for as we know from manifold

evidence the writings of Enoch enjoyed a singular influence on early Christianity. This aggressive attitude of Judaism could hardly have originated before the open rupture of Christianity with the Synagogue and the Pauline controversy. Hence this writing was not earlier than A.D. 50. From lxviii. 5 it is clear that it is prior to A.D. 70. Therefore the limits of its composition are A.D. 50-70.

5. *The depths of the abyss.* A frequent subject in both books of Enoch: Eth. En. xviii. 11; xxi. 7-10, etc.; Slav. En. xxviii. 3.

The weight of the winds. The weighing of the winds is described in the Slav. En. xl. 11; cf. also Eth. xli. 4.

The number of the drops of rain. Slav. En. xlvii. 5; Ecclus. i. 2.

7. *Root of wisdom.* See li. 3, note.

Riches of understanding. lxi. 4.

The fount of knowledge. Bar. iii. 12; 4 Ezra xiv. 47.

8. *The height of the air.* Slav. En. xl. 12: "I have written down the height from the earth to the seventh heaven."

The greatness of Paradise. The measures of Paradise are taken by the angels for Enoch. Cf. Eth. En. lxi. 1-4; lxx. 3, 4.

the consummation of the ages, and the beginning of the day of judgment. 9. And the number of the offerings, and the earths which have not yet come. 10. And the mouth of Gehenna, and the station of vengeance, and the place of faith, and the region of hope. 11. And the likeness of future torment, and the multitude of innumerable angels, and the powers of the flames, and the splendour of the lightnings, and the voice of the thunders, and the orders of the chiefs of the angels, and the treasuries of light, and the changes of the times, and the investigations of the law. 12. These are the bright fourth waters which thou hast seen.

LX. "And the black fifth waters which thou hast

The consummation of the ages. This subject is discussed in every section of the Enochic literature.

The beginning of the day of judgment. This date is fixed according to a definite reckoning in the Slav. En. xxxii. 2-xxxiii. 2; lxv. 7-10; according to certain indefinite measures in Eth. En. lxxxiii.-xc.; xci.-civ.

10. *The mouth of Gehenna.* Eth. En. xxvii. 2, 3; liv. ; lxii. 12; xc. 26, 27.

The station of vengeance. Many places of vengeance are described in the two books of Enoch: Eth. En. xviii. 12-16; xix.; xxi.; xxii. 10-13; liv. 1-6; xc. 24-27; Slav. En. x.; xl. 12.

The place of faith, and the region of hope. These seem to be the places of intermediate bliss. Cf. Eth. En. xxii. 5-9.

11. *The likeness of future torment.* Slav. xl. 12.

The multitude of innumerable angels. See lvi. 14, note. Of early Jewish literature, it is only in Enoch that the angels are described at length.

The splendour of the lightnings, and the voice of the thunders. Eth. En. xli. 3; xliii. 1, 2; xliv.; lix.; lx. 13-15; Slav. En. xl. 9.

The orders of the chiefs of the angels. I have here read the plural ܪ̈ܝܫܝ instead of the singular ܪ̈ܝܫܝ. Ceriani renders the text: "ordines principatus angelorum." The Jews believed in ten orders of angels, the Christians in nine. These orders are mentioned and in part enumerated in the Slav. En. xx. 1, 3 (see note); cf. also Eth. En. lxi. 10; lxxi. 7-9.

The treasuries of light. This expression is unexampled.

The changes of the times, i.e. the seasons. Slav. En. xiii. 5; xl. 6; Eth. En. lxxxii. 11-20.

seen raining are the works which the Amorites wrought, and the spells of their incantations which they wrought, and the wickedness of their mysteries, and the mingling of their pollution. 2. But even Israel was then polluted by sins in the days of the judges, though they saw many signs which were from Him who made them.

LXI. "And the bright sixth waters which thou didst see, this is the time in which David and Solomon were born. 2. And there was at that time the building of Zion, and the dedication of the sanctuary, and the shedding of much blood of the nations that sinned then, and many offerings which were offered then in the dedication of the sanctuary. 3. And peace and tranquillity existed at that time. 4. And wisdom was heard in the assembly, and the riches of understanding were magnified in the congregations. 5. And the holy festivals were fulfilled in goodness and in much joy. 6. And the judgment of the rulers was then seen to be without guile, and the righteousness of the precepts of the Mighty One was accomplished with truth. 7. And because the land was then beloved at that time, and because its inhabitants sinned not, it was glorified beyond all lands, and the city Zion ruled then over all lands and regions. 8. These are the bright waters which thou hast seen.

LX. 1. *Mingling of their pollution.* Cf. Pss. Sol. ii. 14, ἐν φυρμῷ ἀναμίξεως.

2. *Of the judges.* I here follow

Ceriani in correcting ܕܝܢܐ (= "of judgment") into ܕܝܢܐ.

LXI. 4. *Riches of understanding.* lix. 7.

LXII. "And the black seventh waters which thou hast seen, this is the perversion (brought about) by the counsel of Jeroboam, who took counsel to make two calves of gold. 2. And all the iniquities which the kings who were after him iniquitously wrought. 3. And the curse of Jezebel and the worship of idols which Israel practised at that time. 4. And the withholding of rain, and the famines which occurred until women eat the fruit of their wombs. 5. And the time of their captivity which came upon the nine tribes and a half, because they were in many sins. 6. And Salmanasar king of Assyria came and led them away captive. 7. But regarding the Gentiles it were tedious to tell how they always wrought impiety and wickedness, and never wrought righteousness. 8. These are the black seventh waters which thou hast seen.

LXIII. "And the bright eighth waters which thou hast seen, this is the rectitude and uprightness of Hezekiah king of Judah and his benignity which came upon him. 2. For when Sennacherib was stirred up in order that he might perish, and his wrath troubled him in order that he might thereby

LXII. 4. Cf. 2 Kings vi. 28, 29.
5. The captivity of the nine and a half tribes 721 B.C. See lxxviii. note.
6. *I.e.* Shalmaneser, 2 Kings xvii. 3, 6. Cf. 4 Ezra xiii. 40.
7. *Wrought righteousness.* The text is ܩܩ݂ܝܪ = "have been justified." For the grounds for the above restoration, see xxi. 9, note.

LXIII. 1. *His benignity.* So ܣܢ ܠܩܒ݂ܠܘ. But the MS. originally read ܣܢ ܠܩܒ݂ܠܘ = "bounty, kindness." Both readings seem wrong.
2. This verse is translated as it stands in the Syriac. By omitting "for" the word "multitude" could be made the subject of the word "perish."

perish, for the multitude also of the nations which were with him.   3. When, moreover, Hezekiah the king heard those things which the king of Assyria was devising, (*i.e.*) to come and seize him and destroy his people, the two and a half tribes which remained : nay, more he wished to overthrow Zion also : then Hezekiah trusted in his works, and had hope in his righteousness, and spake with the Mighty One and said :   4. 'Behold, for lo ! Sennacherib is prepared to destroy us, and he will be boastful and uplifted when he has destroyed Zion.'   5. And the Mighty One heard him, for Hezekiah was wise, and He had respect unto his prayer, because he was righteous.   6. And thereupon the Mighty One commanded Ramiel His angel who speaks with thee.   7. And I went forth and destroyed their multitude, the number of whose chiefs only was a hundred and eighty-five

---

3. *Hezekiah trusted in his works.* See xiv. 7, note. Observe the play on Hezekiah's name in these words when retranslated into Hebrew, חזקיה התחזק על. There appears to have been one also in Ecclus. xlviii. 22, ἐποίησεν γὰρ Ἐξεκίας . . . καὶ ἐνίσχυσεν. This conjecture as to the probable text in Ecclus. was made in March. It is now (June 20) confirmed by Dr. Neubauer's discovery last week in the Bodley of the Hebrew text of Ecclus. xl.-l. To his kindness and that of Mr. Cowley I owe the following passages where this play on the name occurs twice :—Ecclus. xlviii. 17, יחזקיהו חזק עירו= Ἐξεκίας ὠχύρωσεν τὴν πόλιν αὐτοῦ, and xlviii. 22, (כי עשה יחז)קיהו את הטוב (וי)חחזק

בדרכי דוד =ἐποίησεν γὰρ Ἐξεκίας τὸ ἄρεστον κυρίῳ, καὶ ἐνίσχυσεν ἐν ὁδοῖς Δαυείδ.

4. *Lo, Sennacherib is prepared to destroy us.* There was a play here on the name Sennacherib in the Hebrew, והנה סנחריב עתיד להחריב אותנו,

5. In *Sifre,* 12*b*, and *Jalkut Shim.,* *Beresh.* 27, it is taught that men are heard by God on the ground either of their own merit or on that of others (Weber, 284, 285).

7. In 2 Kings xix. 35 ; Isa. xxxvii. 36, 185,000 is the complete number of the slain. In 2 Chron. xxxii. 21, only the slaughter of the chiefs is mentioned. From these two accounts the writer has worked up the present.

thousand, and each one of them had an equal number (at his command). 8. And at that time I burned their bodies within, but their raiment and arms I preserved outwardly, in order that the still more wonderful deeds of the Mighty One might appear, and that thereby His name might be spoken of throughout the whole earth. 9. Moreover, Zion was saved and Jerusalem delivered : Israel also was freed from tribulation. 10. And all those who were in the holy land rejoiced, and the name of the Mighty One was glorified so that it was spoken of. 11. These are the bright waters which thou hast seen.

LXIV. "And the black ninth waters which thou hast seen, this is all the wickedness which was in the days of Manasseh the son of Hezekiah. 2. For he wrought much impiety, and he slew the righteous, and he wrested judgment, and he shed the blood of the innocent, and wedded women he violently polluted, and he overturned the altars, and destroyed their offerings, and drave forth the priests lest they should minister in the sanctuary. 3. And he made an image with five faces : four of them looked to the

LXIV. 3. *He made an image with five faces : four of,* etc. This is a very peculiar version of 2 Chron. xxxiii. 7. אֶת־פֶּסֶל הַסֶּמֶל וַיָּשֶׂם—"he set the graven image of the. idol." The LXX. implies the Hebrew just given. The Syriac, however, exhibits an early gloss which prepares the way for our text. Thus it gives ܘܐܙ݂ܝ ܠܚܟ݂ܠܐ ܘܣܡܗ ܕ = "and he set the four-fronted image." The Arabic goes still further ; it="and he set a statue having four heads with four faces." But the form of the tradition nearest to the text is found in the Talmud, *Sanh.* 103b : "At first he made for it (the idol) one face and in the end he made for it four faces, that the Shechinah might see and be provoked."

four winds, and the fifth on the summit of the image
as an adversary of the zeal of the Mighty One.   4.
And then wrath went forth from the presence of the
Mighty One to the intent that Zion should be rooted
out, as also it befell in your days.   5. But also against
the two tribes and a half went forth a decree that
they should also be led away captive, as thou hast
now seen.   6. And to such a degree did the impiety
of Manasseh increase, that it removed the praise of
the Most High from the sanctuary.   7. On this
account Manasseh was at that time named 'the
impious,' and finally his abode was in the fire.   8.
For though his prayer was heard with the Most High,
finally, when he was cast into the brazen horse and the
brazen horse was melted, it served as a sign unto him

6. *Removed the praise of the Most High from the sanctuary.* This may be explained by the statement in *Sanh.* 103*b*, that Manasseh erased the divine name and overturned the altar.

7. This verse runs counter to 2 Chron. xxxiii. 11-19, where it is clearly implied that Manasseh was really forgiven on his repentance. This writer declares, on the other hand, that Manasseh's experience in the brazen horse was only a foretaste of his future sufferings in hell.

In the fire. See xliv. 15, note.

8. *His prayer.* 2 Chron. xxxiii. 19 ; *The Prayer of Manasseh* in the Apocrypha.

Cast into the brazen horse and the brazen horse was melted. This tradition appears in the Targum of Chronicles after 2 Chron. xxxiii. 11: "And the Chaldeans made a copper mule and pierced it all over with little holes, and shut him up therein

and kindled fire all around him. . . . And he turned and prayed before the Lord his God. . . . And He shook the world with His word, and the mule burst asunder and he went forth therefrom." Traces of this tradition are also found in the Apostolic Constitutions ii. 22: καὶ ἐπήκουσε τῆς φωνῆς αὐτοῦ κύριος . . . καὶ ἐγένετο περὶ αὐτὸν φλὸξ πυρὸς καὶ ἐτάκησαν πάντα τὰ περὶ αὐτὸν σίδηρα. Also in Anastasius on Ps. vi. (Canisius, *Thesaur. Monum.* iii. 112) φασὶ οἱ ἀρχαῖοι τῶν ἱστοριογράφων, ὅτι ἀπενεχθεὶς Μανασσῆς κατεκλείσθη εἰς ζώδιον χαλκοῦν ἀπὸ βασιλέως Περσῶν καὶ ἔσω ὢν ἐν τοιούτῳ ζωδίῳ προσηύξατο μετὰ δακρύων. In Suidas (see Μανασσῆς): αἰχμάλωτος ἀπήχθη καὶ ἐς τὸ χαλκοῦν ἄγαλμα καθείρχθη . . . ἐδεήθη τοῦ κυρίου . . . καὶ τὸ μὲν ἄγαλμα θείᾳ δυνάμει διερράγη.

Served as a sign. See note on ver. 7.

at the time.   9. For he did not live perfectly, for he was not worthy—but that thenceforward he might know by whom finally he should be tormented.   10. For he who is able to benefit is also able to torment.

LXV. "Thus, moreover, did Manasseh act impiously, and thought that in his time the Mighty One would not inquire into these things.   2. These are the black ninth waters which thou hast seen.

LXVI. "And the bright tenth waters which thou hast seen: this is the purity of the generations of Josiah king of Judah, who was the only one at that time who submitted himself to the Mighty One with all his heart and with all his soul.   2. And he cleansed the land from idols, and hallowed all the vessels which had been polluted, and restored the offerings to the altar, and raised the horn of the holy, and exalted the righteous, and glorified all that were wise in understanding, and brought back the priests to their ministry, and destroyed and removed the magicians and enchanters and fortune-tellers from the land.   3. And not only did he slay the impious that were living, but they also took from the sepulchres

9. Text is corrupt.

LXVI. 1. The writer thus appears to have believed that though Manasseh prayed, yet he did not really repent. This view is found in *Sanh.* 101: "Our Rabbis have taught: there are three who came *with cunning* (before God): they are Cain, Esau, and Manasseh. . . . Manasseh at first called upon many gods, and at last upon the God of his fathers" [Rashi: "He said:

'If Thou save me not, what doth it profit me that I have called on Thee, more than the other gods?'"] (quoted by Ball in his Comm. on *The Prayer of Manasses*).   In *Sanh.* x. three kings are said to have no part in the future life, *i.e.* Jeroboam, Ahab, and Manasseh. Yet in the *Debarim rabba,* ii., salvation is ultimately said to be in store for Manasseh (Weber, 328).

the bones of the dead and burned them with fire. 4. [And the festivals and the sabbaths he established in their sanctity], and their polluted ones he burnt in the fire, and the lying prophets which deceived the people, these also he burnt in the fire, and the people who listened to them when they were living, he cast them into the brook Cedron, and heaped stones upon them. 5. And he was zealous with the zeal of the Mighty One with all his soul, and he alone was firm in the law at that time, so that he left none that was uncircumcised, or that wrought impiety in all the land, all the days of his life. 6. This, moreover, is he that shall receive an eternal reward, and he shall be glorified with the Mighty One beyond many at a later time. 7. For on his account and on account of those who are like him were the inestimable glories, of which thou wast told before, created and prepared. 8. These are the bright waters which thou hast seen.

LXVII. " And the black eleventh waters which thou hast seen: this is the calamity which is now befalling Zion. 2. Dost thou think that there is no anguish to the angels in the presence of the Mighty One, that Zion was so delivered up, and that lo ! the Gentiles boast in their hearts, and assemble before their idols and say : ' She is trodden

---

4. The words which I have bracketed are either interpolated or misplaced. It would perhaps be best to read them after "to their ministry" in verse 2. In that case for "festival" we should read "festivals."

7. See note on xiv. 18.
LXVII. 2. *Boast.* Cf. v. 1 ; vii. 1 ; lxxx. 3.   *Assemble.* The text ܠܐܝܕ = " crowds " is corrupt. I have emended it into ܩܐܝܕ = "assemble."

down who ofttimes trod down, and she has been
reduced to servitude who reduced (others) ?'   3. Dost
thou think that in these things the Most High rejoices,
or that His name is glorified ?   4. But how will it
serve towards His righteous judgment ?   5. Yet after
these things shall those that are dispersed among the
Gentiles be taken hold of by tribulation, and in shame
shall they dwell in every place.   6. Because so far
as Zion is delivered up and Jerusalem laid waste, and
idols prosper in the cities of the Gentiles, and the
vapour of the smoke of the incense of righteousness
which is by the law is extinguished in Zion and in
the region of Zion, lo! in every place there is the
smoke of impiety.   7. But the king of Babylon will
arise who has now destroyed Zion, and he will boast
over the people, and he will speak great things in his
heart in the presence of the Most High.   8. But

5. "The dispersed" here seem to
be the nine and a half tribes.

6-7. With the destruction of Jerusalem, godlessness is triumphant
everywhere. In all the references
in A³ to this destruction of Jerusalem, i.e. in lxiv. 4 ; lxvii. 2, 6, 7,
there is no trace of consciousness in
the mind of the writer that there
was any divine interposition to save
the sacred vessels of the temple and
to destroy Zion by the agency of
angels after the manner described in
B¹, i.e. in vi. 4-10 ; lxxx. 1-3. If,
further, we remark that the declared
object of this interposition was to
prevent the enemies of Zion boasting
before their idols that they had laid
it waste and burnt the temple (vii.
1 ; cf. v. 1 ; lxxx. 3), and if at the
same time we observe that the

writer of A³ represents the angel
Ramiel as admitting that the Gentiles are boasting before their idols
of their destruction of Zion (lxvii.
2), and that the king of Babylon
makes the same vaunt (lxvii. 7), we
can with tolerable certainty conclude that the ideas in B¹, i.e. in v.
1 ; vi. 4-vii. 1 ; lxxx. 1-3, were
either unknown to him or else un-
acknowledged. These ideas seem
foreign to B² also. This writer
would have sympathised with the
remonstrance in 4 Ezra v. 30 :
"Et si odiens odisti populum tuum,
tuis manibus debet castigari." In
the Assumpt. Mosis (iii. 2) the
capture of the sacred vessels by
Nebuchadnezzar is acknowledged.

   Righteousness which is by the law.
See xv. 5, note.

he also shall fall at last.   9. These are the black
waters.

LXVIII. " And the bright twelfth waters which
thou hast seen : this is the word.   2. For after these
things a time will come when thy people shall fall
into distress, so that they shall all run the risk of
perishing together.   3. Nevertheless, they will be
saved, and their enemies will fall in their presence.
4. And they will have in (due) time much joy.   5.
And at that time after a little interval Zion will again
be builded, and its offerings will again be restored, and
the priests will return to their ministry, and again the
Gentiles will come to glorify it.   6. Nevertheless, not
fully as in the beginning.   7. But it will come to pass
after these things that there will be the fall of many
nations.   8. These are the bright waters which thou
hast seen.

LXIX. " For the last waters which thou hast seen
which were darker than all that were before them,
those which were after the twelfth number, which
were collected together, belong to the whole world.
2. For the Most High made division from the beginning, because He alone knows what will befall.   3.

LXVIII. 2, 3. The danger the
Jews encountered according to the
book of Esther, and their subsequent
triumph over their enemies.   We
have here the second earliest
allusion to this O. T. book.   The
earliest is in 2 Macc. xv. 36.

5. The rebuilding of the temple
(535-515).

6. On the lower estimation in
which the second temple was held

see Mal. i.-ii. ; Eth. En. lxxxix. 73,
74 ; Assumpt. Mos. iv. 8.   This
temple, therefore, was standing
when chapters liii.-lxxiv. were
written.

LXIX. 1. *Last.*   I have here
adopted Ceriani's suggestion and
read ‏ܐ‌ܚ‌ܪ‌ܝ‌ܐ‎ instead of ‏ܐ‌ܚ‌ܪ‌ܢ‌ܐ‎ =
" other."

The last waters, etc.   See liii. 7.

For as to the enormities of the impieties which should
be wrought before Him, He foresaw six kinds of them.
4. And of the good works of the righteous which
should be accomplished before Him, He foresaw six
kinds of them, beyond those which He should work at
the consummation of the age. 5. On this account
there were not black waters with black, nor bright
with bright; for it is the consummation.

LXX. "Hear therefore the interpretation of the
last black waters which are to come [after the black]:
this is the word. 2. Behold! the days come, and it
will be when the time of the age has ripened, and the
harvest of its evil and good seeds has come, that the
Mighty One will bring upon the earth and its inhabitants and upon its rulers perturbation of spirit and
stupor of heart. 3. And they will hate one another,
and provoke one another to fight, and the mean will
rule over the honourable, and those of low degree will
be extolled above the famous. 4. And the many will
be delivered into the hands of the few, and those who
are nothing will rule over the strong, and the poor
will have abundance beyond the rich, and the impious

3, 4. This division of the periods of
the world into six good and six evil
recalls Ecclus. xlii. 24 πάντα δισσὰ ἐν
κατέναντι τοῦ ἑνός (cf. also xxxiii. 15).

4. *Foresaw.* So Ceriani rightly
emends from "foresees"—merely a
change of pointing.

Beyond those which, etc. These
woes — the travail pains of the
Messiah—are developed at length
in lxx.-lxxii. (see liii. 7 ; lxix. 1).

LXX. 1. I have bracketed the
words "after the black" as inter-

polated. They misrepresent the
scheme of the writer ; for the "last
black waters" come after the bright
twelfth waters in lxviii.

2. *Its inhabitants.* See xxv. 2, note.
Stupor of heart. Cf. xxv. 2.

3-10. With this notable description of the last woes, cf. xxv. 2-4 ;
xxvii. ; xlviii. 31-39 ; 4 Ezra v. 1-
12 ; vi. 20-24 ; ix. 1-9 ; xiii. 29-31
(see xxvii. 1, note.

3. Cf. xlviii. 37 ; Jubilees xxiii.
19 : 4 Ezra vi. 24.

will exalt themselves above the heroic.   5. And the
wise will be silent, and the foolish will speak, neither
will the thought of men be then confirmed, nor the
counsel of the mighty, nor will the hope of those
who hope be confirmed.   6. Moreover, it will be
when those things which were predicted have come to
pass, that confusion will fall upon all men, and some
of them will fall in battle, and some of them will
perish in anguish, and some of them will be destroyed
by their own.   7. Then the Most High will reveal to
those peoples whom He has prepared before, and they
will come and make war with the leaders that shall
then be left.   8. And it will come to pass that whosoever gets safe out of the war will die in the earthquake, and whosoever gets safe out of the earthquake
will be burned by the fire, and whosoever gets safe
out of the fire will be destroyed by famine.   [9. And
it will come to pass that whosoever of the victors and

5. Cf. xlviii. 33, 36 ; 4 Ezra v. 9-11.
    The mighty. The text which
here reads ܠܐ ܟܣܝܐ = "the Mighty
One," is wrong. We must read the
plural ܠܐ ܟܣܝܐ = "the mighty."
In lxxiv. 1 we must change the plural
into the singular.
    The hope of those who hope, etc.
Cf. 4 Ezra v. 12.
    6. *Destroyed,* etc. Cf. Mic. vii. 6 ;
Matt. x. 35, 36 ; Luke xii. 53. The
Syriac text = "will be hindered" is
corrupt ; for the context requires a
strong expression. The corruption
is traceable to the Hebrew. Thus
"will be hindered " = κωλυθήσονται,
which would be the usual LXX.
rendering of יִכָּלֵא. That יבלאו is a
corruption of יבלו = "will be de-

stroyed " is clear from the fact that
these two verbs are often confused
in Hebrew, combined with the further
fact that יִכְלוּ = "will be destroyed "
gives the exact sense we require.
    7. *Whom He has prepared before.*
Are these the hosts of Gog and
Magog ? if text in verse 9 is
genuine.
    8. *In the earthquake.* Cf. xxvii.
7 ; 4 Ezra ix. 3.
    The fire. Cf. xxvii. 10 ; 4 Ezra, v. 8.
    Will be destroyed. I have here
followed Ceriani's emendation of
ܢܘܣܦ = "he will add," into
ܢܣܘܦ.
    Famine. Cf. xxvii. 6.
    9. I have with some doubt
bracketed this verse as an inter-

the vanquished gets safe out of and escapes all these
things aforesaid will be delivered into the hands of
My servant Messiah.]   10. For all the earth will
devour its inhabitants.

LXXI. "And the holy land will have mercy on
its own, and it will protect its inhabiters at that time.
2. This is the vision which thou hast seen, and this is
the interpretation.   3. For I have come to tell thee
these things, because thy prayer has been heard with
the Most High.

LXXII. "Hear now also regarding the bright lightning which is to come at the consummation after these
black (waters): this is the word.   2. After the signs
have come, of which thou wast told before, when the

polation. The appearance of the
Messiah is premature. His advent
does not really take place till lxxii.
2. Again verse 10 is the natural
sequel to verse 8. Further, the extermination of the Gentiles is here
implied, but only their partial destruction in lxxii. 4-6. Finally,
since the Messiah is the defender of
the righteous, lxxi. 1 is rather in-
appropriate. But lxxi. 1 is fitting
if the Messiah has not yet come.

LXXI. See notes on xxix. 2.
Observe that whereas God protects
the inhabitants of Palestine in xxix.
2, and the Messiah protects them in
xl. 2, it is the land that protects
them here.

2. These words which should not
occur till the end of the interpretation show that the text is dislocated.
This will be obvious on other
grounds as we proceed.

3. Cf. liv. 1.

LXXII. 1. The bright lightning =
‏ܠܘ ܒܪܩܐ‎. So I have emended
by means of liii. 8 the impossible

text ‏ܡܝ̈ܐ ܢܗܝܪܐ‎ = "the bright
waters." It will be remembered
that in the vision in liii. the last
blackest waters (liii. 7) were not
succeeded by bright waters, but by
the lightning which illuminated and
healed the earth and ruled over it
(liii. 8-11). The lightning thus
symbolised the Messiah. But in
the interpretation of the close of the
vision, the lightning is not even
mentioned according to the present
text, but in its place bright waters
are spoken of, though in the vision
in liii. none such are seen and none
such contemplated throughout the
entire interpretation up to the
present chapter. The scheme of the
writer of A³ was as we have seen
above : twelve periods evil and good
alternately, symbolised by black and
bright waters respectively, followed
by a period of woes—the blackest
waters ; and finally, the Messiah's
kingdom which was prefigured by
the lightning. The same emendation must be made in lxxiv. 4.

nations become turbulent, and the time of My Messiah is come, He will both summon all the nations, and some of them He will spare, and some of them He will slay.   3. These things therefore will come upon the nations which are to be spared by Him.   4. Every nation which knows not Israel, and has not trodden down the seed of Jacob, shall indeed be spared.   5. And this because some out of every nation will be subjected to thy people.   6. But all those who have ruled over you, or have known you, shall be given up to the sword.

LXXIII. " And it will come to pass, when He has brought low everything that is in the world, and has sat down in peace for the age on the throne of His kingdom, that joy will then be revealed, and rest appear.   2. And then healing will descend in dew, and disease will withdraw, and anxiety and anguish

Throughout lxxii. 1 the plurals are changed into the singular to agree with the singular subject.

4-6. The Messiah was to extend His dominion over the Gentiles (Ps. lxxii. 11, 17; Isa. xiv. 2; lxvi. 12, 19-21; Zech. xiv.; Eth. En. xc. 30; Pss. Sol. xvii. 32 καὶ ἕξει λαοὺς ἐθνῶν δουλεύειν αὐτῷ). But in the first century B.C. to which the Pss. Sol. belong, a harsher view of the destiny of the Gentiles began to prevail. In Eth. En. xxxvii.-lxx. and Assumpt. Mos. x. it seems to be that of annihilation; it is undoubtedly so in 4 Ezra xiii. 37, 38, 49, and all but universally in later Judaism; cf. Weber, 364-369, 376. A middle line is pursued in the text.

The Messiah here, as in xxxix. 7-xl.; 4 Ezra xii. 32, is a warrior who slays the enemies of Israel with His own hand. This view appears in the Targum of Jon. on Isa. x. 27, and of the pseudo-Jon. on Gen. xlix. 11. In Eth. En. lxii. 2; Pss. Sol. xvii. 27; 4 Ezra xiii. 38; as in Isa. xi. 4, He destroys them by the word of His mouth. But in the Eth. En. xc. 37; Ap. Bar. xxix. 2; 4 Ezra vii. 28, the conception of the Messiah is weak; he does not appear till evil has run its course; he has no active *rôle;* he reigns but does not rule.

LXXIII. 1. Cf. 1 Cor. xv. 24, 25.
Joy will be revealed. The text reads " will be revealed in joy," but this destroys the parallelism with " rest will appear." I have omitted the preposition before "joy."

2. *Healing will descend in dew.* Cf. xxix. 7.

and lamentation will pass from amongst men, and gladness will proceed through the whole earth.   3. And no one shall again die untimely, nor shall any adversity suddenly befall.   4. And judgments, and revilings, and contentions, and revenges, and blood, and passions, and envy, and hatred, and whatsoever things are like these shall go into condemnation when they are removed.   5. For it is these very things which have filled this world with evils, and on account of these the life of man has been greatly troubled.   6. And wild beasts will come from the forest and minister unto men, and asps and dragons will come forth from their holes to submit themselves to a little child.   7. And women will no longer then have pain when they bear, nor will they suffer torment when they yield the fruit of the womb.

LXXIV. "And it will come to pass in those days that the reapers will not grow weary, nor those that build be toilworn; for the works will of themselves speedily advance with those who do them in much tranquillity. 2. For that time is the consummation of that which is corruptible, and the beginning of that which is not corruptible.   3. Therefore those things which were predicted will belong to it: therefore it is far away from evils, and near to those things which die not.   4. This is the bright lightning which came after the last dark waters."

3. *Untimely.* See liv. 15.
4. Cf. *Or. Sibyl.* iii. 376-380, 751-755.
6. Cf. Isa. xi. 6-9 ; lxv. 25 ; *Or. Sibyl.* iii. 620-623, 743-750.

LXXIV. 2. Cf. xl. 2.
4. *This is the bright lightning.* Emended from "these are the last bright waters." See lxxii. 1, note.

LXXV. And I answered and said: "Who can LXXV.-
understand, O Lord, Thy goodness? for it is incompre- LXXVI.=B².
hensible. 2. Or who can search into Thy compassions,
which are infinite? 3. Or who can comprehend Thy
intelligence? 4. Or who is able to recount the
thoughts of Thy mind? 5. Or who of those that are
born can hope to come to those things, unless he is
one to whom Thou art merciful and gracious? 6.
Because, if assuredly Thou didst not have compassion
on man, those who are under Thy right hand, they
could not come to those things, but those who are in
the numbers named can be called. 7. But if, indeed,
we who exist know wherefore we have come, and submit ourselves to Him who brought us out of Egypt,
we shall come again and remember those things which
have passed, and shall rejoice regarding that which has

LXXV. - LXXVI. With these
chapters we return again to B². We
should observe that according to lxxv.
1 Baruch replies to the last speaker
who has interpreted the vision in
liii. for him. This speaker Baruch
addresses as God. But the last
speaker was not God but the angel
Ramiel from whom is derived lv. 4-
lxxiv. Thus we see that lxxv. does
not belong to liii.-lxxiv.

LXXV. 1. *Can understand.* I
have emended ‏‏ܐܬܕ‎ = "can be
likened to" into ‏‏ܐܬܣܬܟܠ‎ = "can
understand," and omitted the ‏ܒ‎ in
‏‏ܒܛܘܒܝܟ‎.

2. The mercies of God are not
dwelt upon much in this book. The
righteous are fully conscious of their
worth (cf. xiv. 7, note). We have,
however, a prayer for God's mercy

in xlviii. 18, and an acknowledgment
of God's long-suffering in xxiv. 2,
but this is shown alike to the
righteous and the wicked. God is
merciful (lxxvii. 7) and His compassions are infinite (lxxv. 2); He has
dealt with Baruch according to the
multitude of the tender mercies
(lxxxi. 4); if God had not compassion on man, he could not attain to
the world to come (lxxv. 5, 6). For
references to mercy in 4 Ezra, see
vii. 132-134; viii. 31, 32, 36, 45;
xii. 48.

5, 6. *Those things.* Probably the
blessed immortality described in li.

6. *Who are under Thy right
hand.* Cf. Ps. lxxx. 17.

7. *We shall come again, i.e.* in
the resurrection described in l.
This verse deals with the destiny of
the obedient and the righteous; the
next with that of the disobedient.

been.   8. But if now we know not wherefore we have
come, and recognise not the principate of Him who
brought us up out of Egypt, we shall come again
and seek after those things which were now, and be
grieved with pain because of those things which have
befallen."

LXXVI. And He answered and said unto me:
[" Inasmuch as the revelation of this vision has been
interpreted to thee as thou besoughtest], hear the word
of the Most High that thou mayest know what is to
befall thee after these things.   2. For thou shalt
surely depart from this earth, nevertheless not unto
death but thou shalt be preserved unto the consummation of the times.   3. Go up therefore to the top
of that mountain, and there will pass before thee all
the regions of that land, and the figure of the inhabited
world, and the top of the mountains, and the depth of
the valleys, and the depths of the seas, and the number
of the rivers, that thou mayest see what thou art leaving, and whither thou art going.   4. Now this will
befall after forty days.   5. Go now therefore during

LXXVI. 1. The earlier half of
this verse is probably due to the
final editor.

Hear the word of the Most High.
This same mode of speech in which
God speaks of Himself in the third
person is found in xiii. 2: "Hear
the word of the Mighty God," and
also in xxv. 1, where the same statements are made in each case.

2. See note on xiii. 3.

*Thou shalt be preserved until the
consummation of the times.*   The
Syr. here ܠܐܬܐܐ ? ܠܡܪ̈ܒܐ = "unto

the observance of the times."   If we
compare the parallel passage, xxv.
1, we see that the above must be
emended into ܠܬܐܐ ; ܠܠܕ̈ܐ,
"thou shalt be preserved unto the
times," or else into the fuller form
we find in xvii. 3.   I have done the
latter in the text.

3. Cf. Deut. xxxiv. 1-8 ; Matt. iv.
8.   Is the mountain here Nebo as
in Deuteronomy ?

4. *Forty days.*   Cf. Exod. xxiv.
18 ; xxxiv. 28 ; Deut. ix. 9, 18.
Analogous to this forty days to be

these days and instruct the people so far as thou art able, that they may learn so as not to die at the last time, but may learn in order that they may live at the last times."

LXXVII. And I, Baruch, went thence and came to the people, and assembled them together from the greatest to the least, and said unto them: 2. "Hear, ye children of Israel, behold how many ye are who remain of the twelve tribes of Israel. 3. For to you and to your fathers the Lord gave a law beyond all peoples. 4. And because your brethren transgressed the commandments of the Most High, He brought vengeance upon you and upon them, and He spared not

LXXVII.-
LXXXII.=B¹.

spent by Baruch in teaching the people are the forty days assigned to Ezra, in which he was to restore the O.T. Scriptures (cf. 4 Ezra xiv. 23, 42, 44, 45).

5. *Live.* See xli. 1, note.

In LXXVIII. - LXXXVII. we have the conclusion of B¹. But of these chapters two are from other sources ; LXXXIII. is from B², and LXXXV. from B³. For the grounds for these conclusions, see the notes *in loc.* For a comprehensive treatment of the two sources, B¹ and B², the reader must consult the Introduction. The chief differences between B¹ and B² are : In the former an earthly felicity is looked for, in the latter not ; in the former the dispersion is to return, in the latter not ; in the former the earthly Jerusalem is to be rebuilt, in the latter not ; in the former Baruch is to die, in the latter to be translated ; in the former Jeremiah is not sent to Babylon, in the latter he is. Thus the portions derived respectively from B¹ and B² are as follows :—

From B¹ i.-iv. 1 ; v.-ix. 1 ; xliii.-xliv. 7 ; xlv.-xlvi. 6 ; lxxvii.-lxxxii. ; lxxxiv., lxxxvi., lxxxvii. From B² ix. 2-xii. (?) ; xiii. 1-3*a* ; xx. ; xxiv. 2-4 ; xiii. 3*b*-12 ; xxv., xiv.-xix. ; xxi.-xxiv. 1 ; xxx. 2-5 ; xli., xlii. ; xlviii. 1-47 ; xlix.-lii. 3 ; lxxv. ; xxxi.-xxxii. 6 ; liv. 17, 18 ; xlviii. 48-50 ; lii. 5-7 ; liv. 16 ; xliv. 8-15 ; lxxxiii. ; xxxii. 7-xxxv. ; lxxvi. The portions derived from B² are restored to what seems to have been their original order in that source.

LXXVII. 1. *From the greatest to the least.* A favourite expression in Jeremiah (cf. vi. 13 ; viii. 10 ; xxxi. 34 ; xlii. 1, 8 ; xliv. 12 ; 4 Ezra xii. 40). Only in these it runs : "From the least to the greatest."

2. The twelve tribes which are here mentioned are treated of in their two main divisions in verse 4. Cf. lxxviii. 4 ; lxxxiv. 3.

3. *A law.* See xv. 5, note.

4. *Upon you. I.e.* the 2½ tribes = "the former" in the next line.

Upon them. The 9½ tribes — "the latter" in the next line.

the former, and the latter also He gave into captivity,
and left not a residue of them.   5. And behold! ye
are here with me.   6. If therefore ye direct your
ways aright, ye also will not depart as your brethren
departed, but they will come to you.   7. For He is
merciful whom ye worship, and He is gracious in
whom ye hope, and He is true, so that He shall do
(you) good and not evil.   8. Lo! have ye not seen
what has befallen Zion?   9. Or do ye perchance think
that the place had sinned, and that on this account it
was overthrown, or that the land had wrought foolishness, and that therefore it was delivered up?   10.
And know ye not that on account of you who did sin,
that which sinned not was overthrown, and, on account
of those who wrought wickedly, that which wrought
not foolishness was delivered up to (its) enemies."   11.
And the whole people answered and said unto me: "So

Hath not left a residue of them.
I.e. of the 9½ tribes. This denies
the Samaritan claim.

5. Cf. lxxx. 5 ; 4 Ezra xiv. 33.
4 Ezra xiv. 30-33 seems to be dependent on lxxvii. 3-6. Those who are
left with Baruch are a remnant of
the 2½ tribes.

6. *As your brethren departed.*
"The brethren" here embrace the 2½
tribes, and so we interpret the subsequent words, "and they will come
to you." On the return of the
9½ tribes see note on lxxviii. 7.

7. *Do (you) good and not evil.*
Cf. Jer. xxi. 10 ; Amos ix. 4.

8. =xliv. 5. Cf. x. 7 ; xiii. 3 ;
lxxix. 1.

9. It was not the place that
sinned. Hence it was destroyed by
the hands of angels before it was
delivered over to the king of Baby-

lon, lest he should glory over it.
Cf. v.-viii., lxxx. ; see note on
lxvii. 6.

10. Observe that the fall of Jerusalem is here attributed not only
to the sins of the 2½ tribes but also
of the 9½. This view appears first
in Jer. xi. 17 : "For the Lord of
hosts that planted thee hath pro-
nounced evil against thee, because
of the evil of the house of Israel
and of the house of Judah." Cf.
Bar. ii. 26 καὶ ἔθηκας τὸν οἶκον οὗ
ἐπεκλήθη τὸ ὄνομά σου ἐπ' αὐτῷ,
ὡς ἡ ἡμέρα αὕτη, διὰ πονηρίαν οἴκου
Ἰσραὴλ καὶ οἴκου Ἰούδα. Assumpt.
Moyseos, iii. 5, where the two tribes
say to the ten : "justus et sanctus
Dominus, quia enim vos peccastis,
et nos pariter abducti sumus vobis-
cum. Cf. also Targ. Jon. on Isa.
liii. 5.

far as we can recall the good things which the Mighty One has done unto us, we do recall them; and those things which we do not remember He in His mercy knows. 12. Nevertheless, do this for us thy people: write also to our brethren in Babylon an epistle of doctrine and a scroll of good tidings, that thou mayest confirm them also before thou dost depart from us. 13. For the shepherds of Israel have perished, and the lamps which gave light are extinguished, and the fountains have withheld their stream whence we used to drink. 14. And we are left in the darkness, and amid the briers of the forest, and the thirst of the wilderness." 15. And I answered and said unto them: "Shepherds and lamps and fountains came (to us) from the law: and though we depart, yet the law abideth. 16. If therefore ye have respect to the law, and are intent upon wisdom, a lamp will not be wanting, and a shepherd will not fail, and a fountain will not dry up. 17. Nevertheless, as ye said unto me, I will write also unto your brethren in Babylon,

12. *To our brethren in Babylon, i.e.* the 2½ tribes. Cf. verse 19; lxxxv. 6. Observe that the writer does not conceive here of Jeremiah being at Babylon. If he had, he would have directed the letter to him. In the Rest of the Words of Baruch, on the other hand, the writer, conceiving Jeremiah to be in Babylon, directs to him the letter intended for the exiles there. This letter (cf. lxxvii. 17, 19; lxxxv. 6) to the 2½ tribes is lost.

Good tidings. Cf. xlvi. 6.

Depart. This refers to an ordinary death (cf. xliii. 2, note; see also xiii. 3, note; lxxviii. 5; lxxxiv. 1).

14. *We are left in darkness.* xlvi. 2; cf. 4 Ezra xiv. 20.

Briers. The text is ⳩ⲟ = ὕλη, which is the LXX. rendering of שמיר in Isa. x. 17. I have supposed a similar rendering here. Or ὕλη may be a rendering of עץ = "trees," and this a corruption of עצ = "thorns." Something is wrong.

15. *The law.* See xv. 5, note.

16. *Shepherd.* The text reads ܪܥܝܢܐ = "mind," which Ceriani has rightly emended into ܪܥܝܐ = "shepherd."

and I will send by means of men, and I will write in like manner to the nine tribes and a half, and send by means of a bird." 18. And it came to pass on the one and twentieth day in the eighth month that I, Baruch, came and sat down under the oak under the shadow of the branches, and no man was with me, but I was alone. 19. And I wrote these two epistles : one I sent by an eagle to the nine and a half tribes ; and the other I sent to those that were at Babylon by means of three men. 20. And I called the eagle, and spake these words unto it : 21. "The Most High hath made thee that thou shouldst be higher than all birds. 22. And now go and tarry not in (any) place, nor enter a nest, nor settle upon any tree, till thou hast passed over the breadth of the many waters of the river Euphrates, and hast gone to the people that dwell there, and cast down to them this epistle. 23. Remember, moreover, that, at the time of the deluge, Noah received from a dove the fruit of the olive, when he sent it forth from the ark. 24. Yea, also the ravens ministered to Elijah, bearing him food, as they had been commanded. 25. Solomon also, in the time

17. *A bird.* This is an eagle (cf. ver. 20). It is worth observing that whereas an eagle carries this letter to the 9½ tribes here, in the Rest of the Words of Baruch vii. it is an eagle that carries Baruch's letter to Jeremiah in Babylon.

18. *The oak.* See vi. 1, note ; cf. 4 Ezra xiv. 1.

21. Cf. Rest of Words of Baruch vii. 3 : "Elect above all the birds of heaven."

22. The 9½ tribes were carried away to Assyria and placed in Halah, and in Habor, on the river of Gozan (2 Kings xvii. 6). Their abode, according to 4 Ezra xiii. 40, 45, was Arzareth, *i.e.* ארץ אחרת of Deut. xxix. 28 ; Joseph. *Ant.* xi. 5, 2.

23. Cf. Gen. viii. 11 ; Rest of Words of Baruch vii. 10 : "Be like the dove which three times brought back word to Noah."

24. Cf. 1 Kings xvii. 6.

of his kingdom, whithersoever he wished to send or
seek for anything, commanded a bird (to go thither),
and it obeyed him as he commanded it.   26. And
now let it not weary thee, and turn not to the right
hand nor to the left, but fly and go by a direct way,
that thou mayest preserve the command of the Mighty
One, according as I said unto thee."

26. Cf. Rest of Words vii. 12.

THE EPISTLE OF BARUCH WHICH HE WROTE TO THE NINE AND A HALF TRIBES

LXXVIII. These are the words of that epistle which Baruch the son of Neriah sent to the nine and a half tribes, which were across the river Euphrates, in which these things were written. 2. Thus saith Baruch the son of Neriah to the brethren carried into captivity: "Mercy and peace." 3. I bear in mind, my brethren, the love of Him who created us, who loved

LXXVIII. 1. *The nine and a half tribes.* In this book the tribes of Israel carried away by the king of Assyria are, except in i. 2, always so designated (cf. lxii. 5; lxxvii. 19). In 4 Ezra xiii. 40 they are called "the ten tribes" only in the Latin Version, but "the nine and a half tribes" in the Syriac and Arabic Versions; in Asc. Isa. iii. 2 and

in the Ethiopic Version of 4 Ezra xiii. 40 they are called the "nine tribes."

2. *Mercy and peace.* 1 Tim. i. 2.

3. It is noteworthy that in the genuine parts of B[1] in chaps. lxxvi.-lxxxvii. Baruch speaks frequently in the first person sing. (see lxxvii. 1, 5, 11, 15, 17-20, 26; lxxviii. 3,

---

of Baruch the scribe'; *k*P, 'the Epistle of Baruch'; *mn*, 'the first Epistle of Baruch.'

LXXVIII. 1. ܘܠܝܢ ܗܠܝܢ 'these are,' *c*; ܘܗܠܝܢ 'and these,' *abdeghiw*P; *f*, ܗܠܝܢ. ܗܝ ܕܐܓܪܬܐ; 'of that Epistle,' *c*; wrongly om. by *abdefghiw*P. ܕܒܗ̇ܝܢ *abcgh*; *defw*P, ܕܒܗܝܢ. ܦܪܬ 'Euphrates,' *abdefghiw*P. *c* om.

2. ܗܘܘ ܘܕܐܬܓܠܝܘ *c*; *abdefhiw*P, ܗܘܘ ܘܕܐܬܓܠܝܘ; *g*, ܗܘܘ ܘܕܐܬܓܠܝܘ. ܫܠܡܐ 'and peace,' *abdefghiw*P; *c.* reads ܫܠܡܐ ܢܗܘܐ ܠܟܘܢ 'and peace be unto you.'

3. ܕܒܪܢ; 'who created us,' *abdefghil*w*P; *c* wrongly ܕܒܪܝܢ;

ܐܓܪܬܐ ܕܒܪܘܟ ܒܪ LXXVIII.
ܢܪܝܐ. ܕܟܬܒ ܠܬܫܥܐ ܫܒܛܝܢ

1 ܘܦܠܓܗ̇. ܗܠܝܢ ܐܢܘܢ
ܦܬܓܡܐ ܕܐܓܪܬܐ
ܗܝ ܕܫܕܪ ܒܪܘܟ ܒܪ ܢܪܝܐ
ܠܬܫܥܐ ܫܒܛܝܢ ܘܦܠܓܗ̇.
ܗܠܝܢ ܕܐܝܬܝܗܘܢ ܗܘܘ
ܠܥܒܪܗ ܕܢܗܪܐ. ܕܒܗ̇ ܕܟܬܝܒܝܢ
2 ܗܘܘ ܒܗ̇ ܗܠܝܢ. ܗܟܢܐ
ܐܡܪ ܒܪܘܟ ܒܪ ܢܪܝܐ.
ܠܐܚܐ ܕܐܫܬܒܝܘ. ܪ̈ܚܡܐ
ܘܫܠܡܐ.
3 ܡܬܕܟܪ ܐܢܐ ܐܚܝ ܠܚܘܒܐ
ܕܗܘ ܕܒܪܝܢ ܕܐܣܪܢ ܚܕ

For some account of the MSS. *abcdefghiklmn* see the General Introduction.

Title.—I have here given *c*, though what the title was is uncertain. *a* reads ܠܘܬ ܐܓܪܬܐ ܩܕܡܝܬܐ ܕܒܪܘܟ ܣܦܪܐ ܕܟܬܒ ܥܠ ܝܕ ܢܫܪܐ ܠܬܫܥܐ ܫܒ̈ܛܝܢ; so *g*, but that it om. ܥܠ ܝܕ, and *b*, but that it om. ܠܘܬ, ܩܕܡܝܬܐ and ܥܠ ܝܕ. *di* give ܠܘܬ ܐܓܪܬܐ ܩܕܡܝܬܐ ܕܒܪܘܟ ܣܦܪܐ ܡܫܠܡܘܢ ܕܐ; so w, but that it om. ܠܘܬ and ܕ before ܐ, and *ef*, but that they om. ܠܘܬ and ܕܐ ܡܫܠܡܘܢ. *l*, ܐܓܪܬܐ ܩܕܡܝܬܐ ܕܒܪܘܟ ܒܪ ܢܪܝܐ 'the first Epistle of Baruch, the son of Neriah'; *h*, 'the Epistle

us from of old, and never hated us, but above all educated us.   4. And truly I know that behold all we the twelve tribes are bound by one chain, inasmuch as we are born from one father.   5. Wherefore I have been the more careful to leave you the words of this epistle before I die, that ye may be comforted regarding the evils which have come upon you, and that ye may be grieved also regarding the evil that has befallen your brethren : and again, also, that ye may justify His judgment which He has decreed against you that ye should be carried away captive—for what ye have suffered is disproportioned to what ye have done—in order that, at the last times, ye may be found

---

4, 5 ; lxxx. 7 ; lxxxi. 2, 4 ; lxxxii. 1 ; lxxxiv. 1, 6, 7 ; lxxxvi. 3 ; lxxxvii.) In the interpolated portions this is not so.

4. *Twelve tribes.*   lxxvii. 2 ; lxxxiv. 3.

5. *Before I die.*   See xiii. 3, note.

Justify. See xxi. 9, note. Cf. Ps. li. 4 ; Dan. ix. 14 ; Baruch ii. 9.

For what ye . . . done is parenthetical.   Cf. lxxix. 2.

That in the last times, etc. These words refer to the return of the 9½ tribes (see note on ver. 7).

---

4. ‏ܗܢ‏, 'that behold,' *abdefghi*wp; *c* wrongly ‏ܕܠܐ‏ ' that not.'
‏ܣܠܝ ܡܚܡܡܝ‏ *bcg* ; *adefh*iwp, ‏ܡܚܡܝܠ‏ .

5. ‏ܗܢܐ‏ ‏ܠܐܝ̈ܢ‏ *abdefghi*wp; *c* trs. ‏ܠܥ‏ *def*iwp om. ‏ܡܚܐܠܒܡܐ‏ *abdefghil*wp; *c*, ‏ܠܣܐܚܠ‏ . ‏ܠܒܣܚ‏ ‏ܕܝܢܡܚ ܠ‏ 'evil that has befallen,' *abdefghi*wp; *c*, ‏ܚܢܡ ܕ‏ ‏ܠܒܢܚ‏ 'evils that have befallen.' ‏ܐܟ ܡܡ ܠܣܘ‏ ‏ܡܡ ܕ‏ *abdefghil*wp ; *c*, ‏ܠܥܣܘ ܕ‏ ‏ܡܡ‏ . ‏ܕܠܐܒܠܕܝ‏ , *a* by a clerical error gives ‏ܠܐܒܠ‏ܘ‏ . ‏ܕܡܣܐܠܘ‏ *acdh* ; *befgi*, ‏ܕܒܒܡܐܠܘ‏ . *c* ‏ܡܠܐ‏ ; *abdefghi*wp, ‏ܡܚܠܥ‏ . ‏ܡܣܚ‏ *ch* ; *b*, ‏ܡܥܡ‏ .

ܩܝܡܢ . ܘܕܢܐ ܡܥܒܕܠܟܘܢ
ܗܫܐ . ܐܢܐ ܝܬܝܪܐܝܬ ܙܕܐ
4 ܗܘܐ ܠܝ . ܘܝܬܝܪܐܝܬ ܡܢܗ
ܐܠܐ ܕܗܘܐ ܐܬܐܣܪܢ ܟܠܢ
ܬܪܥܣܪ ܫܒ̈ܛܝܢ ܒܚܕ
ܐܣܘܪܐ . ܕܐܝܟ ܕܡܢ
ܚܕ ܐܒܐ ܡܬܝܠܕܝܢ ܚܢܢ .
5 ܡܛܠ ܗܢܐ ܝܬܝܪܐܝܬ
ܐܬܒܛܠܬ ܠܝ ܕܐܫܒܘܩ
ܠܟܘܢ . ܡ̈ܠܝܗ ܕܐܓܪܬܐ
ܗܕܐ . ܩܕܡ ܡܐ
ܕܐܡܘܬ . ܕܬܗܘܘܢ ܡܬܒܝܐܝܢ
ܥܠ ܒ̈ܝܫܬܐ ܕܡܛܝܢܟܘܢ .
ܘܬܬܒܝܐܘܢ ܬܘܒ ܥܠ
ܒ̈ܝܫܬܐ ܕܓܕܫ ܠܐܚ̈ܝܟܘܢ .
ܬܘܒ ܕܝܢ ܐܦ ܕܬܕܝܢܘܢ
ܕܝܢܗ ܕܗܘ ܕܓܙܪ ܥܠܝܟܘܢ
ܕܬܫܬܒܘܢ . ܒܝܕ ܗܘ ܓܝܪ
ܡܕܡ ܕܚܫܬܘܢ ܡܢ ܡܐ
ܕܥܒܕܬܘܢ . ܡܛܠ ܕܒܚܪ̈ܬܐ
ܐܫܬܘܐ ܬܬܚܫܒܘܢ ܫܘܝܢ

who created me.' ܝܬܝܪܐܝܬ 'above all,' *abcgh*; *defiwP* om.
ܙܕܐ *acdefi*; *bh*, ܙܪܐ.

worthy of your fathers.   6. Therefore if ye consider
those things which ye have now suffered for your
good, that ye may not finally be condemned and tormented, then ye will receive eternal hope; if above
all ye destroy from your heart vain error, on account
of which ye departed hence.   7. For if ye so do these
things, He will continually remember you, He who
alway promised on our behalf to those who were
more excellent than we, that He will never forget or
forsake us, but with much mercy will gather together
again those who were dispersed.

6. *Departed hence. I.e.* from
Palestine.

7. *Those who were more excellent.*
The patriarchs.

With much mercy. In 4 Ezra
xiv. 34, 35 the righteous are to
obtain mercy after death.   Here
God's mercy will be shown to Israel
by causing them to return from
their captivity.

*Gather together . . . those who were
dispersed.* Cf. lxxvii. 6 ; lxxxiv. 2,
8, 10. The promise that God would
turn again the captivity of Israel is
frequently made in the O. T. (cf.
Deut. xxx. 3 ; Amos ix. 11-15 ; Isa.
xi. 12 ; Jer. xxiii. 8 ; xxix. 14 ;
xxxi. 10 ; xxxii. 37 ; Ezek. xxxvii.
21-28 ; Zeph. iii. 19, 20 ; also in
Bar. iv. 36, 37 ; v. 5-7 ; Pss. Sol.
xi. ; 2 Macc. ii. 18).   The prediction of the return of the exiles
is found also in Tob. xiii. 13 ;
Eth. En. lvii. 1, 2 ; xc. 33 ; *Or.
Sibyl.* ii. 170-173 ; 4 Ezra xiii. 12,
39-47.   Either as in the preceding passages God was to procure

their return directly ; or else indirectly (*a*) through the agency of
the nations who should carry back
to Jerusalem the dispersed as offerings (cf. Isa. xlix. 22 ; lx. 4, 9 ;
lxvi. 20 ; Pss. Sol. xvii. 34) ; (*b*) by
means of the Messiah (cf. Pss. Sol.
xvii. 28, 30, 50 ; Targ. Jon. on Jer.
xxxiii. 13) ; (*c*) by means of Elijah
(cf. Ecclus. xlviii. 10). These different methods are not mutually exclusive.   In the presence of this
strongly attested hope of the restoration of the dispersed it is strange to
find it positively denied by R.
Akiba (*Sanh.* x. 3) : " The ten tribes
will nevermore return ; for it is
said of them (Deut. xxix. 28) : ' He
will cast them into another land, as
this day.'   Hence as this day passes
away and does not return, so shall
they pass away and not return.   So
R. Akiba."

The return of the exiles in B[1]
accords well with the rebuilding of
Jerusalem which is elsewhere expected in B[1].   See i. 4 ; vi. 9, notes.

6 ܐܬܒ̈ܩܘܢ . ܗܟܝܠ ܗܘܐ
ܐܘ ܬܬܚܫܒܘܢ ܗܠܝܢ
ܕܠܛܒ̈ܬܟܘܢ ܚܫܬܘܢ ܗܫܐ .
ܕܠܐ ܠܚܪܬܐ ܬܬܕܝܢܘܢ
ܘܬܫܬܢܩܘܢ . ܗܝܕܝܢ
ܬܣܒܪܘܢ ܣܒܪܐ ܕܠܥܠܡ .
ܐܢܗܘ ܕܡܬܝܪܐܝܬ ܬܥܒܪܘܢ
ܡܢ ܠܒܟܘܢ ܛܘܥܝܬܐ
ܣܪܝܩܬܐ . ܗ̇ܝ ܕܡܛܠܬܗ̇ ܗ̇
7 ܐܬܕܒ̈ܪܬܘܢ ܡܢ ܗܪܟܐ . ܐܘ
ܓܝܪ ܬܥܒܕܘܢ ܗܠܝܢ ܗܟܢܐ .
ܐܡܝܢܐܝܬ ܡܕܟܪ ܗܘ
ܠܟܘܢ . ܗ̇ܘ ܕܒܟܠ̈ ܙܒܢ
ܐܫܬܘܕܝ ܚܠܦܝܢ ܠܐܝܠܝܢ
ܕܡܝܬܪܝܢ ܡܢܢ . ܕܠܐ ܠܥܠܡ
ܢܛܥܝܢ ܐܘ ܢܫܒܩܢ .
ܐܠܐ ܒܪ̈ܚܡܐ ܣܓܝܐ̈ܐ
ܢܟܢܫ ܬܘܒ

6. ܕܠܛܒ̈ܬܟܘܢ, *c*; *bdefgil*WP, ܕܠܛܒܬܟܘܢ ܗܘ; *ah* give conflate reading, ܕܠܛܒ̈ܬܟܘܢ ܗܘ.

7. ܡܕܟܪ, *c* adds ܗܘ. ܢܛܥܝܢ ܐܘ ܢܫܒܩܢ 'will not forget or forsake us,' *abdefghim*WP; *c*, ܢܛܥܐ ܐܘ ܢܫܒܘܩ ܙܪܥܢ 'will not forget or forsake our seed.' ܠܐܝܠܝܢ 'those,' *abdefgh*WP; *c*, ܠܟܠܗܘܢ ܐܝܠܝܢ 'all those.'

LXXIX. Now, my brethren, learn first what befell Zion: how that Nebuchadnezzar king of Babylon came up against us. 2. For we have sinned against Him who made us, and we have not kept the commandments which He commanded us, yet He hath not chastened us as we deserved. 3. For what befell you we also suffered in a pre-eminent degree, for it befell us also.

LXXX. And now, my brethren, I make known unto you that when the enemy had surrounded the city, the angels of the Most High were sent, and they overthrew the fortifications of the strong wall, and they

LXXIX. 1. *What befell Zion.* See lxxvii. 8, note.
2. *We have sinned*, etc. Cf. Baruch i. 17, 18.
Chastened. Cf. i. 5 ; xiii. 10.
As we deserved. Cf. lxxviii. 5.

LXXX. This chapter closely resembles and implies vi.-viii., but lxvii. proceeds upon different presuppositions. See lxvii. 6, note.
1. *Fortifications of the strong wall.* Cf. vii. 1.

---

*bdefghi*wP. *bdefghi*wP read ܟ ܐܘܕܥ ܥܟܡ ܘܡܡܝ ܕܚ̣ܣܐ ܐܦ ܠܐܬܐ 'but likewise that which has befallen you has overtaken us : in a pre-eminent degree have we suffered also'; so also *a*, but that it inserts ܘ before ܠܐܬܐ, a conflate reading as in lxxviii. 6: all readings seem corrupt. ܚܣܘ *ce*; *bh*, ܚܣܘ; *fi*, ܚܣܘ̣. ܡܟܝ *abg*; *cdh*, ܟܡܢ̣; *fi*, ܟܡܢܢ̣; wP, ܟܡܢܢ̣ 'our calamity.'

LXXX. 1. ܥܕܘܝܠ ܐܠ ܚܣܘ̣ ܘ 'I make known unto you that,' *abdefghi*wP; *c* wrongly om. ܘܡܣܚܩ *abcdfghilm*; *e*wP om. ס 'and.' ܫܘܪ̈ܐ 'fortifications,' *abdefghilm*wP; *c,*

LXXIX. 1 ܠܐܡܠܟܝܢ ܕܐܬܒܪܘ . — . ܡܛܠ
ܐܢܫ ܕܗܘܝܬܘܢ ܚܝܒܝܢ
ܠܘܩܒܠ ܕܡܪܝܐ ܚܛܝܢ ܗ̇ܘ
ܠܒܪܘܝܢ . ܕܣܠܩ ܥܠܝܢ
ܢܒܘܟܕܢܨܪ ܡܠܟܐ ܕܒܒܠ .
2 ܚܛܝܢ ܓܝܪ ܠܗܘ ܕܒܪܢ .
ܘܠܐ ܢܛܪܢ ܦܘܩܕܢܐ
ܕܦܩܕܢ ܐܠܐ ܐܦ ܠܐ
ܪܕܢ ܐܝܟ ܕܚܛܗܝܢ ܗ̈ܘܝܢ .
3 ܡܛܠ ܓܝܪ ܕܚܛܗܝܢ
⁘ ܡܬܡܪܬ ܠܥܠ ܢܦܫ .
.. ܐܦ ܠܢ ܓܝܪ ܚܛܝܢ ܀

LXXX. 1 ܘܗܫܐ ܐܚ̈ܝ ܡܘܕܥ ܐܢܐ ܠܟܘܢ ܕܟܕ ܚܕܪܘܗ̇
ܒܥܠܕܒܒܐ ܠܡܕܝܢܬܐ .
ܐܫܬܕܪܘ ܡܠܐܟܐ
ܕܡܪܘܡܐ ܘܥܩܪܘ ܫܘ̈ܪܝܗ̇ܝܢ

LXXIX. 1. ܠܘܩܒܠ *abdefghi*WP; *c*, ܩܕܡ. ܕܡܪܝܐ *abcgh*; *defi*WP, ܡܪܝܐ. ܢܒܘܟܕܢܨܪ *cfhi*; *bg*, ܢܒܘܟܘܕܢܨܪ.

2. ܚܛܝܢ *bdfghi*WP; *ac*, ܚܛܝܢܢ. ܕܒܪܢ *b(ad ?)efghi*WP; *c*, ܕܒܪ̈ܢ. ܦܘܩܕܢ̈ܐ 'commandments,' *ch*WP; *abdefgil*, ܦܘܩܕܢܐ 'commandment.'

2—3. ܡܬܡܪܬ . . . . ܠܐ 'yet He hath not chastened . . . . degree'; so *c*, save that I have om. ܘ before ܡܬܡܪܬ, with

destroyed the firm iron corners, which could not be
rooted out.   2. Nevertheless, they hid all the vessels of
the sanctuary, lest the enemy should get possession
of them.   3. And when they had done these things,
they delivered thereupon to the enemy the overthrown
wall, and the plundered house, and the burnt temple,
and the people who were overcome because they were
delivered up, lest the enemy should boast and say:
" Thus by force have we been able to lay waste even
the house of the Most High in war."   4. Your brethren

Its . . . corners. Cf. vi. 4 ; viii. 1.
2. *Hid all the vessels.* Cf. vi. 7,
8. The ultimate motive for hiding
the holy vessels can only be that
given in vi. 9.
All the vessels of the sanctuary.
The Syriac gives the impossible
text, "the vessels of the vessels."
The corruption becomes obvious
when we retranslate into Hebrew.
Thus the words = כלים מכלי הקרש
corrupted from כל־כלי הקרש. I have
emended accordingly.
*Lest the enemy should get posses-
sion of them.*   The Syriac = "lest
they should be polluted by the
enemies." But the parallel passage

in vi. 8, "So that strangers may not
get possession of them," expresses
the idea we should find here ; for
the object with which the vessels
are hidden is their preservation for
use in the restored temple (vi. 7-10).
Further, we find that the corrupt text
which = פן יחלו מאריבים becomes by
the addition of a single letter
פן יחלם אויבים ="lest the enemy
should get possession of them."
3. *Plundered house, and the burnt
temple.* Cf. v. 3 ; vi. 6, 7.
Should boast. Cf. vii. 1. Contrast lxvii. 2, 7.
4. Cf. viii. 5. Observe that there
is no mention here of Jeremiah

' who were overcome,' *abdefgiw*P; so *h*, but that it gives the
plural; *c*, ܘܟܠܐ . ܘ ܡܟܠܐ 'because,' *abcgh*; *defiw*P, ܘ ܡܟܠܐ
' when.' ܘܐܡܠܟܡ *b* reads ܘܐܡܠܟܡܘ . ܐܡܟܘ ܡܠܝ
b ; *adefghiw*P, ܡܟܘܡܠ ; *c*, ܡܟܘܡܠ . ܟܡܠܐ ' by force,'
*abdefghiw*P; *c* wrongly om. ܟܡܘܠܐ *bdefghiw*P; *a*, ܟܡܘܠܐ .

ܕܫܘܪܐ ܒܥܓܠ . ܘܗܦܟܘ
ܘܐܫܝܬܐ ܫܪܝܪܬܐ ܕܩܘܕܫܐ .
ܗܠܝܢ ܕܠܐ ܡܫܬܡܛܝܢ ܗܘܘ

2 ܕܢܬܚܒܠܘܢ . ܛܫܘ ܕܝܢ ܡܐܢܐ ܡܢ ܡܐܢܐ
ܕܩܘܕܫܐ ܠܡܛܫܘ . ܐܝܟ ܕܠܐ
ܢܬܛܡܐܘܢ ܡܢ ܒܥܠܕܒܒܐ .

3 ܘܟܕ ܥܒܕܘ ܗܠܝܢ . ܗܝܕܝܢ
ܐܫܠܡܘ ܠܗܘܢ ܠܒܥܠܕܒܒܐ ܫܘܪܐ .
ܟܕ ܫܚܝܦ ܘܒܝܬܐ ܟܕ
ܒܙܝܙ . ܘܗܝܟܠܐ ܟܕ ܡܘܩܕ .
ܘܥܡܐ ܕܐܙܕܟܝ ܡܛܠ
ܕܐܫܬܠܡ . ܕܠܐ ܢܗܘܘܢ
ܡܫܬܒܗܪܝܢ ܒܥܠܕܒܒܐ
ܘܢܐܡܪܘܢ ܕܗܢܘܢ ܐܬܟܒܫܘ ܚܝܠܐ ܒܚܝܠܐ
ܒܩܪܒܐ ܕܐܦ ܠܒܝܬܗ
ܕܥܫܝܢܐ ܢܨܚܘ ܒܩܪܒܐ .

ܚܘܣܢܗ 'fortification.' ܘܗܦܟܘ *abdefghiwP*; *c*, ܘܗܦܟ. ܘܐܫܝܬܐ *abdefgiwP*; *c*, ܘܐܫܝܬܗ. ܫܪܝܪܬܐ *abcgh*; *defgiwP*, ܫܪܝܪܬܐ.

2. ܡܐܢܐ ܡܢ ܡܐܢܐ ܕ 'some vessels of the vessels,' *abdefghiwP*; *c*, ܡܐܢܝܢ. ܢܬܛܡܐܘܢ 'should be polluted,' *abcdfghi*; *d*, ܢܬܛܡܐܘܢ; *ewP*, ܢܬܛܡܘܢ.

3. *f* om. ܘܟܕ .... ܠܒܥܠܕܒܒܐ through hmt. ܥܒܕܘ *abc'deghiwP*; *c*, ܥܒܕܘ. ܠܗܘܢ *abdeghiwP*; *c* om. ܕܐܙܕܟܝ

also have they bound and led away to Babylon, and
have caused them to dwell there. 5. But we have
been left here, being very few. 6. This is the tribulation about which I wrote to you. 7. For assuredly
I know that the habitation of Zion gave you consolation: so far as ye knew that it was prospered (your
consolation) was greater than the tribulation which ye
endured in having departed from it.

LXXXI. But regarding consolation, hear ye the
word. 2. For I was mourning regarding Zion, and
I prayed for mercy from the Most High, and I said:

though, according to x. 5, he went
with the captivity to Babylon. See
x. 2, note.

5. From Jer. xlii. 2, where the
words are spoken of the remnant in
Jerusalem (cf. Deut. iv. 27; Baruch
ii. 13). The two latter passages
deal with the remnant among the
Gentiles.

LXXXI. As in lxxx. 7 the 9½
tribes had consolation in the fact
that Jerusalem prospered and were
proportionately grieved on its over-

throw, Baruch has now a word of
consolation for them touching Zion
(lxxxi. 1) ; for, when in his grief over
it (lxxxi. 2), he asked God how long
should this desolation last (lxxxi.
3), God, to give him consolation,
vouchsafed a revelation as to the
mysteries of the times and removed
his anguish (lxxxi. 4).

1. *Regarding consolation.* This
word refers to the restoration
of Zion. Cf. xliv. 7; lxxxi. 4;
lxxxii. 1.

---

*bdefghil*wP ; *ac*, ܐ̈ܘܢܬ̈ܐ 'habitations.'   ܡܢ ܠܘܬ '(your
consolation) was greater than,' *abcdeghi* ; *f*wP, ܐܠܘܬܐ ܣܟ,
which requires the following rendering: 'the more assured ye
were that it prospered, the greater was the tribulation.'

LXXXI. 1. ܒܘܝܐ *abcefghi*; *d*wP, ܒܘܠܒ.

2. ܘܟܣܐ *c*; *abdefghi*wP, ܘܟܣܐ.

1 LXXXI.

4.] *acdefhiwp*; *bg,* *bcdefghilwp*; *a,*
. For *l* reads *abc*;
defgiwp, ; *h,* .

5. *abcg*; *defhwp,* *bc*; *adfhwp* om.

6. *cefghi*; *b,* .

7. *abcdfghi*; *lwp,* 'habitation,'

3. "How long will these things endure for us ? and will these evils come upon us always?"   4. And the Mighty One did according to the multitude of His mercies, and the Most High according to the greatness of His compassion, and He revealed unto me the word, that I might receive consolation, and He showed me visions that I should not again endure anguish, and He made known to me the mystery of the times, and the advent of the hours He showed me.

LXXXII. Therefore, my brethren, I have written to you, that ye may comfort yourselves regarding the multitude of your tribulations.   2. For know ye that our Maker will assuredly avenge us on all our enemies, according to all that they have done to us, also that

4. *The multitude . . . compassion.* Cf. Dan. ix. 18 ; Bar. ii. 27 ; cf. lxxvi. 6.
Consolation. See verse 1.
Mystery of the times. Cf. lxxxv. 8.

LXXXII. I am doubtful as to whether lxxxii. 2-9 belongs to B[1] or B[2]. I am inclined to believe the latter. But the evidence is not decisive either way.

---

4. ܘܟܠܡ 'and ... did,' c ; *abdefghi*wp, ܘܟܠܡ 'who did.'
ܘܙܣܬܟܚܣܘܗܝ 'of His mercies,' *abcgh* ; *defi*wp, ܘܙܣܚܕܐ 'of mercies.' ܘܙܐܠܬܐ *abgh* ; *cdefil*wp, ܘܐܠܬܐ. ܐܙ|ܙ 'mystery,' *abdefgi*wp ; *ch*, ܐܙ|ܙ 'mysteries.'

LXXXII. 1. ܘܕܥܩܬܟ 'of your tribulations,' *abgh* ; *defi*wp, ܘܟܥܩܬܟ 'of your tribulation'; c, ܐܩܬܟ 'of tribulations.'
2. ܗܣܘܩܠܘ *abdfgh*wp ; c, ܠܗܣܘܘ. ܠܙܥ c ; *abefghlm*wp, ܠܙܥ ; *di* om. point.   ܠ 'us,' *abdefghilm*wp ; c om.   ܘܕܠ c ; *abdefghi*wp, ܠܣ.   ܠ 'to us'; c adds ܘܣ 'and in us,' against *abdefghi*wp.   ܠܐ *abdefghi*wp ; c, ܘ.   ܘܣ

3 ܥܕܡܡܬܐ ܘܐܬܪܓܙܬ . ܘܥܕܡܡܬܐ
ܠܐܡܬܟܠܢ ܗܠܝܢ ܡܩܦܢ
ܥܠܝܢ . ܘܒܒܠܒܘܠܝܢ ܐܬܝܢ ܒܟܠܝܢ
4 ܒܣܘܓܐܐ ܗܠܝܢ . ܘܒܥܝ
ܡܡܠܠܬܐ ܐܝܟ ܗܘܝܬ
ܕܬܡܝܗܘܬܗ . ܘܡܬܪܥܡܢܘ
ܐܝܟ ܣܘܓܐܐ ܕܚܢܢܗ .
ܘܓܠܐ ܠܝ ܡܠܬܐ ܐܝܟ
ܕܐܬܒܝܐ . ܘܚܘܝܢܝ
ܚܙܘܢܐ ܐܝܟ ܕܬܘܒ ܠܐ
ܐܬܬܥܝܩ . ܘܐܘܕܥܢܝ
ܐܪܙܐ ܕܙܒܢܐ . ܘܡܐܬܝܬܗܘܢ
LXXXII. 1 .. ܕܫܥܬܐ ܚܘܝܢܝ . ܐܚܝ ܡܟܝܠ
ܗܢܐ ܐܟܬܒܬ ܒܥܠܬ ܠܟܘܢ
ܕܐܝܟܢܐ ܬܬܒܝܐܘܢ ܡܢ ✤
2 ܣܘܓܐܐ ܕܥܩܬܟܘܢ . ܗܘ ܝܕܥܘܢ
ܕܝܢ ܡܬܒܥܢ ܕܥܒܕܢ ܦܪܥ ܠܢ
ܒܟܘܠ ܥܠ ܟܠܗܘܢ
ܒܥܠܕܒܒܝܢ . ܐܝܟ ܕܟܠ ܡܐ
ܕܥܒܕܘ ܠܢ . ܐܦ ܕܫܘܠܡܬ

3. ܕܥܕܡܡܬܐ ܠܐܡܬܟܠܢ ܗܠܝܢ 'how long . . . these things?' *abdefghilm*wP; *c*, ܕܗܠܝܢ ܥܕܡܐ ܠܐܫܬܘܠܡܬ '(will) these things ... to the end?' ܥܠܝܢ 'upon us,' *acdefhi*wP; *bg*, ܥܠܝ 'upon me.'

the consummation which the Most High will make is very nigh, and His mercy that is coming, and the consummation of His judgment, is by no means far off. 3. For lo! we see now the multitude of the prosperity of the Gentiles, though they act impiously, but they will be like a vapour. 4. And we behold the multitude of their power, though they do wickedly, but they will be made like unto a drop. 5. And we see the firmness of their might, though they resist the Mighty One every hour, but they will be accounted as spittle. 6. And we consider the glory of their greatness, though they do not keep the statutes of the Most High, but as smoke will they pass away. 7. And we meditate

3. *Like a vapour.* 4 Ezra vii. 61.

4. *Like unto a drop.* Isa. xl. 15; 4 Ezra vi. 56.

5. *Accounted as spittle.* Here certainly, and in 4 Ezra vi. 56, the text agrees with the LXX.; for in Isa. xl. 15 it has ὡς σίελος λογισθήσονται against the Hebrew יִטּוֹל כַּדַּק.

---

bg, ܚܙܝܢ ܚܢܢ. ܗܫܐ 'now,' *abdfghi*WP; *c* om. here as it has already inserted ܗܫܐ in place of ܗܘ; *e* om. ܗܫܐ ܚܙܝܢܢ ܣܘܓܐܐ. ܕܡܫܝܢܘܬܐ *c*; *abdgh*WP, ܕܡܫܝܢܘܬܗܘܢ; *efi*, ܕܡܫܝܢܘ̈ܬܗܘܢ.

4. ܘܣܟܝܢܢ *cdefgim*WP; *abh*, ܘܣܟܝܢ ܚܢܢ. ܠܢܛܘܦܬܐ 'unto a drop,' *abdefghil*WP; *c* wrongly ܠܛܢܦܘܬܐ 'unto pollution.'

5. ܘܚܙܝܢܢ *cdefgh*WP; *ab*, ܘܚܙܝܢ ܚܢܢ. ܫܘܪܪܗ 'firmness,' *abdefghi*WP; *c* wrongly ܫܪܪܗ 'truth.' ܫܥܐ 'hour,' *abdefghi*WP; *c* wrongly ܫܢܐ 'year.'

6. ܘܡܬܒܩܝܢܢ *cdefghi*WP; *ab*, ܘܡܬܒܩܝܢ ܚܢܢ. ܦܘܩܕ̈ܢܝܗܘܢ 'commands,' *abdefgh*WP; *c*, ܡܦܩ̈ܕܢܘܬܗܘܢ 'statutes.'

ܡܪܝܡ ܗܘ ܫܘܠܛܢܐ ܕܒܪܢ

ܡܪܝܡܐ ܘܪ̈ܚܡܘܗܝ

ܕܠܥܠܡ . ܘܠܐ ܗܘܐ

ܪ̈ܚܡܝܢ ܫܘܠܛܢܗ ܕܒܪܝܬܗ .

3 ܗܐ ܓܝܪ ܚܙܝܢܢ ܗܫܐ ܣܘܓܐܐ

ܕܡܬܓܘܣܘܬܐ ܕܥܡ̈ܡܐ

ܟܕ ܗܢܘܢ ܡܪܫܥܝܢ . ܐܠܐ

4 ܠܗܒܠܐ ܗܘ ܕܡܝܢ . ܘܡܫܬܪܚܝܢ

ܒܥܘܫܢܐ ܕܐܘܚܕܢܗܘܢ

ܟܕ ܗܢܘܢ ܡܚܒܠܝܢ . ܐܠܐ

5 ܠܢܘܛܦܬܐ ܢܬܕܡܘܢ . ܘܚܙܝܢܢ

ܥܘܙܐ ܕܚܝܠܗܘܢ . ܟܕ ܗܢܘܢ

ܠܘܩܒܠܗ ܚܝܠܬܢܐ ܩܝܡܝܢ

ܒܟܠ ܫܥܐ . ܐܠܐ ܐܝܟ

6 ܪܘܩܐ ܢܬܚܫܒܘܢ . ܘܡܬܚܫܒܝܢ

ܒܟܠ ܫܘܒܚܐ ܕܪܒܘܬܗܘܢ .

ܟܕ ܗܢܘܢ ܠܐ ܢܛܪܝܢ

ܦܘܩ̈ܕܢܘܗܝ ܕܡܪܝܡܐ . ܐܠܐ

ܐܝܟ ܬܢܢܐ ܕܥܒܪܝܢ .

acghWP; bdefi, ܗܘܐ. ܕܒܪܢ abcdefhiWP; bg, ܕܒܪ̈ܢ. ܫܘܠܛܢܗ c; abdefhilWP, ܫܘܠܛܢܐ.

3. ܗܐ 'lo!' abdefghiWP; c, ܗܫܐ 'now.' ܡܪܫܥܝܢ acdfhWP;

on the beauty of their gracefulness, though they have
to do with pollutions, but as grass that withers will
they fade away.　8. And we consider the strength of
their cruelty, though they remember not the end
(thereof), but as a wave that passes will they be broken.
9. And we remark the boastfulness of their might,
though they deny the beneficence of God, who gave
(it) to them, but they will pass away as a passing
cloud.

LXXXIII. =
B².

[LXXXIII. For the Most High will assuredly hasten
His times, and He will assuredly bring on His hours.
2. And He will assuredly judge those who are in His

7. *As grass*, etc. Isa. xl. 6, 7.

LXXXIII. This chapter seems
to belong to B². Thus the times
will be cut short (lxxxiii. 1, 6),
and everything brought into judgment (lxxxiii. 2, 3, 7); let not,
therefore, earthly interests engage
them (lxxxiii. 4), but let them fix
their thoughts on the promised
consummation (lxxxiii. 4, 5), and
devote themselves to their faith of
aforetime, lest to their captivity in
this world there should be added
torment in the next (lxxxiii. 8); for

the world passeth away with its
strength and its weakness, its virtues,
and its lusts (lxxxiii. 9-23).

The connection between lxxxiii.
and xx. is close. Cf. lxxxiii. 1, 6;
xx. 1; lxxxiii. 2; xx. 2; lxxxiii.
7; xx. 4. This chapter seems to
have formed originally part of
Baruch's address to the people
(xxxi. 3 - xxxii. 6; xliv. 8 - 15),
and to have followed immediately
on xliv. 8-15.

1. This and verse 6 are related to
xx. 1. Cf. liv. 1; Ep. Barn. iv. 3.

---

8. ܣܠܩ ܣܡܬܐܣܟ ‍c; *abdefghiw*P, ܣܡܬܐܣܟ. ܠܟܠ،

ܘܟܬܒ cdefhi; abg, ܘܟܬܒ، ܠܝ; WP give plural.

9. ܣ݈ܠܡܠܬܣܐܟ݈ܣ cdfghi; ab, ܣܠܡܠܬܣܐܟ݈ܣ; ewP,
ܣܠܡܠܬܐܟ݈ܣ. ܣܘܨܘܪܐ 'the boastfulness,' c; *abdefghiw*P,
ܣܘܨܘܪ 'the beauty.' ܗܘܢ ܘܓܠܗ 'of God—Him,' c; *abdefghiw*P,
ܘܗܢ 'of Him.'

LXXXIII. 2. ܣܥܝ ܢܘܝ 'will assuredly judge,' *acdefhiw*P;

7 ܘܢܚܫܘܒ ܥܠ ܫܘܦܪܐ
ܕܝܐܝܘܬܗܘܢ . ܗܝ ܕܗܘܢ
ܒܛܢ̈ܦܘܬܐ ܡܛܠ ܕܛܢܦܝܢ . ܐܠܐ
ܐܝܟ ܥܣܒܐ ܕܝܒܫܐ
8 ܢܐܒܕܘܢ . ܘܢܬܚܫܒ ܚܢܢ
ܥܠ ܥܘܫܢܐ ܕܥܫܝܢܘܬܗܘܢ .
ܗܝ ܕܗܘܢ ܚܙܬܐ ܠܐ
ܡܛܠ ܕܥܒܪܝܢ . ܐܠܐ ܐܝܟ
ܓܠܠܐ ܕܥܒܪ ܢܬܚܫܒܘܢ .
9 ܘܢܬܒܝܢܢ ܥܠ ܫܘܒܗܪܐ
ܕܚܝܠܗܘܢ . ܗܝ ܕܗܘܢ ܥܒܪܝܢ
ܒܡܫܘܚܬܗ ܕܐܠܗܐ ܗܘ
ܕܡܩܒܠ ܠܗܘܢ . ܐܠܐ ܐܝܟ
.. ܒܒܝܬܐ ܕܥܒܪܐ ܢܥܒܪܘܢ . ܫܠܡ .
LXXXIII. 1 ܡܣܪܗܒܐ ܓܝܪ ܡܣܪܗܒܘ
ܡܣܪܗܒ ܙܒܢܘܗܝ . ܘܡܬܝܬܝܢ
2 ܡܬܝܬܐ ܫܥܘܗܝ . ܘܕܝܢ
ܢܕܘܢ ܠܐܢܫܐ ܕܒܥܠܡܗ .

7. ܘܢܚܫܘܒ *abdefgi*WP; *bhl*, ܘܢܚܫܘܒ ܚܠܦ. ܕܝܐܝܘܬܗܘܢ 'of their gracefulness,' *c*; *abdefghil*WP, ܕܚܝܘܬܗܘܢ 'of their life.' ܒܛܢ̈ܦܘܬܐ 'with pollutions,' *c*; *abdefghil*WP, ܒܛܢܦܘܬܐ 'with pollution.'

world, and will visit in truth all things by means of all their hidden works. 3. And He will assuredly examine the secret thoughts, and that which is laid up in the secret chambers of all the members of man, and will make (them) manifest in the presence of all with reproof. 4. Let none therefore of these present things ascend into your hearts, but above all let us be expectant, because that which is promised to us will come. 5. And let us not now look unto the delights of the Gentiles in the present, but let us remember what has been promised to us in the end. 6. For the ends of the times and of the seasons and whatsoever is together with them will assuredly pass

2. *Visit.* See xx. 2, note.
3. See 4 Ezra xvi. 65. Cf. 1 Cor. iv. 5; also Heb. iv. 12; 1 Cor. xiv. 25.
4. *Let none therefore*, etc. Cf. Col. iii. 3: τὰ ἄνω φρονεῖτε.
That which is promised, etc. See xiv. 13, note; xxi. 25; xliv. 13.
6. See xx. 1, note.

---

which in all'; *dei*WP, ܕܒܟܠܗܘܢ. ܕܠܒܘܬܐ. ܕܒܪܢܫܐ 'of man,' *abdefghil*WP; *c*, ܕܒܪܘܫܥܐ 'which in wickedness.' ܟܠ ܐܢܫ *cdh*; *abgil*, ܟܠܢܫ.

4. ܡܟܝܠ, *bdefghi*WP add ܝܬܝܪ against *ac*. ܕܩܢܘ̈ܡܟ *cl*; *bgh*, ܕܡܬ̈ܩܢܟ. ܗܘ̇ *ach*WP; *bdegi*, ܗܘ; *f*, ܗܘ̣. ܠܢ 'to us,' *abdefghi*WP; *c* om.

5. ܗܫܐ 'now,' *abdfghi*WP; *c*. om. *e* om. ver. 5 through hmt. ܠܒܘ̈ܣܡܝܗܘܢ 'the delights,' *c*; *abdfghi*WP, ܠܒܘܣܡܗܘܢ 'the delight.' ܕܡܬ̈ܩܢܐ, *c* adds ܕܗܫܐ against *abdefghi*WP.

6. ܘܙܒ̈ܢܐ *bcdefghi*WP; *a*, ܘܙܒܢܐ. ܐܝܟ ܚܕܐ *c*; *abdefghi*WP, ܐܟܚܕܐ.

ܘܢܒܩܘܪ ܒܫܪܪܐ ܠܟܠܡܕܡ .
ܒܐܝܕܐ ܕܟܠ ܥܒ̈ܕܝܗܘܢ
3 ܕܟܣܝܬܐ ܘܡܒܚܢܘ
ܢܒܚܢ ܡܚܫܒ̈ܬܐ ܟܣ̈ܝܬܐ
ܘܟܠ ܕܒܬܘ̈ܢܐ . ܕܒܗܕܡܝܗܘܢ
ܗܕ̈ܡܐ ܕܒܪܢܫܐ ܢܦܩ .
ܘܢܓܠܐ ܩܕܡ ܟܠ ܐܢܫ
4 ܟܕ ܐܬܐ ܢܟܣ . ܡܟܝܠ ܠܐ
ܢܣܩ ܥܠ ܠܒܟܘܢ ܡܕܡ
܀ ܡܢ ܗܠܝܢ ܕܩܝܡܝܢ . ܐܠܐ
ܝܬܝܪܐܝܬ ܢܣܟܐ . ܡܛܠ
ܕܐܬܐ ܗܘ ܡܠܝܟ
5 ܕܡܠܝܟ ܠܢ . ܘܠܐ ܢܚܘܪ ܗܫܐ
ܒܒ̈ܘܣܡܝܗܘܢ ܕܥ̈ܡܡܐ
. ܐܠܐ ܢܬܕܟܪ ܡܠܝܟ
6 ܕܠܚܪܬܐ ܡܠܝܟ ܠܢ . ܡܛܠ
ܕܡܫܠܡܝܢ ܙܒ̈ܢܝܢ ܠܫܘܠ̈ܡܝܗܘܢ
. ܕܥܕ̈ܢܐ ܘܙܒ̈ܢܐ . ܘܟܘܠ
ܕܐܝܬ ܒܗܘܢ ܐܟܚܕܐ .

bg, ܘܕܐܢ ܡܪܢ 'our Lord will judge.' ܕܟܣܝܬܐ 'hidden,' *abdefghi*WP; c, ܕܚܛܗ̈ܐ ܗܘܘ 'which were sins.'

3. ܕܒܬܘ̈ܢܐ ܕܗܕ̈ܡܝܗܘܢ 'which in the secret chambers of all,' c; *abfghl*, ܕܒܬܘܢܐ ܕܒܗܕܡܝܗܘܢ 'which in the secret chamber

by.   7. The consummation, moreover, of the age will
then show the great might of its ruler, when all things
come to judgment.   8. Do ye therefore prepare your
hearts for that which before ye believed, lest ye come
to be in bondage in both worlds, so that ye be led
away captive here and be tormented there.   9. For
that which exists now or which has passed away, or
which is to come in all these things, neither is the
evil fully evil, nor again the good fully good.   10. For
all healthinesses of this time are turning into diseases.
11. And all might of this time is turning into weakness,

7. Cf. xx. 4.
8. *Prepare your hearts.* See xxxii.
1, note.
   That which ye before believed.
This seems to refer to apostates, *i.e.*
Christians who had left Judaism.
Cf. xli. 3 ; xlii. 4.

Come to be in bondage, etc. Cf.
lxxxv. 9.
10. Contrast xxix. 7.
11. *All might of this time,* etc.
Cf. xxi. 14.

ܚܥ‌ܠܐ ܘܐܬܐ ܗܪܝܢ ܀ܐܠܐ‌ܟܐܕ؛ 'that ye be led away captive and
... there,' *c* ; *abdefghik*wP, ܘܐܠܐ‌ܟܐܕ؛ ܀ܘܗܐ.   *e* om.
ܐܠܐܡܚ‌ܝܐ.

9. At the beginning of this verse *ef* insert ܒ in red,
w inserts ܚܛܐܠܐ؛ as also *di*, but that they add ܝ before
ܒ.   ܝܚܢܩ؛ ch ; *bg,* ܝܚܢܩܢ؛ ; *efi,* ܝܚܢܩܢ؛ ; *k,* ܝܚܐܡܩ .
cefh ; *b,* ܝܚܕܡ؛ ; *adgik*wP, ܝܚܕܡ . ܐܠܐ‌ܟܐܡܚܟܠ ܀ܟܕܐ ܠܐܙܘ *c* ;
*abdefgik*wP, ܐܠܐܡܐ؛ܝܚܕܡܟ ܠܐܙܘ ܟܐܠܐ ܀ܟܠ؛ ; *h,* ܠܐܙܘ
ܟܐܠܐ . ܟܐܠܐ .

10. ܟܚܛܙܢܩܗ 'diseases,' *abcdeghk* ; *d'fi*wP, ܟܚܛܙܢܩܗ
'disease.'

11. ܠܟ‌ܐܘܠ; 'to misery,' *bg* : so also *a,* ܠܟ‌ܐܘܘܠ; and *defhi,*

7 ܫܘܠܡܗ ܕܝܢ ܕܥܠܡܐ
ܗܝܕܝܢ ܢܚܘܐ ܚܝܠܗ ܪܒܐ
ܕܡܕܒܪܢܘܬܗ . ܟܕ ܒܟܠܡܕܡ
8 ܢܐܬܐ ܠܕܝܢܐ . ܐܢܬܘܢ
ܗܟܝܠ ܐܬܛܝܒܘ ܠܒܘ̈ܬܟܘܢ
ܠܡܕܡ ܕܡܢ ܩܕܝܡ
ܗܝܡܢܬܘܢ ܕܠܐ ܡܢ
ܬܪܬܝܗܘܢ ܥ̈ܠܡܐ ܬܬܚܪܡܘܢ
ܕܐܫܬܒܝܬܘܢ ܗܪܟܐ . ܘܬܡܢ
9 ܬܫܬܢܩܘܢ . ܡܕܡ ܓܝܪ
ܕܡܟܐ ܗܫܐ ܐܘ ܕܥܒܪ
ܐܘ ܕܐܬܐ ܒܟܘܠܗܝܢ
ܗܠܝܢ . ܐܦ ܠܐ ܒܝܫܬܐ
ܒܝܫܐ ܡܫܠܡܐܝܬ . ܐܦ ܠܐ
ܬܘܒ ܛܒܬܐ ܡܫܠܡܐܝܬ
10 ܛܒܬܐ ܐܝܬܝܗ . ܟܠ ܓܝܪ
ܚܘܠܡ̈ܢܐ ܕܗܫܐ ܗܦܟܝܢ
11 ܠܟܘܪ̈ܗܢܐ . ܘܟܠ
ܚܝܠܬܢܘܬܐ ܕܗܫܐ ܗܦܟܐ

7. ܫܘܠܡܗ 'the consummation,' *c*; *e*, ܘܫܘܠܡܗ; *abdfghik*WP, ܒܫܘܠܡܗ 'in the consummation.'

8. ܥ̈ܠܡܐ 'worlds,' *abdefghik*WP; *c*, ܥܠܡܐ 'world.'

and all force of this time is turning into misery.   12.
And every energy of youth is turning into old age and
consummation, and every beauty of gracefulness of
this time is turning faded and hateful.   13. And every
proud dominion of the present is turning into humilia-
tion and shame.   14. And every praise of the glory
of this time is turning into the shame of silence, and
every splendour and insolence of this time is turning
into voiceless ruin.   15. And every delight and joy
of this time is turning to worms and corruption.   16.
And every clamour of the pride of this time is turning
into dust and stillness.   17. And every possession of
riches of this time is being turned into Sheol alone.

12. *Every beauty*, etc. Cf. xxi.   13. Cf. xlviii. 35.
14 ; xlviii. 35.

---

so also *i*, but defectively ; *c* reads corruptly |ﺄﻤﺤﺝ، ﻮﺝﺭ؛ﻢﺳ
'swelling of pride': we must emend |ﺄﻤﺤﺝ؛ﻮﺝﺭ، into
|ﺄﻤﺤﺝ؛ﻮﺝﺭ.

14. *e*WP om. |ﺄﻤﻟﺄ ... ﻮﻤﺳ through h m t.

15. |ﺄﺳﻤﻤﺩﻤ٥ |ﺄﻤﻟﻮﻤ 'delight and joy,' *bdefghi*WP ; *ack*,
|ﺄﻤﻤﺳﻤﻤﺩﻤ٥ |ﺄﻤﻟﻮﻤ 'delights and joys.' |ﺄﺩﻤﺏﺳ 'to worms,'
*abdefghik*WP ; *c*, |ﺄﺩﻤﺝﺳ 'to rejection.'   For |ﺄﺳﻤﺳﻮ *f*
reads |ﺄﺳﻤﻤﺳﻮ.

16. |ﺄﻤﺳ، ﻮﻤﺩﺳﻤﻮﺝ، 'of the pride of this time,' *abdefghik*WP ;
c, |ﺝﺳﻮﻤﻤﺝ، 'of the proud.' |ﺄﻤﻤﺳﻮ |؛ﺩﺳﻤ 'to dust and
stillness,' *abdefghikm*WP ; *c*, |ﺄﻤﻤﺳﻤﻤ |؛ﺩﺳﻤ 'to the still dust.'

17. |؛ﺄﻮﺳﺝ، 'of riches,' *cdefi*WP ; *abghk*, |؛ﺄﻮﺳﻮ 'and
riches.'

ܟܡܘܩܐ; c, ܟܡܐܘܩܠ 'to miseries.' k om. . . . ܟܘܐܦܠܐ
ܘܗܒܪ through hmt.

12. ܟܟܘܟܘܐ c; abfghikwp, ܟܟܘܟܘܐܘ.

13. ܘܟܟܘܟܗܐ ܐܣܝܟܐ 'proud dominion,' abdefghkwp;

18. And all the rapine of passion of this time is turning into involuntary death, and every passion of the lusts of this time is turning into a judgment of torment. 19. And every artifice and craftiness of this time is turning into a proof of the truth. 20. And every sweetness of unguents of this time is turning into judgment and condemnation. 21. And every love of lying is turning to shame through truth. 22. Since therefore all these things are done now, does any one think that they will not be avenged? 23. But the consummation of all things will come to the truth.]

LXXXIV = B¹.   LXXXIV. Behold! I have therefore made known unto you (these things) whilst I live: for I said that

---

19. ‏|ܐܠܕܝ‏, *c*; *abdefghiklw*P, ‏|ܙܐܠܕܝ‏. ‏|ܙܐܡܝܟܐܣܘ‏ 'and craftiness,' *abdefghikln*WP; *c*, ‏|ܙܐܡܝܟܐܣܘ‏ 'of craftiness.' *f* om. ‏|ܗܥܘܗ‏ ‏|ܗܘܢ‏ ‏: ‏ܘܥܟܡܬܢܐ‏ ... ‏|ܙܐܘܗܗܗܘܢ‏ ‏ܟܐܗܟܟܬܬܐ‏ through *hmt*.

20. ‏|ܙܐܘܗܣܡܡܟܣ‏o *c*; *h*, ‏|ܗܣܡܣܣܟ‏o.

21. ‏|ܝܐܘܣܡ‏ ‏: ‏ܘܗܣܡ‏ 'of lying,' *abdefghik*WP; *c* wrongly om. ‏|ܟܢܬܢܣ‏ *c*; *abdefghik*WP, ‏|ܗܣܡܣ‏. ‏|ܐܣܣܣܣ‏ 'through truth,' *abdefgik*WP; *c*, ‏ܟܐܠܐܣ‏ 'in silence.'

22. ‏ܣܟܣ ܝܐܣܣ‏ *c*; *abhk* trs.; *di*, ‏ܣܟܣ ܝܐܣܣ‏; *efgl*WP, ‏ܝܐܣܣ‏. For ‏ܣܘܣ‏ *efilw* read ‏ܣܘܣ‏. ‏ܐܠܐ ܣܣܙ‏ 'does anyone think?' *abdefghiklw*P; *c*, ‏|ܐܠܐ ܣܣܙ‏ 'dost thou think?'

23. ‏ܣܘܣ‏, 'of all,' *abcdefghik*; WP, ‏ܣܟܣ‏ 'all.'

LXXXIV. 1. ‏|ܗܣ‏ *abdefghik*WP; *c* om. ‏ܘܝܐܣܐܠܐ ܐܠܟܟܣܣܘܢ‏

LXXXIV. 1

18. ‏‎ abcwp; defghi, ‏‎ 'of the lusts,'
abcegh ; dfiwp, ‏‎ 'of the lust.' ‏‎ 'of this time,'
abdefghikwp; c wrongly om. k om. ‏‎
through hmt., and for ‏‎ reads ‏‎.

ye should above all things learn the commandments
of the Mighty One, wherein I shall instruct you: and
I will set before you some of the commandments of
His judgment before I die.   2. Remember that
formerly Moses assuredly called heaven and earth
to witness against you, and said: "if ye transgress the
law ye shall be dispersed, but if ye keep it ye shall
be kept."   3. And other things also he used to say
unto you when ye the twelve tribes were together
in the desert.   4. And after his death ye cast
them away from you: on this account there came

LXXXIV. 1. *Before I die.* See
lxxviii. 5.

*The commandments of the Mighty
One* (cf. ver. 7 ; xliv. 3).

2. See xix. 2, 3, note. In this
verse there are several traces of the
Hebrew original. First the Syr.
for "assuredly called . . . to witness" = διαμαρτυρόμενος διεμαρτύ-
ρατο = הָעֵד הֵעִיד. Next we have

the play on the two senses of שָׁמַר :
"if ye keep it, ye shall be kept" =
אם תשמרוה תשמרו, Finally, there
seems to be a paronomasia intended
in "if ye transgress the law, ye
shall be dispersed" = אם תמרו מתורה
תזורו.

3. *Twelve tribes.* Cf. lxxviii. 4 ;
James i. 1.

ܠܡܣܘܗ ܚܘܣܡ, *e* save in reading ܚܡܣ, *f* save in reading ܡܣܚ݂,
and *k* save in reading ܚܒܡܚ݂ܠ݀ܕ (for ܚܒܡܚ݂ܠ݀ܙܐܕ).   ܠܡ݂ܣܘܚ *ce*;
*dfgi*wp, ܠܡ݂ܣܘܚ ; *k*, ܣܗܣ݂ܘܡ݂ܣܘܚ.

2. ܡܘ݂ܣ *abcefghil*wp ; *b*, ܐ݂ܡܘ݂ܣ.   ܠܚ݂ *abdefghi*wp ; *c* om.
ܠܠ݂ܢܚ݂ܘ 'ye shall be kept,' *abdefghi*wp ; *c*, ܠܠܚ݂ܒ݂ܘ 'ye
shall be planted.'

3. ܐ݂ܟ ܠܝ݂ ܐ݂ *abdefghi*wp ; *c*, ܟ݂ܐ.   ܡܚ *ach* ; *bdefgi*wp,
ܡܕ݂.   ܠܡ݂ܟ݂ܚ *c* ; *abdefghi*wp, ܠܡܟ݂ܚ.

4. ܘܟܠܣ݂ܡ 'therefore,' *abdefgi*wp ; *ch*, ܘܟܠܣ݂ܡܘ 'and

www.ingramcontent.com/pod-product-compliance
Lightning Source LLC
Chambersburg PA
CBHW060309100426
42812CB00003B/711